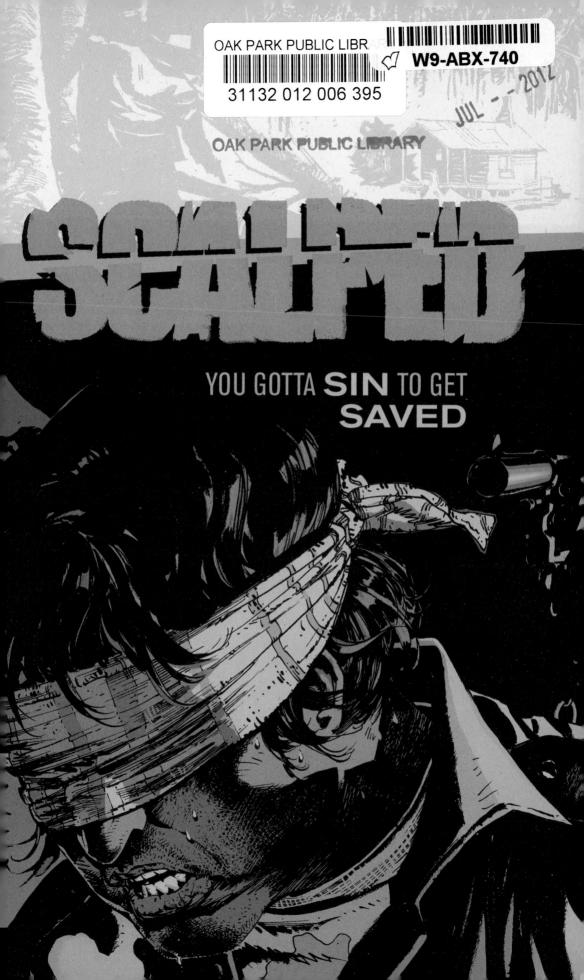

SCALPED

YOU GOTTA **SIN** TO GET
SAVED

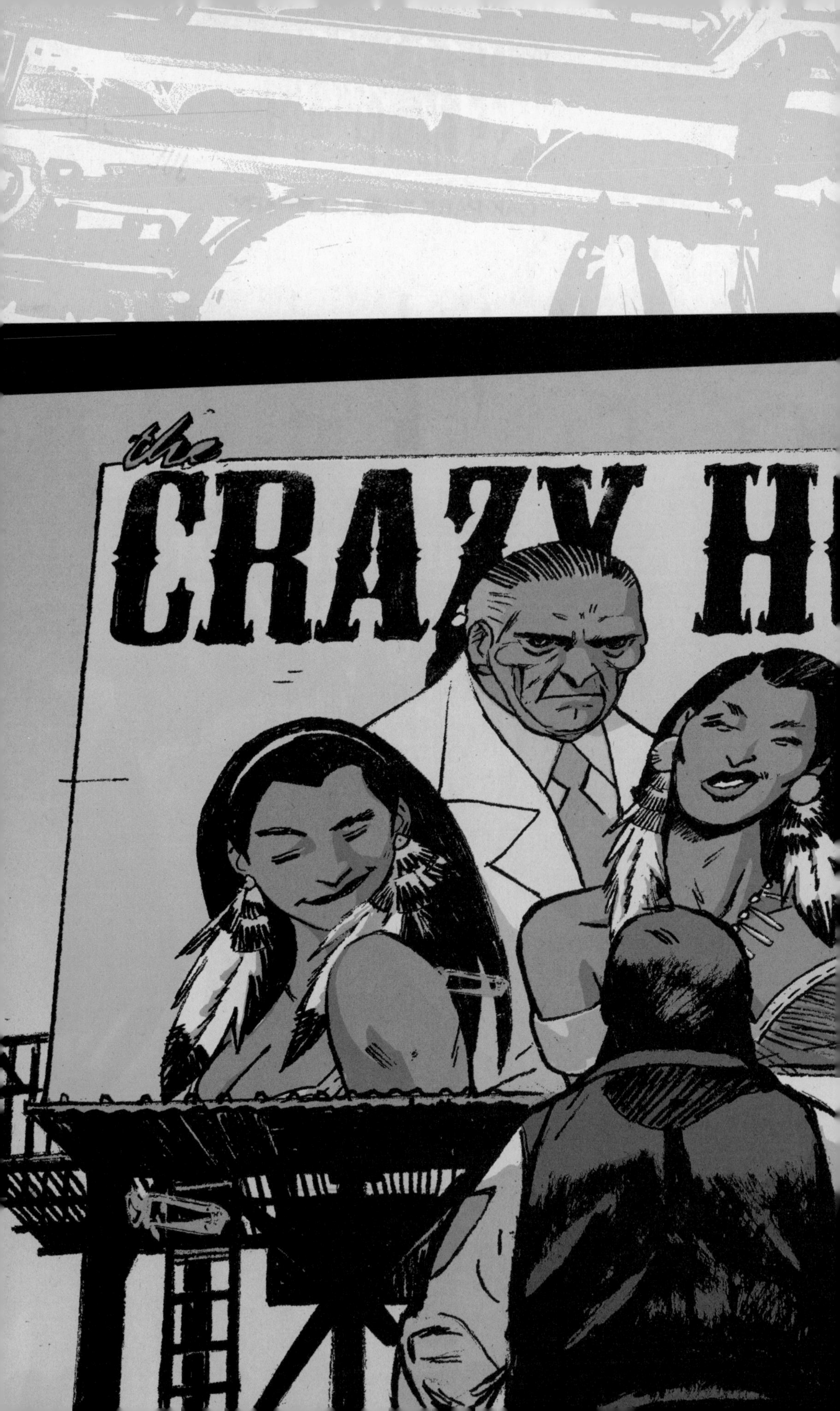
the
CRAZY

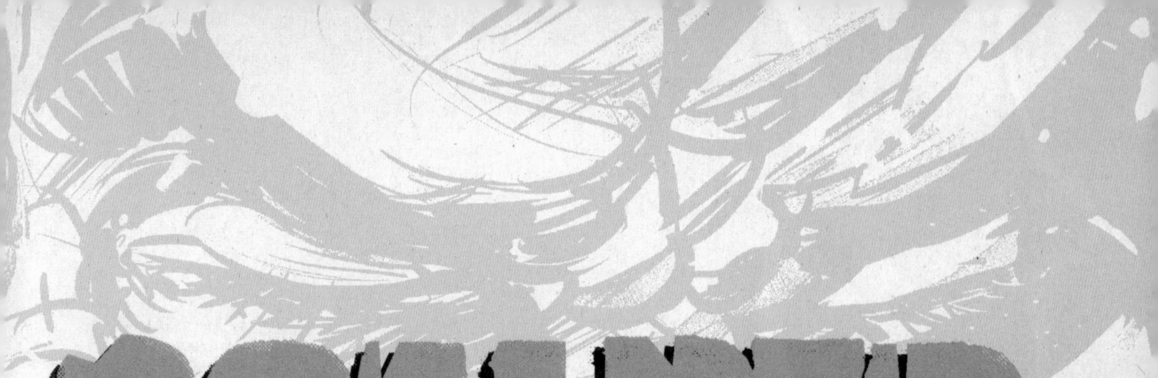

SCALPED

YOU GOTTA SIN TO GET SAVED

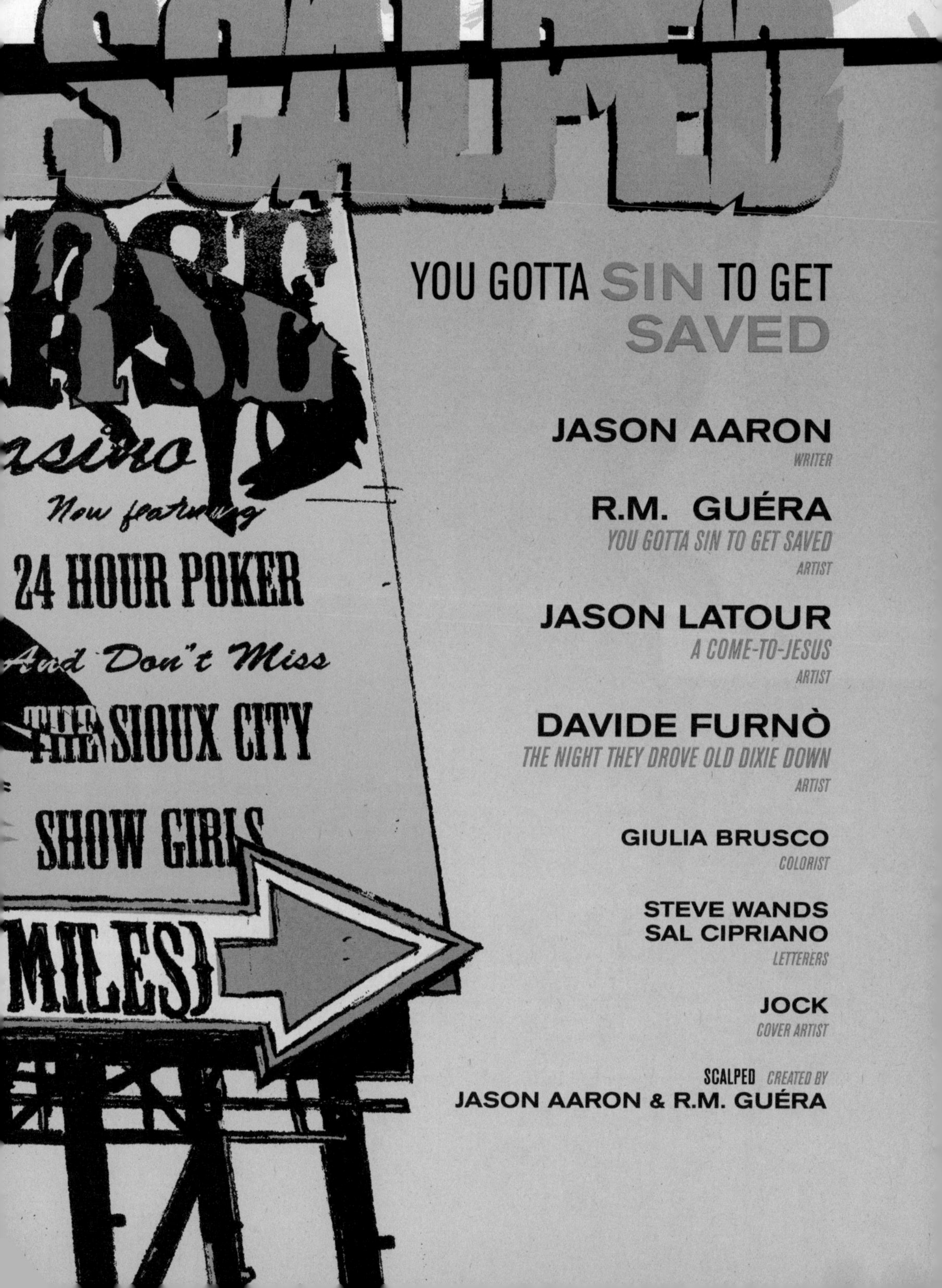

asino
24 HOUR POKER
And Don't Miss
THE SIOUX CITY
SHOW GIRL
MILES)

JASON AARON
WRITER

R.M. GUÉRA
YOU GOTTA SIN TO GET SAVED
ARTIST

JASON LATOUR
A COME-TO-JESUS
ARTIST

DAVIDE FURNÒ
THE NIGHT THEY DROVE OLD DIXIE DOWN
ARTIST

GIULIA BRUSCO
COLORIST

STEVE WANDS
SAL CIPRIANO
LETTERERS

JOCK
COVER ARTIST

SCALPED *CREATED BY*
JASON AARON & R.M. GUÉRA

WILL DENNIS
Editor – Original Series
MARK DOYLE
Associate Editor – Original Series
IAN SATTLER
Director – Editorial, Special Projects and Archival Editions
ROBBIN BROSTERMAN
Design Director – Books

KAREN BERGER
Senior VP – Executive Editor, Vertigo
BOB HARRAS
VP – Editor in Chief

DIANE NELSON
President
DAN DIDIO and JIM LEE
Co-Publishers

GEOFF JOHNS
Chief Creative Officer
JOHN ROOD
Executive VP – Sales, Marketing and Business Development
AMY GENKINS
Senior VP – Business and Legal Affairs
NAIRI GARDINER
Senior VP – Finance
JEFF BOISON
VP – Publishing Operations
MARK CHIARELLO
VP – Art Direction and Design
JOHN CUNNINGHAM
VP – Marketing
TERRI CUNNINGHAM
VP – Talent Relations and Services
ALISON GILL
Senior VP – Manufacturing and Operations

DAVID HYDE
VP – Publicity
HANK KANALZ
Senior VP – Digital
JAY KOGAN
VP – Business and Legal Affairs, Publishing
JACK MAHAN
VP – Business Affairs, Talent
NICK NAPOLITANO
VP – Manufacturing Administration
SUE POHJA
VP – Book Sales
COURTNEY SIMMONS
Senior VP – Publicity
BOB WAYNE
Senior VP – Sales

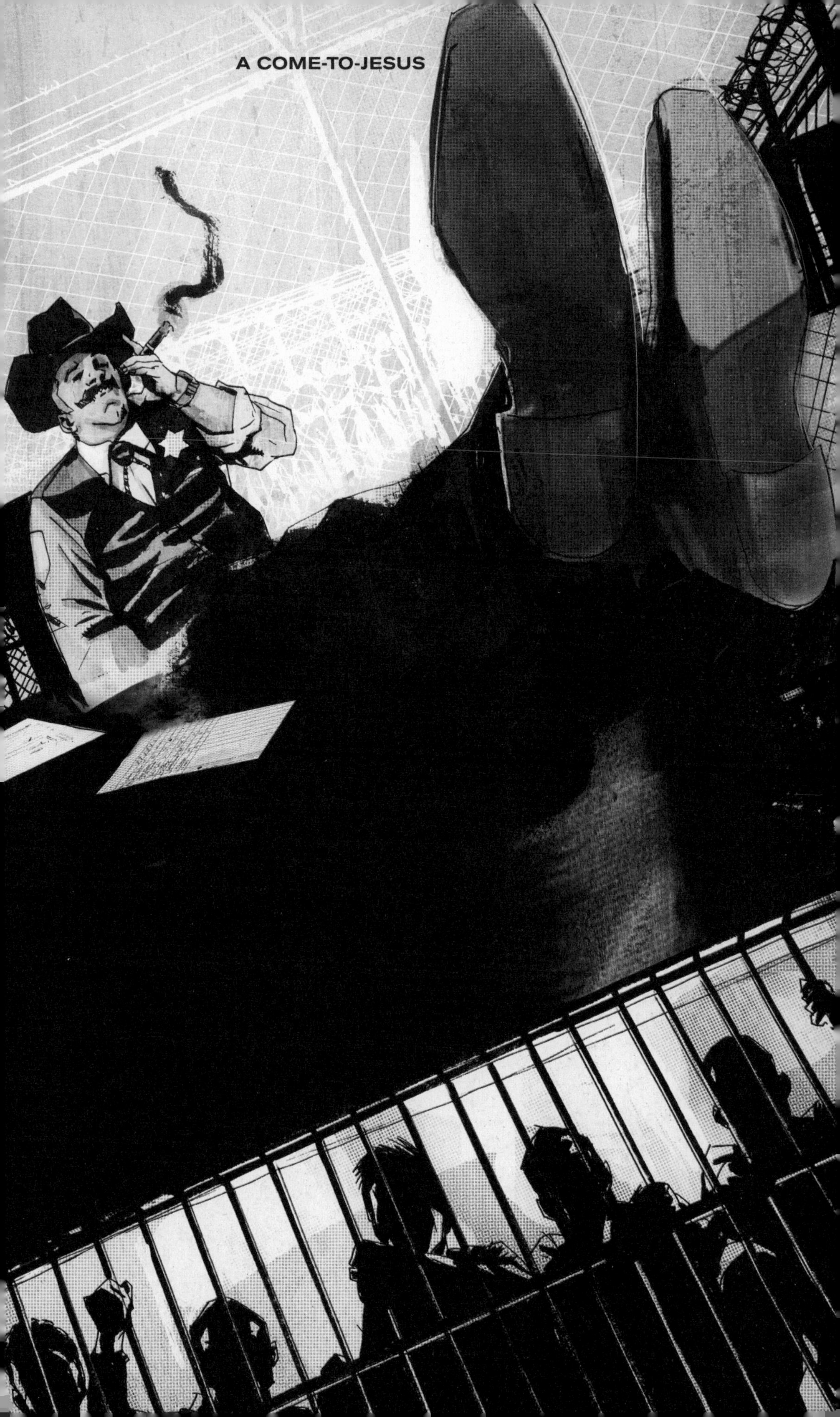
A COME-TO-JESUS

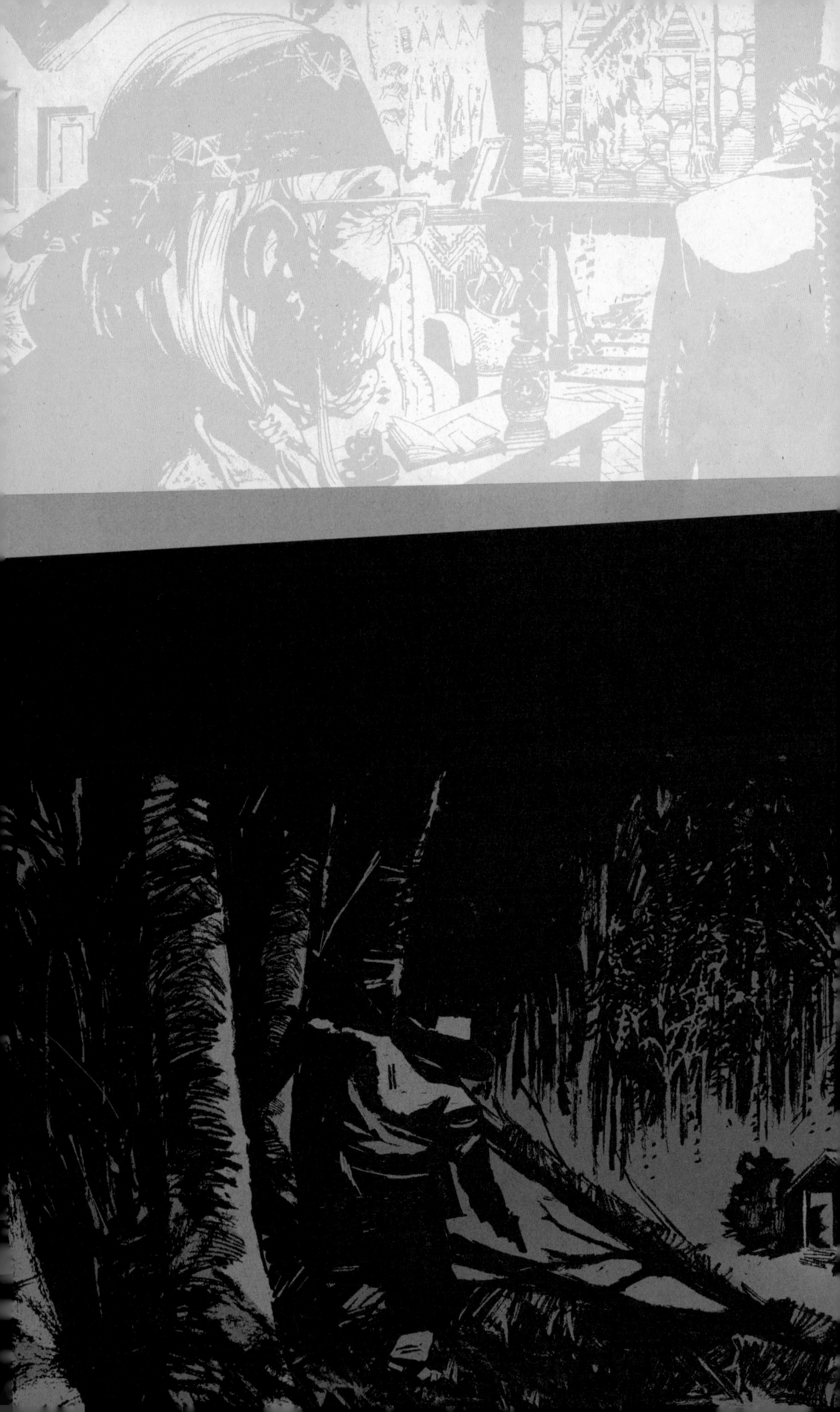

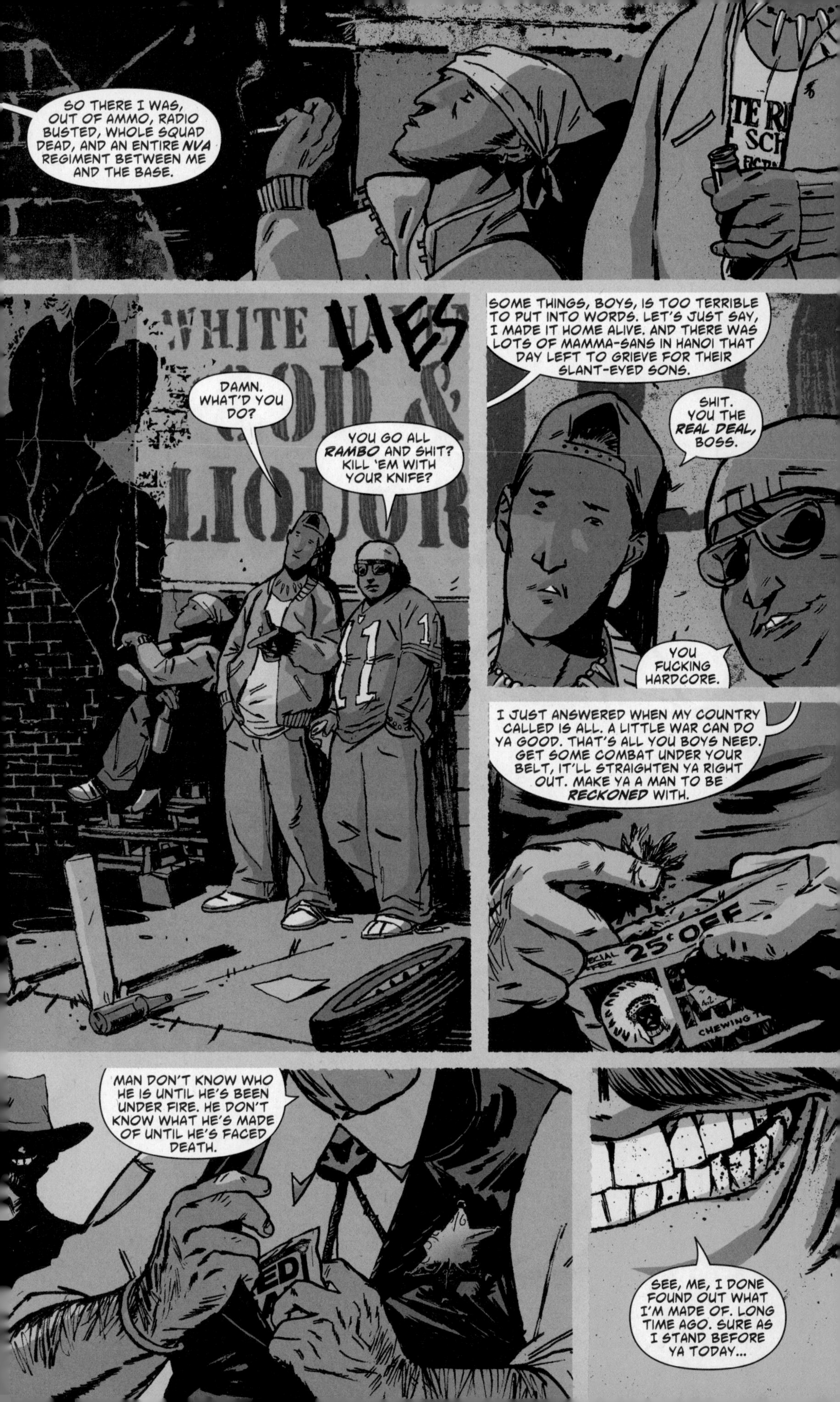
SO THERE I WAS, OUT OF AMMO, RADIO BUSTED, WHOLE SQUAD DEAD, AND AN ENTIRE NVA REGIMENT BETWEEN ME AND THE BASE.
WHITE HAVEN FOOD & LIQUOR
LIES
DAMN. WHAT'D YOU DO?
YOU GO ALL RAMBO AND SHIT? KILL 'EM WITH YOUR KNIFE?
SOME THINGS, BOYS, IS TOO TERRIBLE TO PUT INTO WORDS. LET'S JUST SAY, I MADE IT HOME ALIVE. AND THERE WAS LOTS OF MAMMA-SANS IN HANOI THAT DAY LEFT TO GRIEVE FOR THEIR SLANT-EYED SONS.
SHIT. YOU THE REAL DEAL, BOSS.
YOU FUCKING HARDCORE.
I JUST ANSWERED WHEN MY COUNTRY CALLED IS ALL. A LITTLE WAR CAN DO YA GOOD. THAT'S ALL YOU BOYS NEED. GET SOME COMBAT UNDER YOUR BELT, IT'LL STRAIGHTEN YA RIGHT OUT. MAKE YA A MAN TO BE RECKONED WITH.
25¢ OFF
CHEWING
MAN DON'T KNOW WHO HE IS UNTIL HE'S BEEN UNDER FIRE. HE DON'T KNOW WHAT HE'S MADE OF UNTIL HE'S FACED DEATH.
SEE, ME, I DONE FOUND OUT WHAT I'M MADE OF. LONG TIME AGO. SURE AS I STAND BEFORE YA TODAY...

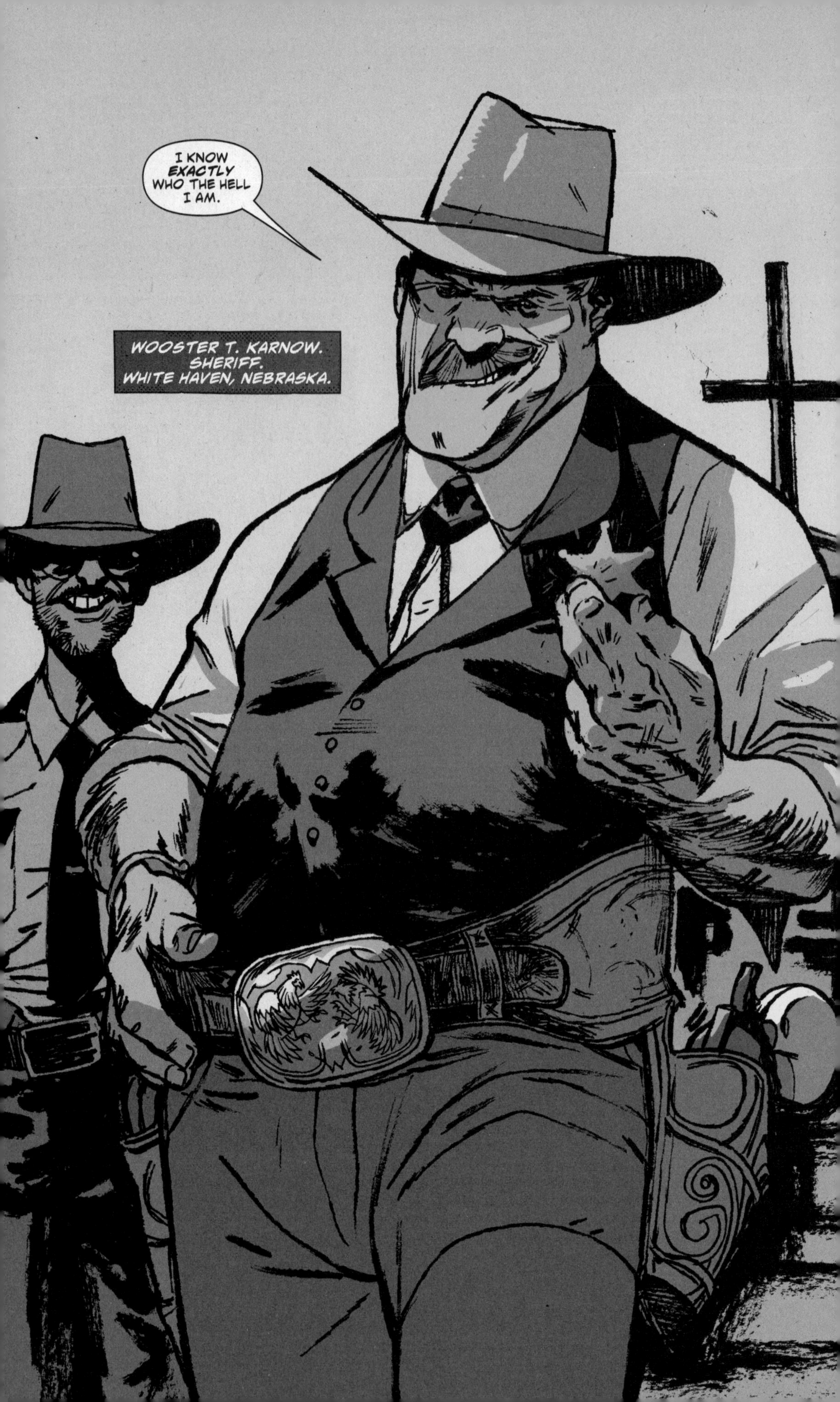
I KNOW EXACTLY WHO THE HELL I AM.
WOOSTER T. KARNOW. SHERIFF. WHITE HAVEN, NEBRASKA.

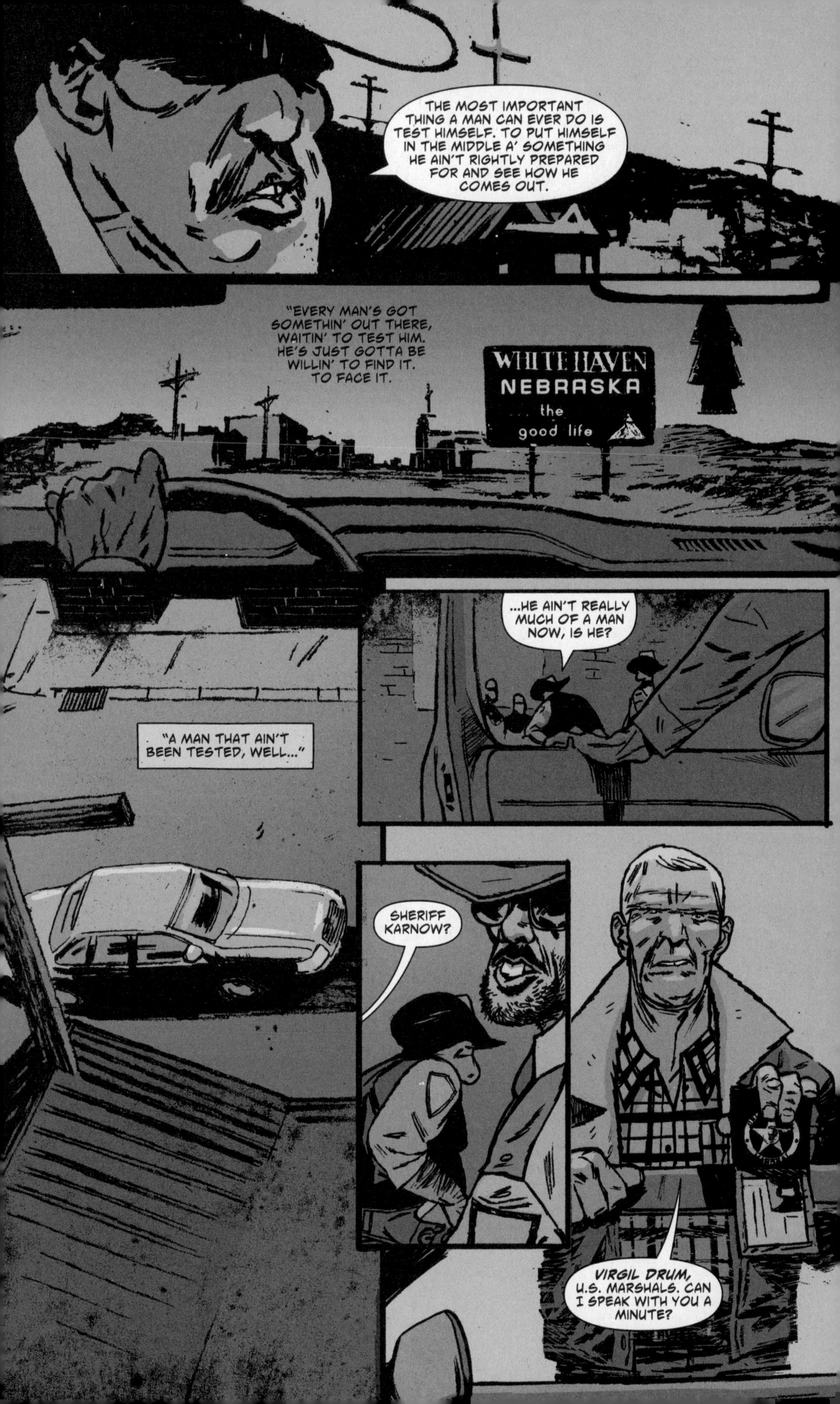

THE MOST IMPORTANT THING A MAN CAN EVER DO IS TEST HIMSELF. TO PUT HIMSELF IN THE MIDDLE A' SOMETHING HE AIN'T RIGHTLY PREPARED FOR AND SEE HOW HE COMES OUT.
"EVERY MAN'S GOT SOMETHIN' OUT THERE, WAITIN' TO TEST HIM. HE'S JUST GOTTA BE WILLIN' TO FIND IT. TO FACE IT.
WHITE HAVEN NEBRASKA the good life
"A MAN THAT AIN'T BEEN TESTED, WELL..."
...HE AIN'T REALLY MUCH OF A MAN NOW, IS HE?
SHERIFF KARNOW?
VIRGIL DRUM, U.S. MARSHALS. CAN I SPEAK WITH YOU A MINUTE?

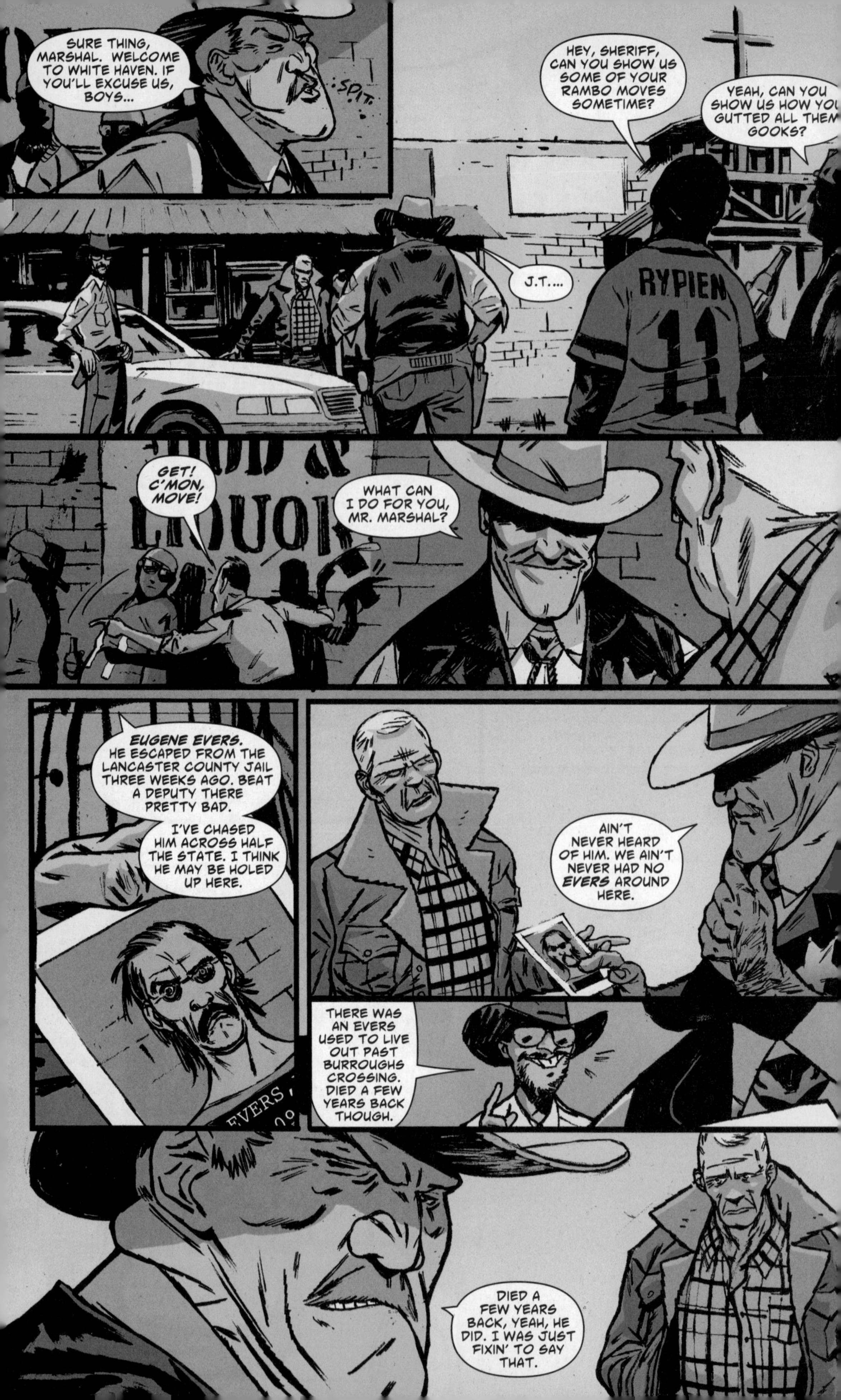
SURE THING, MARSHAL. WELCOME TO WHITE HAVEN. IF YOU'LL EXCUSE US, BOYS...
SPIT.
HEY, SHERIFF, CAN YOU SHOW US SOME OF YOUR RAMBO MOVES SOMETIME?
YEAH, CAN YOU SHOW US HOW YOU GUTTED ALL THEM GOOKS?
J.T....
RYPIEN
11
GET! C'MON, MOVE!
WHAT CAN I DO FOR YOU, MR. MARSHAL?
EUGENE EVERS. HE ESCAPED FROM THE LANCASTER COUNTY JAIL THREE WEEKS AGO. BEAT A DEPUTY THERE PRETTY BAD.
I'VE CHASED HIM ACROSS HALF THE STATE. I THINK HE MAY BE HOLED UP HERE.
EVERS
AIN'T NEVER HEARD OF HIM. WE AIN'T NEVER HAD NO EVERS AROUND HERE.
THERE WAS AN EVERS USED TO LIVE OUT PAST BURROUGHS CROSSING. DIED A FEW YEARS BACK THOUGH.
DIED A FEW YEARS BACK, YEAH, HE DID. I WAS JUST FIXIN' TO SAY THAT.

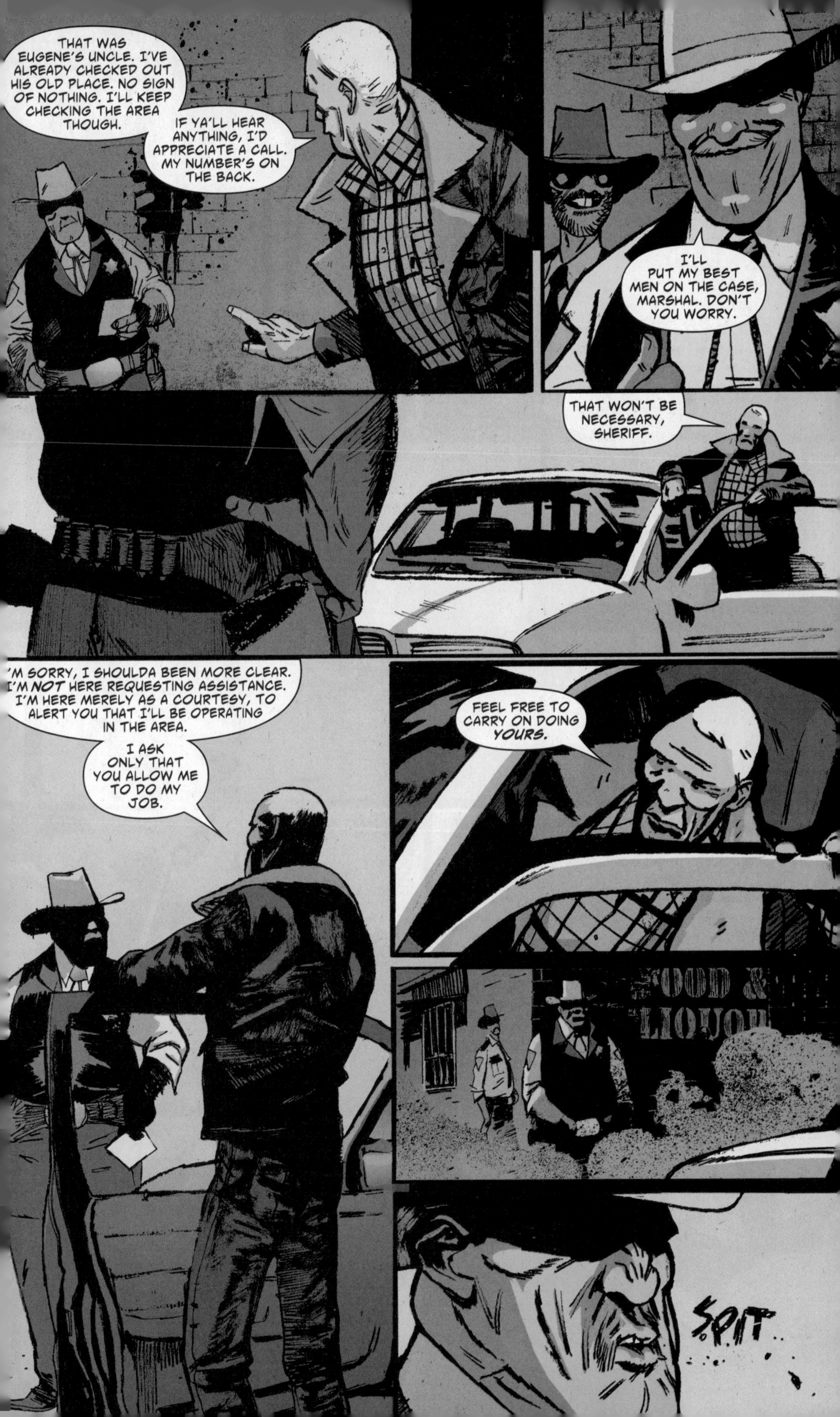
THAT WAS EUGENE'S UNCLE. I'VE ALREADY CHECKED OUT HIS OLD PLACE. NO SIGN OF NOTHING. I'LL KEEP CHECKING THE AREA THOUGH.
IF YA'LL HEAR ANYTHING, I'D APPRECIATE A CALL. MY NUMBER'S ON THE BACK.
I'LL PUT MY BEST MEN ON THE CASE, MARSHAL. DON'T YOU WORRY.
THAT WON'T BE NECESSARY, SHERIFF.
I'M SORRY, I SHOULDA BEEN MORE CLEAR. I'M NOT HERE REQUESTING ASSISTANCE. I'M HERE MERELY AS A COURTESY, TO ALERT YOU THAT I'LL BE OPERATING IN THE AREA.
I ASK ONLY THAT YOU ALLOW ME TO DO MY JOB.
FEEL FREE TO CARRY ON DOING YOURS.
SPIT

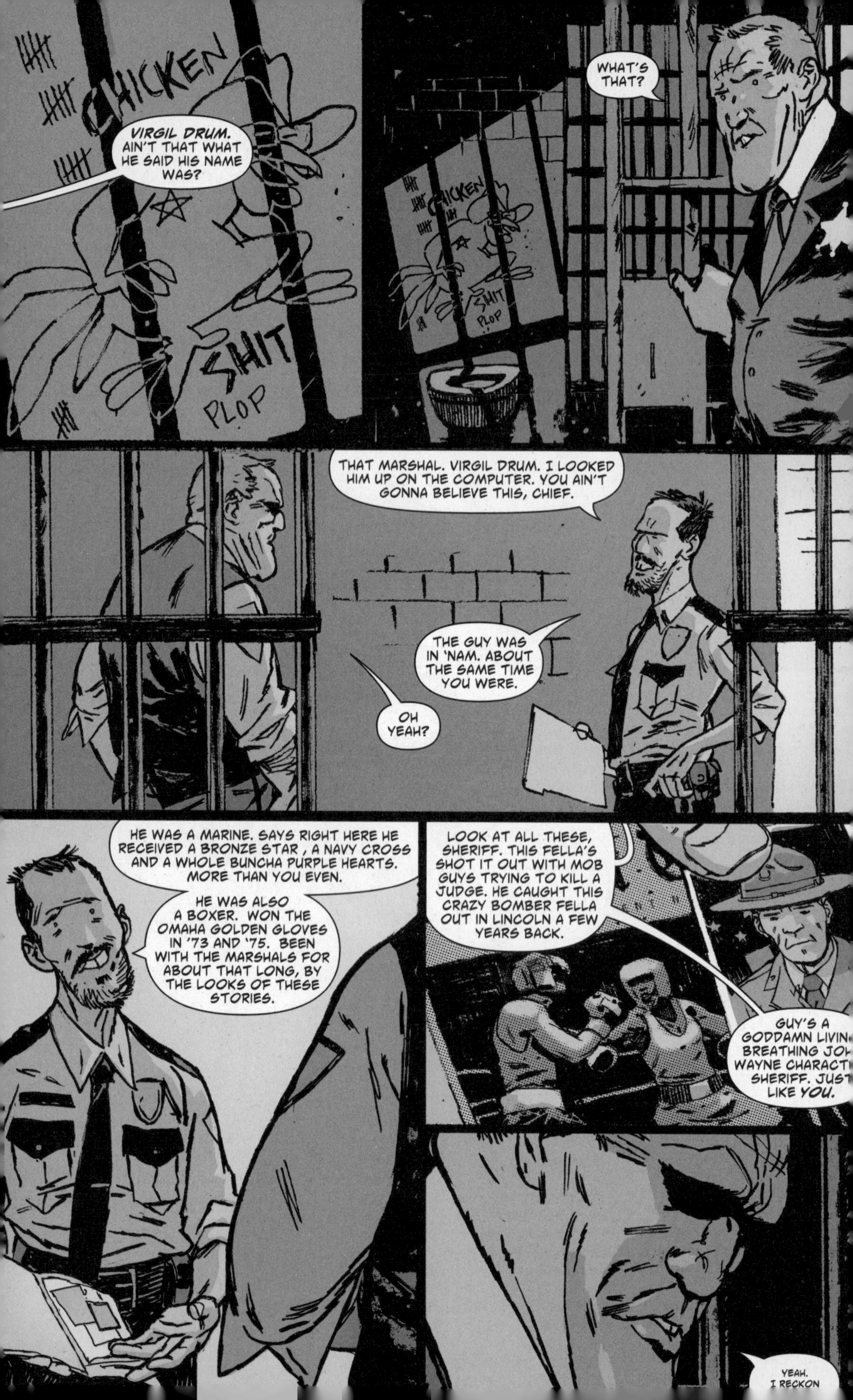
CHICKEN
VIRGIL DRUM. AIN'T THAT WHAT HE SAID HIS NAME WAS?
SHIT
PLOP
WHAT'S THAT?
THAT MARSHAL. VIRGIL DRUM. I LOOKED HIM UP ON THE COMPUTER. YOU AIN'T GONNA BELIEVE THIS, CHIEF.
THE GUY WAS IN 'NAM. ABOUT THE SAME TIME YOU WERE.
OH YEAH?
HE WAS A MARINE. SAYS RIGHT HERE HE RECEIVED A BRONZE STAR , A NAVY CROSS AND A WHOLE BUNCHA PURPLE HEARTS. MORE THAN YOU EVEN.
HE WAS ALSO A BOXER. WON THE OMAHA GOLDEN GLOVES IN '73 AND '75. BEEN WITH THE MARSHALS FOR ABOUT THAT LONG, BY THE LOOKS OF THESE STORIES.
LOOK AT ALL THESE, SHERIFF. THIS FELLA'S SHOT IT OUT WITH MOB GUYS TRYING TO KILL A JUDGE. HE CAUGHT THIS CRAZY BOMBER FELLA OUT IN LINCOLN A FEW YEARS BACK.
GUY'S A GODDAMN LIVIN BREATHING JOH WAYNE CHARACT SHERIFF. JUST LIKE YOU.
YEAH. I RECKON

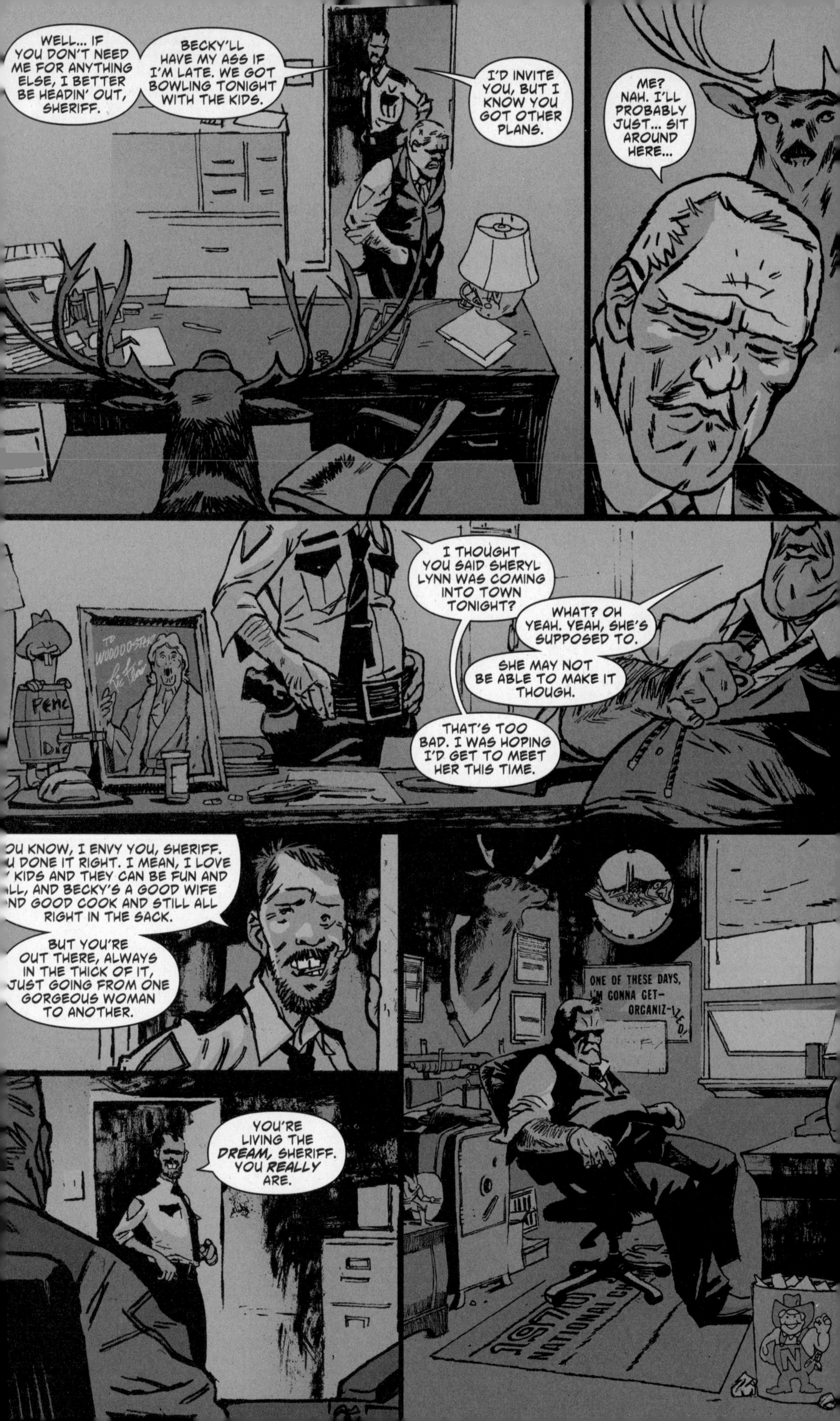
WELL... IF YOU DON'T NEED ME FOR ANYTHING ELSE, I BETTER BE HEADIN' OUT, SHERIFF.
BECKY'LL HAVE MY ASS IF I'M LATE. WE GOT BOWLING TONIGHT WITH THE KIDS.
I'D INVITE YOU, BUT I KNOW YOU GOT OTHER PLANS.
ME? NAH. I'LL PROBABLY JUST... SIT AROUND HERE...
I THOUGHT YOU SAID SHERYL LYNN WAS COMING INTO TOWN TONIGHT?
WHAT? OH YEAH. YEAH, SHE'S SUPPOSED TO.
SHE MAY NOT BE ABLE TO MAKE IT THOUGH.
THAT'S TOO BAD. I WAS HOPING I'D GET TO MEET HER THIS TIME.
OU KNOW, I ENVY YOU, SHERIFF. U DONE IT RIGHT. I MEAN, I LOVE KIDS AND THEY CAN BE FUN AND LL, AND BECKY'S A GOOD WIFE ND GOOD COOK AND STILL ALL RIGHT IN THE SACK.
BUT YOU'RE OUT THERE, ALWAYS IN THE THICK OF IT, JUST GOING FROM ONE GORGEOUS WOMAN TO ANOTHER.
YOU'RE LIVING THE DREAM, SHERIFF. YOU REALLY ARE.
ONE OF THESE DAYS, I'M GONNA GET- ORGANIZ-IZED!

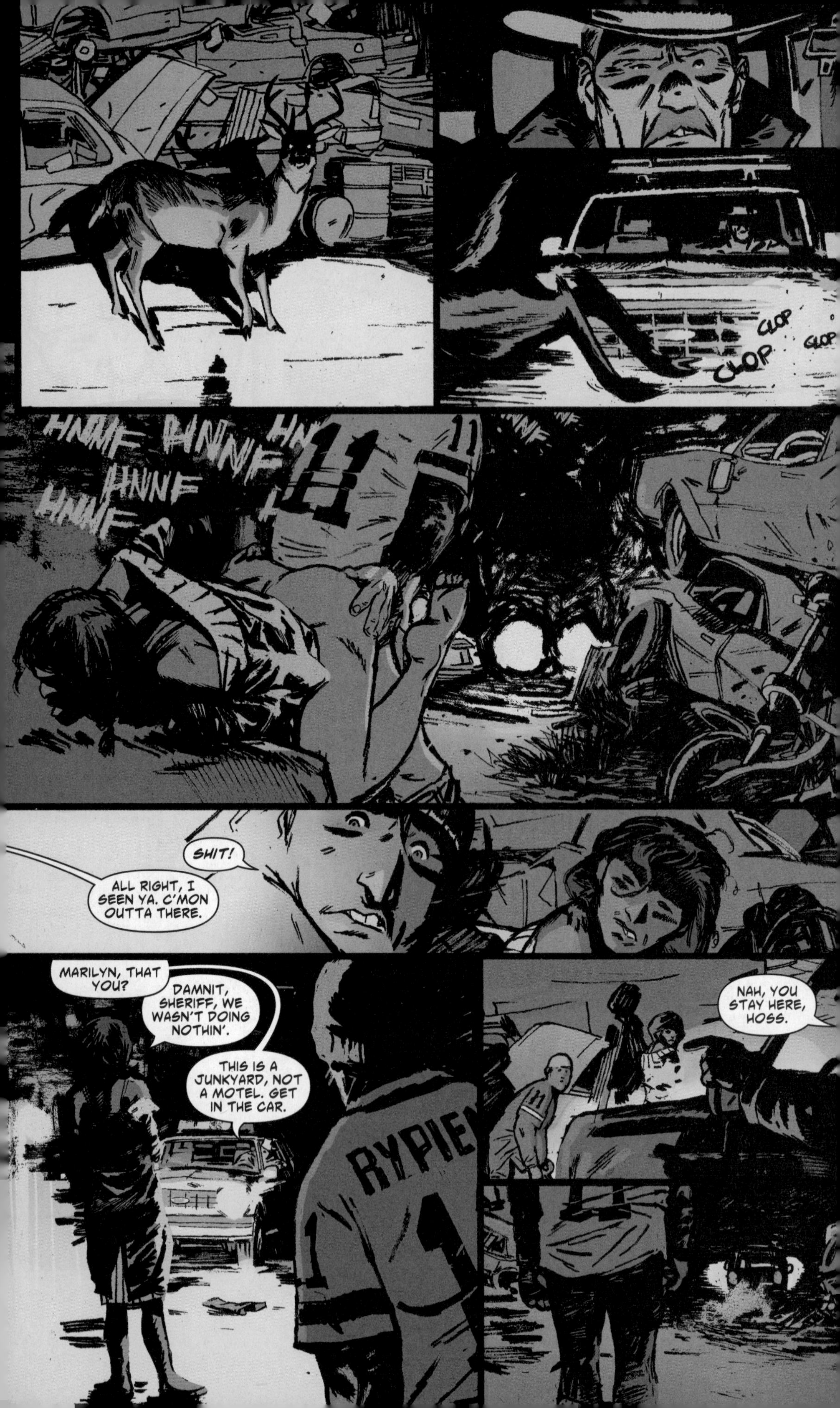
CLOP
CLOP
CLOP
CLOP
HNNF HNNF HN
HNNF
HNNF
HNNF
SHIT!
ALL RIGHT, I SEEN YA. C'MON OUTTA THERE.
MARILYN, THAT YOU?
DAMNIT, SHERIFF, WE WASN'T DOING NOTHIN'.
THIS IS A JUNKYARD, NOT A MOTEL. GET IN THE CAR.
RYPIE
NAH, YOU STAY HERE, HOSS.

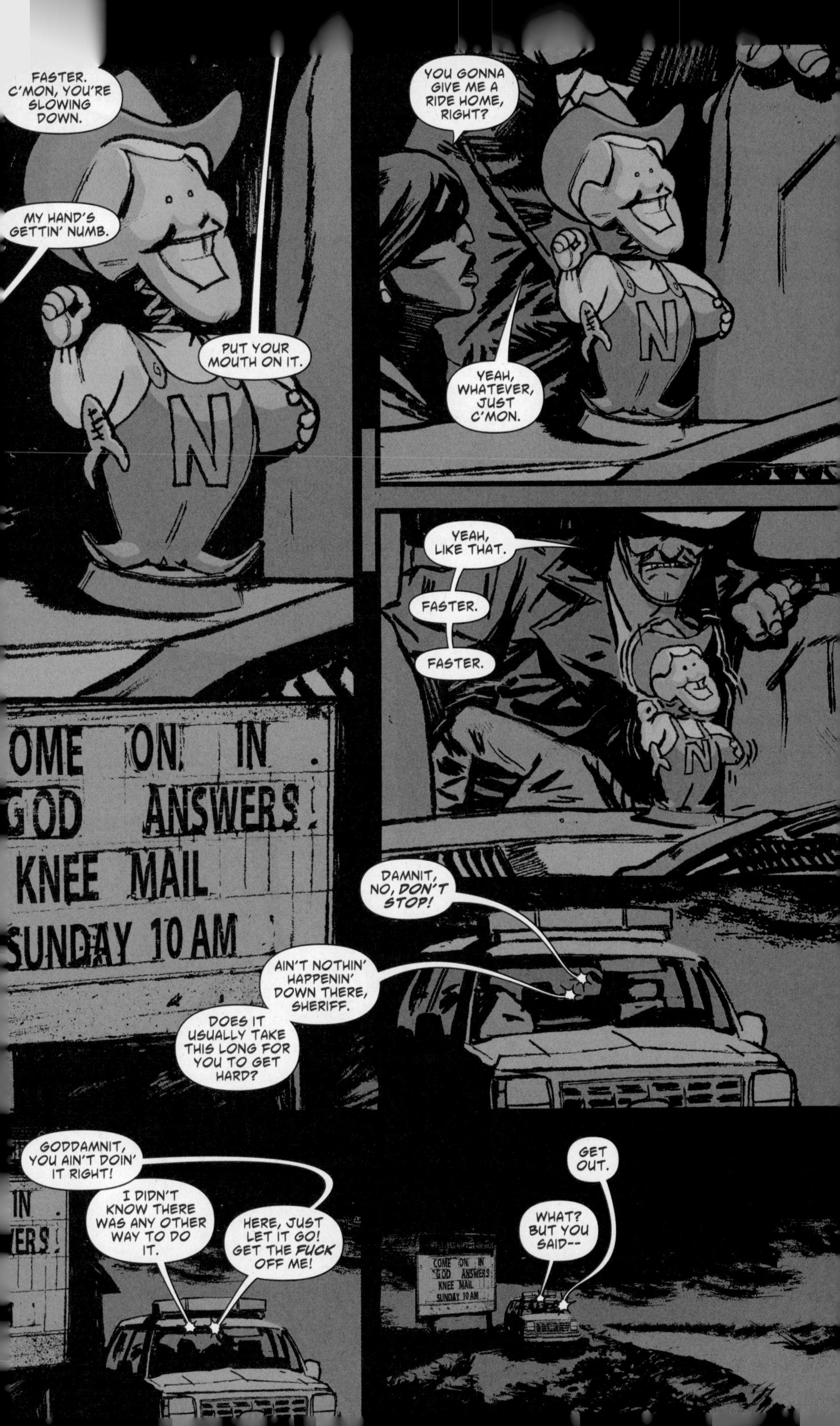

FASTER. C'MON, YOU'RE SLOWING DOWN.
MY HAND'S GETTIN' NUMB.
PUT YOUR MOUTH ON IT.
YOU GONNA GIVE ME A RIDE HOME, RIGHT?
YEAH, WHATEVER, JUST C'MON.
YEAH, LIKE THAT.
FASTER.
FASTER.
OME ON IN
GOD ANSWERS
KNEE MAIL
SUNDAY 10 AM
DAMNIT, NO, *DON'T STOP!*
AIN'T NOTHIN' HAPPENIN' DOWN THERE, SHERIFF.
DOES IT USUALLY TAKE THIS LONG FOR YOU TO GET HARD?
GODDAMNIT, YOU AIN'T DOIN' IT RIGHT!
I DIDN'T KNOW THERE WAS ANY OTHER WAY TO DO IT.
HERE, JUST LET IT GO! GET THE *FUCK* OFF ME!
GET OUT.
WHAT? BUT YOU SAID--

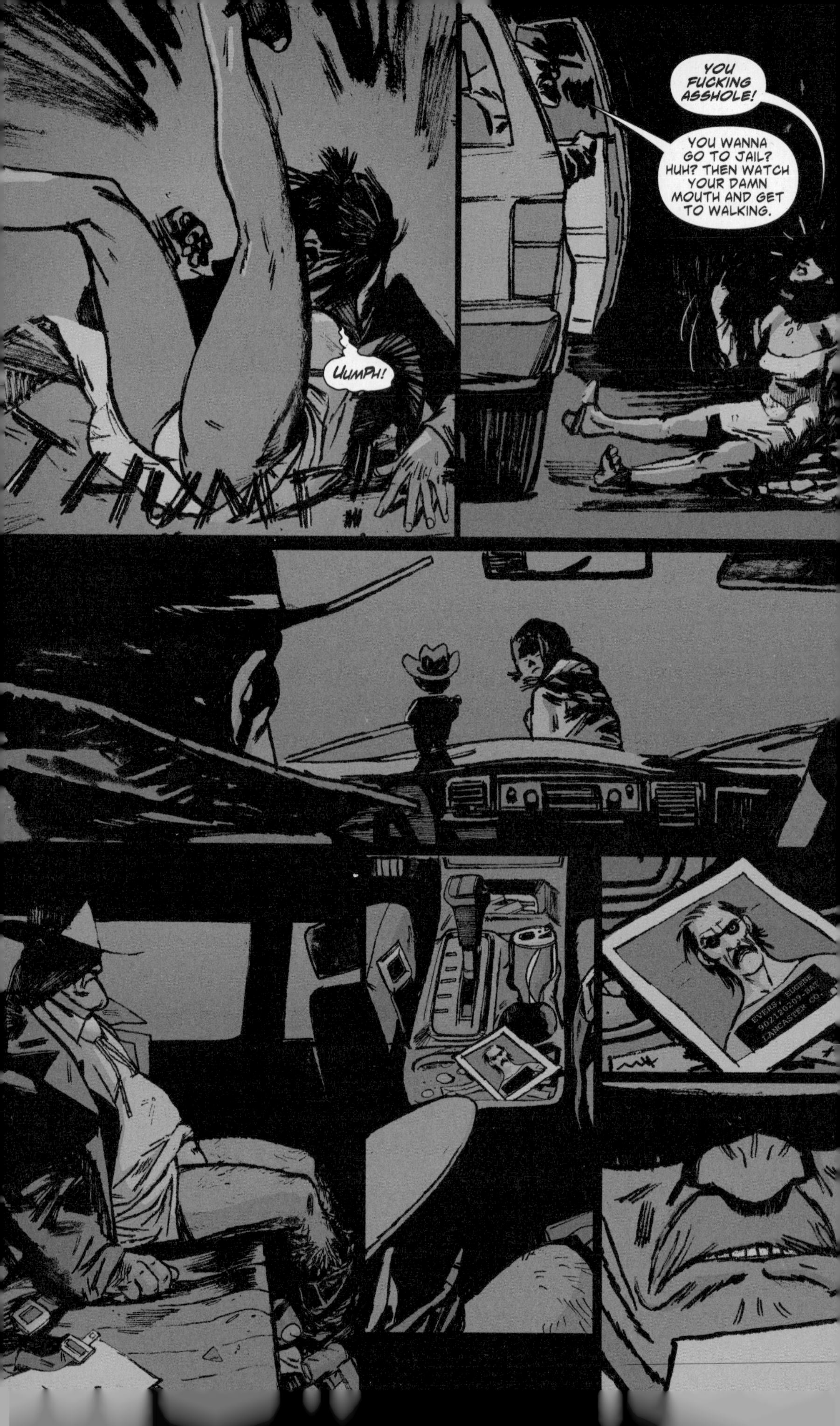
THUMP
UUMPH!
YOU FUCKING ASSHOLE!
YOU WANNA GO TO JAIL? HUH? THEN WATCH YOUR DAMN MOUTH AND GET TO WALKING.
EVERS, EUGENE
902120209-BA
LANCASTER CO.

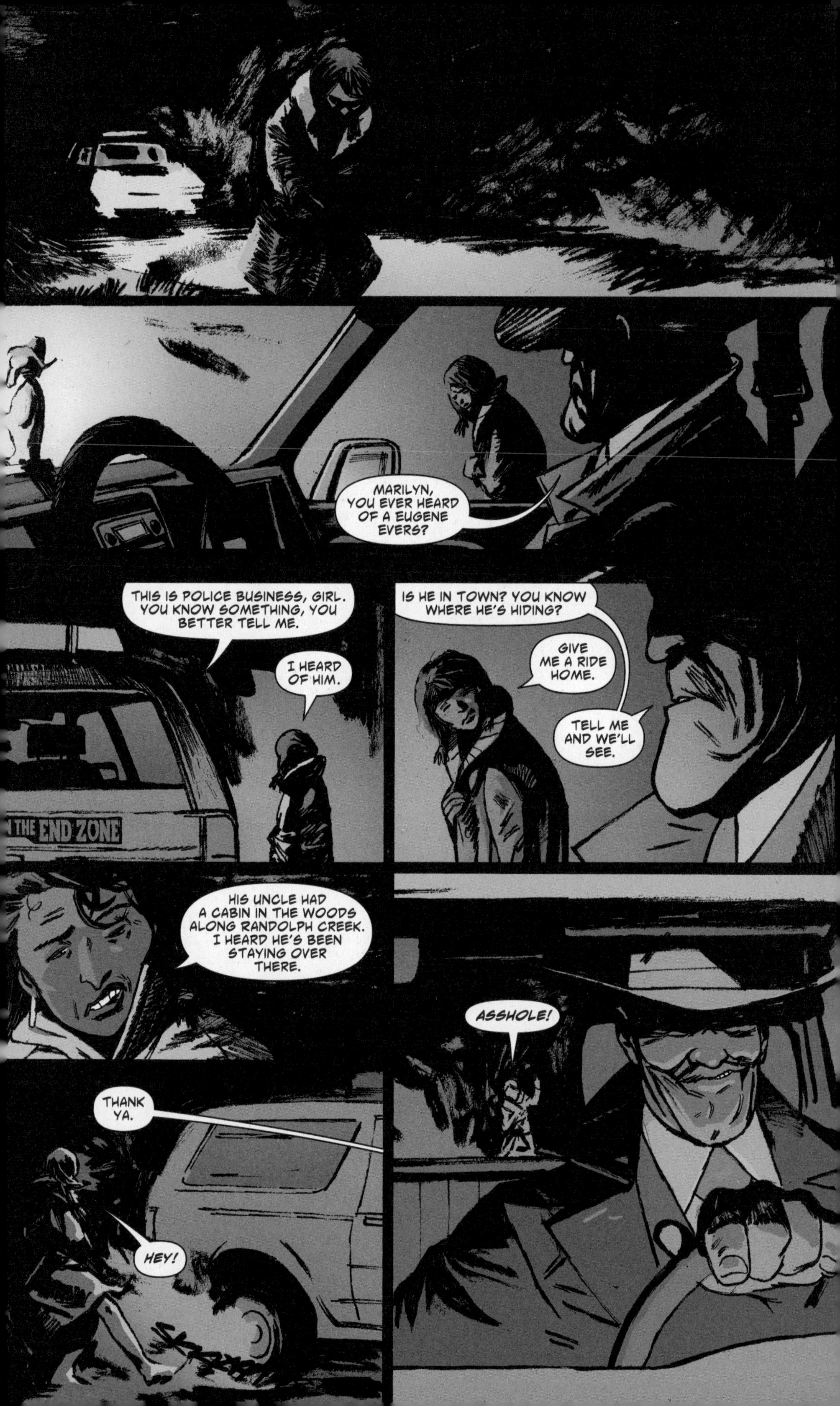
MARILYN, YOU EVER HEARD OF A EUGENE EVERS?
THIS IS POLICE BUSINESS, GIRL. YOU KNOW SOMETHING, YOU BETTER TELL ME.
I HEARD OF HIM.
THE END ZONE
IS HE IN TOWN? YOU KNOW WHERE HE'S HIDING?
GIVE ME A RIDE HOME.
TELL ME AND WE'LL SEE.
HIS UNCLE HAD A CABIN IN THE WOODS ALONG RANDOLPH CREEK. I HEARD HE'S BEEN STAYING OVER THERE.
ASSHOLE!
THANK YA.
HEY!

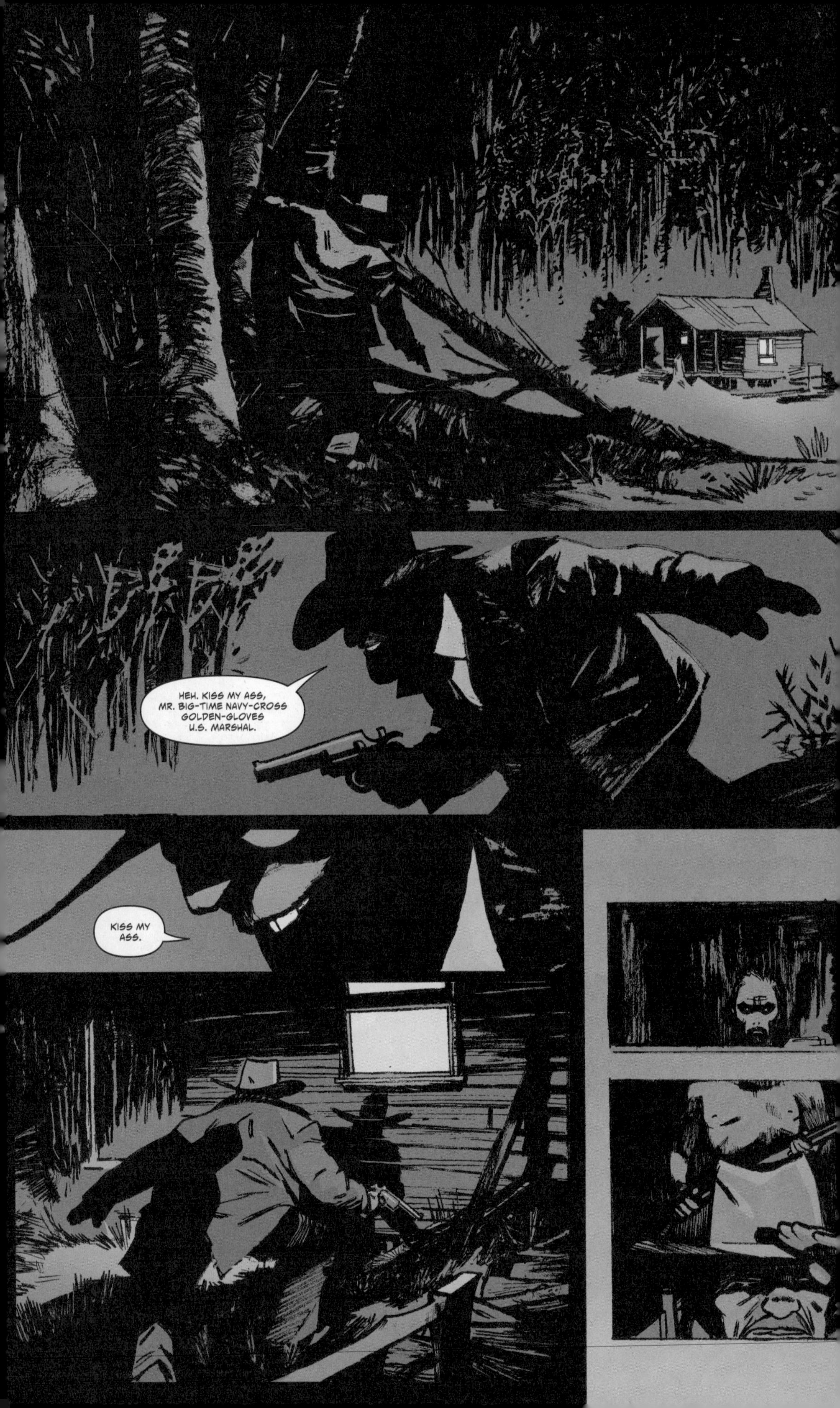
HEH. KISS MY ASS, MR. BIG-TIME NAVY-CROSS GOLDEN-GLOVES U.S. MARSHAL.
KISS MY ASS.

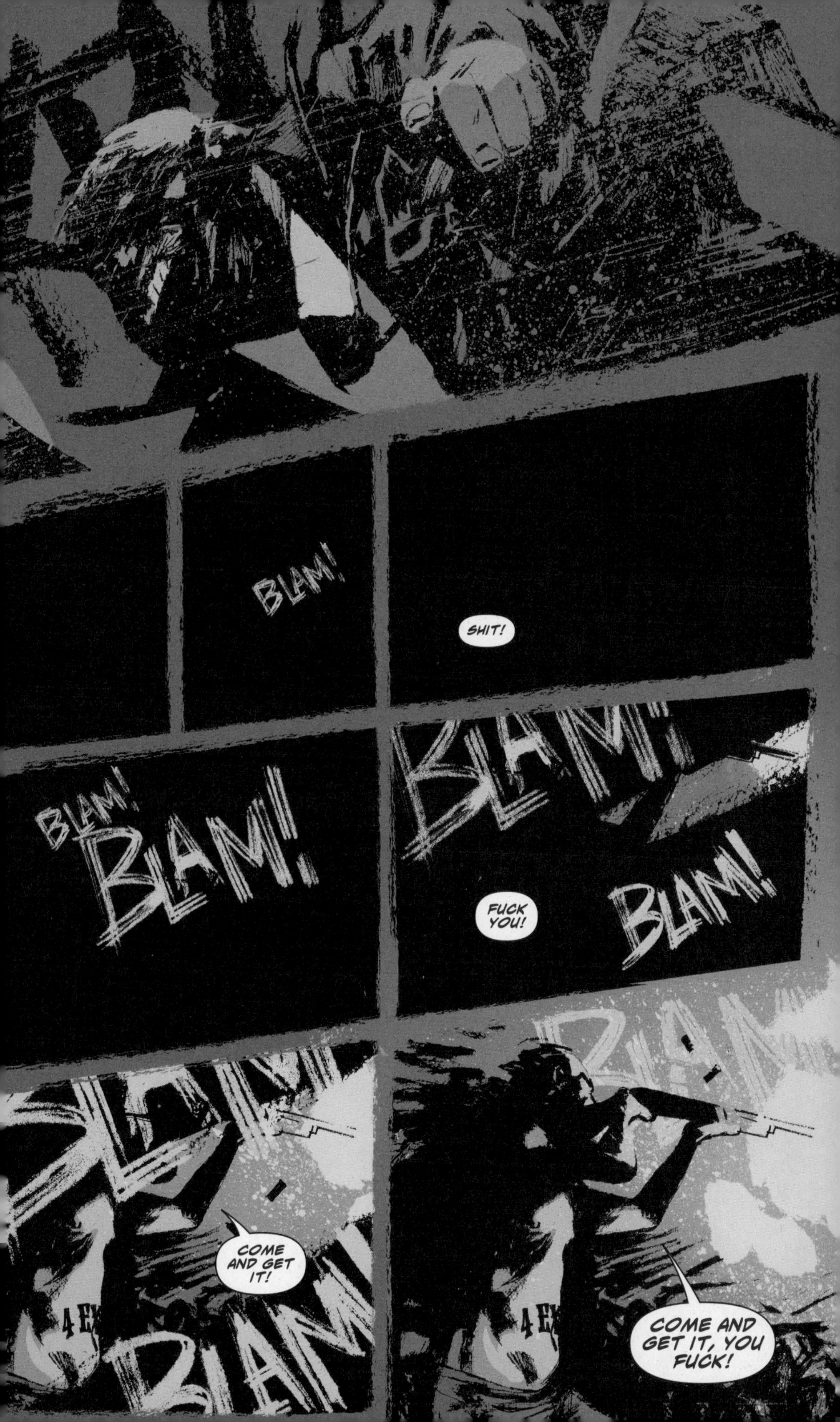
BLAM!
SHIT!
BLAM!
BLAM!
BLAM!
FUCK YOU!
BLAM!
COME AND GET IT!
COME AND GET IT, YOU FUCK!

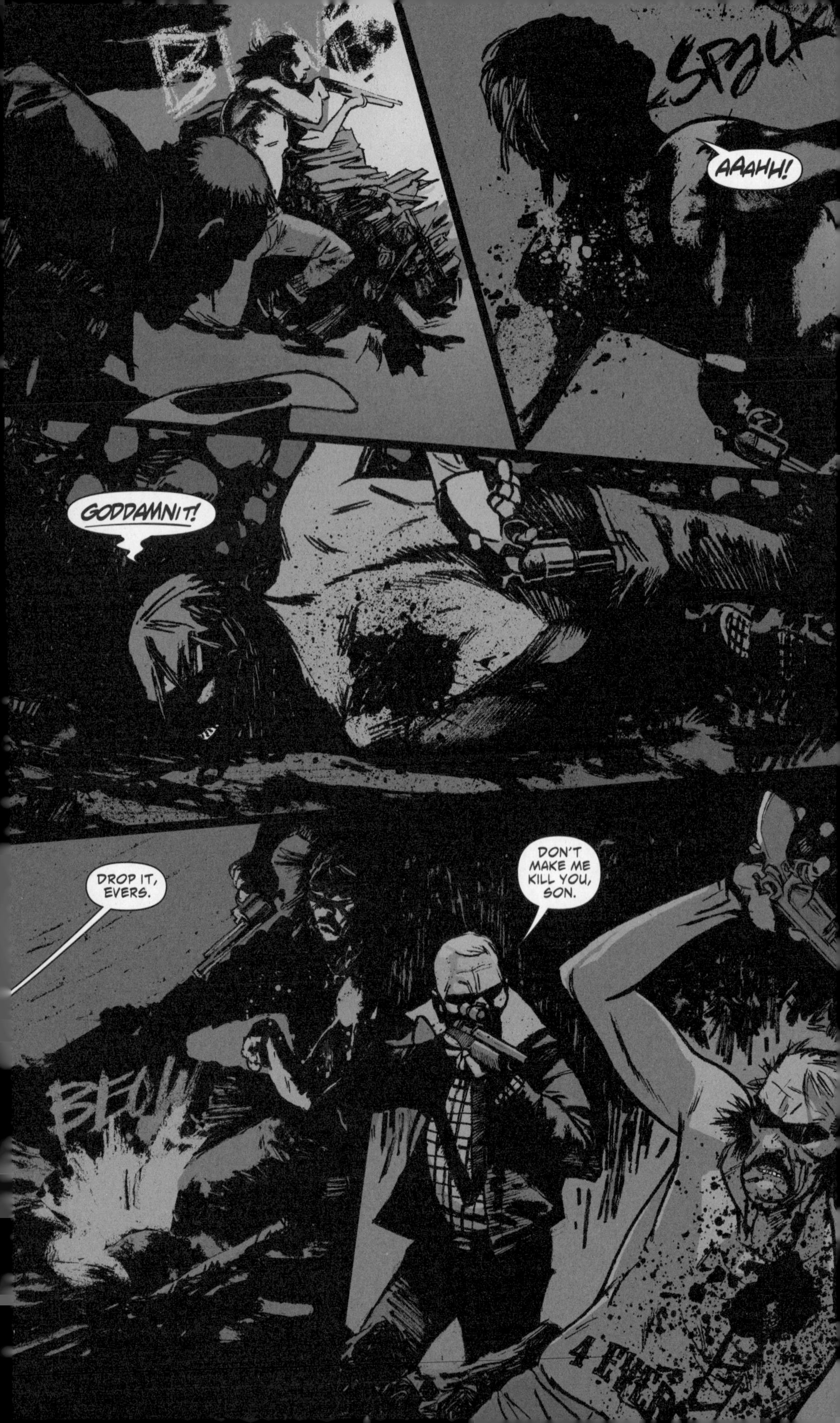
BLAM
SPLAT
AAAHH!
GODDAMNIT!
DROP IT, EVERS.
DON'T MAKE ME KILL YOU, SON.
BLAM
4 EVER

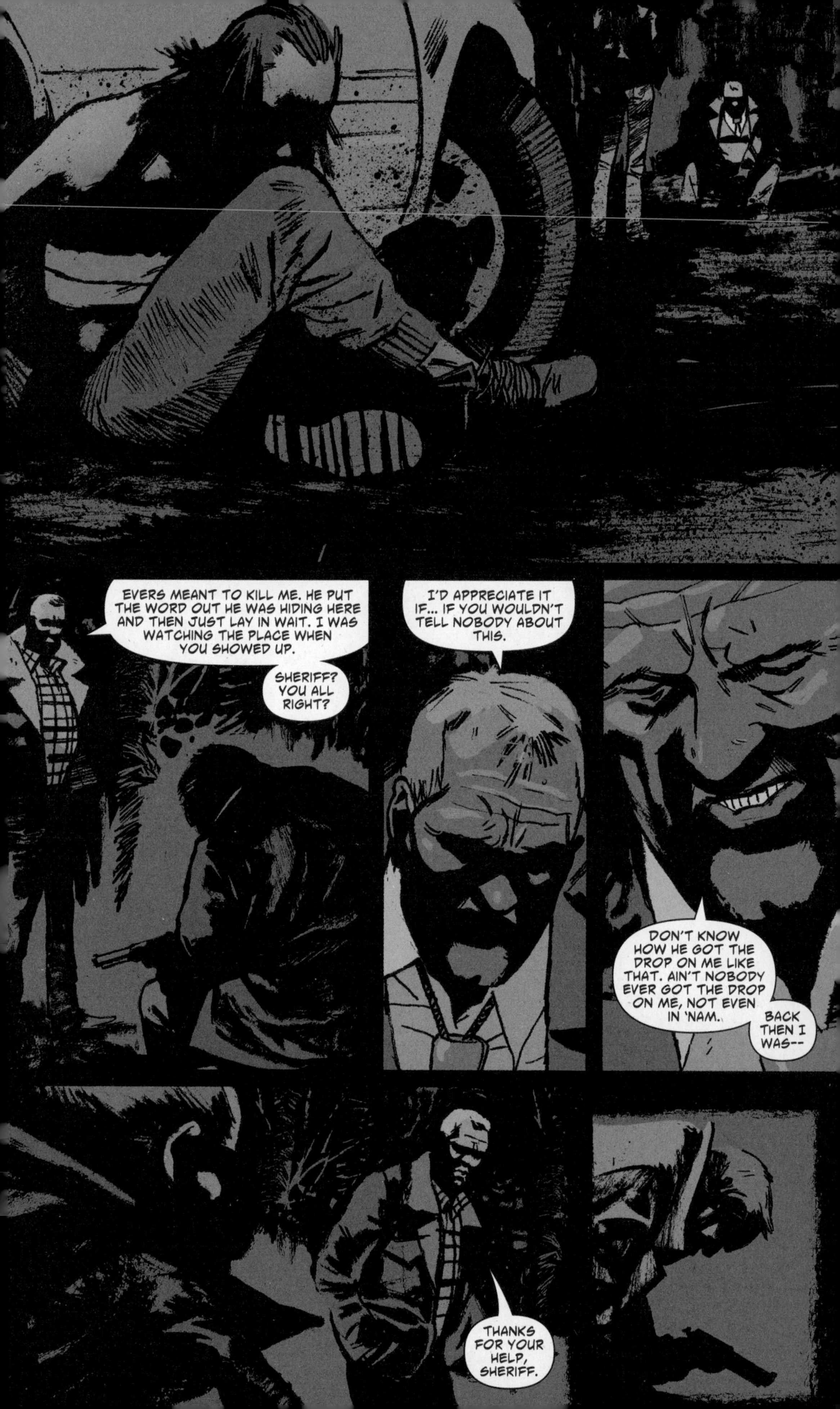
EVERS MEANT TO KILL ME. HE PUT THE WORD OUT HE WAS HIDING HERE AND THEN JUST LAY IN WAIT. I WAS WATCHING THE PLACE WHEN YOU SHOWED UP.
SHERIFF? YOU ALL RIGHT?
I'D APPRECIATE IT IF... IF YOU WOULDN'T TELL NOBODY ABOUT THIS.
DON'T KNOW HOW HE GOT THE DROP ON ME LIKE THAT. AIN'T NOBODY EVER GOT THE DROP ON ME, NOT EVEN IN 'NAM.
BACK THEN I WAS--
THANKS FOR YOUR HELP, SHERIFF.

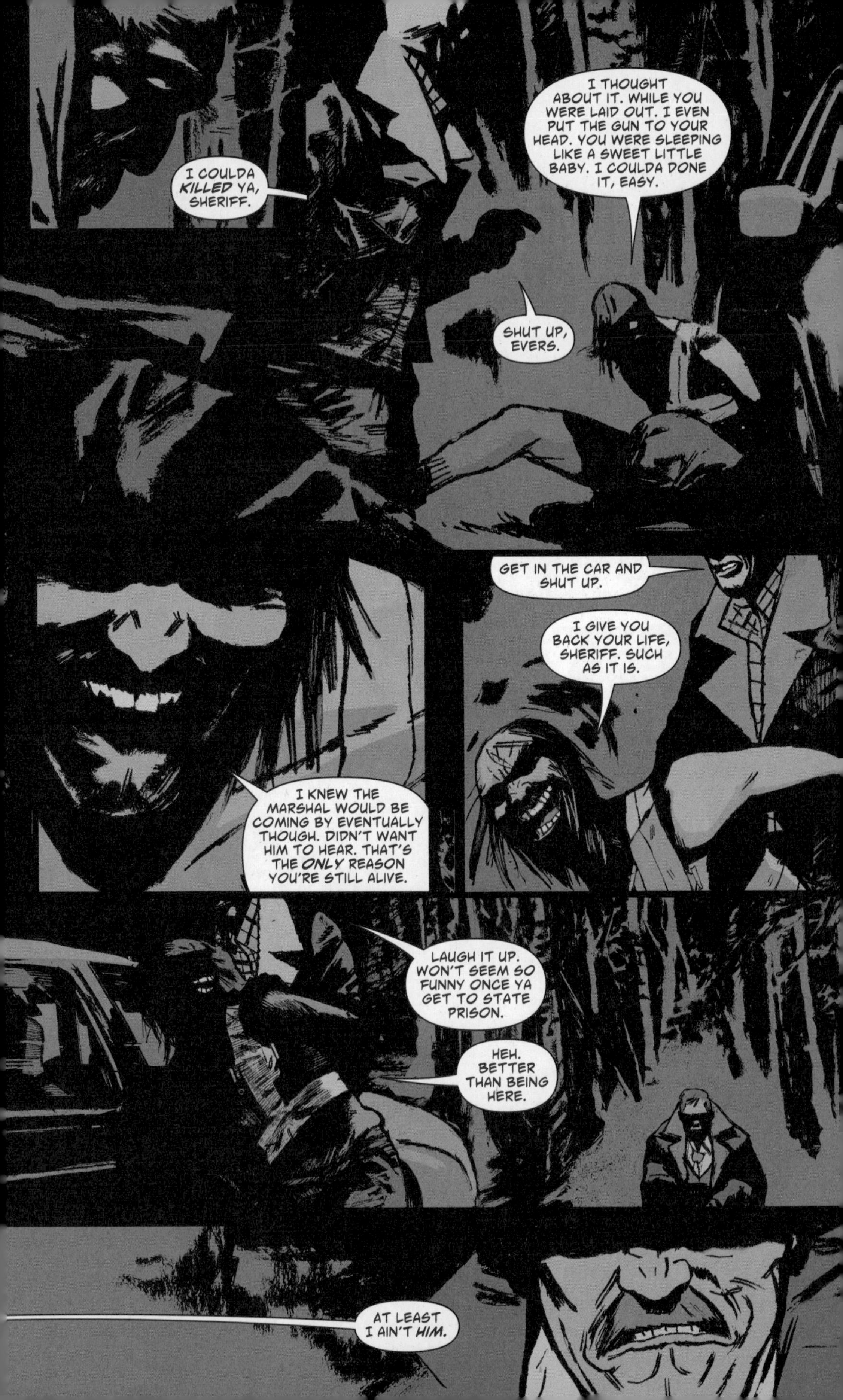
I COULDA KILLED YA, SHERIFF.
I THOUGHT ABOUT IT. WHILE YOU WERE LAID OUT. I EVEN PUT THE GUN TO YOUR HEAD. YOU WERE SLEEPING LIKE A SWEET LITTLE BABY. I COULDA DONE IT, EASY.
SHUT UP, EVERS.
I KNEW THE MARSHAL WOULD BE COMING BY EVENTUALLY THOUGH. DIDN'T WANT HIM TO HEAR. THAT'S THE ONLY REASON YOU'RE STILL ALIVE.
GET IN THE CAR AND SHUT UP.
I GIVE YOU BACK YOUR LIFE, SHERIFF. SUCH AS IT IS.
LAUGH IT UP. WON'T SEEM SO FUNNY ONCE YA GET TO STATE PRISON.
HEH. BETTER THAN BEING HERE.
AT LEAST I AIN'T HIM.

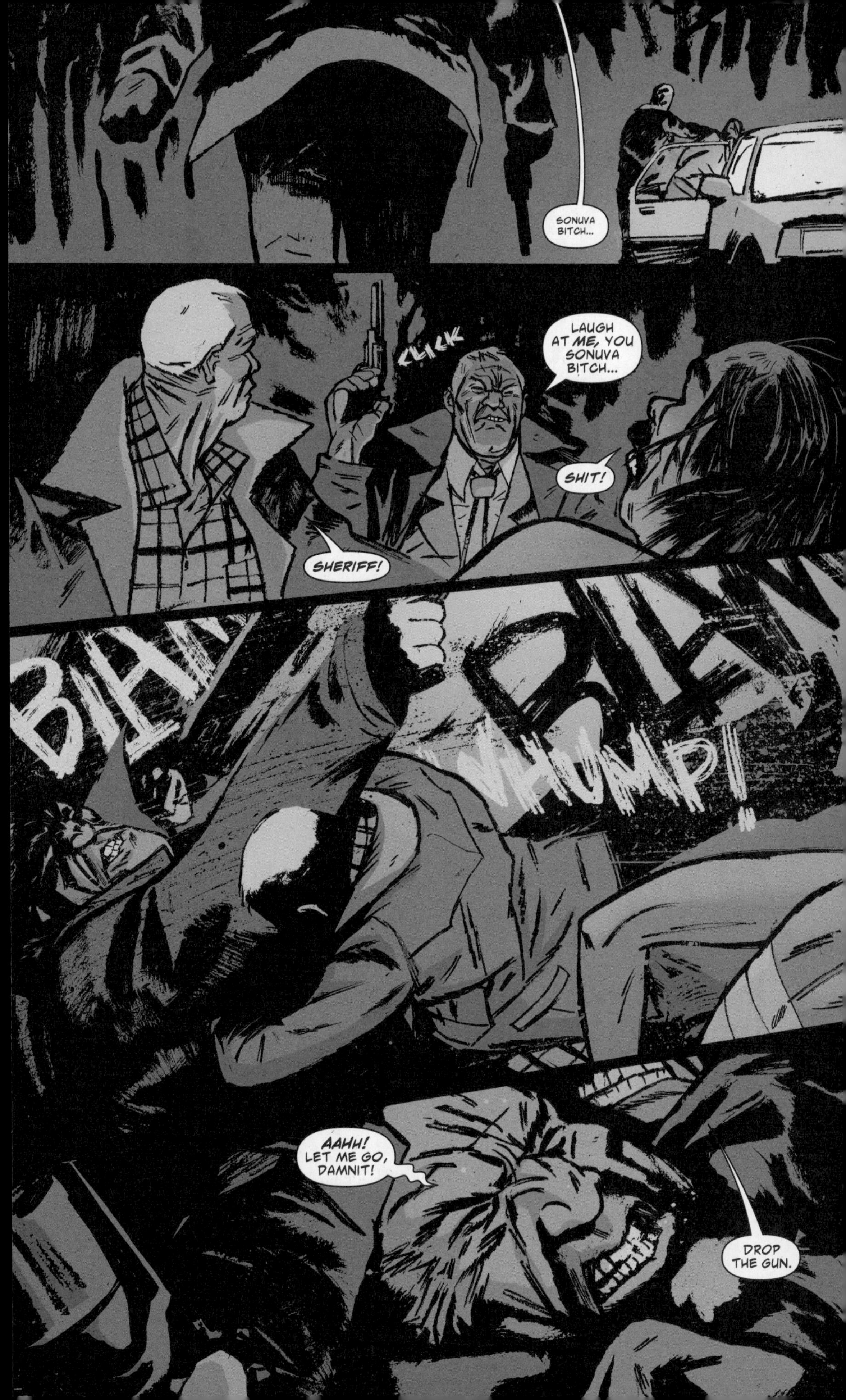

SONUVA BITCH...
CLICK
LAUGH AT ME, YOU SONUVA BITCH...
SHIT!
SHERIFF!
BLAM
BLAM
WHUMP!
AAHH! LET ME GO, DAMNIT!
DROP THE GUN.

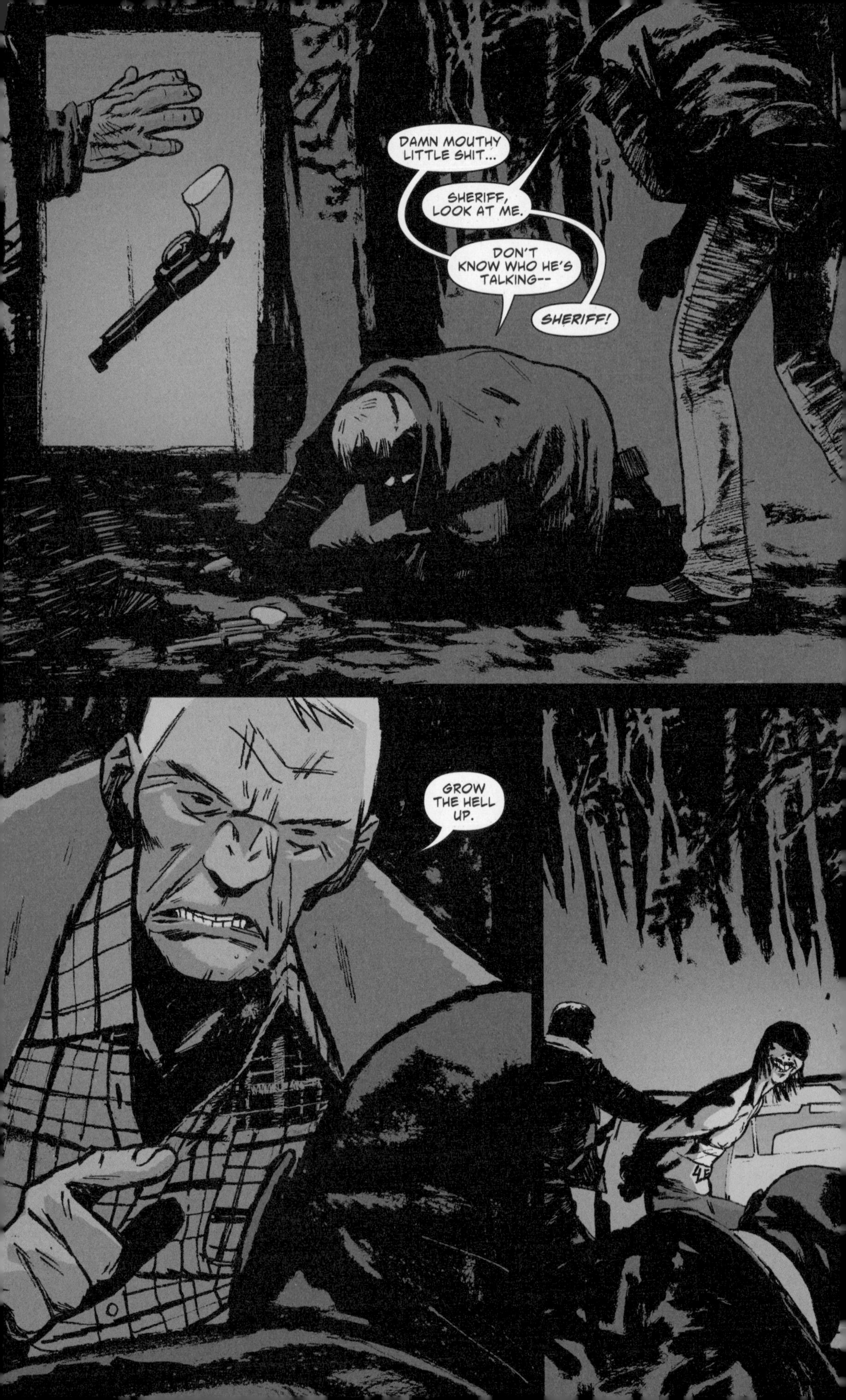
DAMN MOUTHY LITTLE SHIT...
SHERIFF, LOOK AT ME.
DON'T KNOW WHO HE'S TALKING--
SHERIFF!
GROW THE HELL UP.

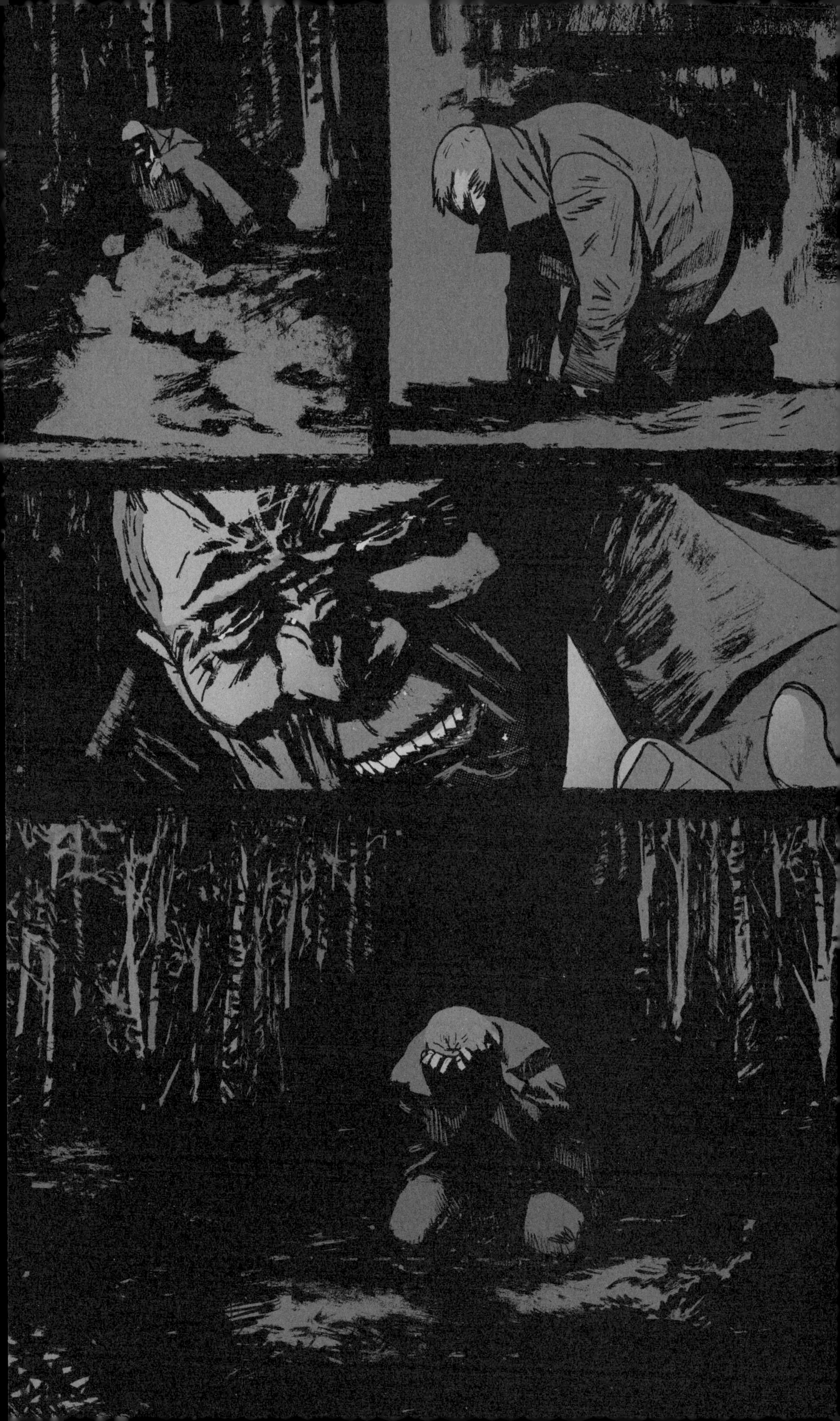

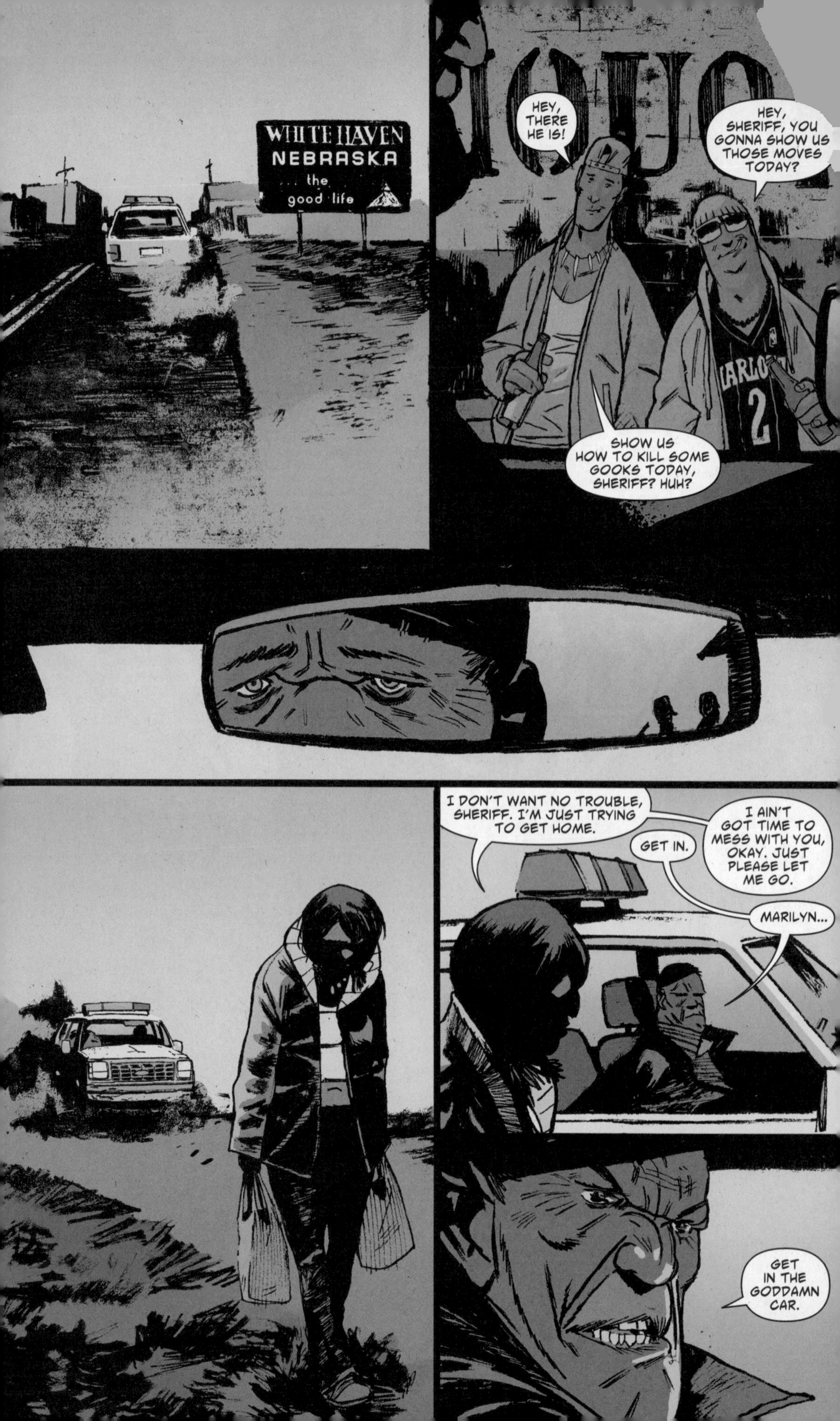
WHITE HAVEN
NEBRASKA
... the good life
HEY, THERE HE IS!
HEY, SHERIFF, YOU GONNA SHOW US THOSE MOVES TODAY?
SHOW US HOW TO KILL SOME GOOKS TODAY, SHERIFF? HUH?
I DON'T WANT NO TROUBLE, SHERIFF. I'M JUST TRYING TO GET HOME.
I AIN'T GOT TIME TO MESS WITH YOU, OKAY. JUST PLEASE LET ME GO.
GET IN.
MARILYN...
GET IN THE GODDAMN CAR.

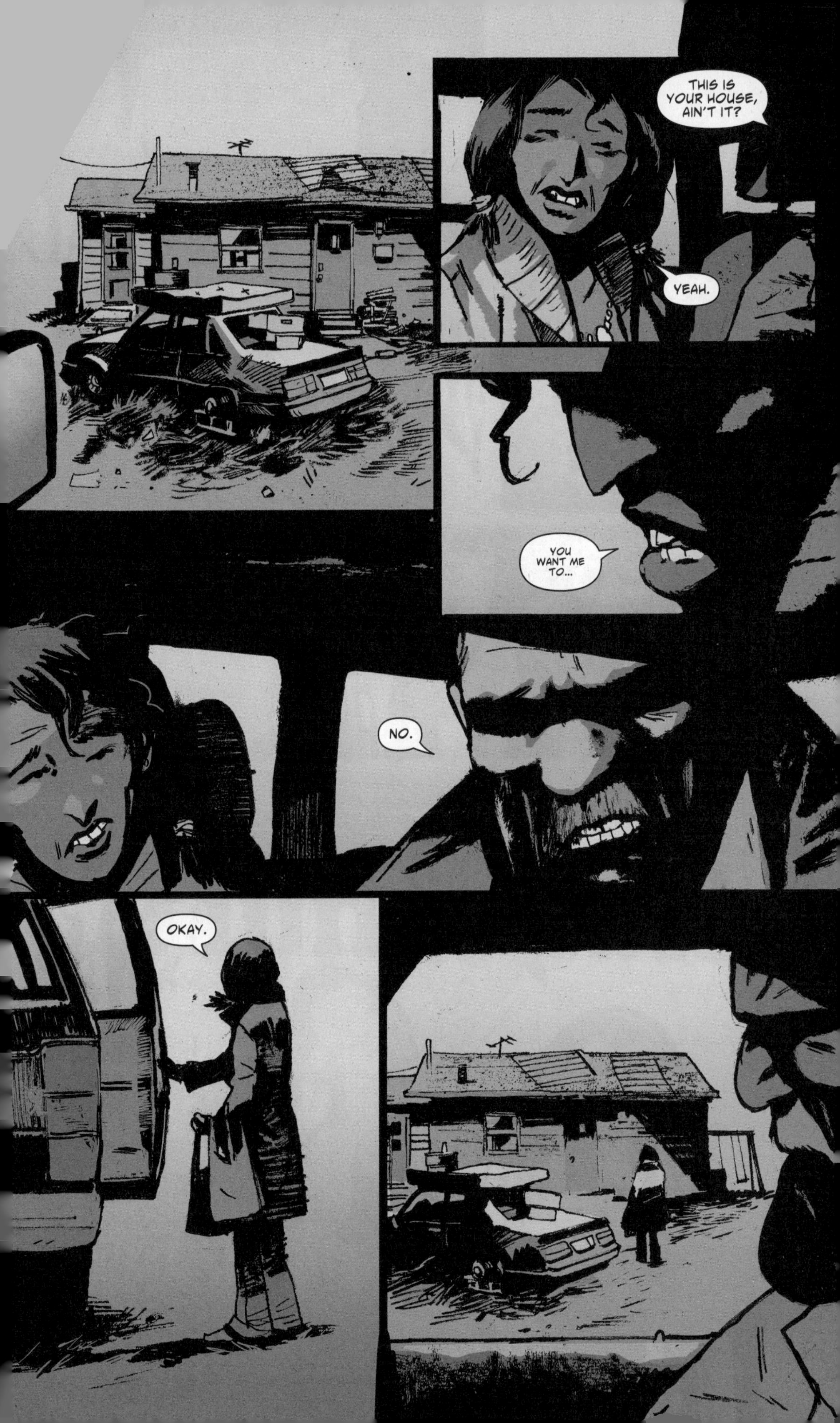
THIS IS YOUR HOUSE, AIN'T IT?
YEAH.
YOU WANT ME TO...
NO.
OKAY.

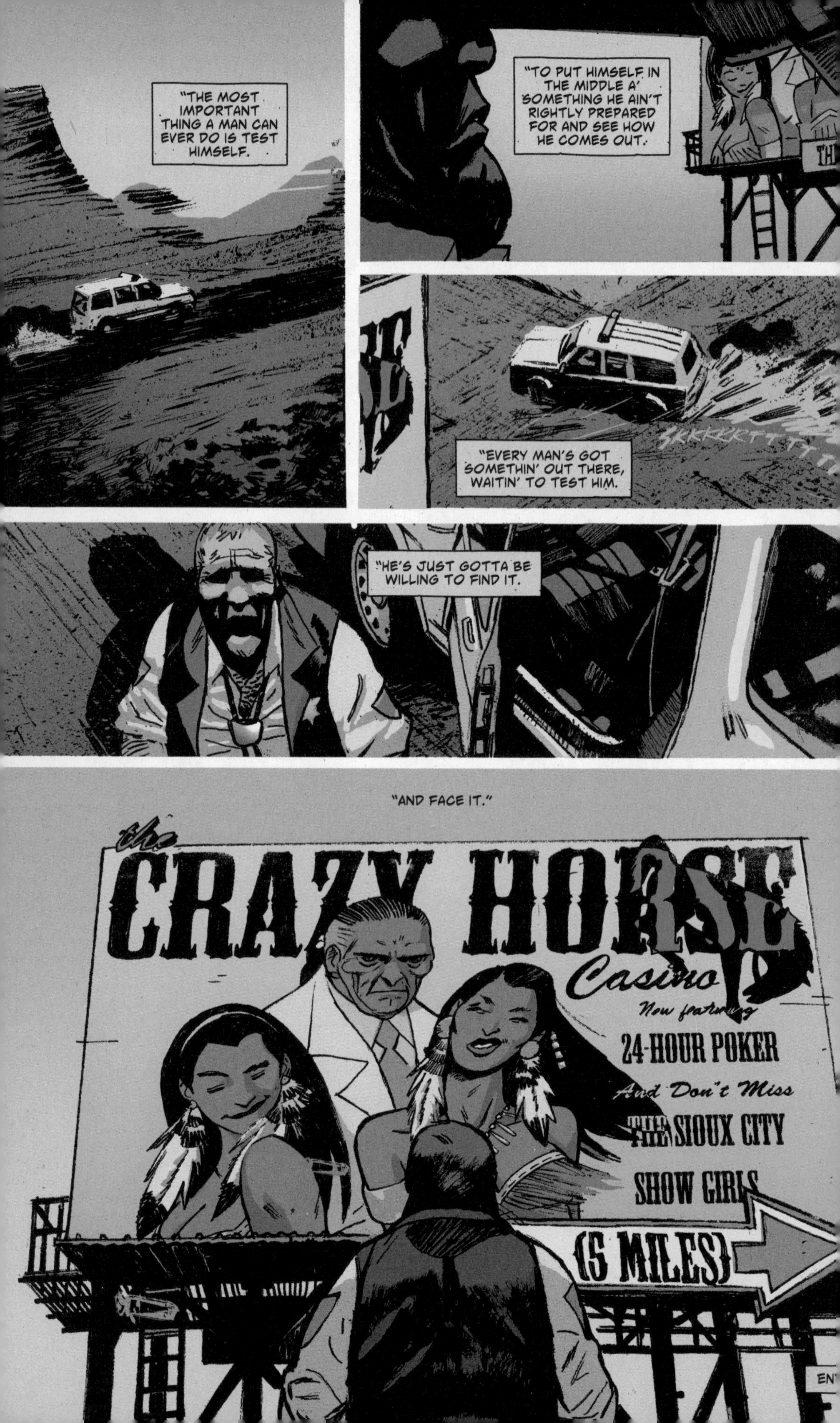
"THE MOST IMPORTANT THING A MAN CAN EVER DO IS TEST HIMSELF.
"TO PUT HIMSELF IN THE MIDDLE A' SOMETHING HE AIN'T RIGHTLY PREPARED FOR AND SEE HOW HE COMES OUT.
SKKKRRTTTTT
"EVERY MAN'S GOT SOMETHIN' OUT THERE, WAITIN' TO TEST HIM.
"HE'S JUST GOTTA BE WILLING TO FIND IT.
"AND FACE IT."
the CRAZY HORSE Casino
24-HOUR POKER
And Don't Miss
THE SIOUX CITY
SHOW GIRLS
(5 MILES)

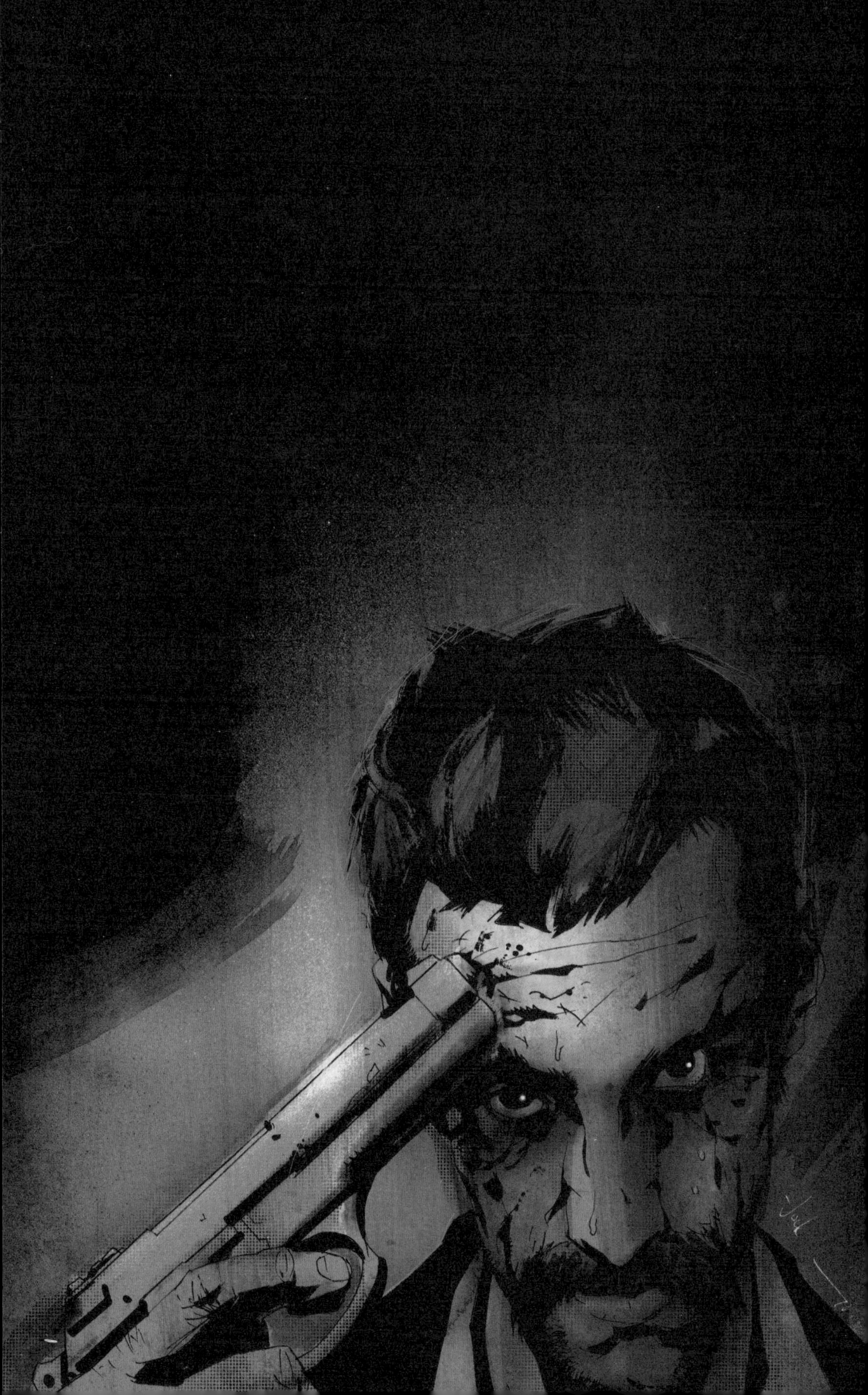

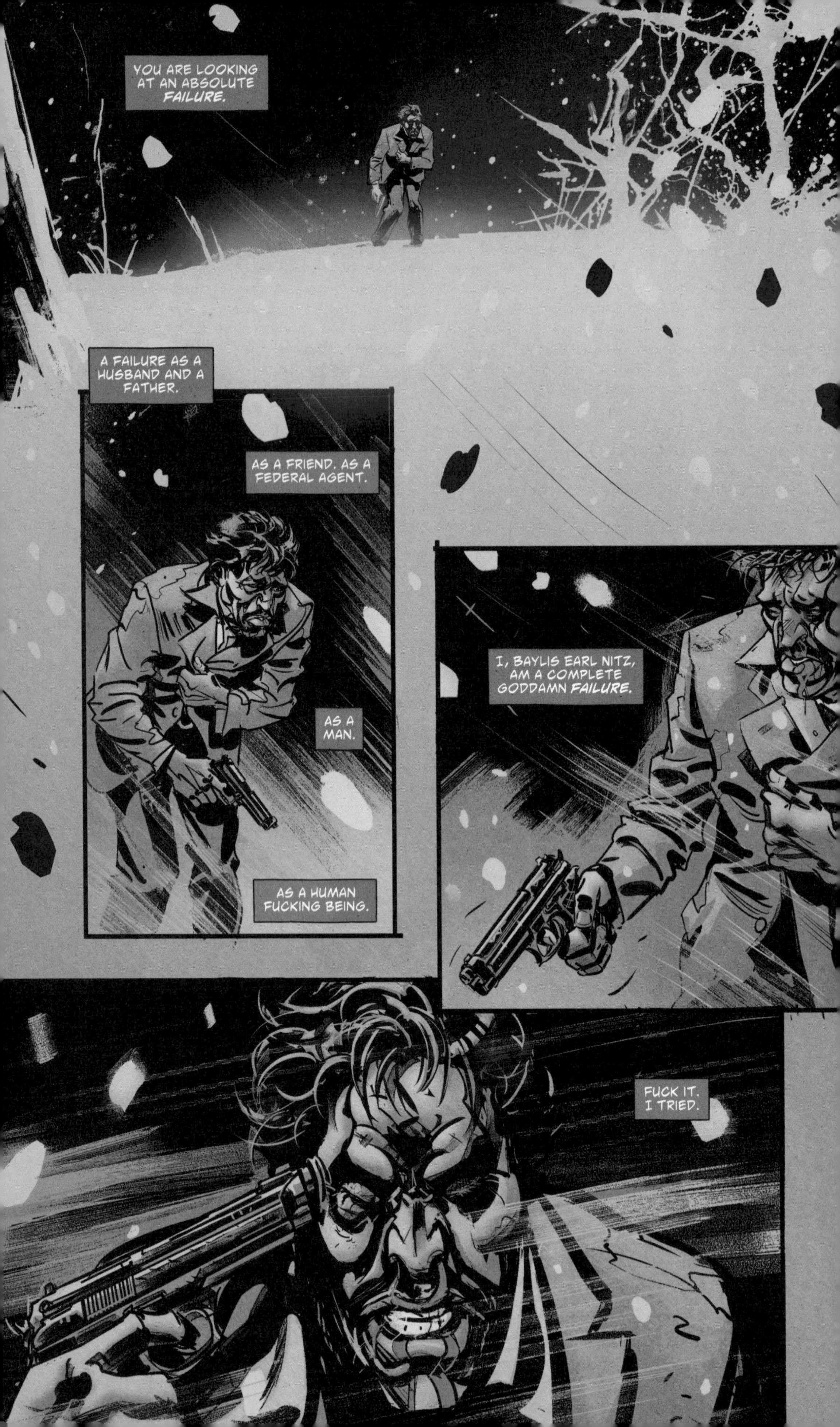
YOU ARE LOOKING AT AN ABSOLUTE *FAILURE.*
A FAILURE AS A HUSBAND AND A FATHER.
AS A FRIEND. AS A FEDERAL AGENT.
AS A MAN.
AS A HUMAN FUCKING BEING.
I, BAYLIS EARL NITZ, AM A COMPLETE GODDAMN *FAILURE.*
FUCK IT. I TRIED.

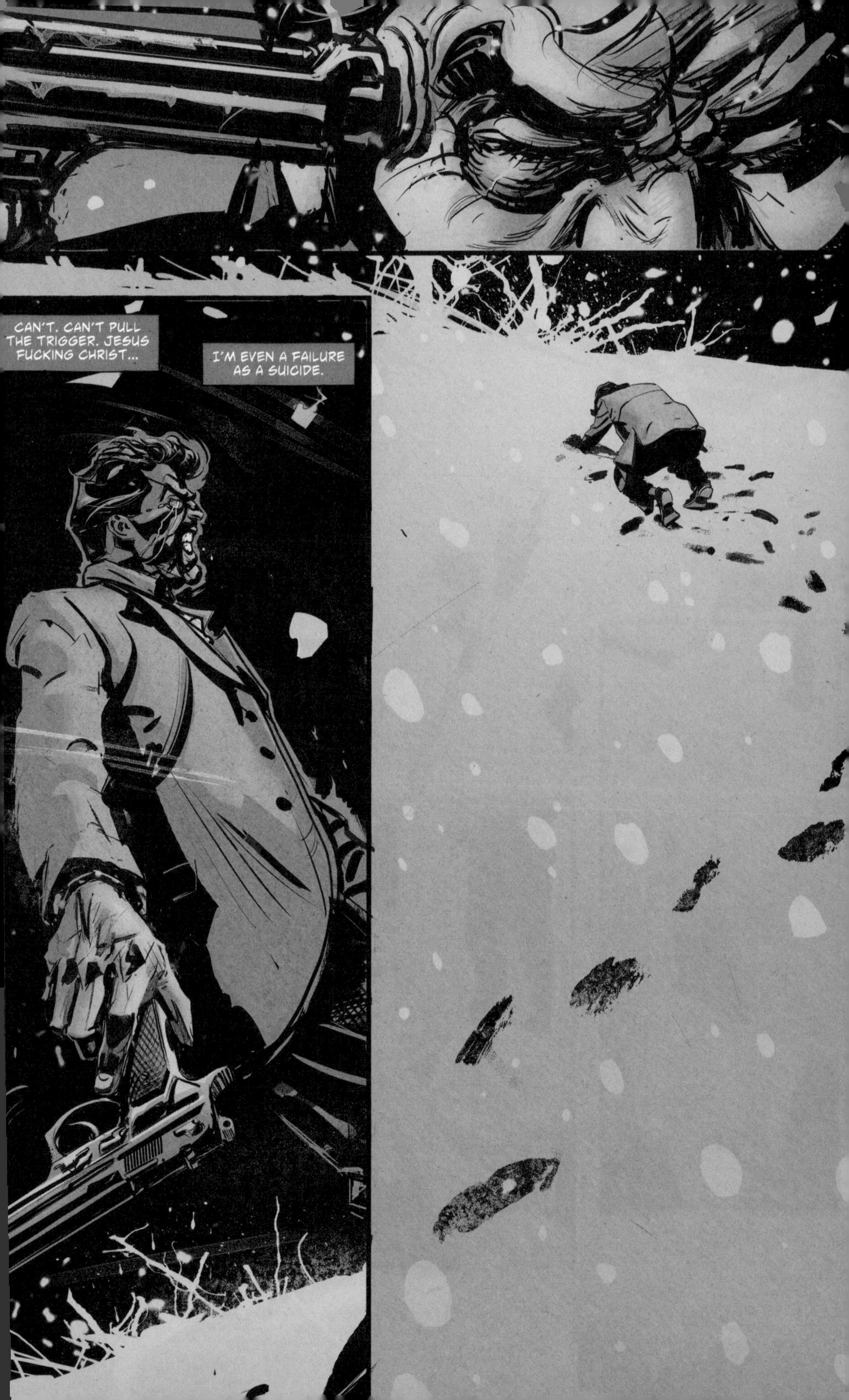
CAN'T. CAN'T PULL THE TRIGGER. JESUS FUCKING CHRIST...
I'M EVEN A FAILURE AS A SUICIDE.

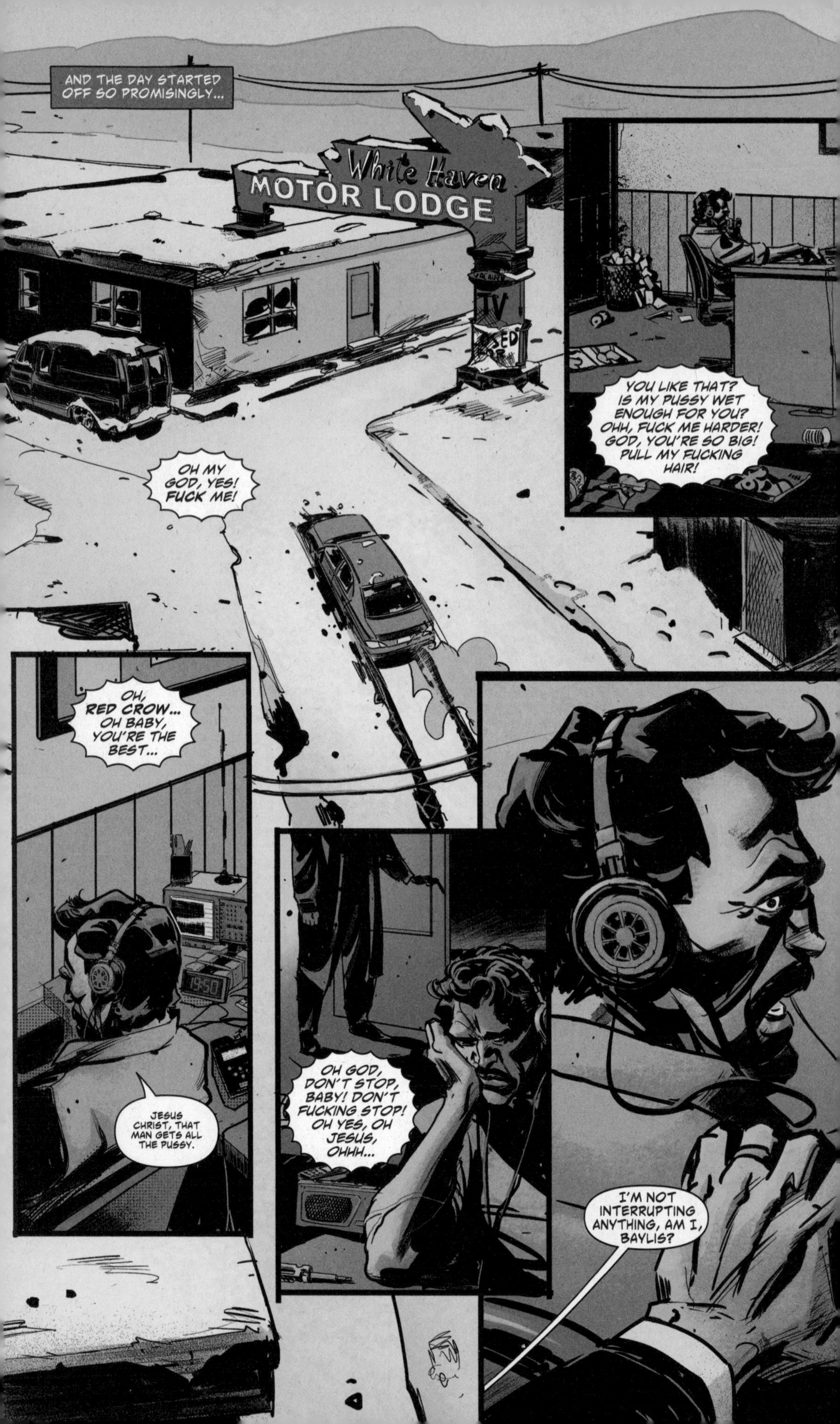
AND THE DAY STARTED OFF SO PROMISINGLY...
White Haven
MOTOR LODGE
TV
OH MY GOD, YES! FUCK ME!
YOU LIKE THAT? IS MY PUSSY WET ENOUGH FOR YOU? OHH, FUCK ME HARDER! GOD, YOU'RE SO BIG! PULL MY FUCKING HAIR!
OH, RED CROW... OH BABY, YOU'RE THE BEST...
19:50
JESUS CHRIST, THAT MAN GETS ALL THE PUSSY.
OH GOD, DON'T STOP, BABY! DON'T FUCKING STOP! OH YES, OH JESUS, OHHH...
I'M NOT INTERRUPTING ANYTHING, AM I, BAYLIS?

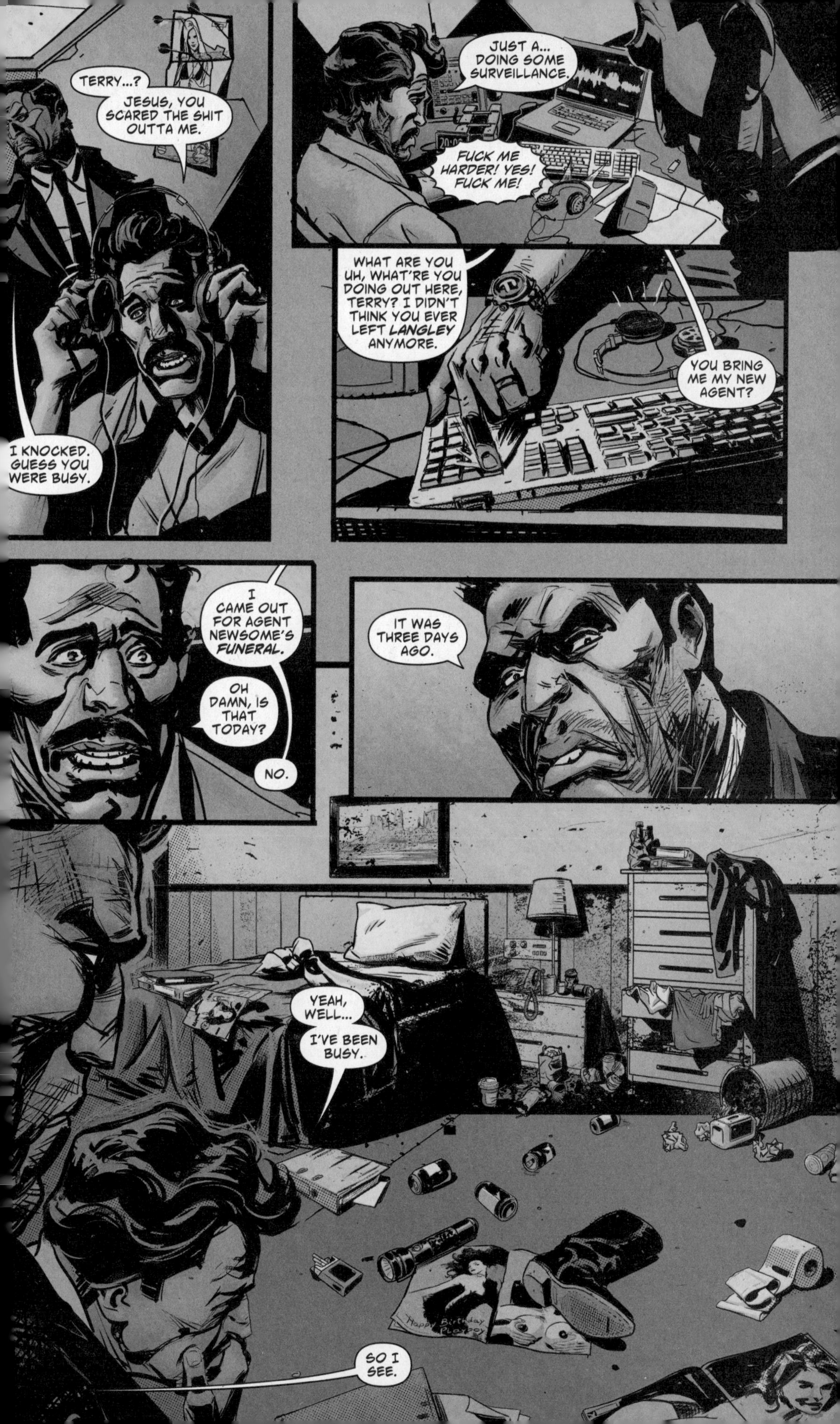
TERRY...?
JESUS, YOU SCARED THE SHIT OUTTA ME.
I KNOCKED. GUESS YOU WERE BUSY.
JUST A... DOING SOME SURVEILLANCE.
FUCK ME HARDER! YES! FUCK ME!
WHAT ARE YOU UH, WHAT'RE YOU DOING OUT HERE, TERRY? I DIDN'T THINK YOU EVER LEFT LANGLEY ANYMORE.
YOU BRING ME MY NEW AGENT?
I CAME OUT FOR AGENT NEWSOME'S FUNERAL.
OH DAMN, IS THAT TODAY?
NO.
IT WAS THREE DAYS AGO.
YEAH, WELL...
I'VE BEEN BUSY.
Happy Birthday Playboy
SO I SEE.

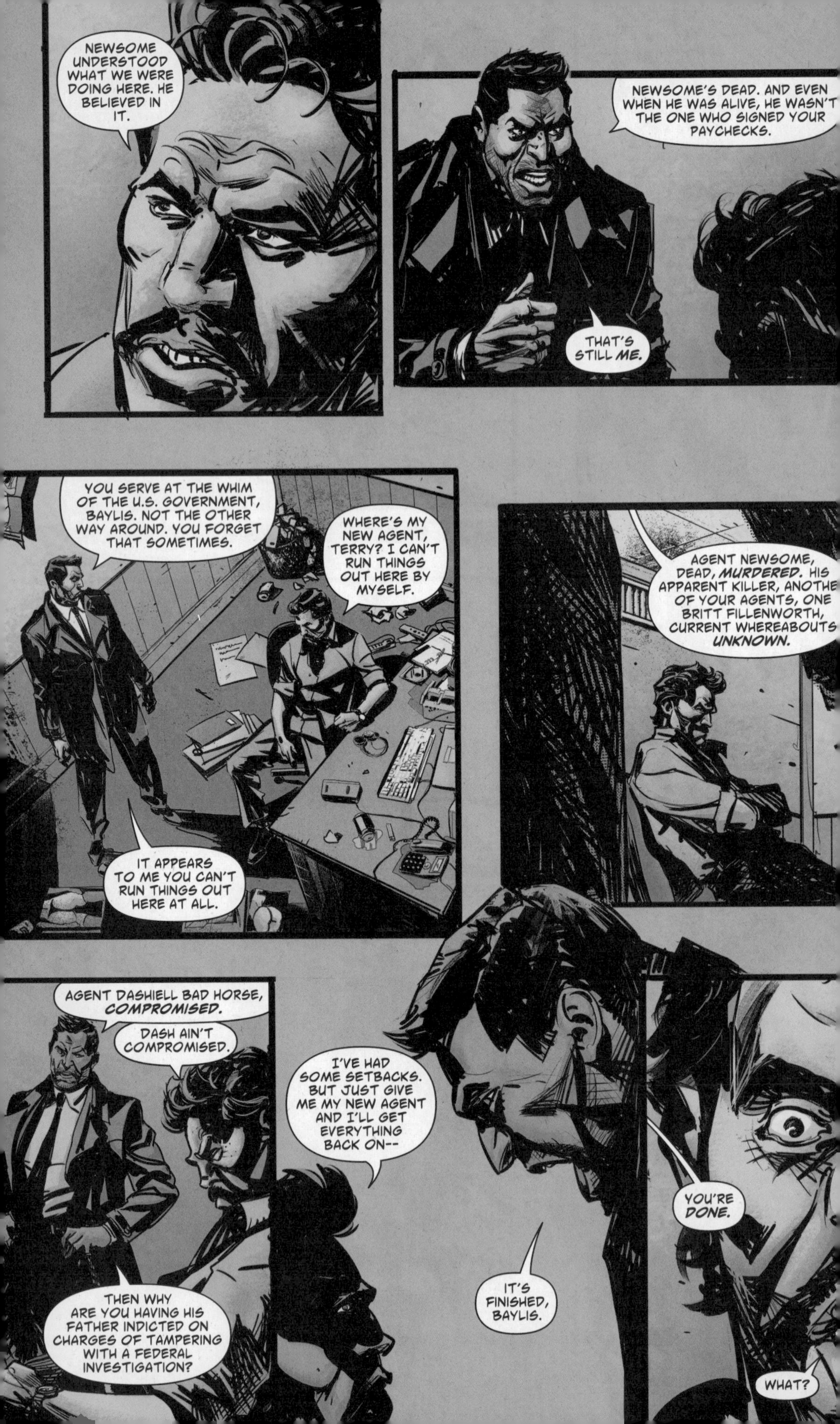
NEWSOME UNDERSTOOD WHAT WE WERE DOING HERE. HE BELIEVED IN IT.
NEWSOME'S DEAD. AND EVEN WHEN HE WAS ALIVE, HE WASN'T THE ONE WHO SIGNED YOUR PAYCHECKS.
THAT'S STILL *ME*.
YOU SERVE AT THE WHIM OF THE U.S. GOVERNMENT, BAYLIS. NOT THE OTHER WAY AROUND. YOU FORGET THAT SOMETIMES.
WHERE'S MY NEW AGENT, TERRY? I CAN'T RUN THINGS OUT HERE BY MYSELF.
IT APPEARS TO ME YOU CAN'T RUN THINGS OUT HERE AT ALL.
AGENT NEWSOME, DEAD, ***MURDERED.*** HIS APPARENT KILLER, ANOTHE OF YOUR AGENTS, ONE BRITT FILLENWORTH, CURRENT WHEREABOUTS ***UNKNOWN.***
AGENT DASHIELL BAD HORSE, ***COMPROMISED.***
DASH AIN'T COMPROMISED.
THEN WHY ARE YOU HAVING HIS FATHER INDICTED ON CHARGES OF TAMPERING WITH A FEDERAL INVESTIGATION?
I'VE HAD SOME SETBACKS. BUT JUST GIVE ME MY NEW AGENT AND I'LL GET EVERYTHING BACK ON--
IT'S FINISHED, BAYLIS.
YOU'RE *DONE.*
WHAT?

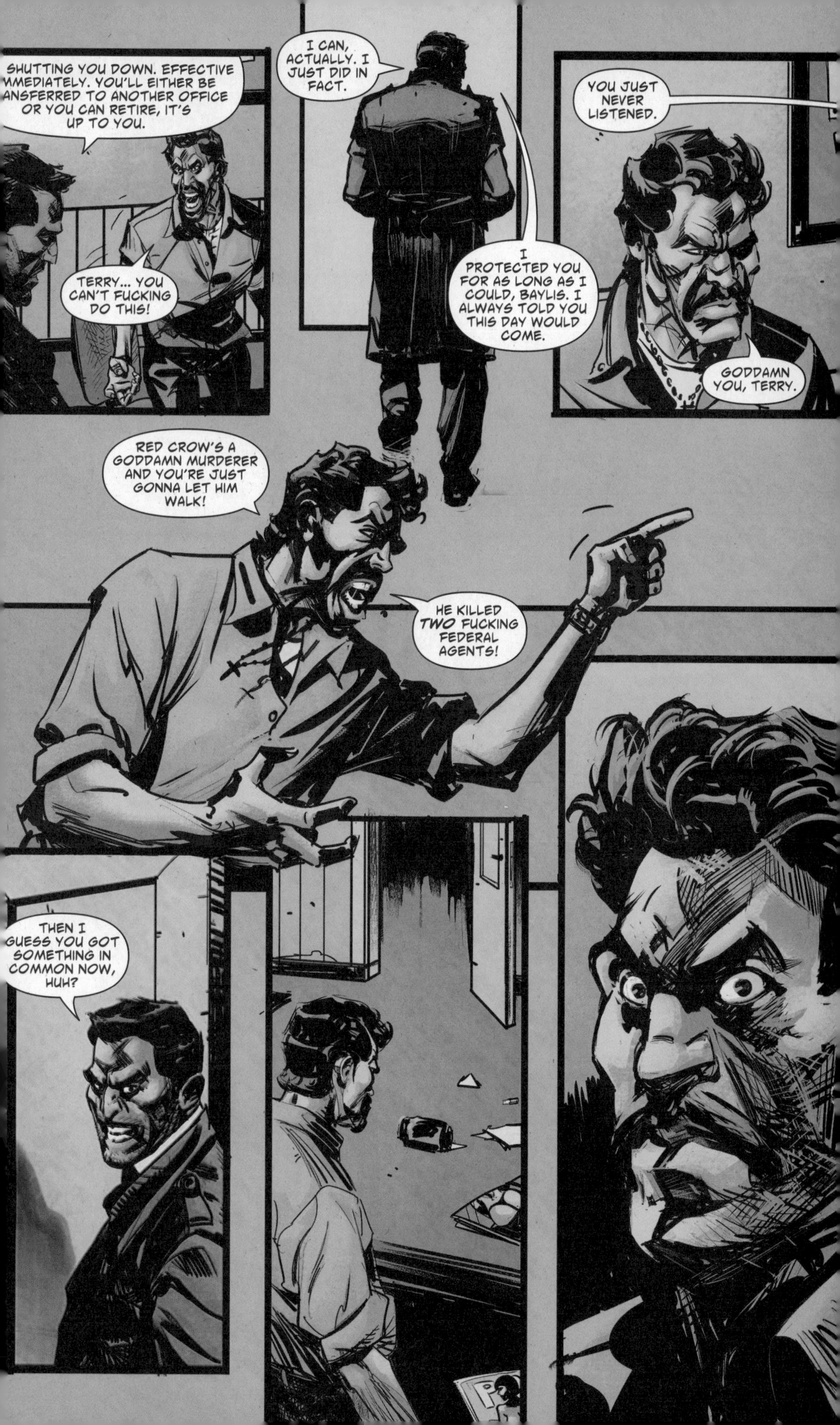
SHUTTING YOU DOWN. EFFECTIVE MMEDIATELY. YOU'LL EITHER BE ANSFERRED TO ANOTHER OFFICE OR YOU CAN RETIRE, IT'S UP TO YOU.
TERRY... YOU CAN'T FUCKING DO THIS!
I CAN, ACTUALLY. I JUST DID IN FACT.
I PROTECTED YOU FOR AS LONG AS I COULD, BAYLIS. I ALWAYS TOLD YOU THIS DAY WOULD COME.
YOU JUST NEVER LISTENED.
GODDAMN YOU, TERRY.
RED CROW'S A GODDAMN MURDERER AND YOU'RE JUST GONNA LET HIM WALK!
HE KILLED TWO FUCKING FEDERAL AGENTS!
THEN I GUESS YOU GOT SOMETHING IN COMMON NOW, HUH?

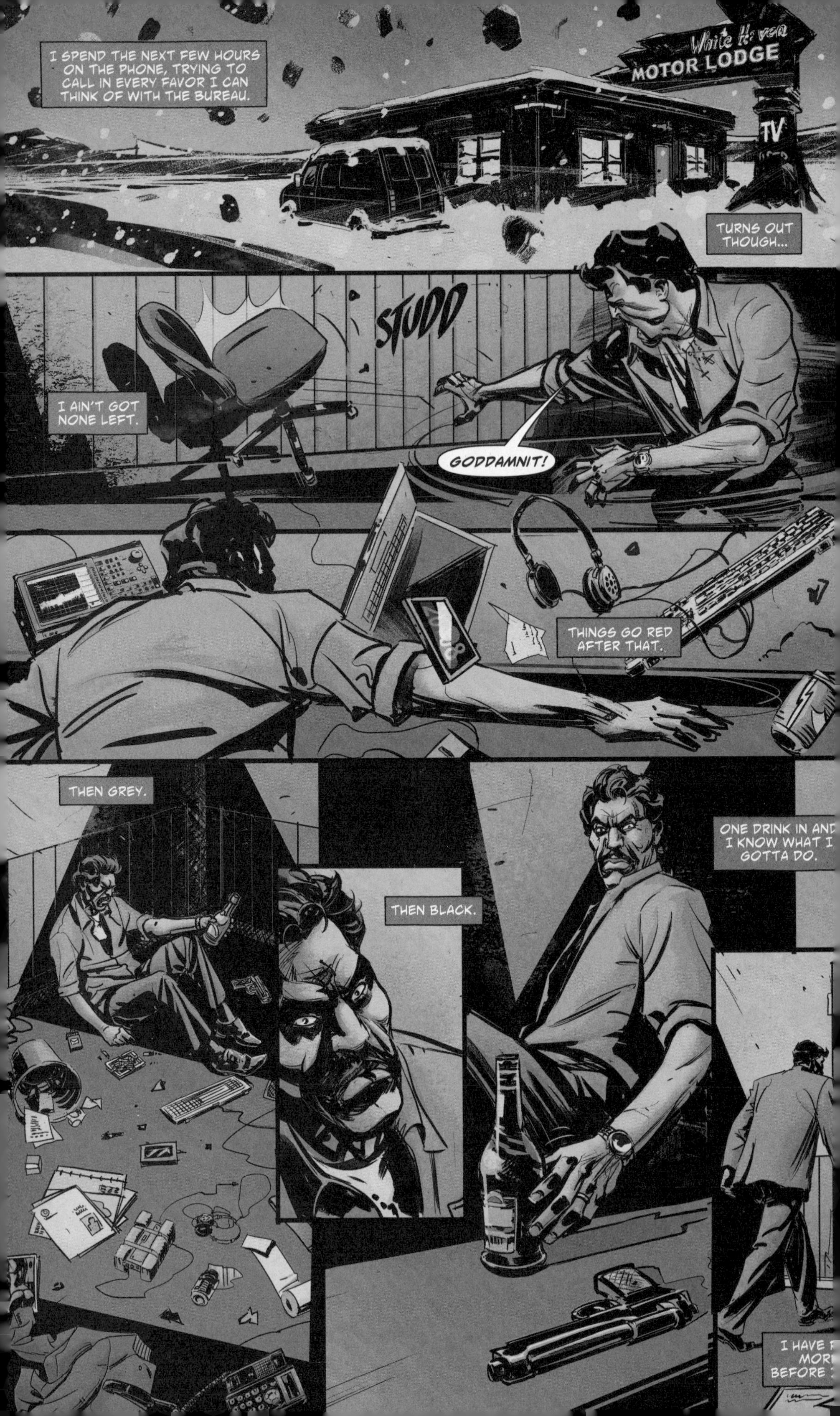
I SPEND THE NEXT FEW HOURS ON THE PHONE, TRYING TO CALL IN EVERY FAVOR I CAN THINK OF WITH THE BUREAU.
MOTOR LODGE
TV
TURNS OUT THOUGH...
STUDD
I AIN'T GOT NONE LEFT.
GODDAMNIT!
THINGS GO RED AFTER THAT.
THEN GREY.
THEN BLACK.
ONE DRINK IN AND I KNOW WHAT I GOTTA DO.
I HAVE
MORE
BEFORE

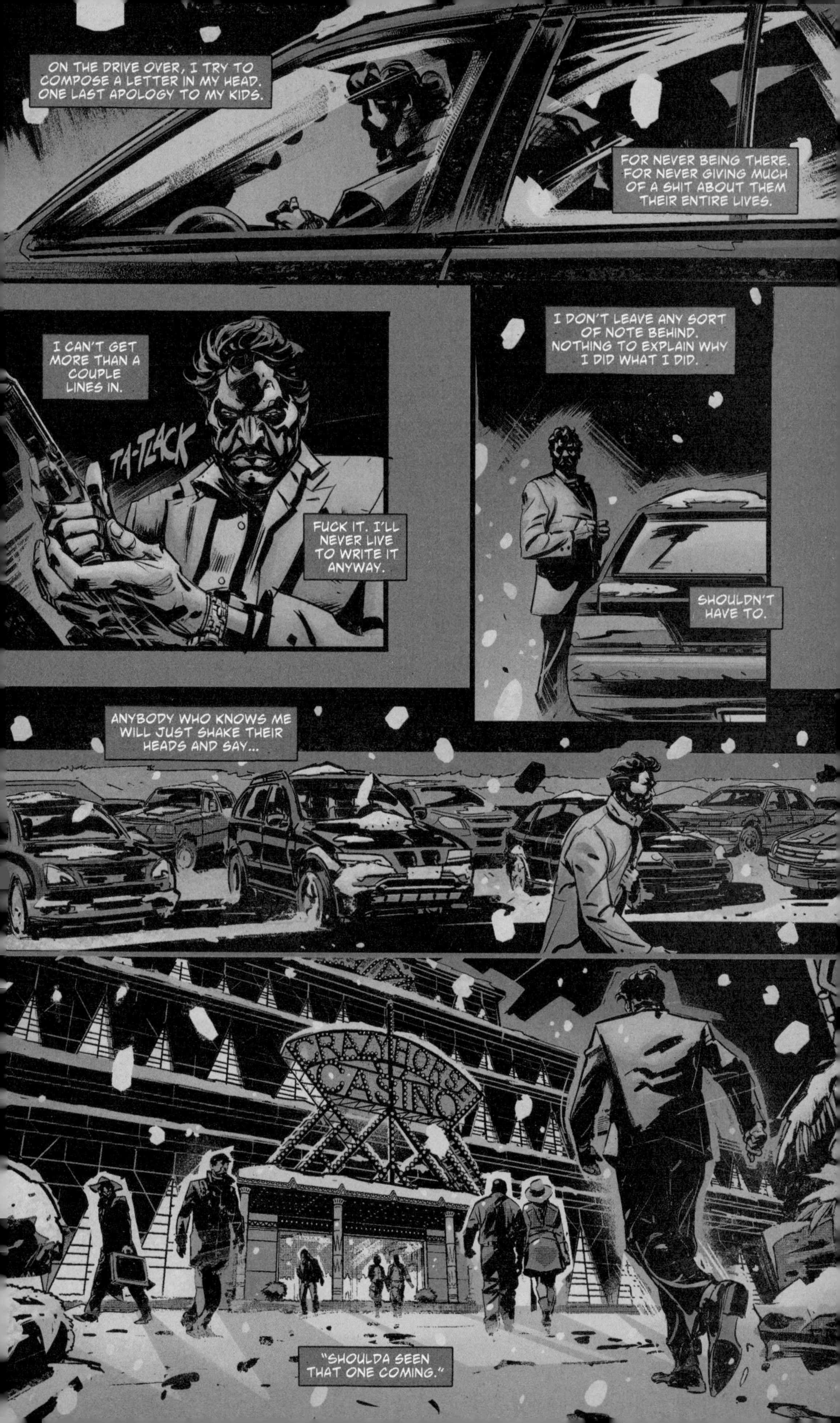
ON THE DRIVE OVER, I TRY TO COMPOSE A LETTER IN MY HEAD. ONE LAST APOLOGY TO MY KIDS.
FOR NEVER BEING THERE. FOR NEVER GIVING MUCH OF A SHIT ABOUT THEM THEIR ENTIRE LIVES.
I CAN'T GET MORE THAN A COUPLE LINES IN.
TA-TLACK
FUCK IT. I'LL NEVER LIVE TO WRITE IT ANYWAY.
I DON'T LEAVE ANY SORT OF NOTE BEHIND. NOTHING TO EXPLAIN WHY I DID WHAT I DID.
SHOULDN'T HAVE TO.
ANYBODY WHO KNOWS ME WILL JUST SHAKE THEIR HEADS AND SAY...
"SHOULDA SEEN THAT ONE COMING."

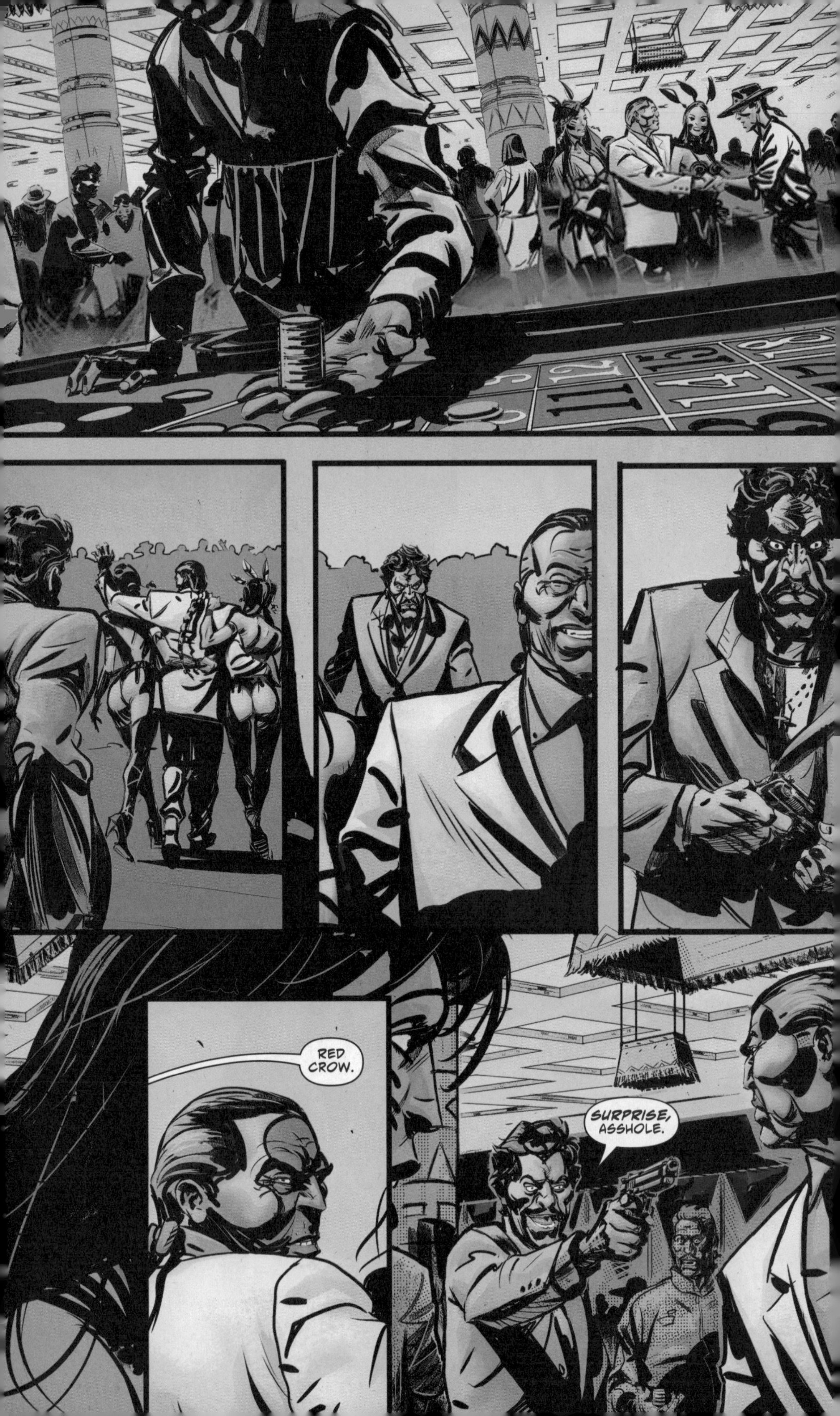
RED CROW.
SURPRISE, ASSHOLE.

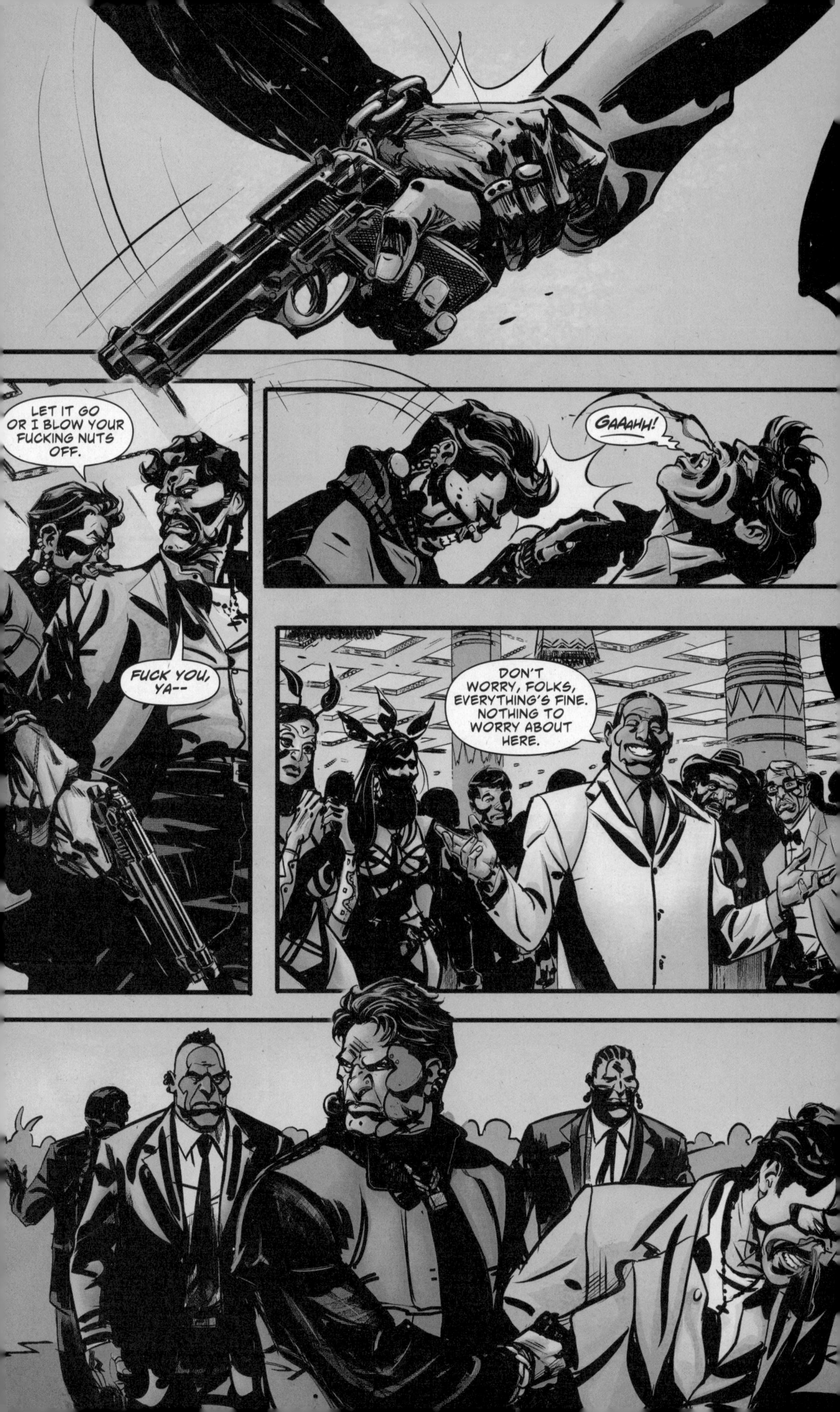
LET IT GO OR I BLOW YOUR FUCKING NUTS OFF.
FUCK YOU, YA--
GAAAHH!
DON'T WORRY, FOLKS, EVERYTHING'S FINE. NOTHING TO WORRY ABOUT HERE.

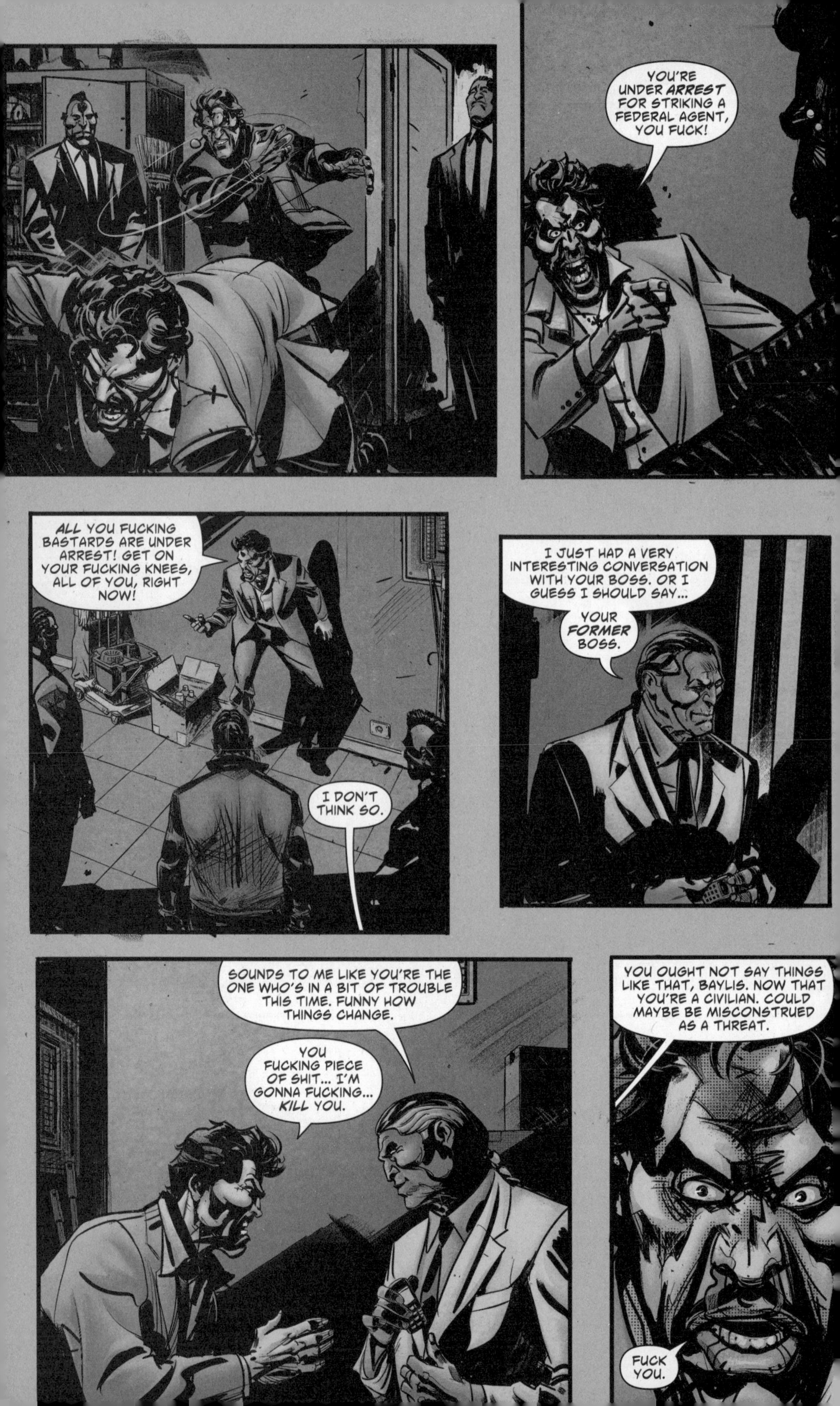
YOU'RE UNDER *ARREST* FOR STRIKING A FEDERAL AGENT, YOU FUCK!
ALL YOU FUCKING BASTARDS ARE UNDER ARREST! GET ON YOUR FUCKING KNEES, ALL OF YOU, RIGHT NOW!
I DON'T THINK SO.
I JUST HAD A VERY INTERESTING CONVERSATION WITH YOUR BOSS. OR I GUESS I SHOULD SAY...
YOUR *FORMER* BOSS.
SOUNDS TO ME LIKE YOU'RE THE ONE WHO'S IN A BIT OF TROUBLE THIS TIME. FUNNY HOW THINGS CHANGE.
YOU FUCKING PIECE OF SHIT... I'M GONNA FUCKING... *KILL* YOU.
YOU OUGHT NOT SAY THINGS LIKE THAT, BAYLIS. NOW THAT YOU'RE A CIVILIAN. COULD MAYBE BE MISCONSTRUED AS A THREAT.
FUCK YOU.

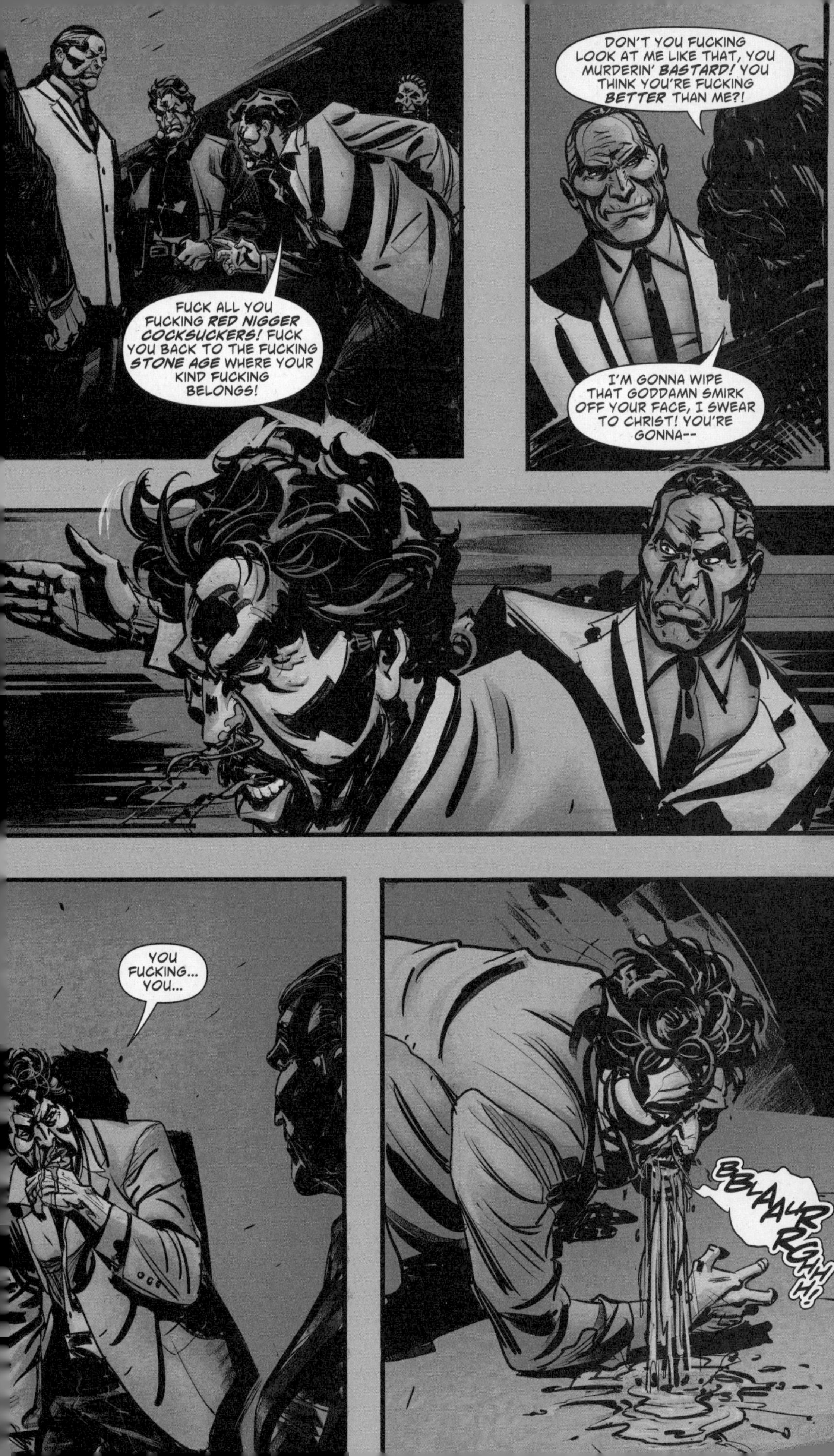
FUCK ALL YOU FUCKING RED NIGGER COCKSUCKERS! FUCK YOU BACK TO THE FUCKING STONE AGE WHERE YOUR KIND FUCKING BELONGS!
DON'T YOU FUCKING LOOK AT ME LIKE THAT, YOU MURDERIN' BASTARD! YOU THINK YOU'RE FUCKING BETTER THAN ME?!
I'M GONNA WIPE THAT GODDAMN SMIRK OFF YOUR FACE, I SWEAR TO CHRIST! YOU'RE GONNA--
YOU FUCKING... YOU...
BBLAAURRGHH!

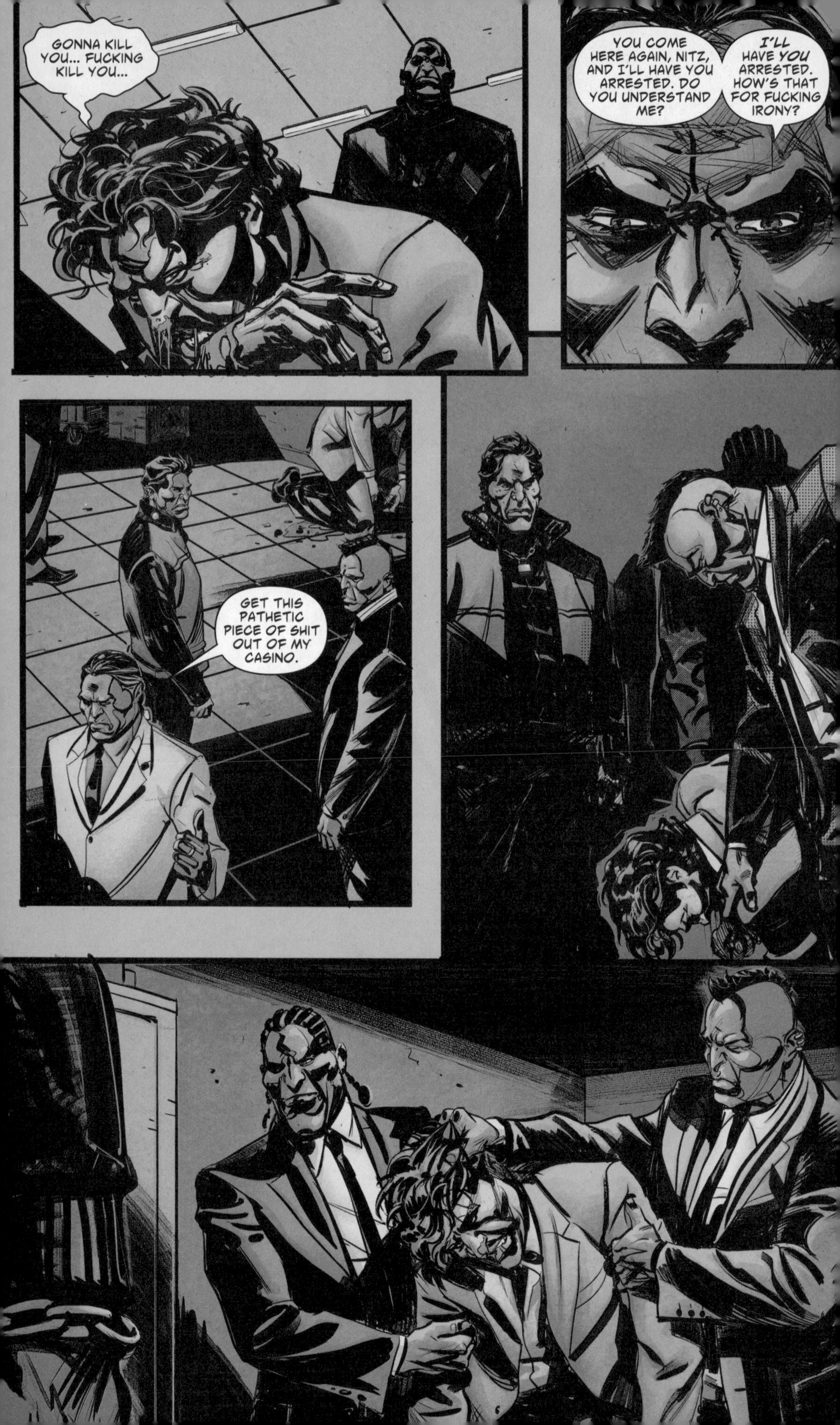
GONNA KILL YOU... FUCKING KILL YOU...
YOU COME HERE AGAIN, NITZ, AND I'LL HAVE YOU ARRESTED. DO YOU UNDERSTAND ME?
I'LL HAVE YOU ARRESTED. HOW'S THAT FOR FUCKING IRONY?
GET THIS PATHETIC PIECE OF SHIT OUT OF MY CASINO.

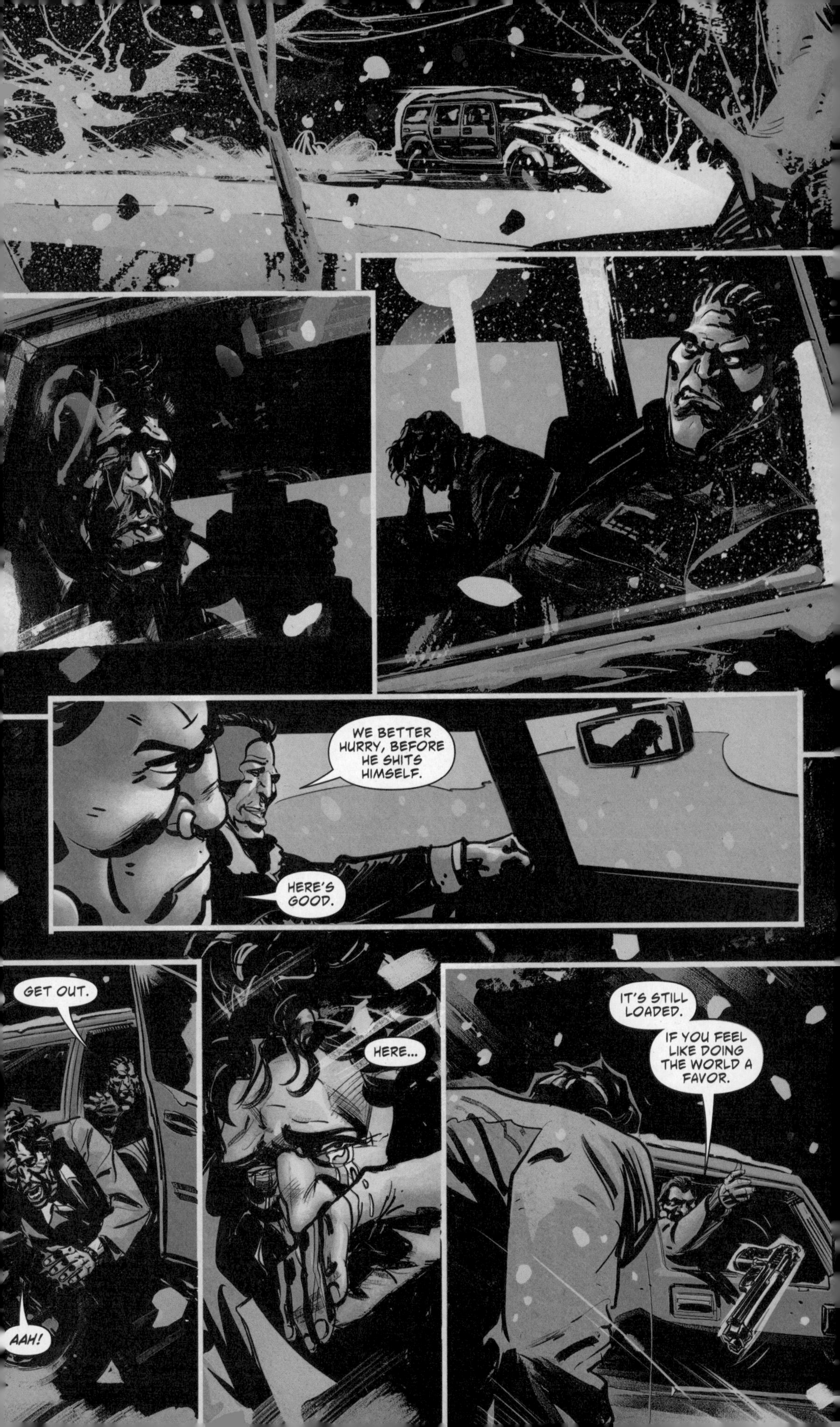

WE BETTER HURRY, BEFORE HE SHITS HIMSELF.
HERE'S GOOD.
GET OUT.
AAH!
HERE...
IT'S STILL LOADED.
IF YOU FEEL LIKE DOING THE WORLD A FAVOR.

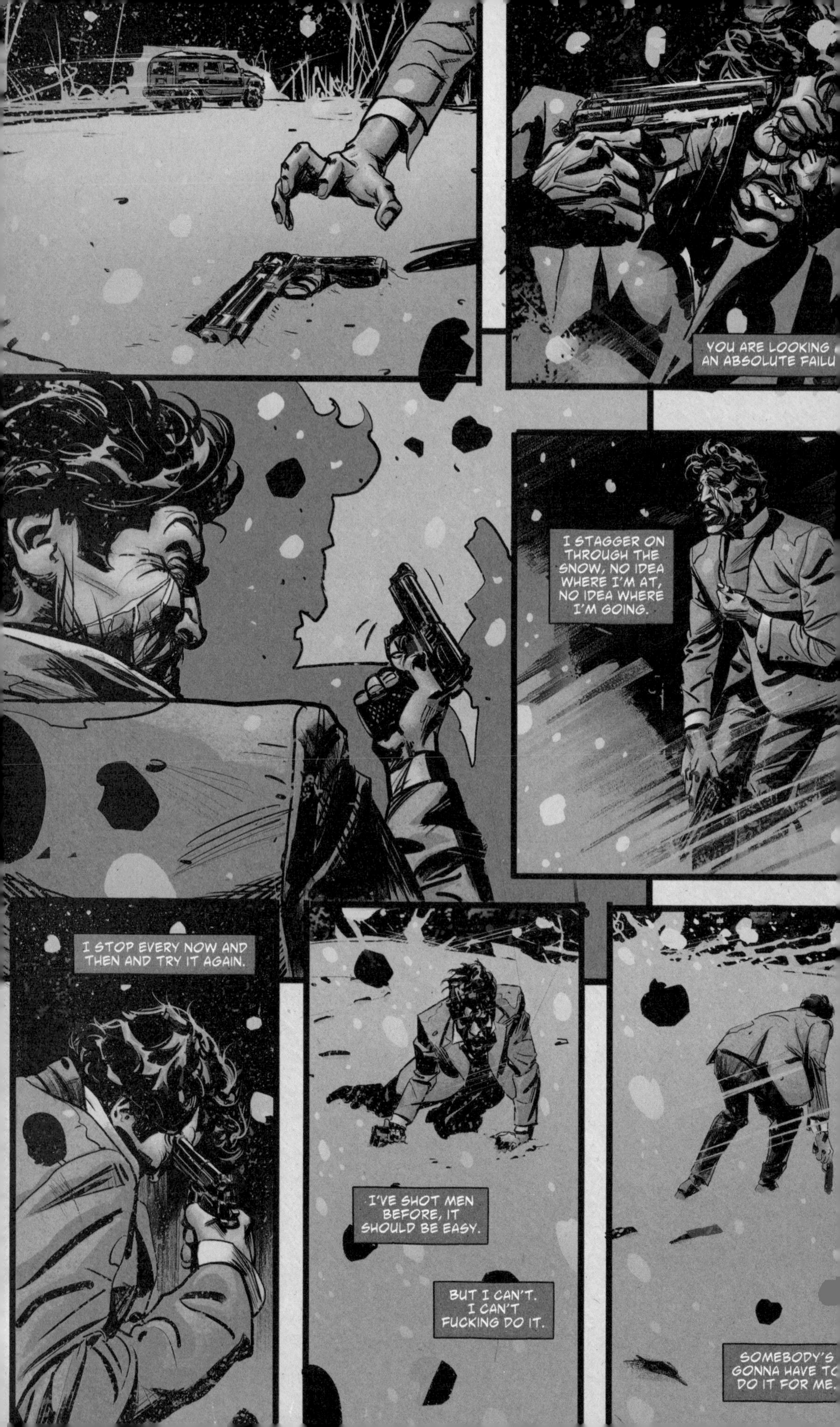
YOU ARE LOOKING AN ABSOLUTE FAILU
I STAGGER ON THROUGH THE SNOW, NO IDEA WHERE I'M AT, NO IDEA WHERE I'M GOING.
I STOP EVERY NOW AND THEN AND TRY IT AGAIN.
I'VE SHOT MEN BEFORE, IT SHOULD BE EASY.
BUT I CAN'T. I CAN'T FUCKING DO IT.
SOMEBODY'S GONNA HAVE TO DO IT FOR ME.

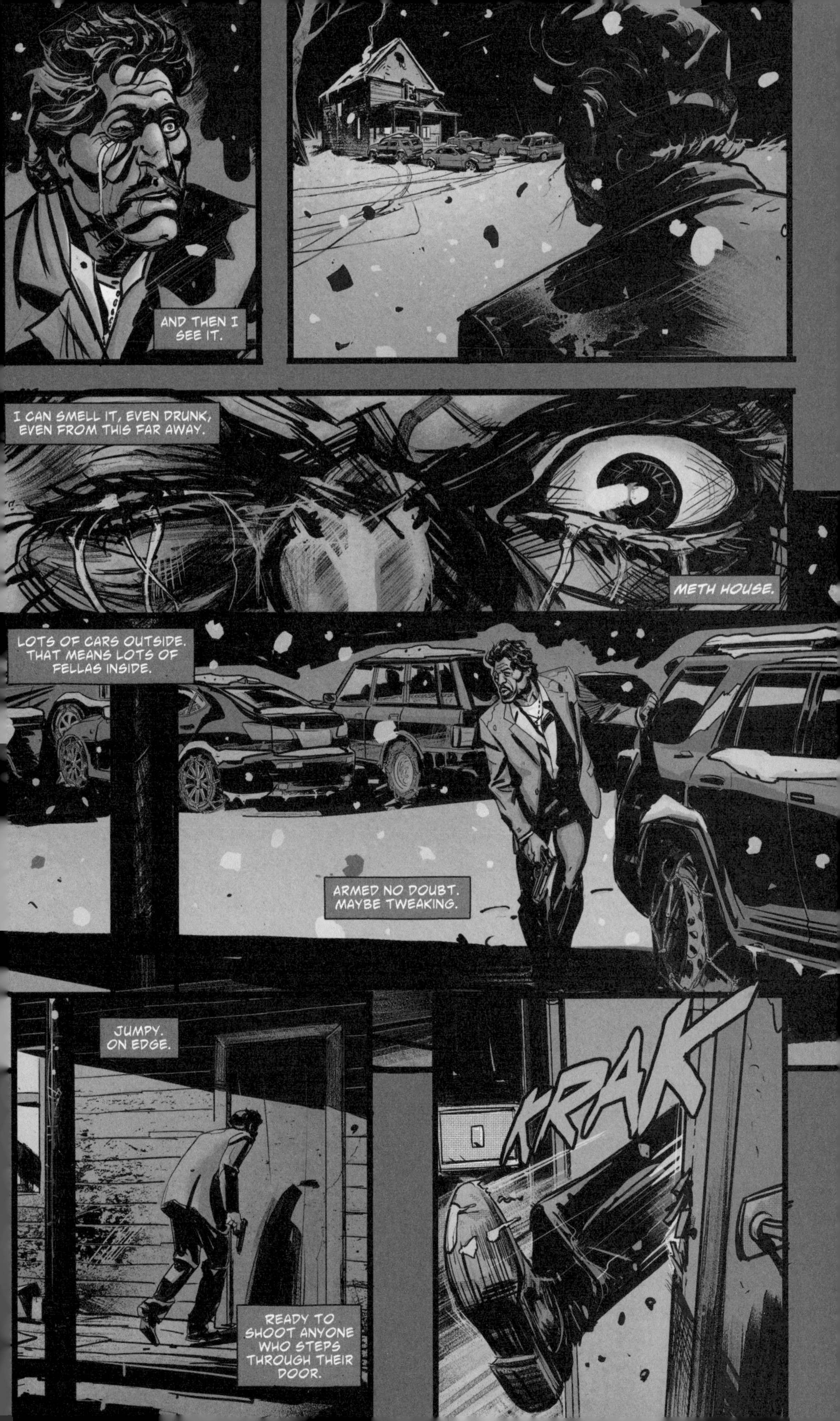
AND THEN I SEE IT.
I CAN SMELL IT, EVEN DRUNK, EVEN FROM THIS FAR AWAY.
METH HOUSE.
LOTS OF CARS OUTSIDE. THAT MEANS LOTS OF FELLAS INSIDE.
ARMED NO DOUBT. MAYBE TWEAKING.
JUMPY. ON EDGE.
READY TO SHOOT ANYONE WHO STEPS THROUGH THEIR DOOR.
KRAK

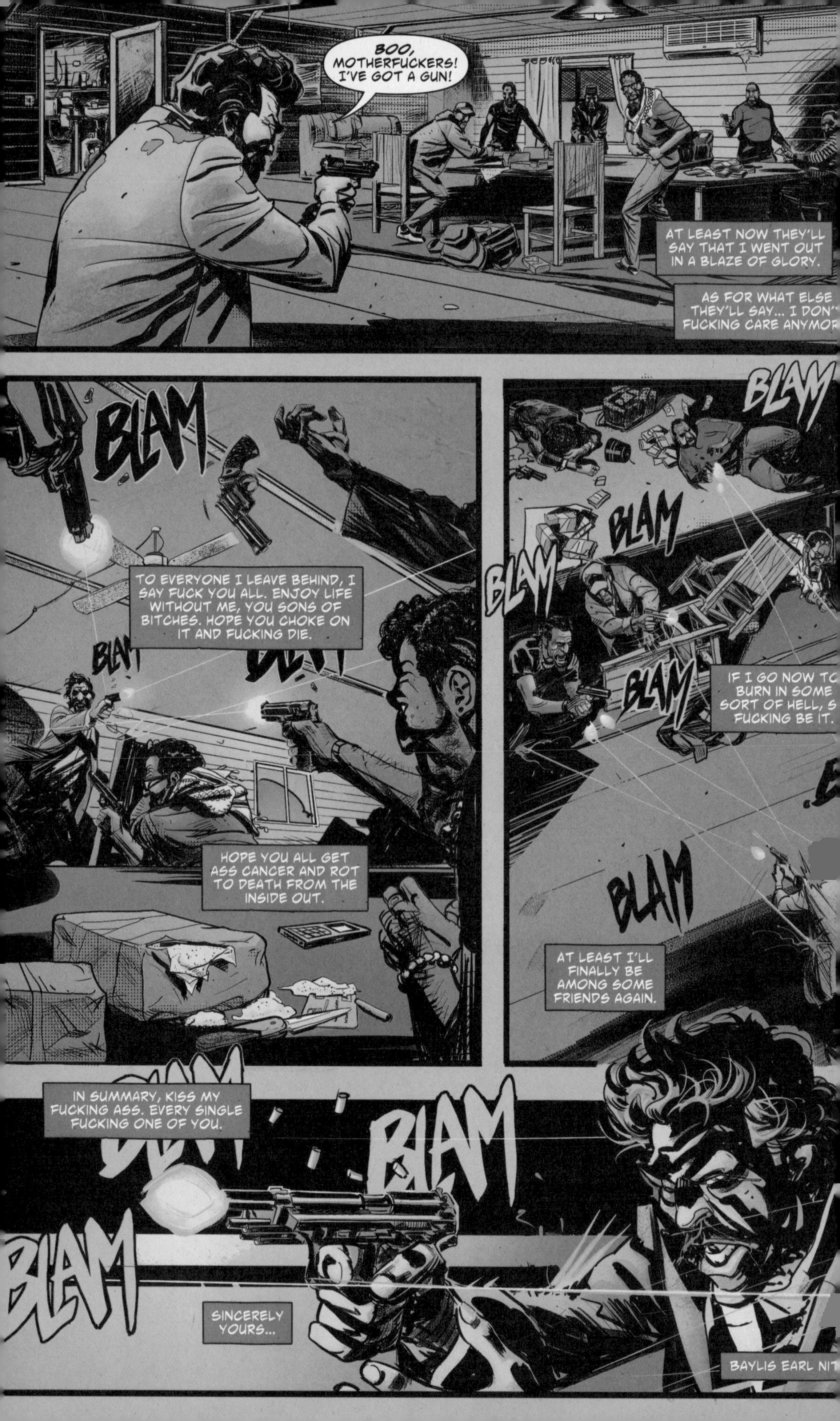

BOO, MOTHERFUCKERS! I'VE GOT A GUN!
AT LEAST NOW THEY'LL SAY THAT I WENT OUT IN A BLAZE OF GLORY.
AS FOR WHAT ELSE THEY'LL SAY... I DON'T FUCKING CARE ANYMOR
BLAM
TO EVERYONE I LEAVE BEHIND, I SAY FUCK YOU ALL. ENJOY LIFE WITHOUT ME, YOU SONS OF BITCHES. HOPE YOU CHOKE ON IT AND FUCKING DIE.
BLAM
HOPE YOU ALL GET ASS CANCER AND ROT TO DEATH FROM THE INSIDE OUT.
BLAM
BLAM
BLAM
BLAM
IF I GO NOW TO BURN IN SOME SORT OF HELL, S FUCKING BE IT.
BLAM
AT LEAST I'LL FINALLY BE AMONG SOME FRIENDS AGAIN.
IN SUMMARY, KISS MY FUCKING ASS. EVERY SINGLE FUCKING ONE OF YOU.
BLAM
BLAM
SINCERELY YOURS...
BAYLIS EARL NIT

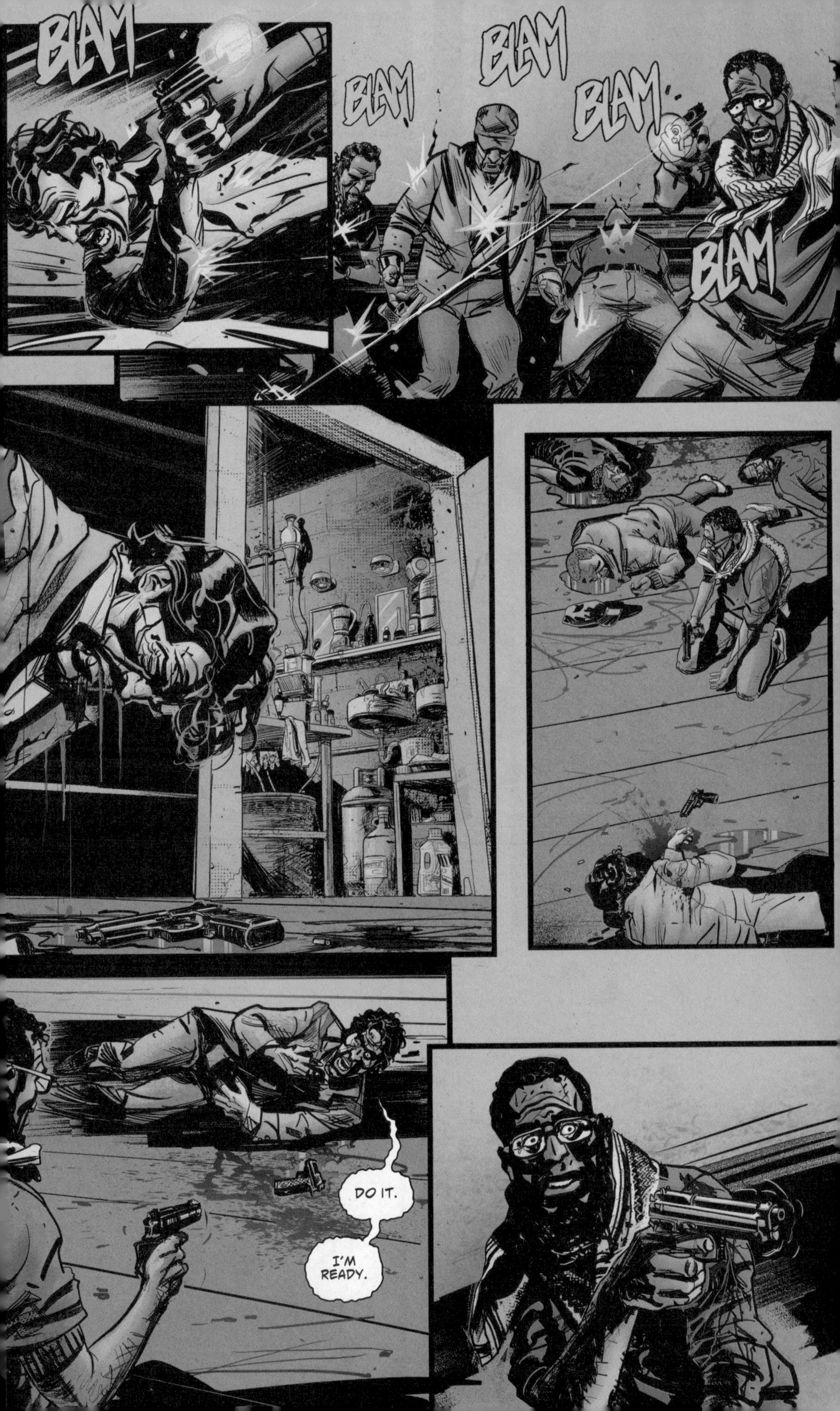
BLAM
BLAM
BLAM
BLAM
BLAM
DO IT.
I'M READY.

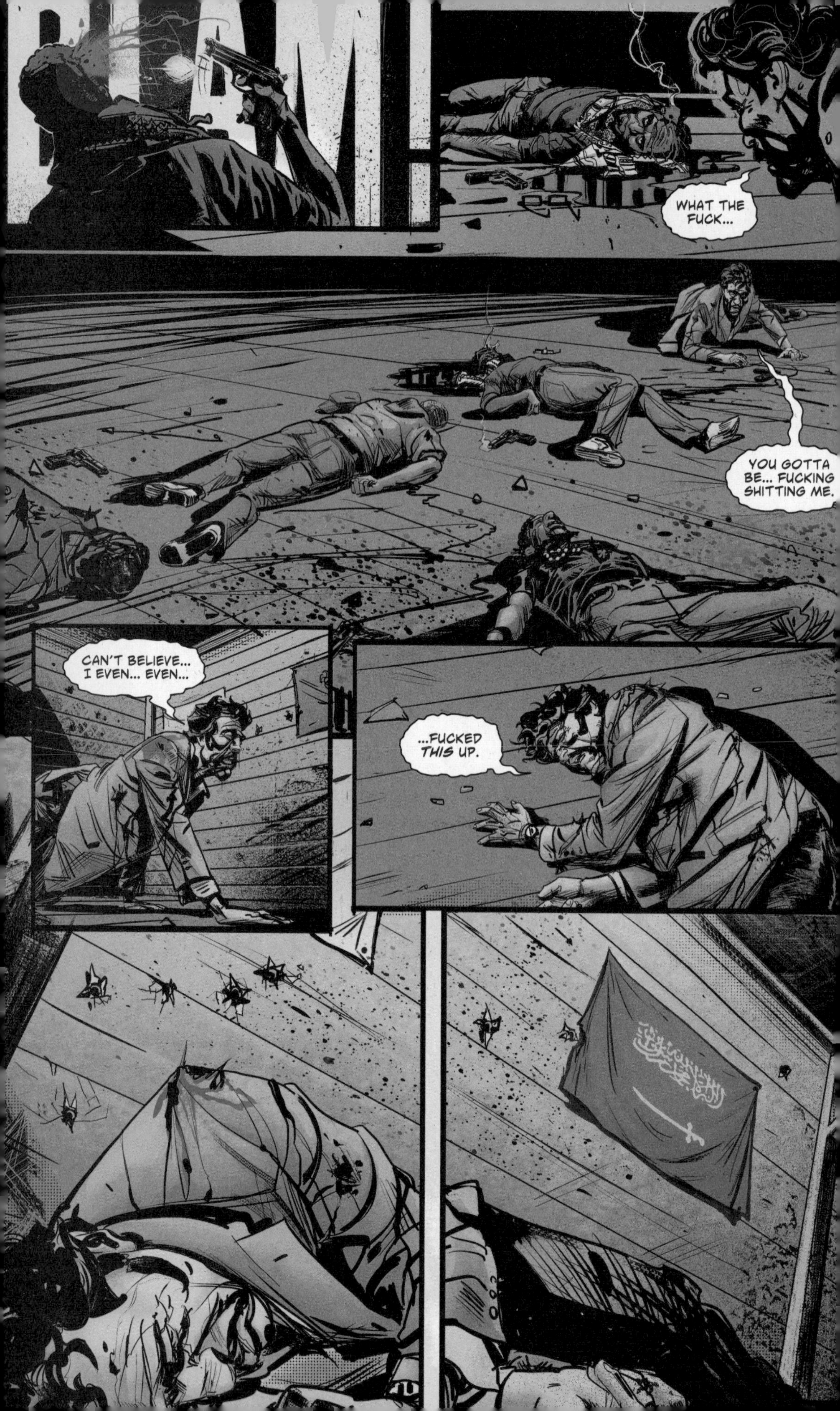
BLAM!
WHAT THE FUCK...
YOU GOTTA BE... FUCKING SHITTING ME.
CAN'T BELIEVE... I EVEN... EVEN...
...FUCKED THIS UP.

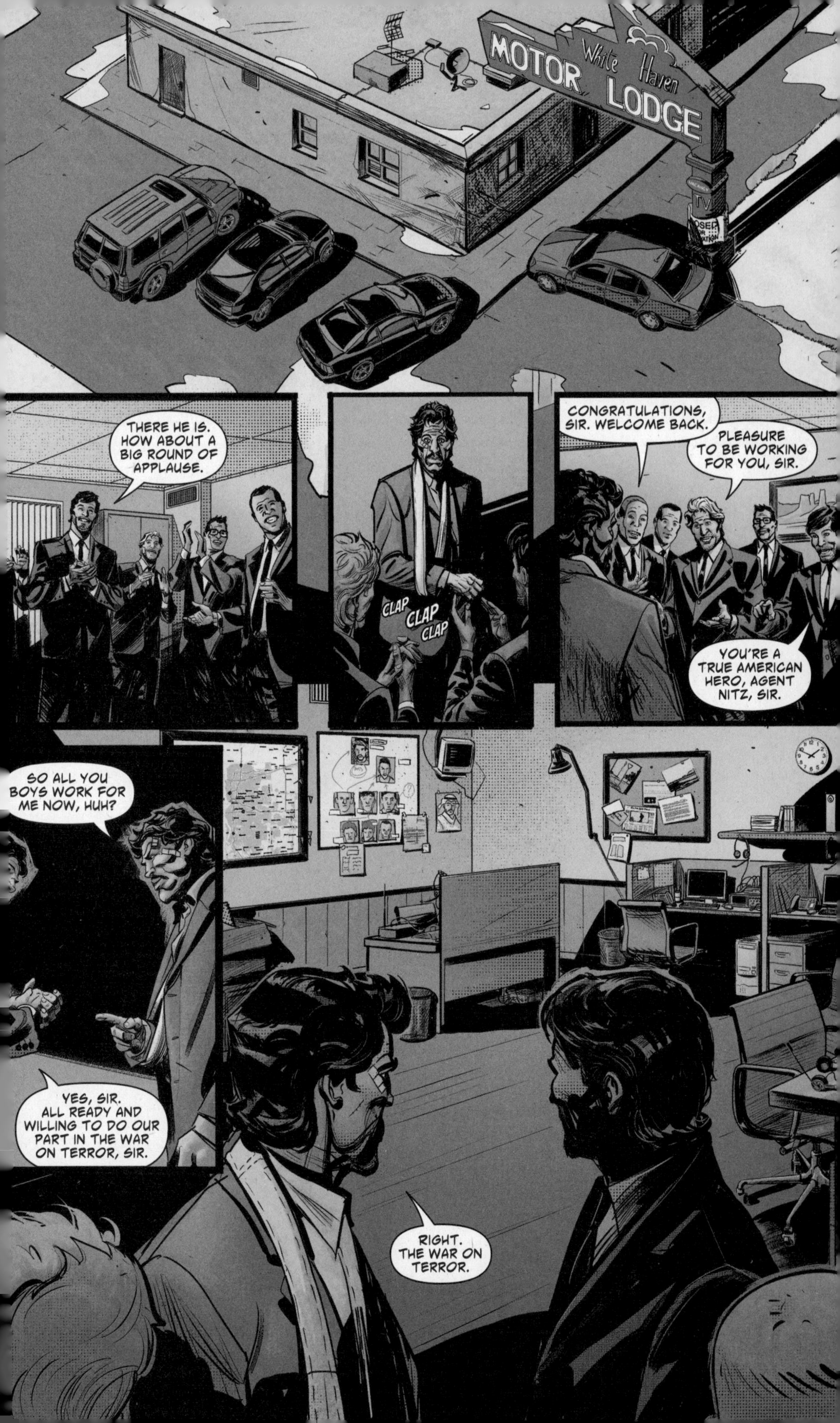
White Haven
MOTOR LODGE
TV
THERE HE IS. HOW ABOUT A BIG ROUND OF APPLAUSE.
CLAP CLAP CLAP
CONGRATULATIONS, SIR. WELCOME BACK.
PLEASURE TO BE WORKING FOR YOU, SIR.
YOU'RE A TRUE AMERICAN HERO, AGENT NITZ, SIR.
SO ALL YOU BOYS WORK FOR ME NOW, HUH?
YES, SIR. ALL READY AND WILLING TO DO OUR PART IN THE WAR ON TERROR, SIR.
RIGHT. THE WAR ON TERROR.

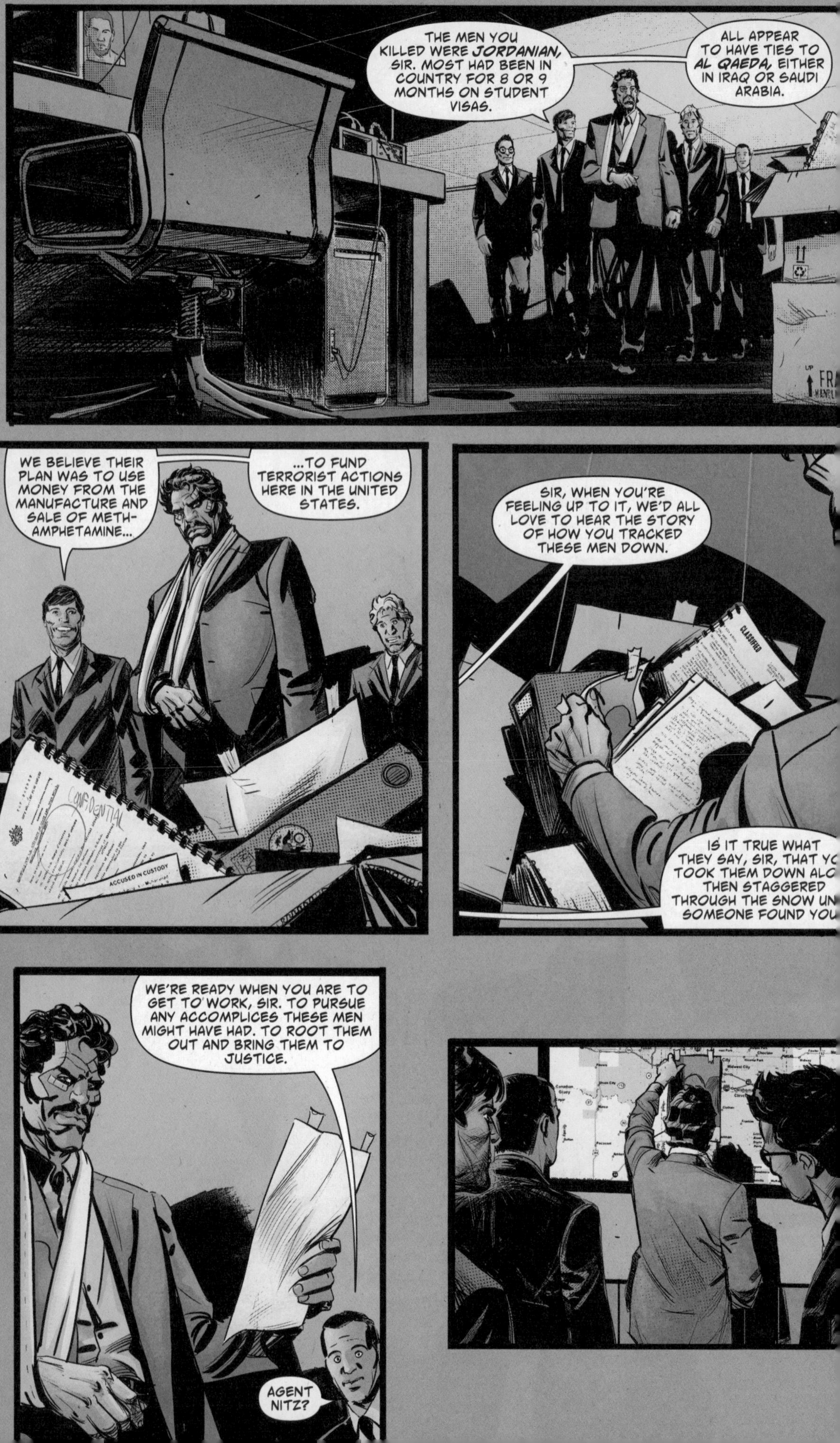
THE MEN YOU KILLED WERE JORDANIAN, SIR. MOST HAD BEEN IN COUNTRY FOR 8 OR 9 MONTHS ON STUDENT VISAS.
ALL APPEAR TO HAVE TIES TO AL QAEDA, EITHER IN IRAQ OR SAUDI ARABIA.
WE BELIEVE THEIR PLAN WAS TO USE MONEY FROM THE MANUFACTURE AND SALE OF METH-AMPHETAMINE...
...TO FUND TERRORIST ACTIONS HERE IN THE UNITED STATES.
CONFIDENTIAL
ACCUSED IN CUSTODY
SIR, WHEN YOU'RE FEELING UP TO IT, WE'D ALL LOVE TO HEAR THE STORY OF HOW YOU TRACKED THESE MEN DOWN.
CLASSIFIED
IS IT TRUE WHAT THEY SAY, SIR, THAT YC TOOK THEM DOWN ALC THEN STAGGERED THROUGH THE SNOW UN SOMEONE FOUND YOU
WE'RE READY WHEN YOU ARE TO GET TO WORK, SIR. TO PURSUE ANY ACCOMPLICES THESE MEN MIGHT HAVE HAD. TO ROOT THEM OUT AND BRING THEM TO JUSTICE.
AGENT NITZ?

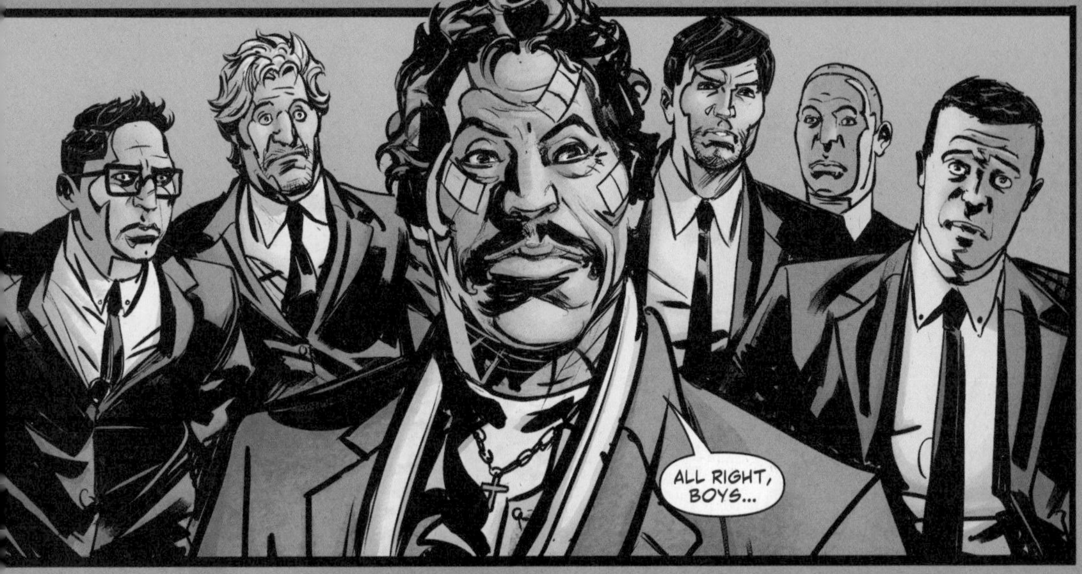
ALL RIGHT, BOYS...

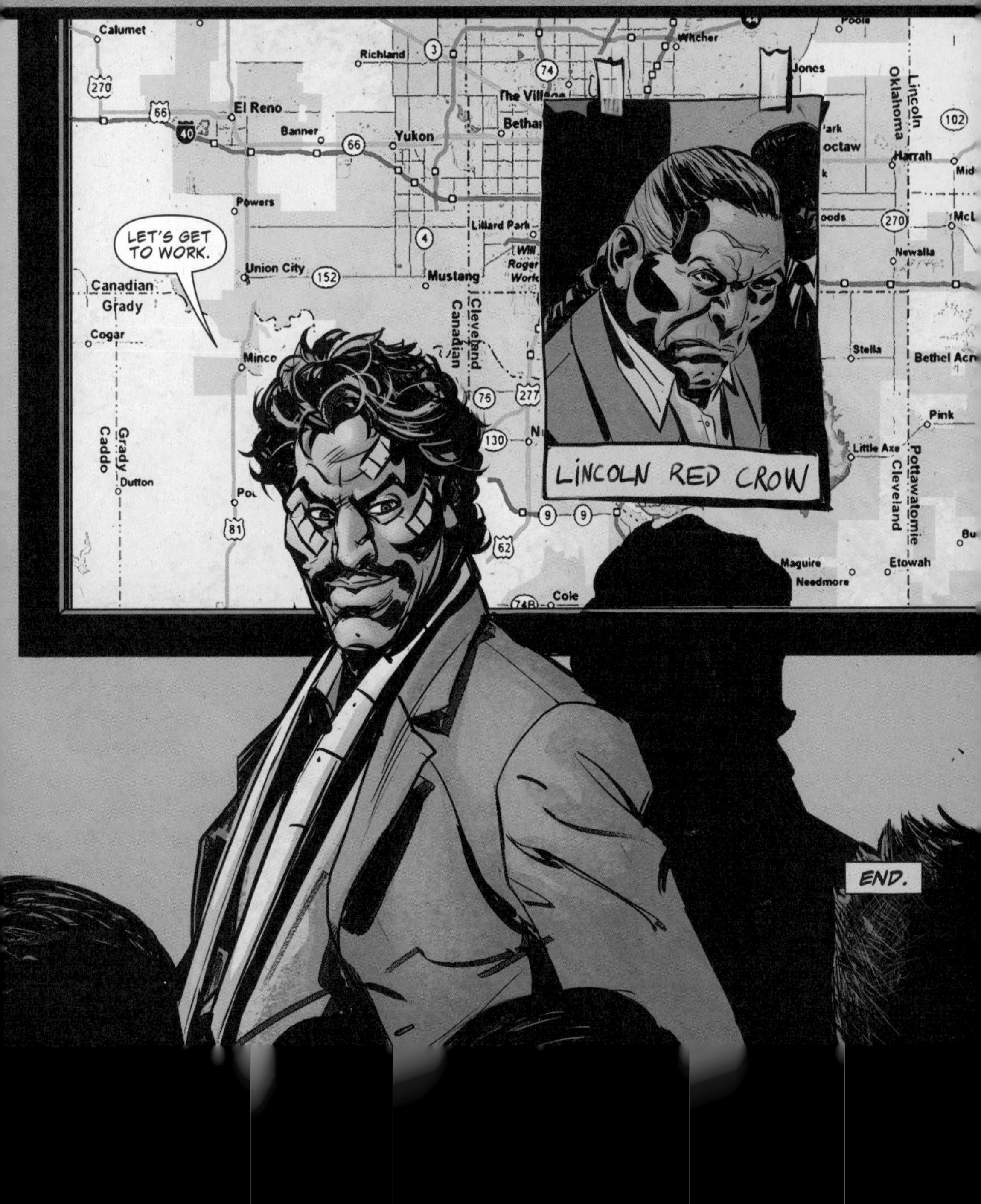
Calumet
Richland
El Reno
Banner
Yukon
Powers
Union City
Canadian
Grady
Cogar
Minco
Mustang
Lillard Park
Cleveland
Canadian
Caddo
Grady
Dutton
Whcher
Jones
Oklahoma
Lincoln
Harrah
Newalla
Stella
Bethel Acr
Pink
Little Axe
Pottawatomie
Cleveland
Maguire
Needmore
Etowah
Cole
LET'S GET TO WORK.
LINCOLN RED CROW
END.

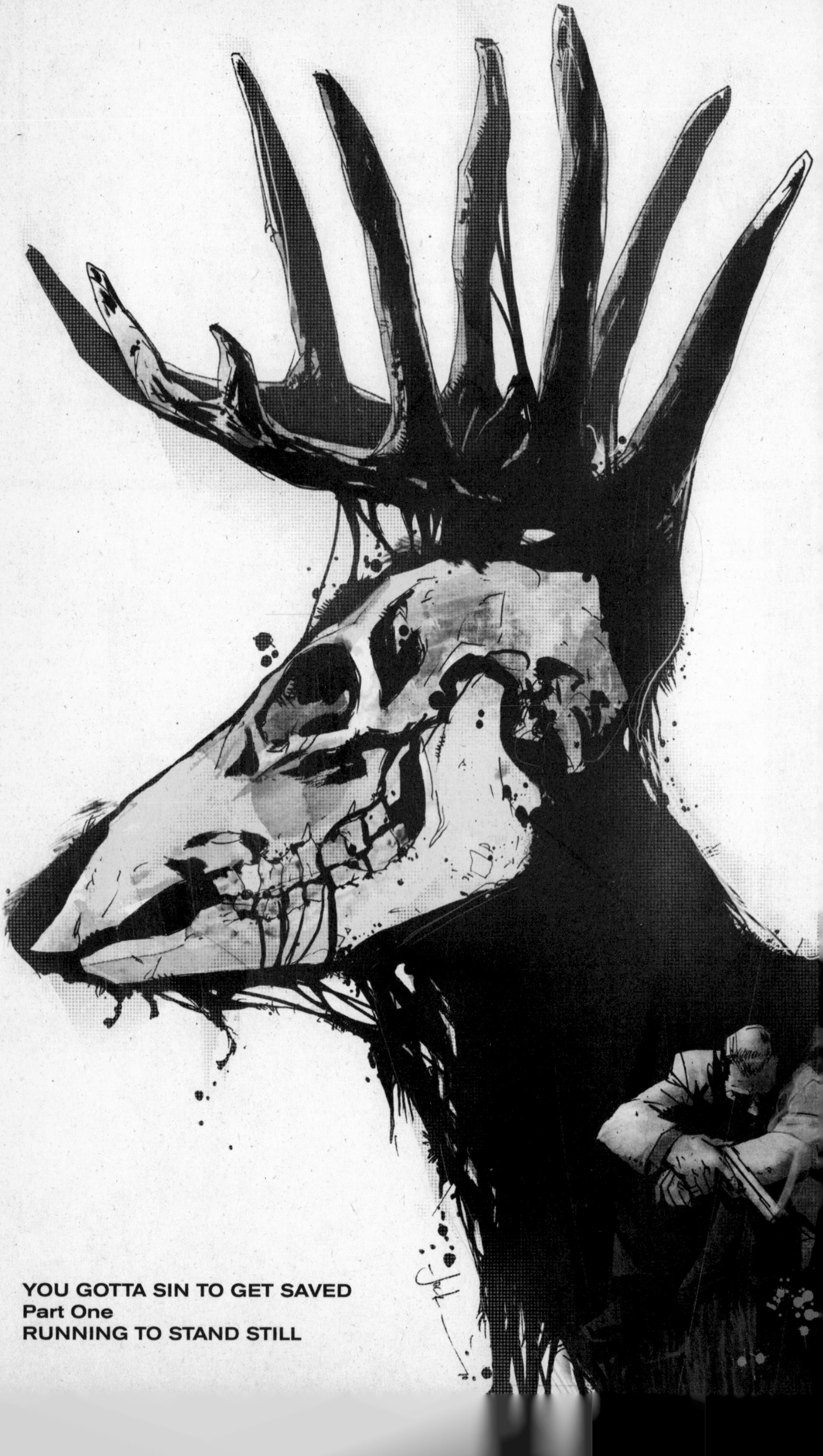

YOU GOTTA SIN TO GET SAVED
Part One
RUNNING TO STAND STILL

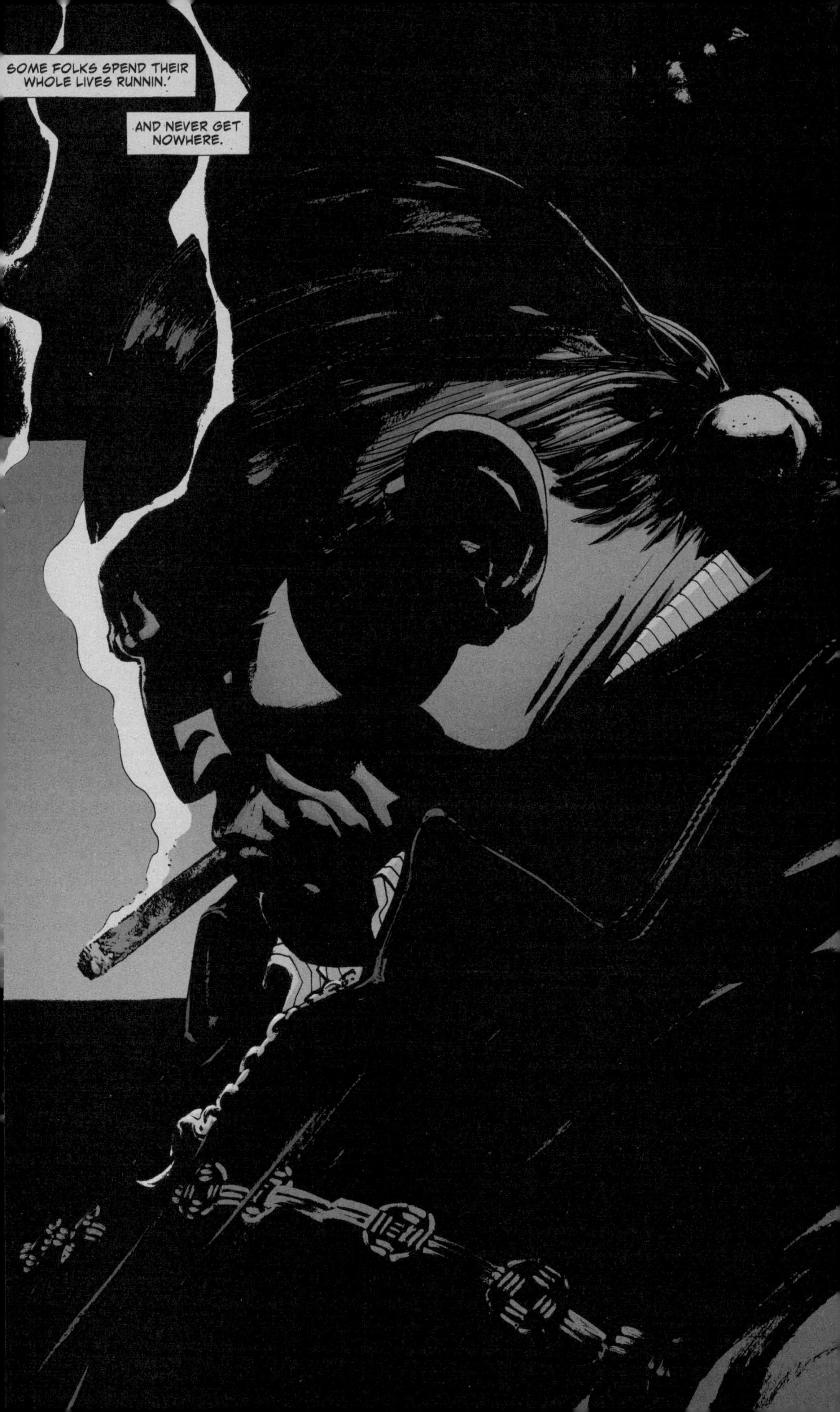
SOME FOLKS SPEND THEIR WHOLE LIVES RUNNIN.'
AND NEVER GET NOWHERE.

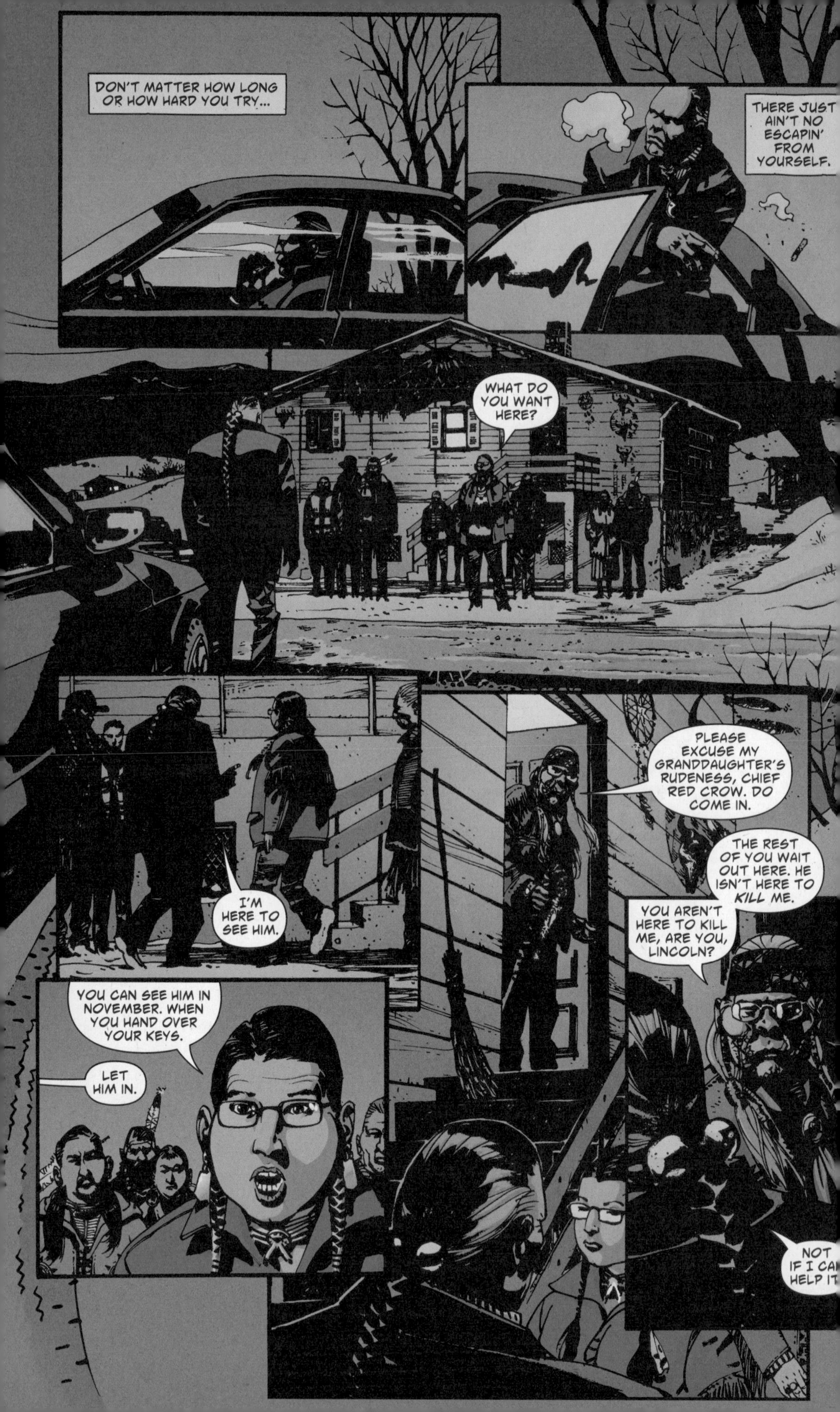
DON'T MATTER HOW LONG OR HOW HARD YOU TRY...
THERE JUST AIN'T NO ESCAPIN' FROM YOURSELF.
WHAT DO YOU WANT HERE?
I'M HERE TO SEE HIM.
PLEASE EXCUSE MY GRANDDAUGHTER'S RUDENESS, CHIEF RED CROW. DO COME IN.
YOU CAN SEE HIM IN NOVEMBER. WHEN YOU HAND OVER YOUR KEYS.
LET HIM IN.
THE REST OF YOU WAIT OUT HERE. HE ISN'T HERE TO *KILL* ME.
YOU AREN'T HERE TO KILL ME, ARE YOU, LINCOLN?
NOT IF I CA HELP IT

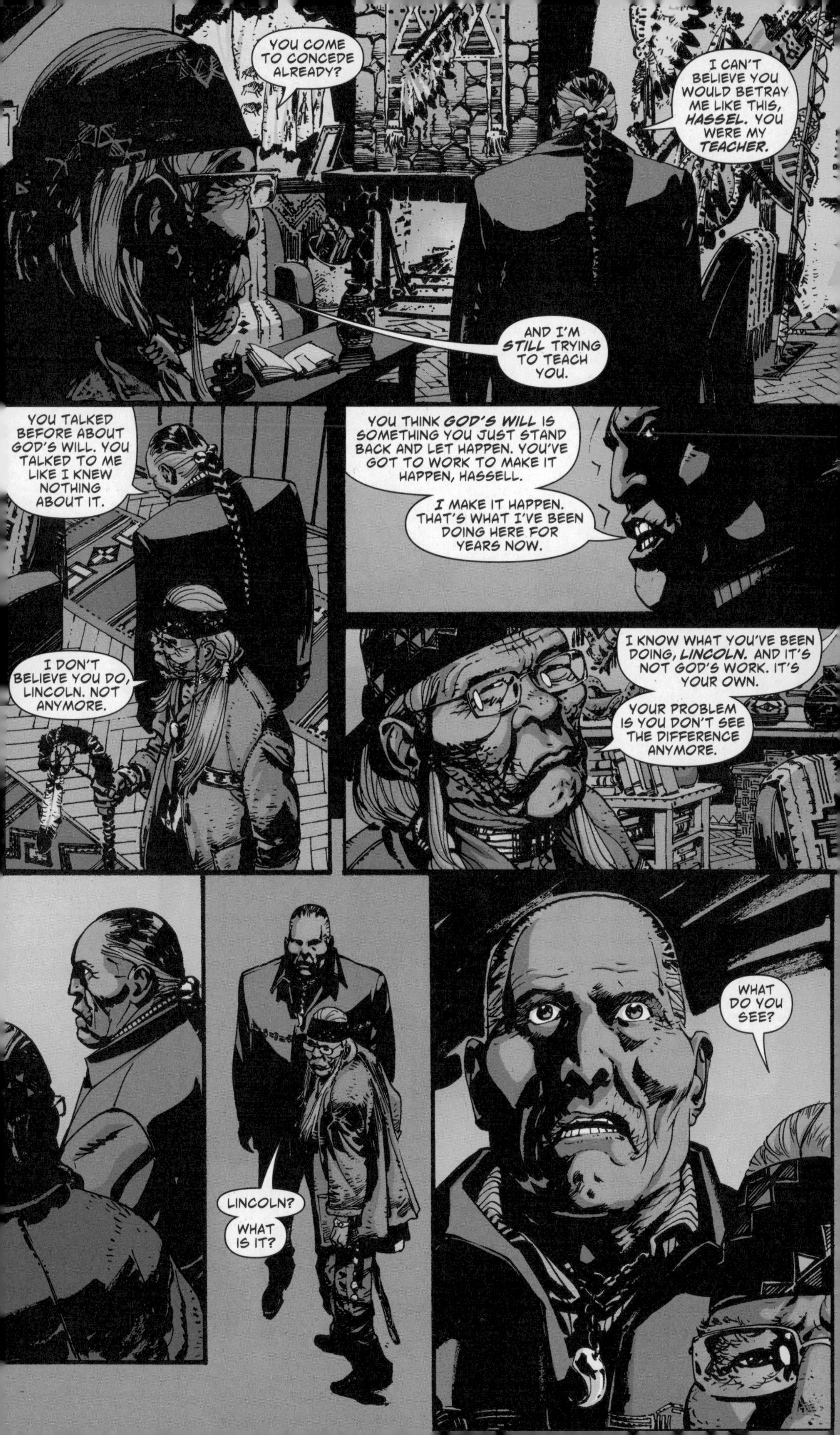
YOU COME TO CONCEDE ALREADY?
I CAN'T BELIEVE YOU WOULD BETRAY ME LIKE THIS, HASSEL. YOU WERE MY TEACHER.
AND I'M STILL TRYING TO TEACH YOU.
YOU TALKED BEFORE ABOUT GOD'S WILL. YOU TALKED TO ME LIKE I KNEW NOTHING ABOUT IT.
I DON'T BELIEVE YOU DO, LINCOLN. NOT ANYMORE.
YOU THINK GOD'S WILL IS SOMETHING YOU JUST STAND BACK AND LET HAPPEN. YOU'VE GOT TO WORK TO MAKE IT HAPPEN, HASSELL.
I MAKE IT HAPPEN. THAT'S WHAT I'VE BEEN DOING HERE FOR YEARS NOW.
I KNOW WHAT YOU'VE BEEN DOING, LINCOLN. AND IT'S NOT GOD'S WORK. IT'S YOUR OWN.
YOUR PROBLEM IS YOU DON'T SEE THE DIFFERENCE ANYMORE.
LINCOLN? WHAT IS IT?
WHAT DO YOU SEE?

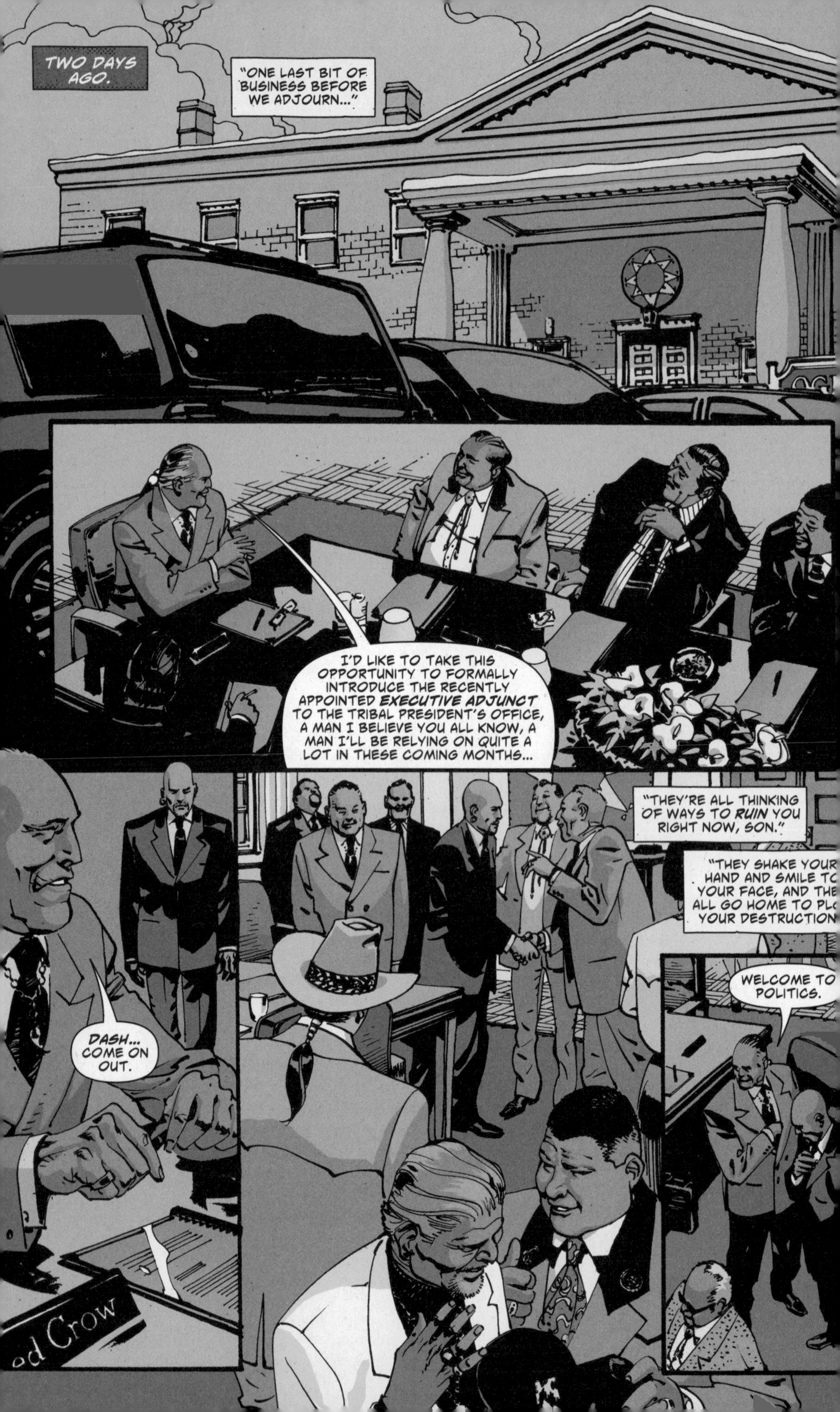
TWO DAYS AGO.
"ONE LAST BIT OF BUSINESS BEFORE WE ADJOURN..."
I'D LIKE TO TAKE THIS OPPORTUNITY TO FORMALLY INTRODUCE THE RECENTLY APPOINTED EXECUTIVE ADJUNCT TO THE TRIBAL PRESIDENT'S OFFICE, A MAN I BELIEVE YOU ALL KNOW, A MAN I'LL BE RELYING ON QUITE A LOT IN THESE COMING MONTHS...
DASH... COME ON OUT.
"THEY'RE ALL THINKING OF WAYS TO RUIN YOU RIGHT NOW, SON."
"THEY SHAKE YOUR HAND AND SMILE TO YOUR FACE, AND THE ALL GO HOME TO PL YOUR DESTRUCTION
WELCOME TO POLITICS.
od Crow

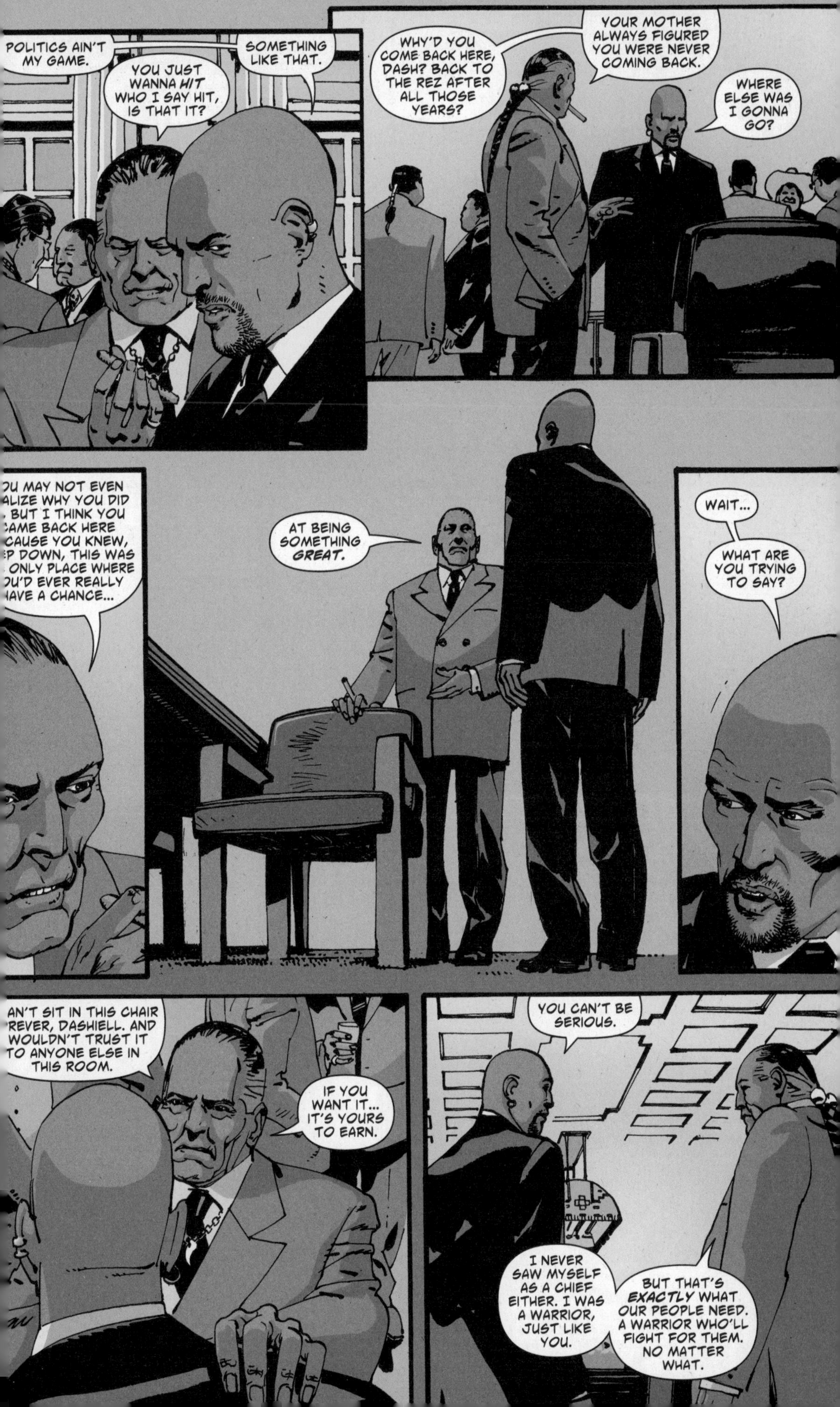
POLITICS AIN'T MY GAME.
YOU JUST WANNA HIT WHO I SAY HIT, IS THAT IT?
SOMETHING LIKE THAT.
WHY'D YOU COME BACK HERE, DASH? BACK TO THE REZ AFTER ALL THOSE YEARS?
YOUR MOTHER ALWAYS FIGURED YOU WERE NEVER COMING BACK.
WHERE ELSE WAS I GONNA GO?
OU MAY NOT EVEN ALIZE WHY YOU DID . BUT I THINK YOU CAME BACK HERE CAUSE YOU KNEW, EP DOWN, THIS WAS ONLY PLACE WHERE OU'D EVER REALLY HAVE A CHANCE...
AT BEING SOMETHING GREAT.
WAIT...
WHAT ARE YOU TRYING TO SAY?
AN'T SIT IN THIS CHAIR REVER, DASHIELL. AND WOULDN'T TRUST IT TO ANYONE ELSE IN THIS ROOM.
IF YOU WANT IT... IT'S YOURS TO EARN.
YOU CAN'T BE SERIOUS.
I NEVER SAW MYSELF AS A CHIEF EITHER. I WAS A WARRIOR, JUST LIKE YOU.
BUT THAT'S EXACTLY WHAT OUR PEOPLE NEED. A WARRIOR WHO'LL FIGHT FOR THEM. NO MATTER WHAT.

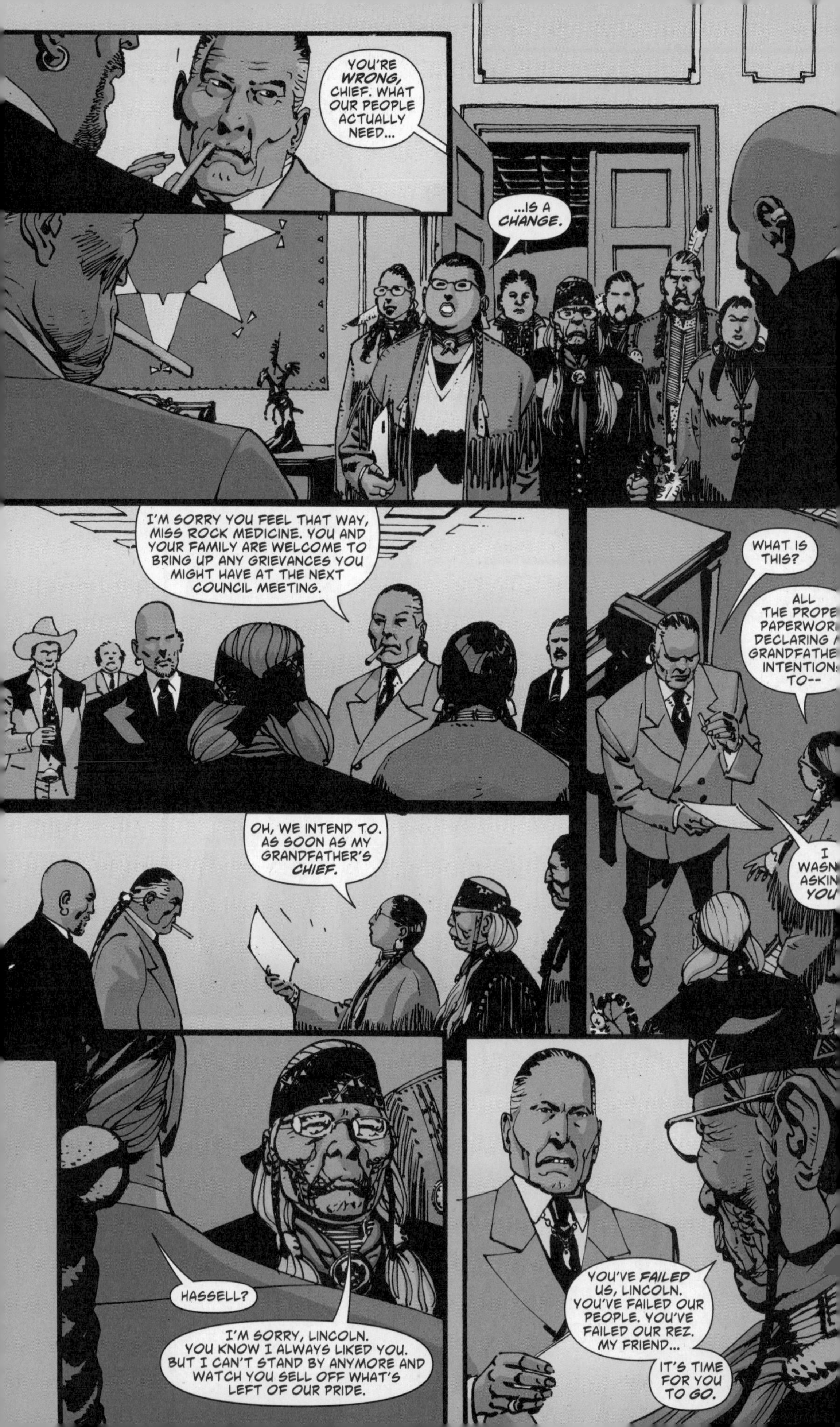
YOU'RE WRONG, CHIEF. WHAT OUR PEOPLE ACTUALLY NEED...
...IS A CHANGE.
I'M SORRY YOU FEEL THAT WAY, MISS ROCK MEDICINE. YOU AND YOUR FAMILY ARE WELCOME TO BRING UP ANY GRIEVANCES YOU MIGHT HAVE AT THE NEXT COUNCIL MEETING.
OH, WE INTEND TO. AS SOON AS MY GRANDFATHER'S CHIEF.
WHAT IS THIS?
ALL THE PROPE PAPERWOR DECLARING GRANDFATHE INTENTION TO--
I WASN ASKIN YOU
HASSELL?
I'M SORRY, LINCOLN. YOU KNOW I ALWAYS LIKED YOU. BUT I CAN'T STAND BY ANYMORE AND WATCH YOU SELL OFF WHAT'S LEFT OF OUR PRIDE.
YOU'VE FAILED US, LINCOLN. YOU'VE FAILED OUR PEOPLE. YOU'VE FAILED OUR REZ. MY FRIEND...
IT'S TIME FOR YOU TO GO.

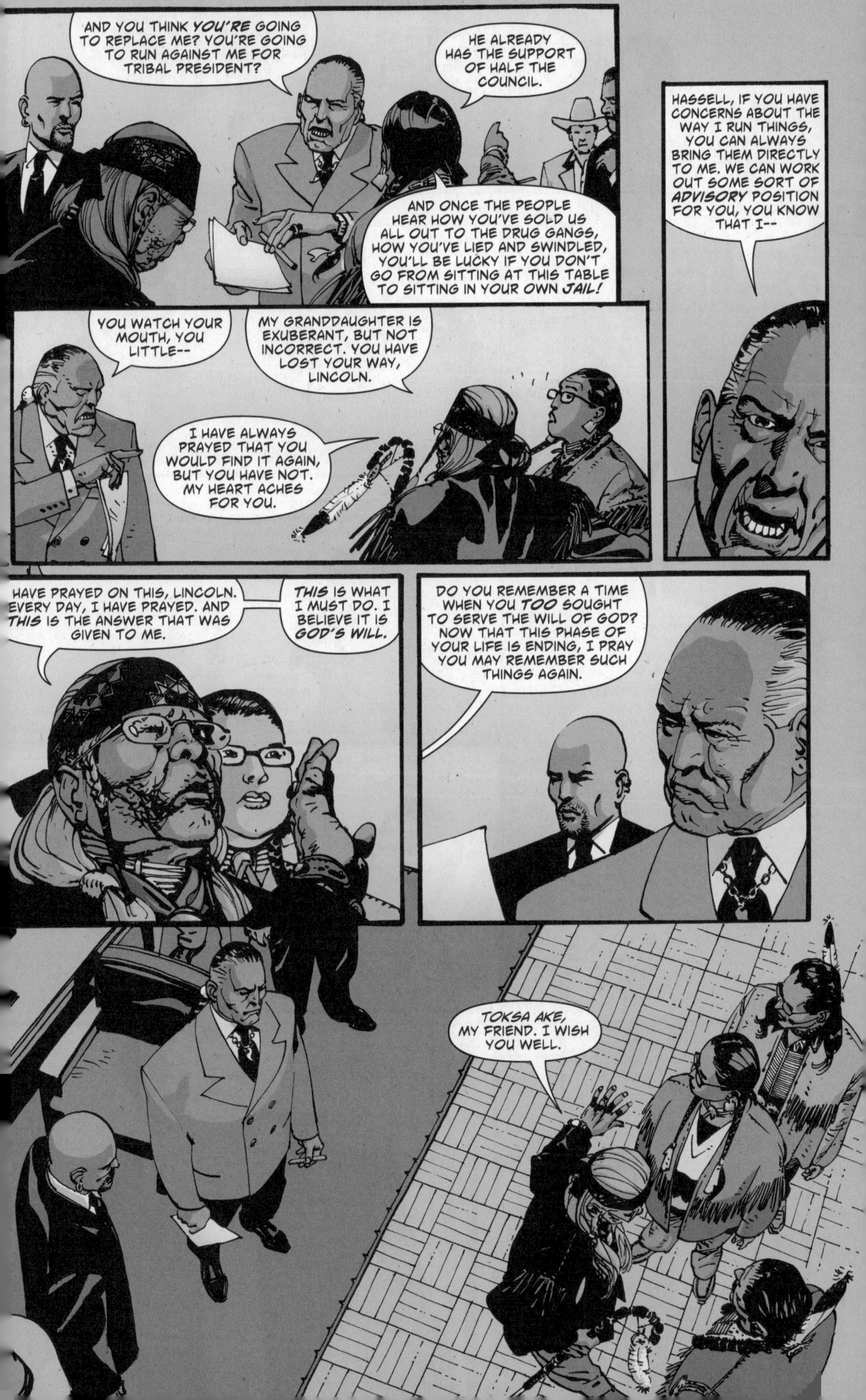
AND YOU THINK YOU'RE GOING TO REPLACE ME? YOU'RE GOING TO RUN AGAINST ME FOR TRIBAL PRESIDENT?
HE ALREADY HAS THE SUPPORT OF HALF THE COUNCIL.
AND ONCE THE PEOPLE HEAR HOW YOU'VE SOLD US ALL OUT TO THE DRUG GANGS, HOW YOU'VE LIED AND SWINDLED, YOU'LL BE LUCKY IF YOU DON'T GO FROM SITTING AT THIS TABLE TO SITTING IN YOUR OWN JAIL!
YOU WATCH YOUR MOUTH, YOU LITTLE--
MY GRANDDAUGHTER IS EXUBERANT, BUT NOT INCORRECT. YOU HAVE LOST YOUR WAY, LINCOLN.
I HAVE ALWAYS PRAYED THAT YOU WOULD FIND IT AGAIN, BUT YOU HAVE NOT. MY HEART ACHES FOR YOU.
HASSELL, IF YOU HAVE CONCERNS ABOUT THE WAY I RUN THINGS, YOU CAN ALWAYS BRING THEM DIRECTLY TO ME. WE CAN WORK OUT SOME SORT OF ADVISORY POSITION FOR YOU, YOU KNOW THAT I--
HAVE PRAYED ON THIS, LINCOLN. EVERY DAY, I HAVE PRAYED. AND THIS IS THE ANSWER THAT WAS GIVEN TO ME.
THIS IS WHAT I MUST DO. I BELIEVE IT IS GOD'S WILL.
DO YOU REMEMBER A TIME WHEN YOU TOO SOUGHT TO SERVE THE WILL OF GOD? NOW THAT THIS PHASE OF YOUR LIFE IS ENDING, I PRAY YOU MAY REMEMBER SUCH THINGS AGAIN.
TOKSA AKE, MY FRIEND. I WISH YOU WELL.

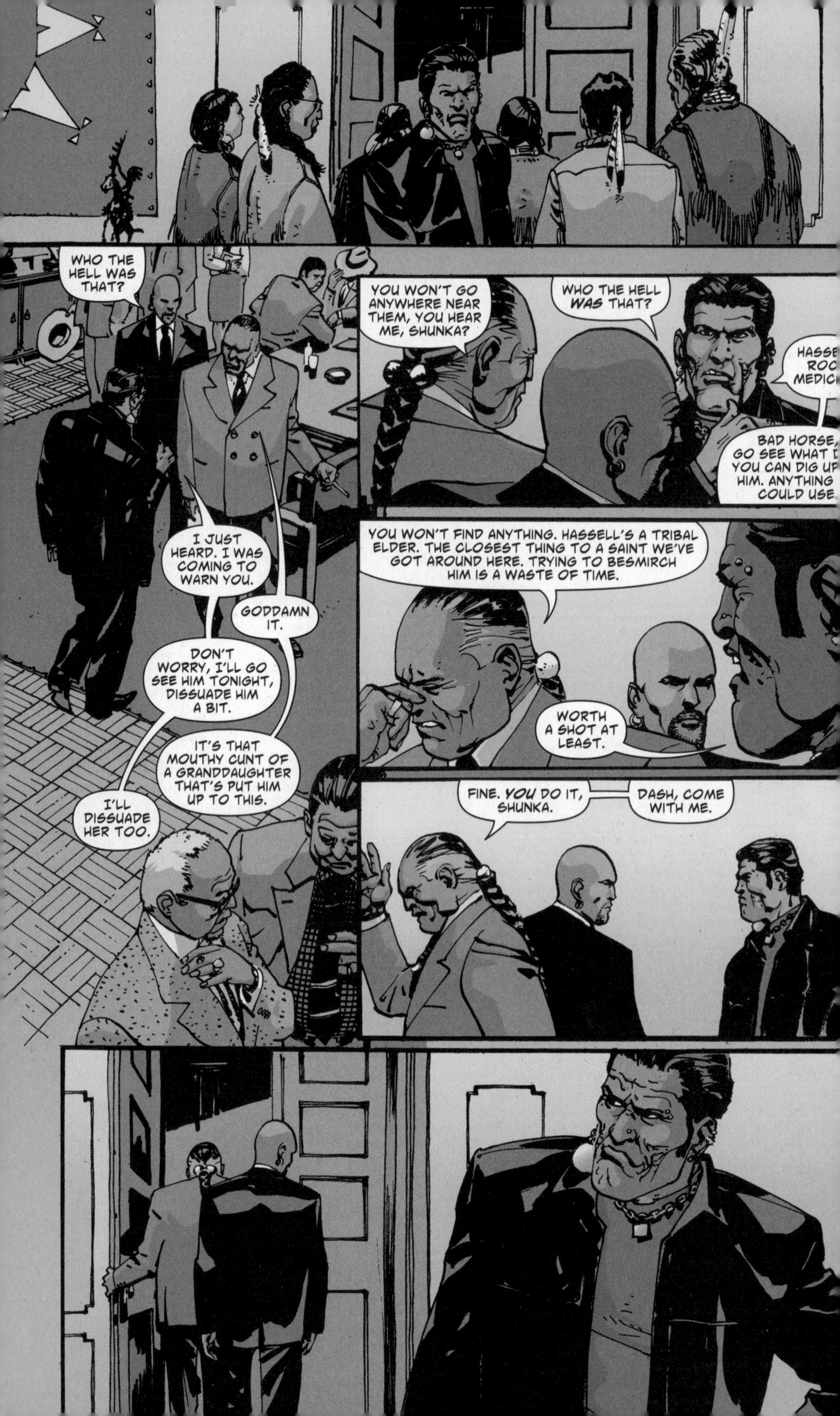
WHO THE HELL WAS THAT?
YOU WON'T GO ANYWHERE NEAR THEM, YOU HEAR ME, SHUNKA?
WHO THE HELL WAS THAT?
BAD HORSE, GO SEE WHAT YOU CAN DIG UP HIM. ANYTHING COULD USE.
YOU WON'T FIND ANYTHING. HASSELL'S A TRIBAL ELDER. THE CLOSEST THING TO A SAINT WE'VE GOT AROUND HERE. TRYING TO BESMIRCH HIM IS A WASTE OF TIME.
WORTH A SHOT AT LEAST.
I JUST HEARD. I WAS COMING TO WARN YOU.
GODDAMN IT.
DON'T WORRY, I'LL GO SEE HIM TONIGHT, DISSUADE HIM A BIT.
IT'S THAT MOUTHY CUNT OF A GRANDDAUGHTER THAT'S PUT HIM UP TO THIS.
I'LL DISSUADE HER TOO.
FINE. YOU DO IT, SHUNKA.
DASH, COME WITH ME.

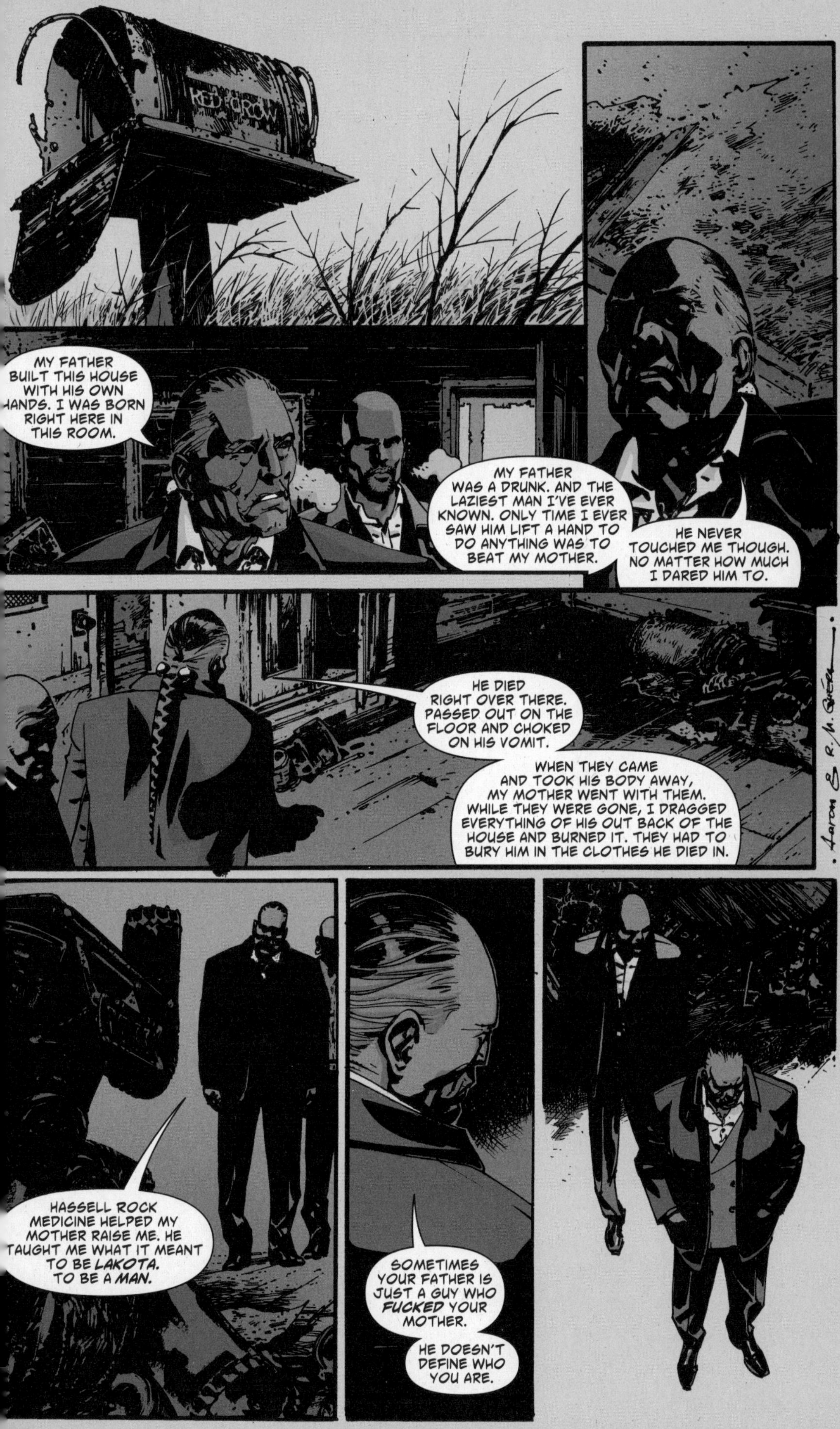
RED CROW
MY FATHER BUILT THIS HOUSE WITH HIS OWN HANDS. I WAS BORN RIGHT HERE IN THIS ROOM.
MY FATHER WAS A DRUNK. AND THE LAZIEST MAN I'VE EVER KNOWN. ONLY TIME I EVER SAW HIM LIFT A HAND TO DO ANYTHING WAS TO BEAT MY MOTHER.
HE NEVER TOUCHED ME THOUGH. NO MATTER HOW MUCH I DARED HIM TO.
HE DIED RIGHT OVER THERE. PASSED OUT ON THE FLOOR AND CHOKED ON HIS VOMIT.
WHEN THEY CAME AND TOOK HIS BODY AWAY, MY MOTHER WENT WITH THEM. WHILE THEY WERE GONE, I DRAGGED EVERYTHING OF HIS OUT BACK OF THE HOUSE AND BURNED IT. THEY HAD TO BURY HIM IN THE CLOTHES HE DIED IN.
HASSELL ROCK MEDICINE HELPED MY MOTHER RAISE ME. HE TAUGHT ME WHAT IT MEANT TO BE *LAKOTA*. TO BE A *MAN*.
SOMETIMES YOUR FATHER IS JUST A GUY WHO ***FUCKED*** YOUR MOTHER.
HE DOESN'T DEFINE WHO YOU ARE.

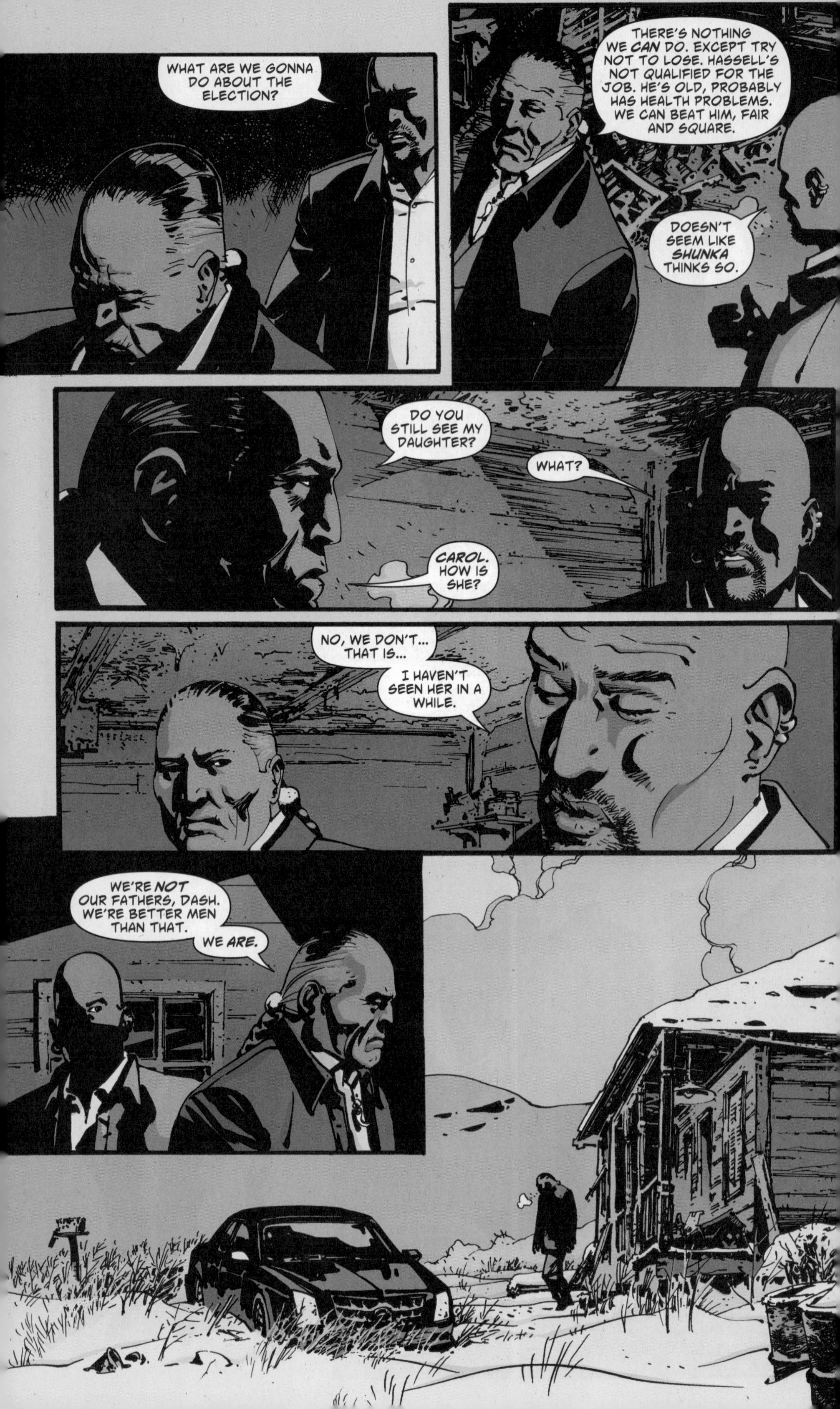
WHAT ARE WE GONNA DO ABOUT THE ELECTION?
THERE'S NOTHING WE CAN DO. EXCEPT TRY NOT TO LOSE. HASSELL'S NOT QUALIFIED FOR THE JOB. HE'S OLD, PROBABLY HAS HEALTH PROBLEMS. WE CAN BEAT HIM, FAIR AND SQUARE.
DOESN'T SEEM LIKE SHUNKA THINKS SO.
DO YOU STILL SEE MY DAUGHTER?
WHAT?
CAROL. HOW IS SHE?
NO, WE DON'T... THAT IS...
I HAVEN'T SEEN HER IN A WHILE.
WE'RE NOT OUR FATHERS, DASH. WE'RE BETTER MEN THAN THAT.
WE ARE.

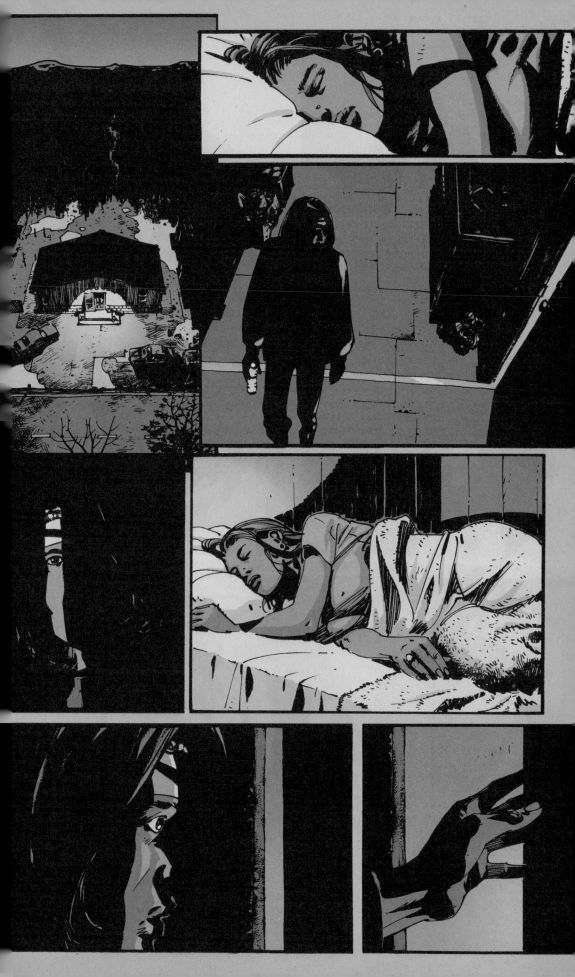

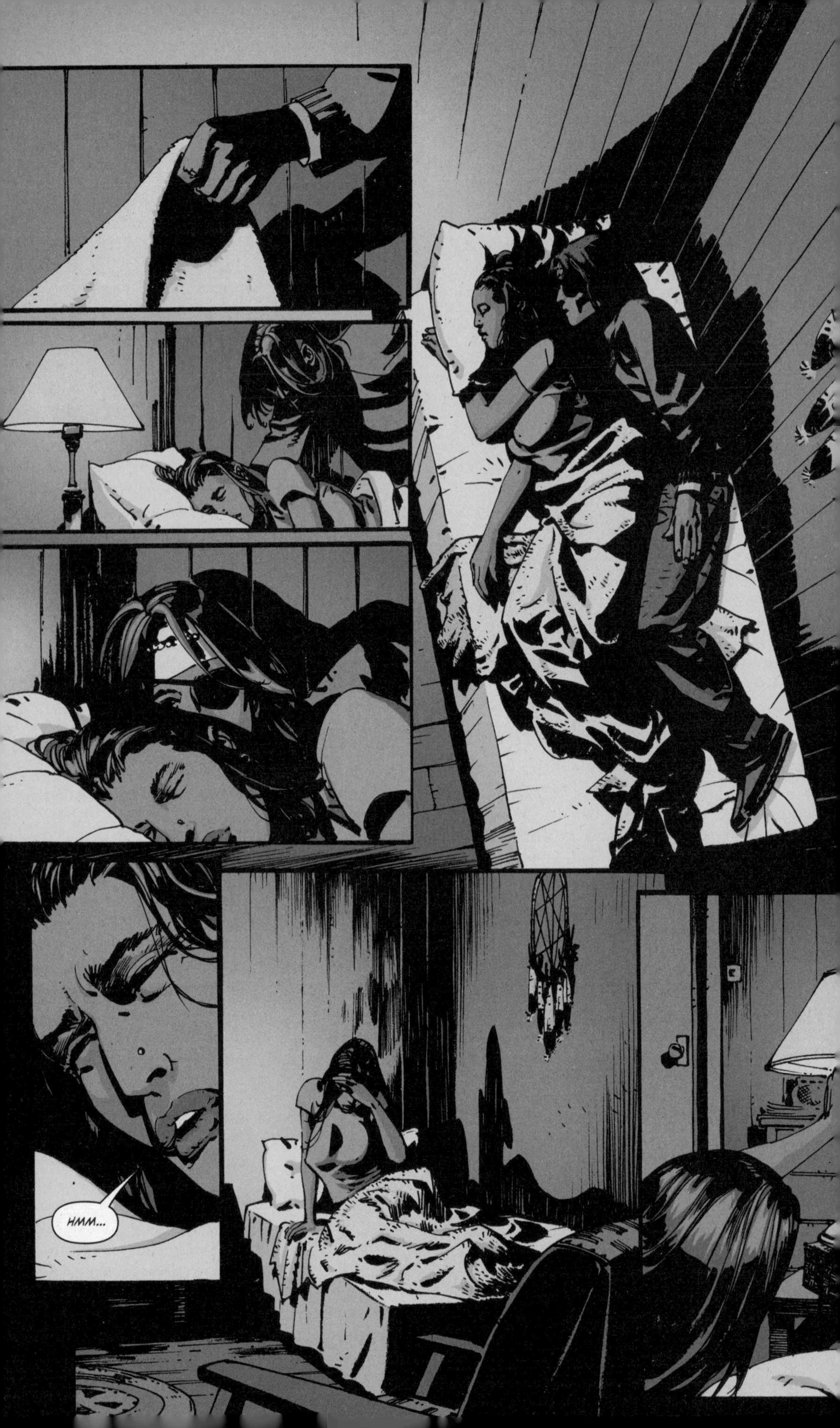
HMM...

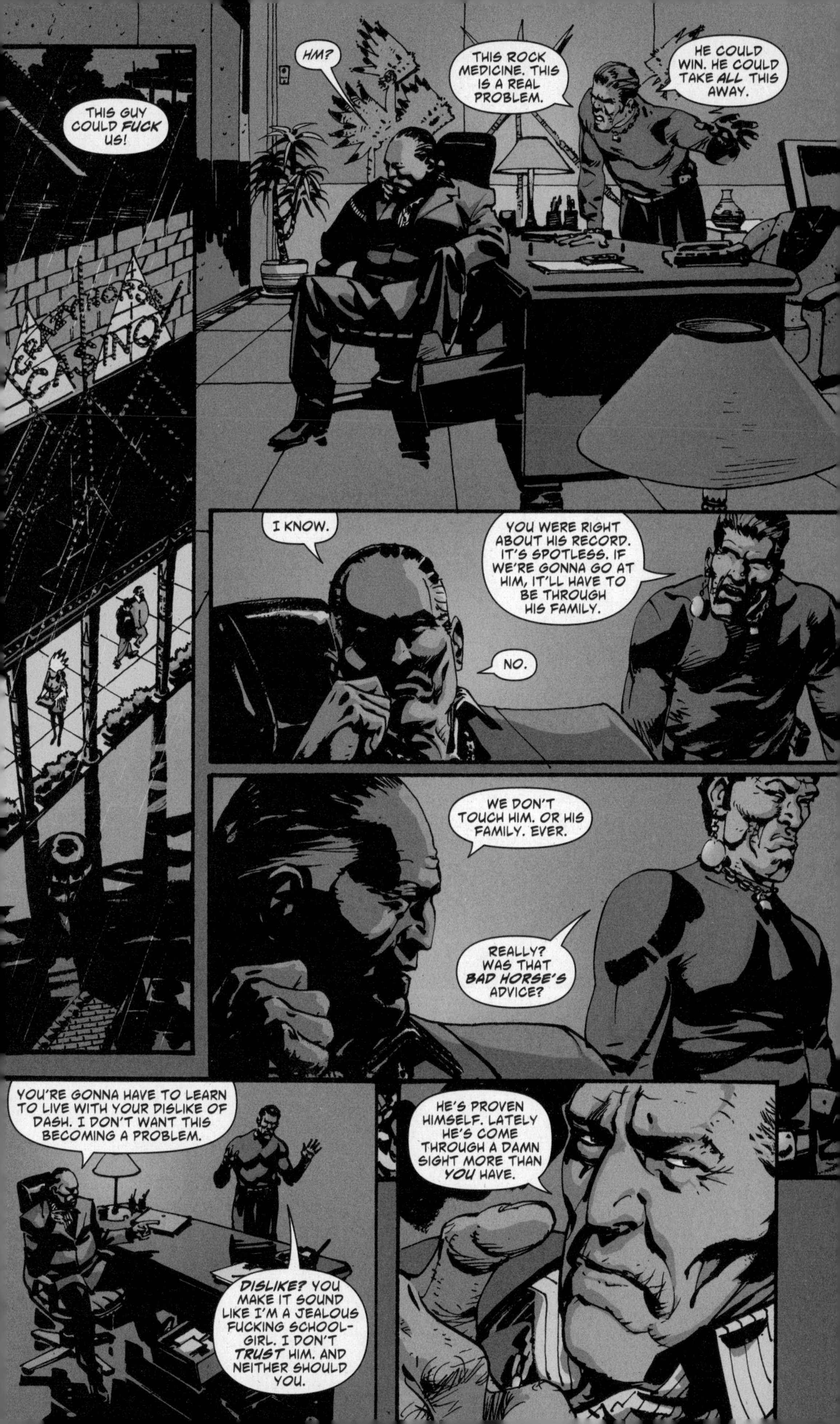
THIS GUY COULD FUCK US!
HM?
THIS ROCK MEDICINE. THIS IS A REAL PROBLEM.
HE COULD WIN. HE COULD TAKE ALL THIS AWAY.
GRAYHORSE CASINO
I KNOW.
YOU WERE RIGHT ABOUT HIS RECORD. IT'S SPOTLESS. IF WE'RE GONNA GO AT HIM, IT'LL HAVE TO BE THROUGH HIS FAMILY.
NO.
WE DON'T TOUCH HIM. OR HIS FAMILY. EVER.
REALLY? WAS THAT BAD HORSE'S ADVICE?
YOU'RE GONNA HAVE TO LEARN TO LIVE WITH YOUR DISLIKE OF DASH. I DON'T WANT THIS BECOMING A PROBLEM.
DISLIKE? YOU MAKE IT SOUND LIKE I'M A JEALOUS FUCKING SCHOOL-GIRL. I DON'T TRUST HIM. AND NEITHER SHOULD YOU.
HE'S PROVEN HIMSELF. LATELY HE'S COME THROUGH A DAMN SIGHT MORE THAN YOU HAVE.

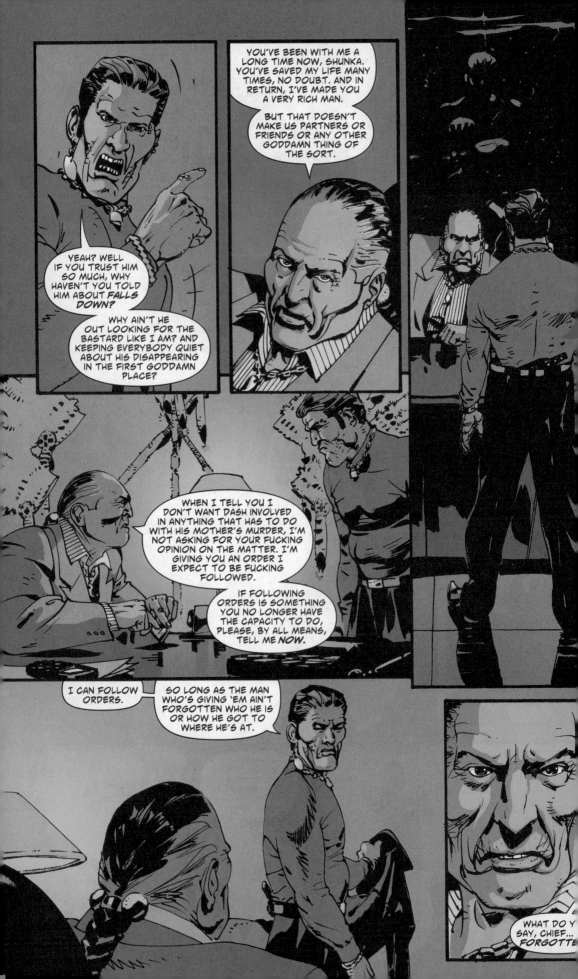

YOU'VE BEEN WITH ME A LONG TIME NOW, SHUNKA. YOU'VE SAVED MY LIFE MANY TIMES, NO DOUBT. AND IN RETURN, I'VE MADE YOU A VERY RICH MAN.

BUT THAT DOESN'T MAKE US PARTNERS OR FRIENDS OR ANY OTHER GODDAMN THING OF THE SORT.

YEAH? WELL IF YOU TRUST HIM SO MUCH, WHY HAVEN'T YOU TOLD HIM ABOUT FALLS DOWN?

WHY AIN'T HE OUT LOOKING FOR THE BASTARD LIKE I AM? AND KEEPING EVERYBODY QUIET ABOUT HIS DISAPPEARING IN THE FIRST GODDAMN PLACE?

WHEN I TELL YOU I DON'T WANT DASH INVOLVED IN ANYTHING THAT HAS TO DO WITH HIS MOTHER'S MURDER, I'M NOT ASKING FOR YOUR FUCKING OPINION ON THE MATTER. I'M GIVING YOU AN ORDER I EXPECT TO BE FUCKING FOLLOWED.

IF FOLLOWING ORDERS IS SOMETHING YOU NO LONGER HAVE THE CAPACITY TO DO, PLEASE, BY ALL MEANS, TELL ME NOW.

I CAN FOLLOW ORDERS.

SO LONG AS THE MAN WHO'S GIVING 'EM AIN'T FORGOTTEN WHO HE IS OR HOW HE GOT TO WHERE HE'S AT.

WHAT DO Y SAY, CHIEF... FORGOTTE

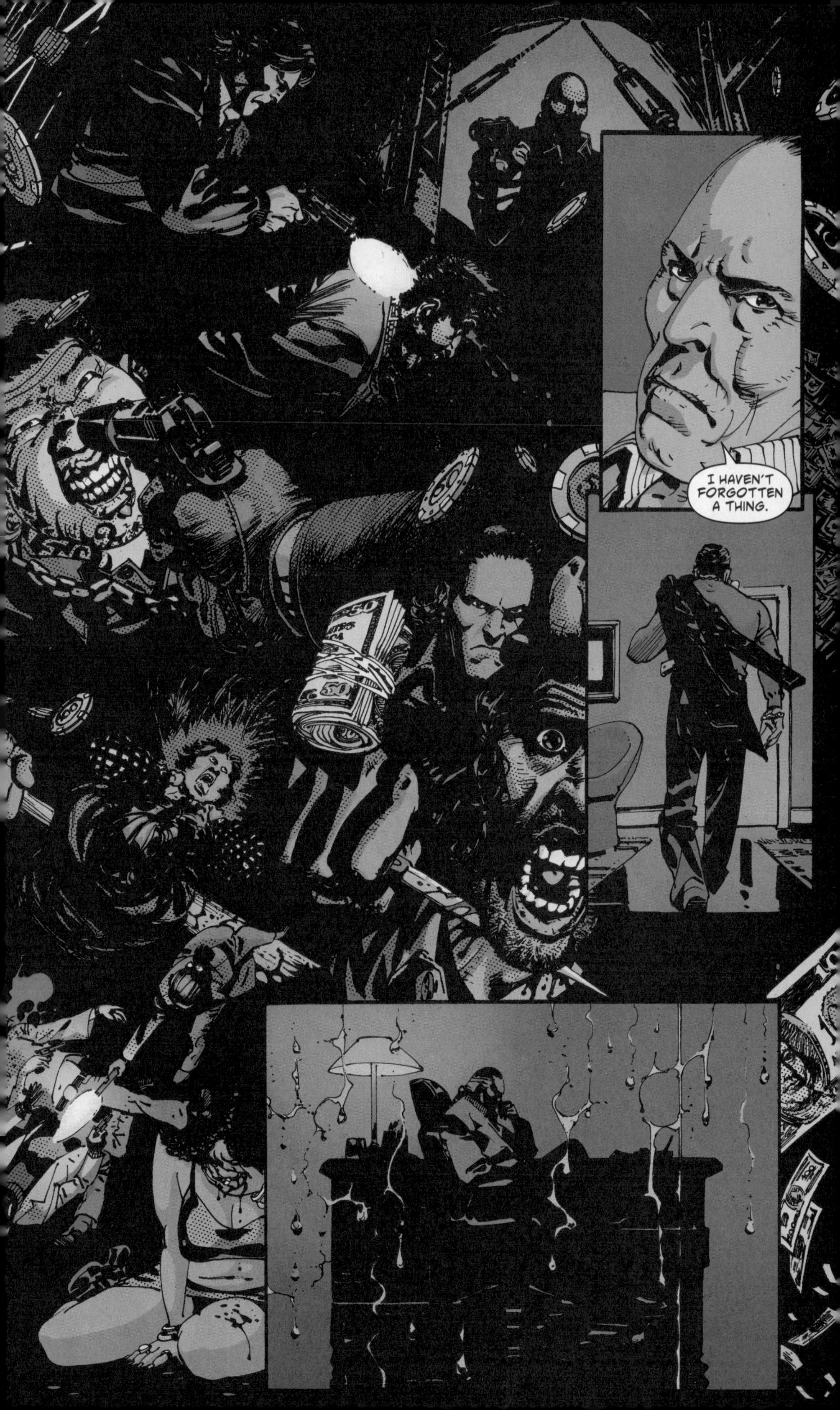
I HAVEN'T FORGOTTEN A THING.

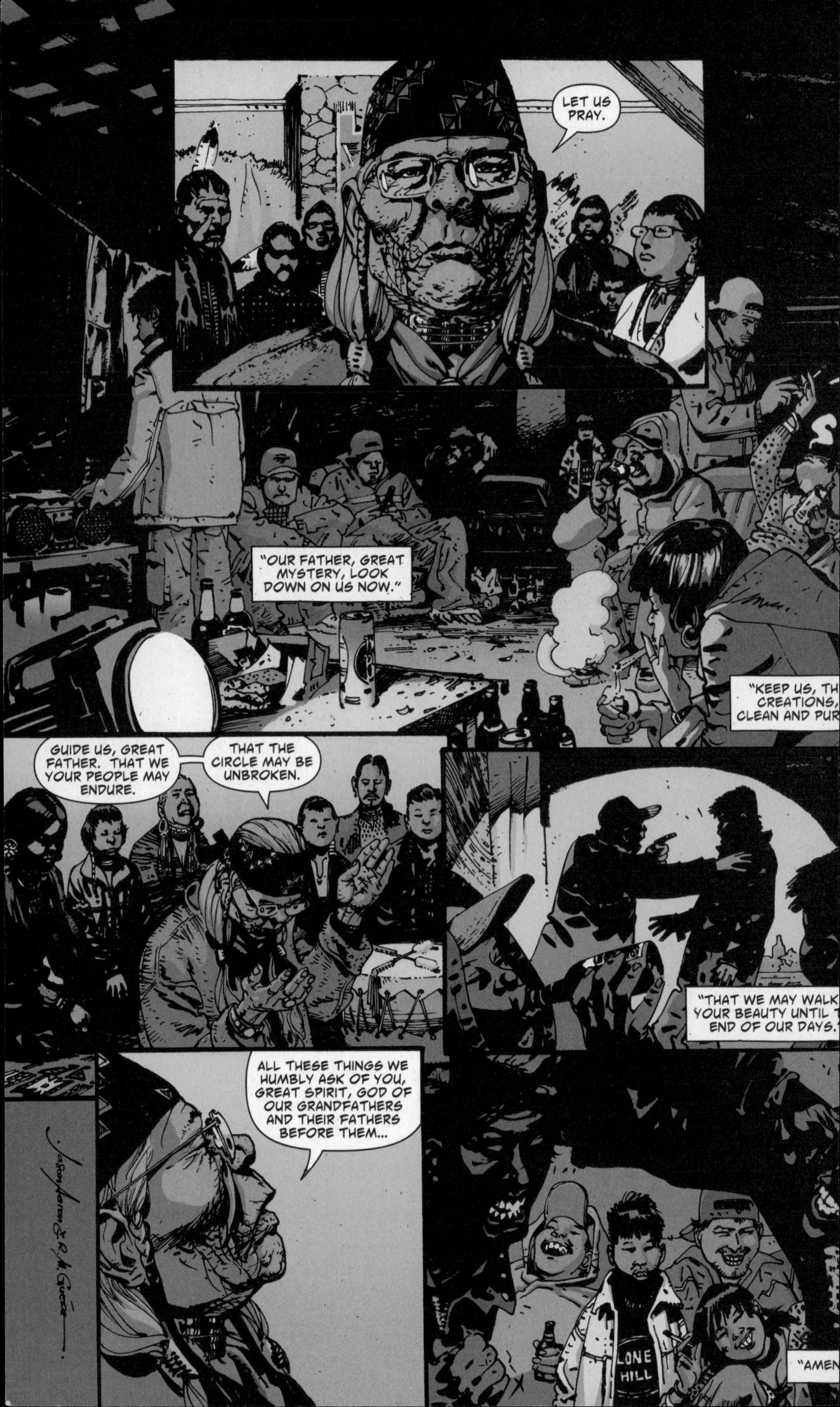
LET US PRAY.
"OUR FATHER, GREAT MYSTERY, LOOK DOWN ON US NOW."
"KEEP US, TH CREATIONS, CLEAN AND PUR
GUIDE US, GREAT FATHER. THAT WE YOUR PEOPLE MAY ENDURE.
THAT THE CIRCLE MAY BE UNBROKEN.
"THAT WE MAY WALK YOUR BEAUTY UNTIL T END OF OUR DAYS."
ALL THESE THINGS WE HUMBLY ASK OF YOU, GREAT SPIRIT, GOD OF OUR GRANDFATHERS AND THEIR FATHERS BEFORE THEM...
LONE HILL
"AMEN

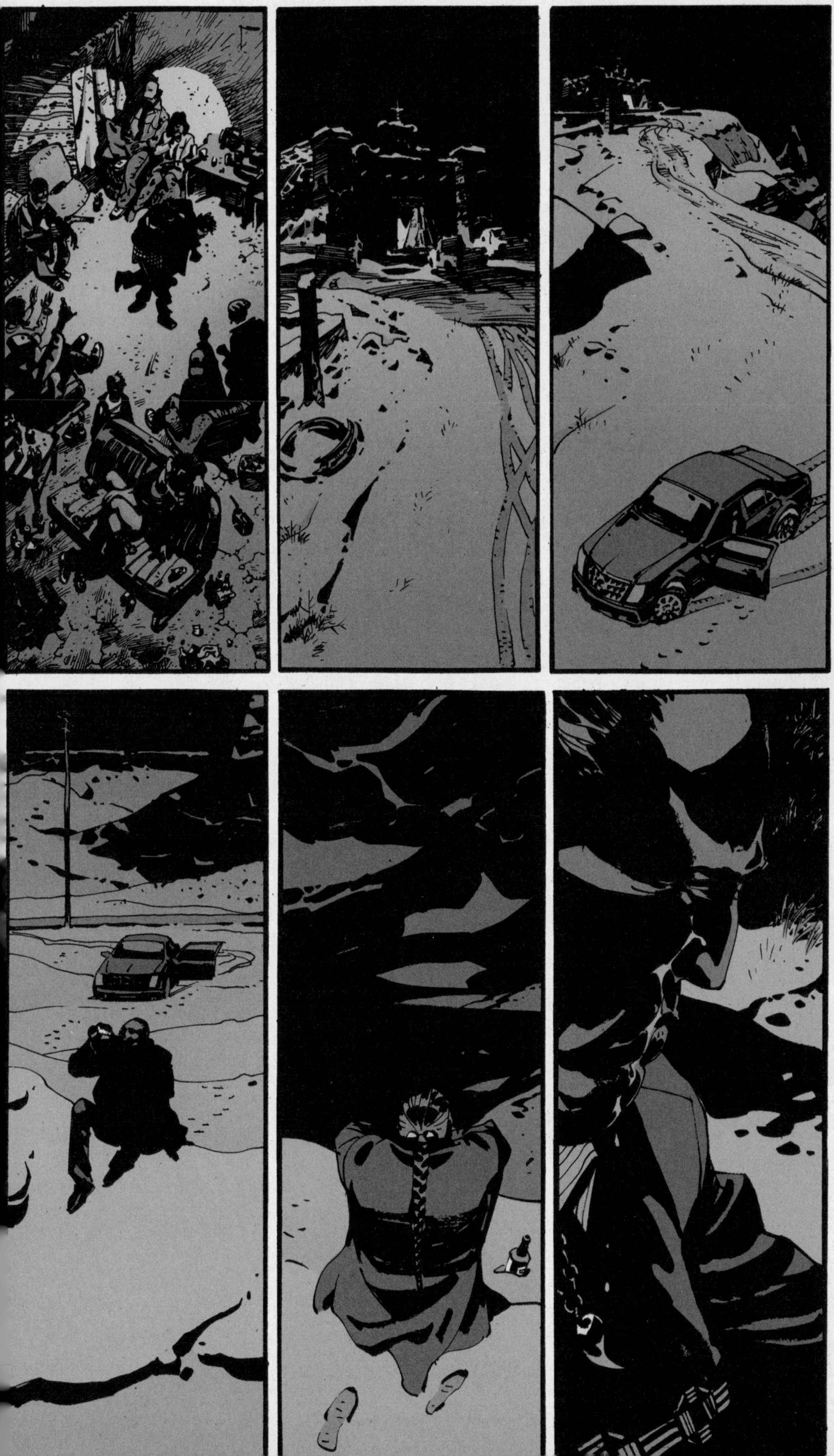

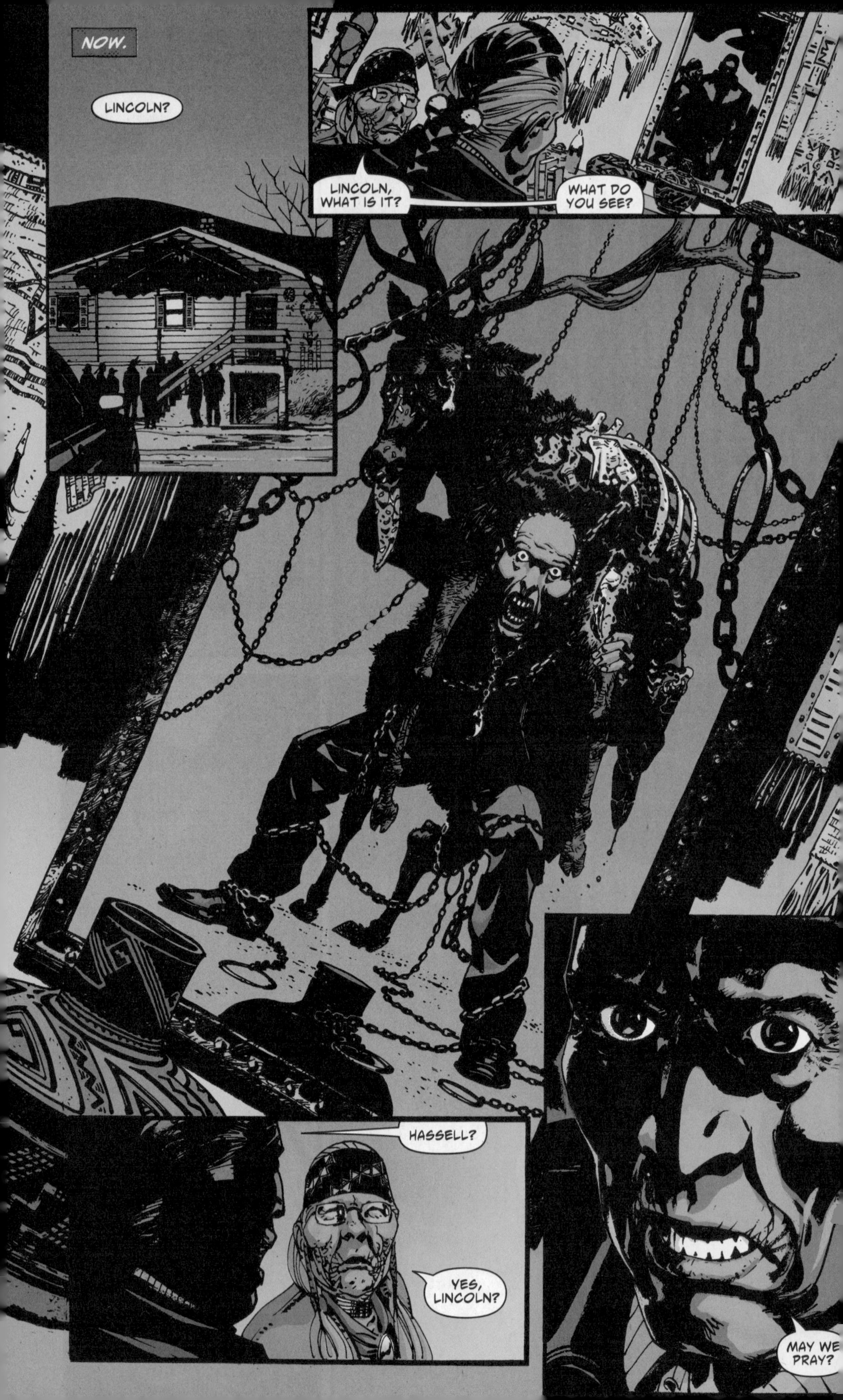
NOW.
LINCOLN?
LINCOLN, WHAT IS IT?
WHAT DO YOU SEE?
HASSELL?
YES, LINCOLN?
MAY WE PRAY?

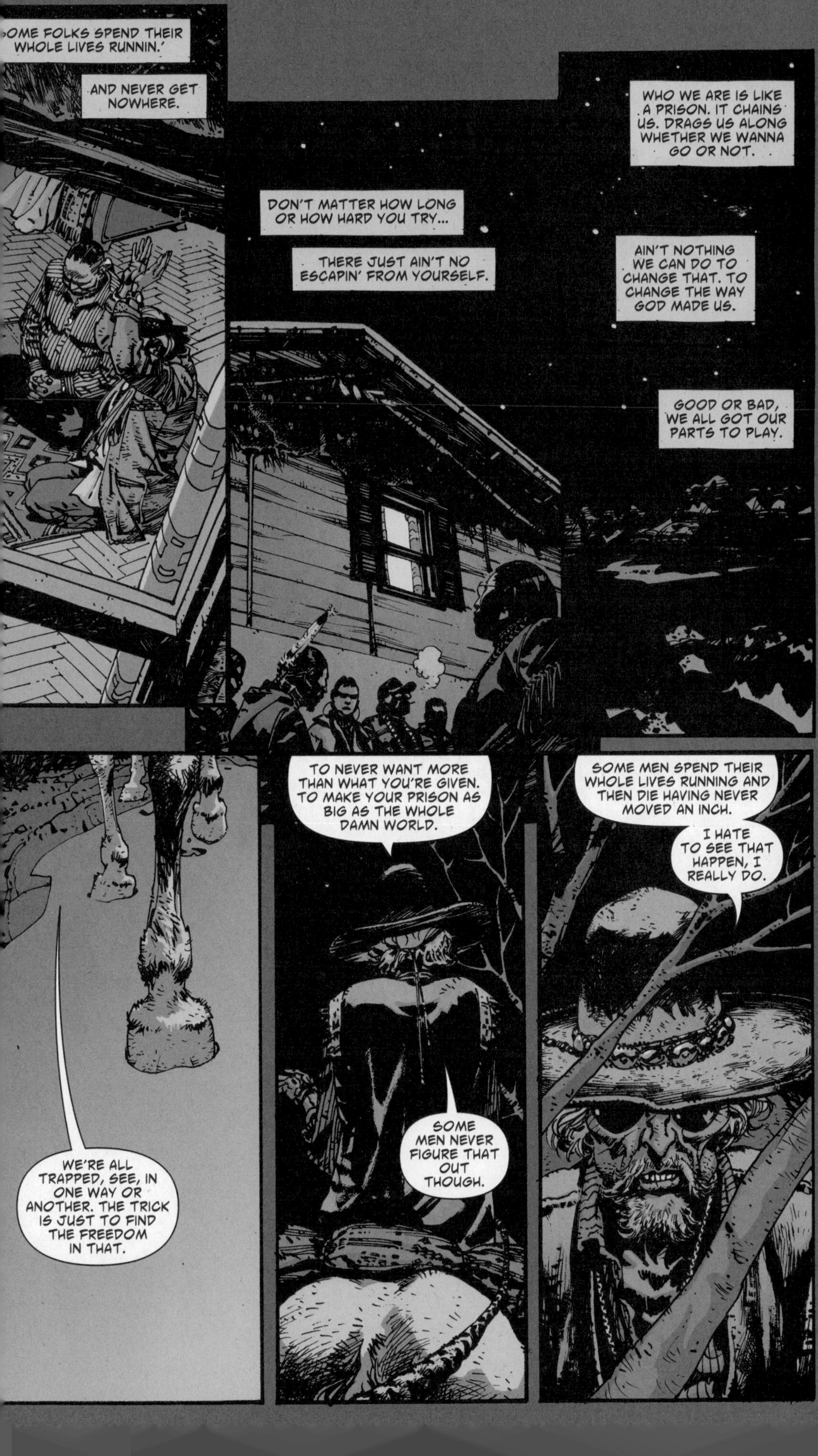
SOME FOLKS SPEND THEIR WHOLE LIVES RUNNIN.'
AND NEVER GET NOWHERE.
DON'T MATTER HOW LONG OR HOW HARD YOU TRY...
THERE JUST AIN'T NO ESCAPIN' FROM YOURSELF.
WHO WE ARE IS LIKE A PRISON. IT CHAINS US. DRAGS US ALONG WHETHER WE WANNA GO OR NOT.
AIN'T NOTHING WE CAN DO TO CHANGE THAT. TO CHANGE THE WAY GOD MADE US.
GOOD OR BAD, WE ALL GOT OUR PARTS TO PLAY.
WE'RE ALL TRAPPED, SEE, IN ONE WAY OR ANOTHER. THE TRICK IS JUST TO FIND THE FREEDOM IN THAT.
TO NEVER WANT MORE THAN WHAT YOU'RE GIVEN. TO MAKE YOUR PRISON AS BIG AS THE WHOLE DAMN WORLD.
SOME MEN NEVER FIGURE THAT OUT THOUGH.
SOME MEN SPEND THEIR WHOLE LIVES RUNNING AND THEN DIE HAVING NEVER MOVED AN INCH.
I HATE TO SEE THAT HAPPEN, I REALLY DO.

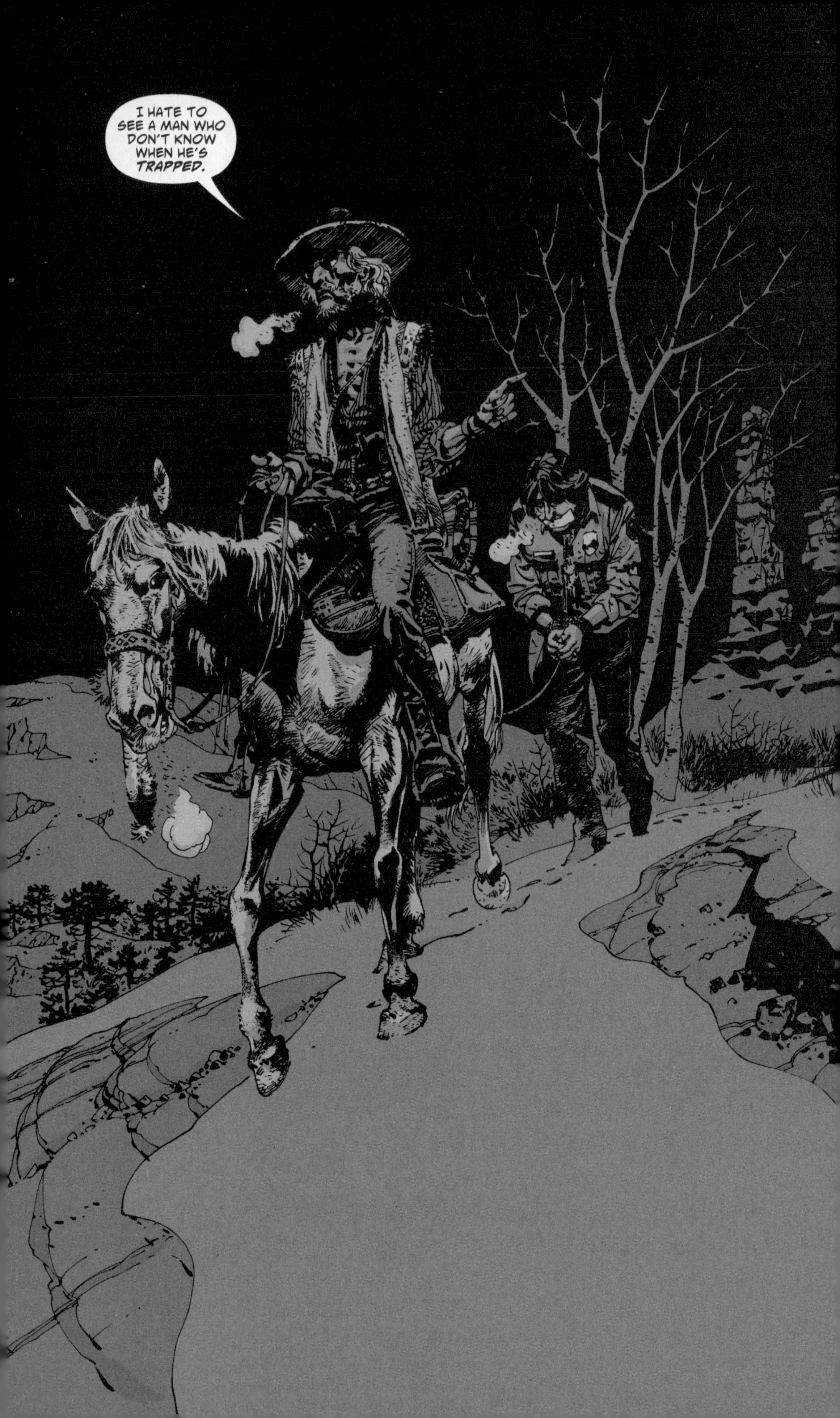
I HATE TO SEE A MAN WHO DON'T KNOW WHEN HE'S *TRAPPED*.

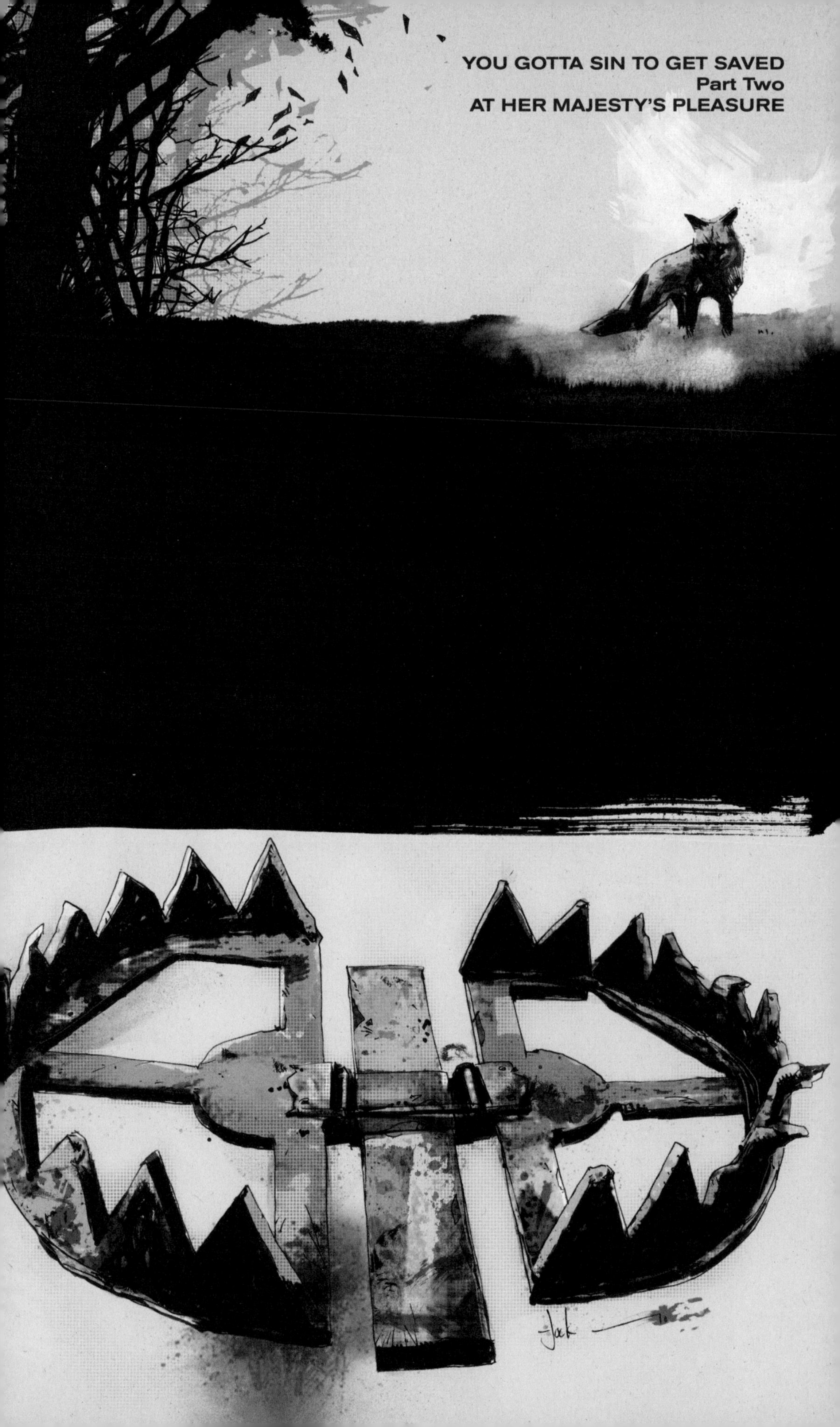
YOU GOTTA SIN TO GET SAVED
Part Two
AT HER MAJESTY'S PLEASURE
Jock

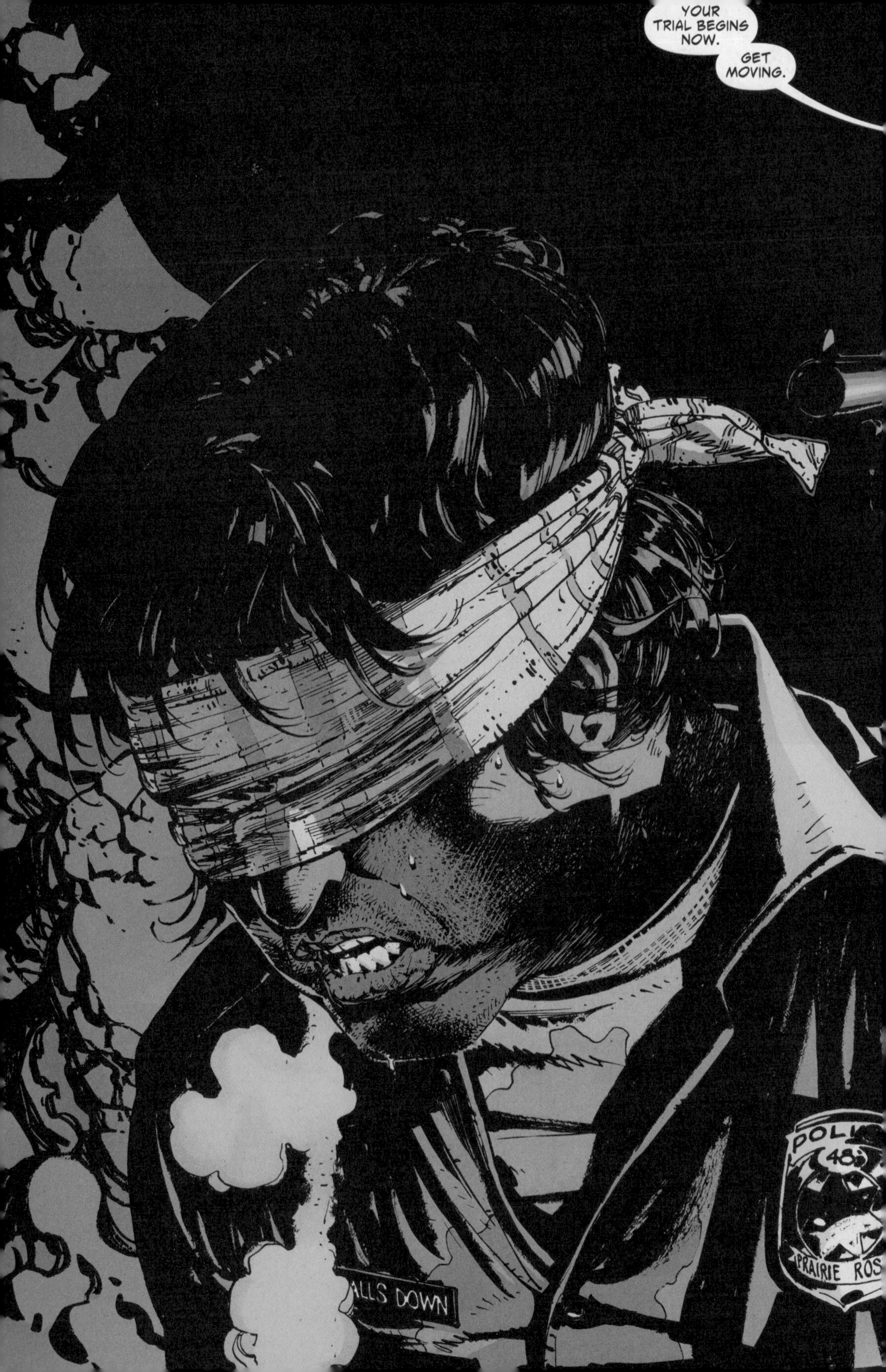
YOUR TRIAL BEGINS NOW.
GET MOVING.
POLI
48
PRAIRIE ROS
ALLS DOWN

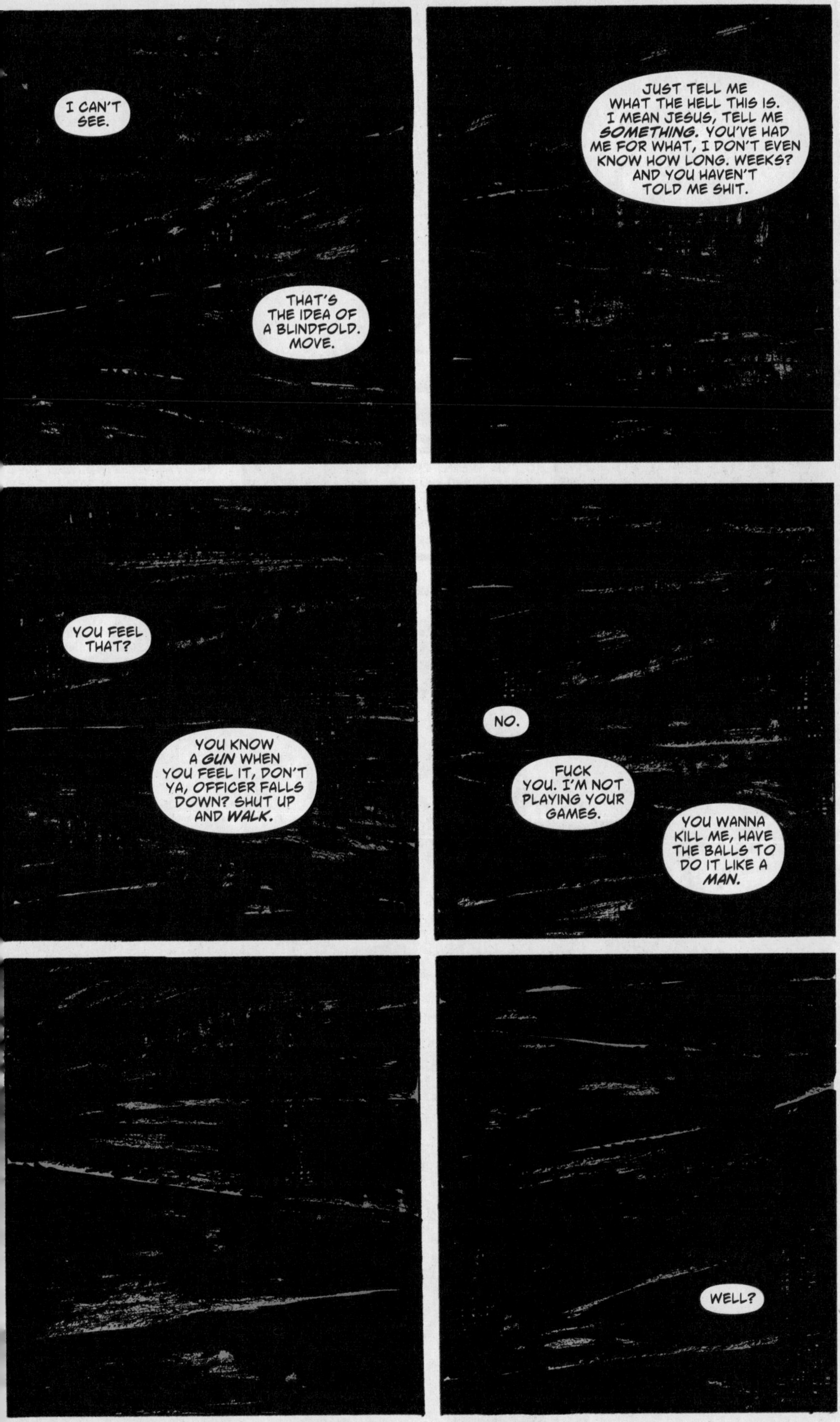
I CAN'T SEE.
THAT'S THE IDEA OF A BLINDFOLD. MOVE.
JUST TELL ME WHAT THE HELL THIS IS. I MEAN JESUS, TELL ME *SOMETHING.* YOU'VE HAD ME FOR WHAT, I DON'T EVEN KNOW HOW LONG. WEEKS? AND YOU HAVEN'T TOLD ME SHIT.
YOU FEEL THAT?
YOU KNOW A *GUN* WHEN YOU FEEL IT, DON'T YA, OFFICER FALLS DOWN? SHUT UP AND *WALK.*
NO.
FUCK YOU. I'M NOT PLAYING YOUR GAMES.
YOU WANNA KILL ME, HAVE THE BALLS TO DO IT LIKE A *MAN.*
WELL?

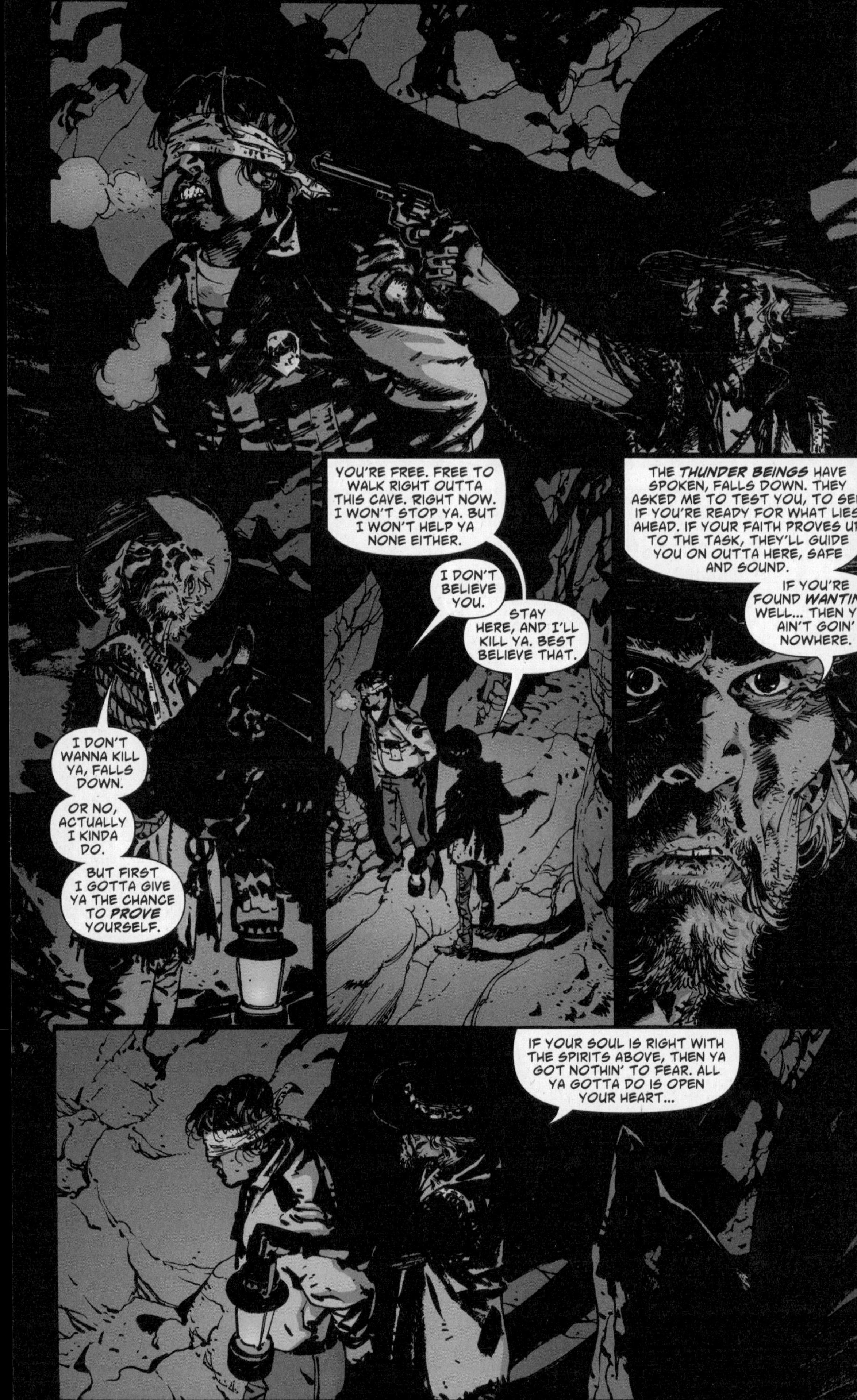
I DON'T WANNA KILL YA, FALLS DOWN.
OR NO, ACTUALLY I KINDA DO.
BUT FIRST I GOTTA GIVE YA THE CHANCE TO *PROVE* YOURSELF.
YOU'RE FREE. FREE TO WALK RIGHT OUTTA THIS CAVE. RIGHT NOW. I WON'T STOP YA. BUT I WON'T HELP YA NONE EITHER.
I DON'T BELIEVE YOU.
STAY HERE, AND I'LL KILL YA. BEST BELIEVE THAT.
THE *THUNDER BEINGS* HAVE SPOKEN, FALLS DOWN. THEY ASKED ME TO TEST YOU, TO SE IF YOU'RE READY FOR WHAT LIES AHEAD. IF YOUR FAITH PROVES U TO THE TASK, THEY'LL GUIDE YOU ON OUTTA HERE, SAFE AND SOUND.
IF YOU'RE FOUND *WANTIN* WELL... THEN Y AIN'T GOIN' NOWHERE.
IF YOUR SOUL IS RIGHT WITH THE SPIRITS ABOVE, THEN YA GOT NOTHIN' TO FEAR. ALL YA GOTTA DO IS OPEN YOUR HEART...

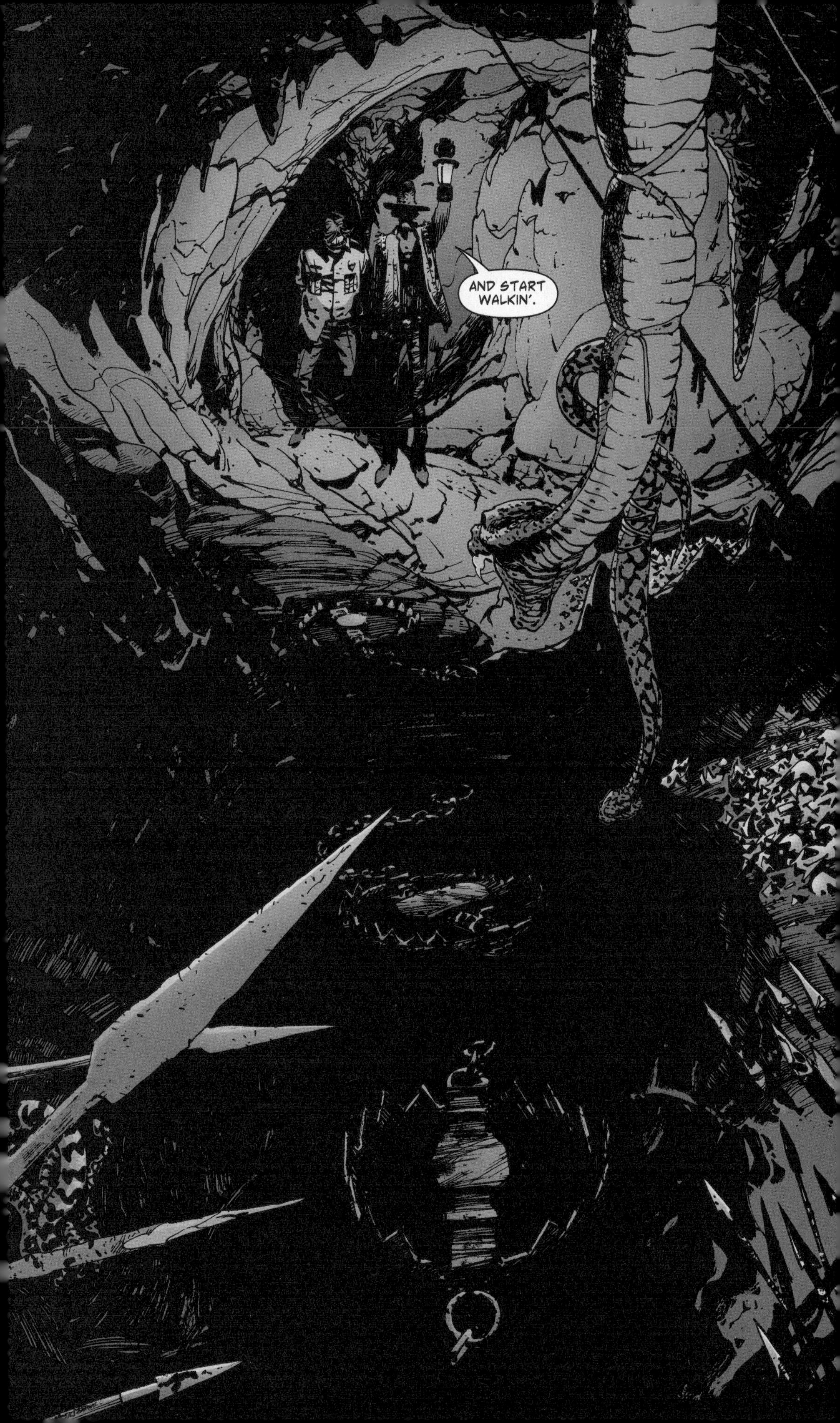
AND START WALKIN'.

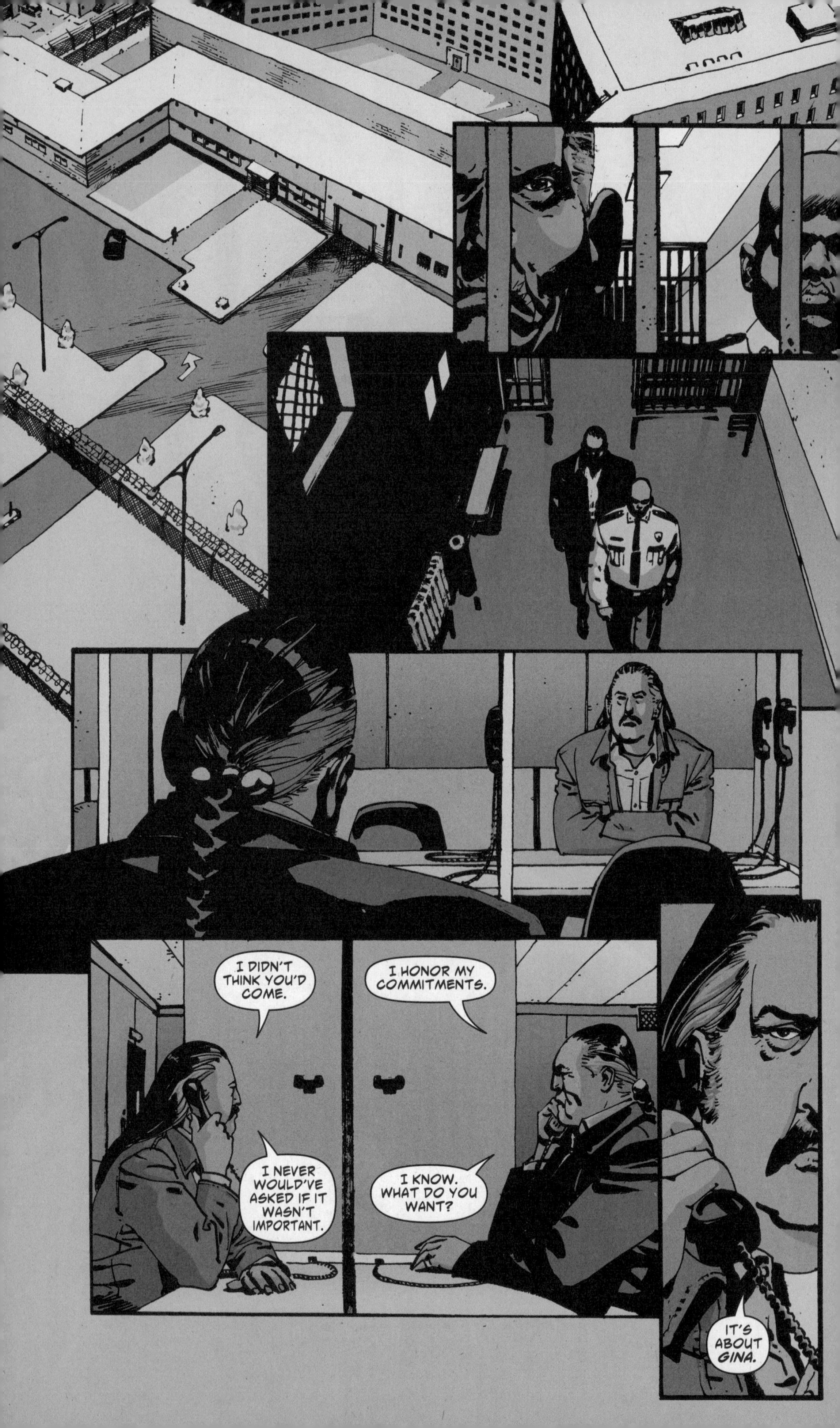
I DIDN'T THINK YOU'D COME.
I HONOR MY COMMITMENTS.
I NEVER WOULD'VE ASKED IF IT WASN'T IMPORTANT.
I KNOW. WHAT DO YOU WANT?
IT'S ABOUT GINA.

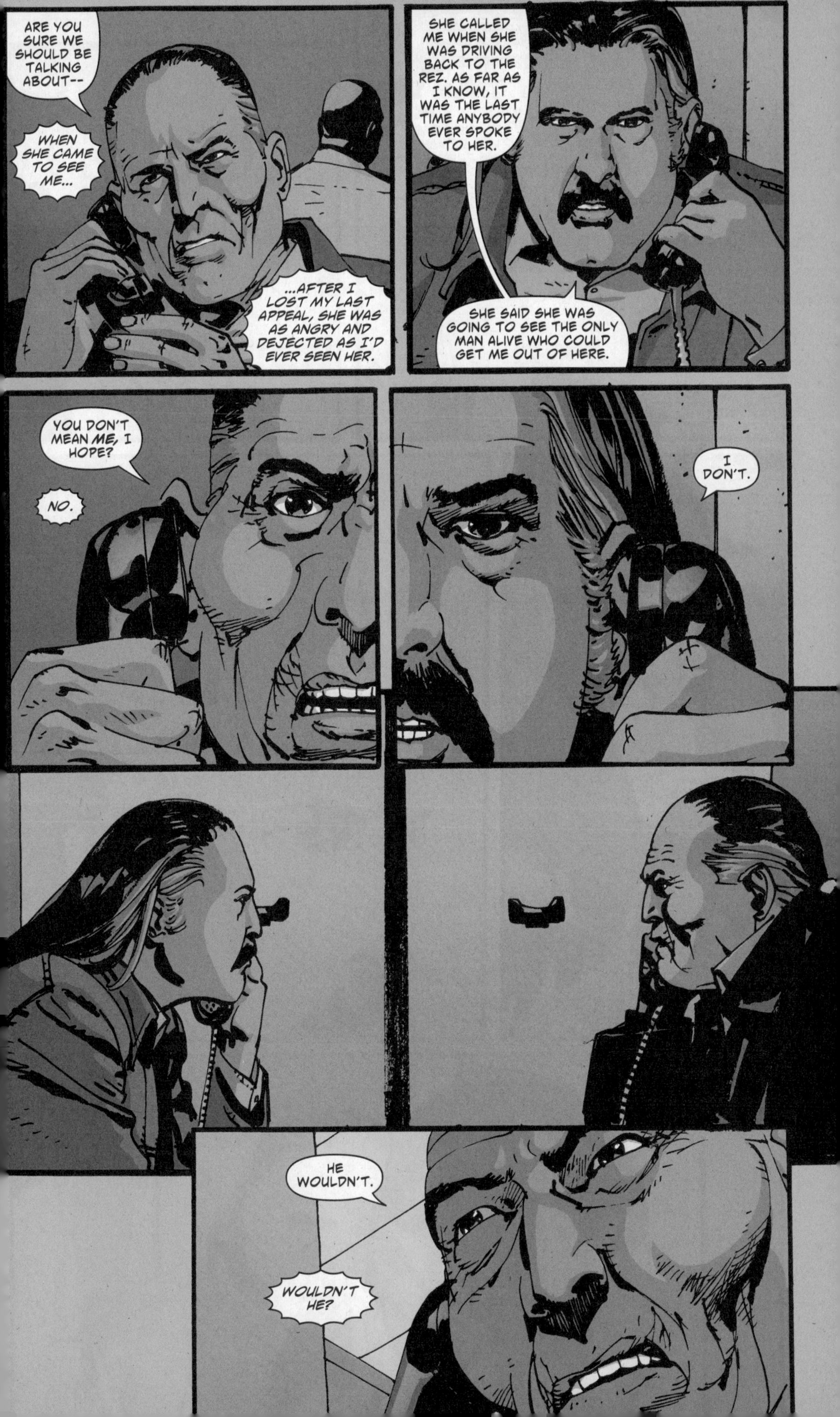
ARE YOU SURE WE SHOULD BE TALKING ABOUT--
WHEN SHE CAME TO SEE ME...
...AFTER I LOST MY LAST APPEAL, SHE WAS AS ANGRY AND DEJECTED AS I'D EVER SEEN HER.
SHE CALLED ME WHEN SHE WAS DRIVING BACK TO THE REZ. AS FAR AS I KNOW, IT WAS THE LAST TIME ANYBODY EVER SPOKE TO HER.
SHE SAID SHE WAS GOING TO SEE THE ONLY MAN ALIVE WHO COULD GET ME OUT OF HERE.
YOU DON'T MEAN ME, I HOPE?
NO.
I DON'T.
HE WOULDN'T.
WOULDN'T HE?

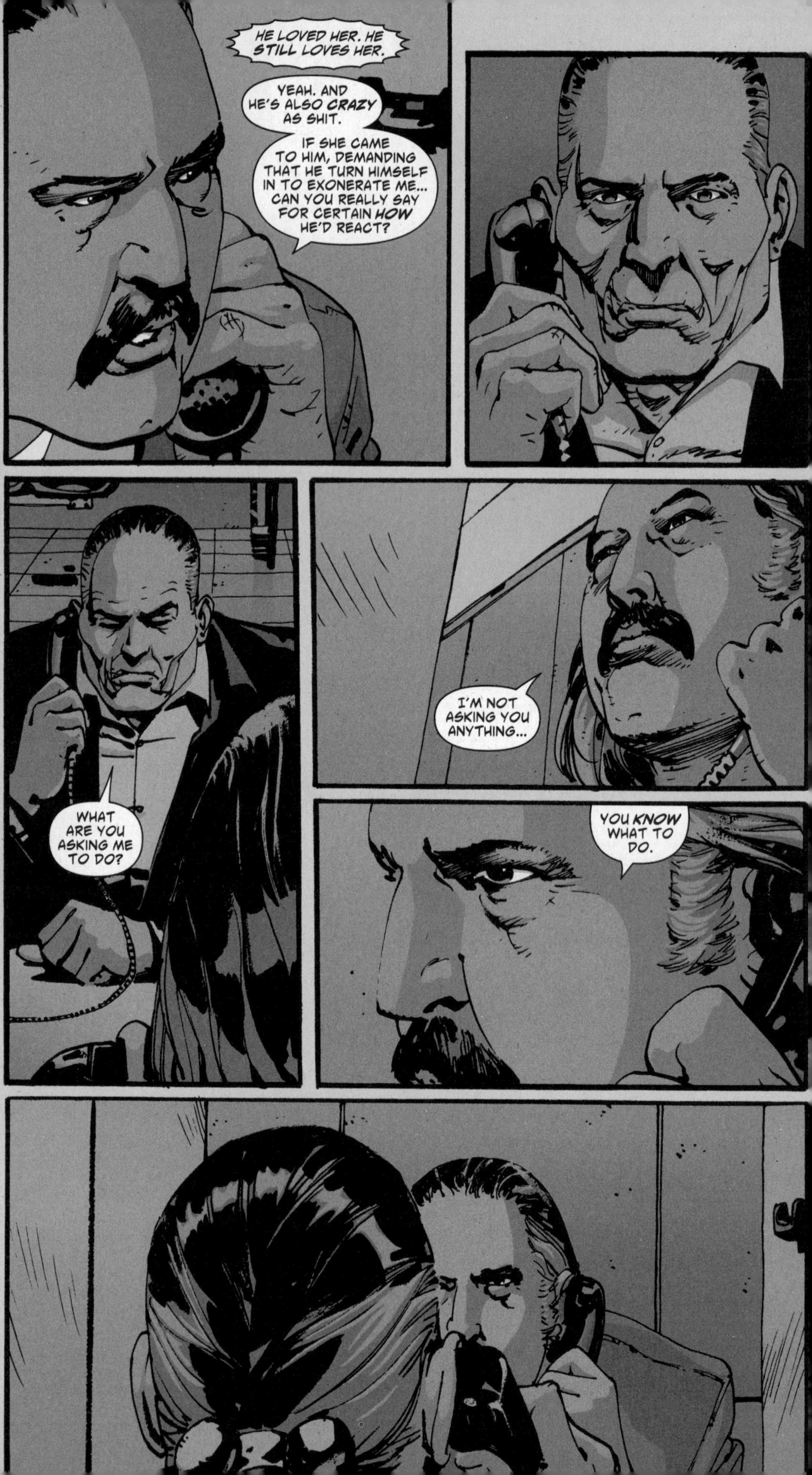
HE LOVED HER. HE STILL LOVES HER.
YEAH. AND HE'S ALSO CRAZY AS SHIT.
IF SHE CAME TO HIM, DEMANDING THAT HE TURN HIMSELF IN TO EXONERATE ME... CAN YOU REALLY SAY FOR CERTAIN HOW HE'D REACT?
WHAT ARE YOU ASKING ME TO DO?
I'M NOT ASKING YOU ANYTHING...
YOU KNOW WHAT TO DO.

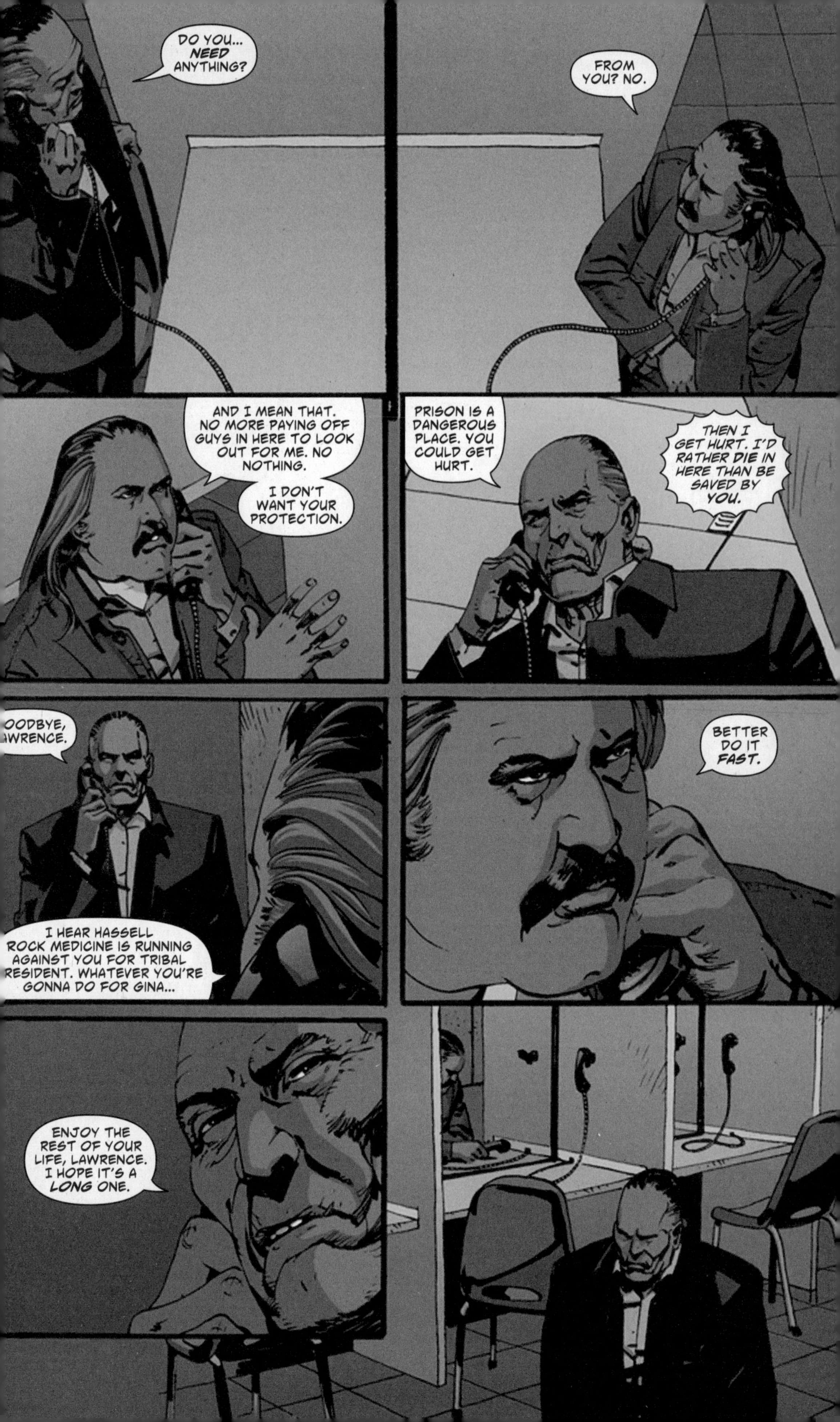
DO YOU... NEED ANYTHING?
FROM YOU? NO.
AND I MEAN THAT. NO MORE PAYING OFF GUYS IN HERE TO LOOK OUT FOR ME. NO NOTHING.
I DON'T WANT YOUR PROTECTION.
PRISON IS A DANGEROUS PLACE. YOU COULD GET HURT.
THEN I GET HURT. I'D RATHER DIE IN HERE THAN BE SAVED BY YOU.
OODBYE, AWRENCE.
I HEAR HASSELL ROCK MEDICINE IS RUNNING AGAINST YOU FOR TRIBAL RESIDENT. WHATEVER YOU'RE GONNA DO FOR GINA...
BETTER DO IT FAST.
ENJOY THE REST OF YOUR LIFE, LAWRENCE. I HOPE IT'S A LONG ONE.

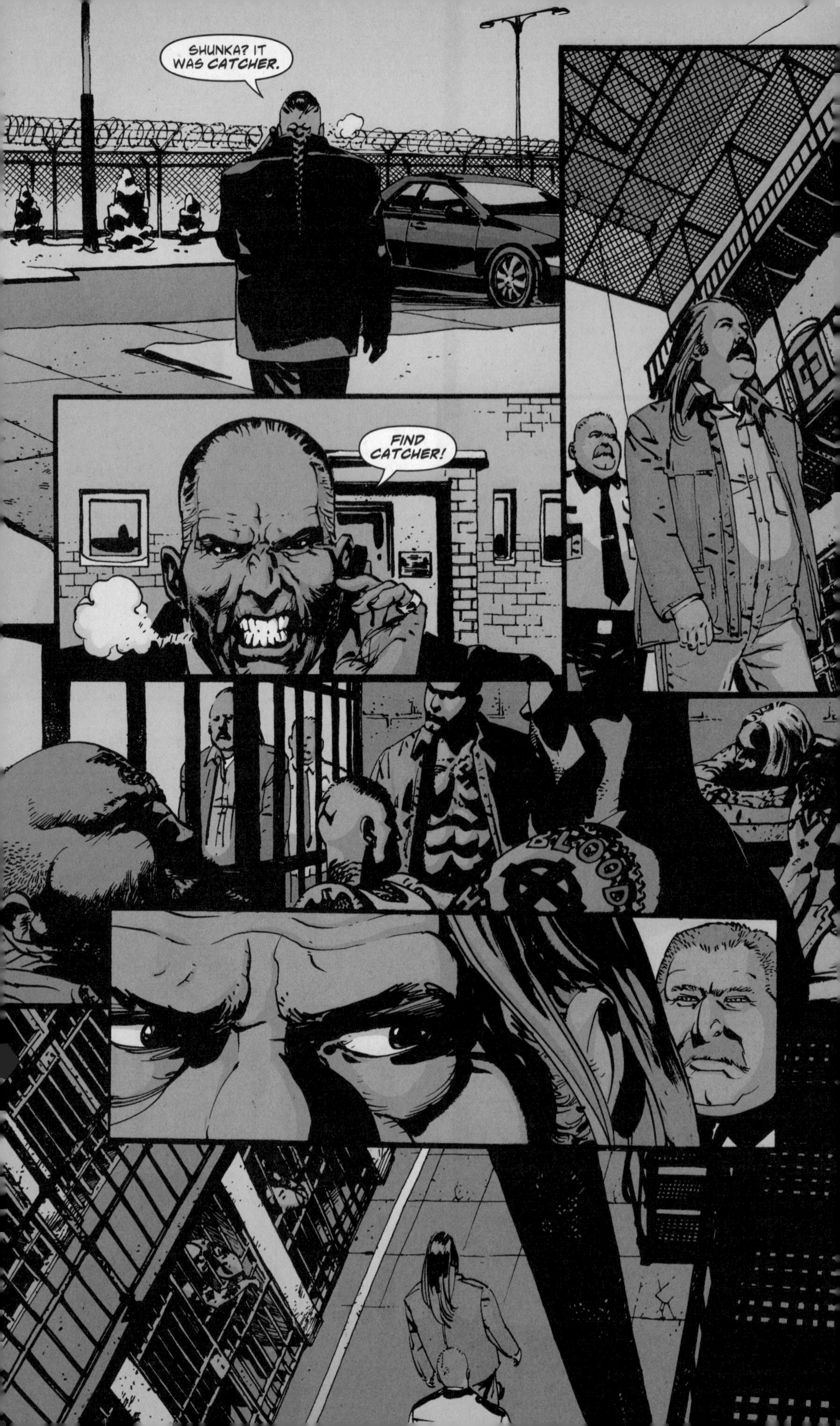

SHUNKA? IT WAS CATCHER.
FIND CATCHER!
BLOOD

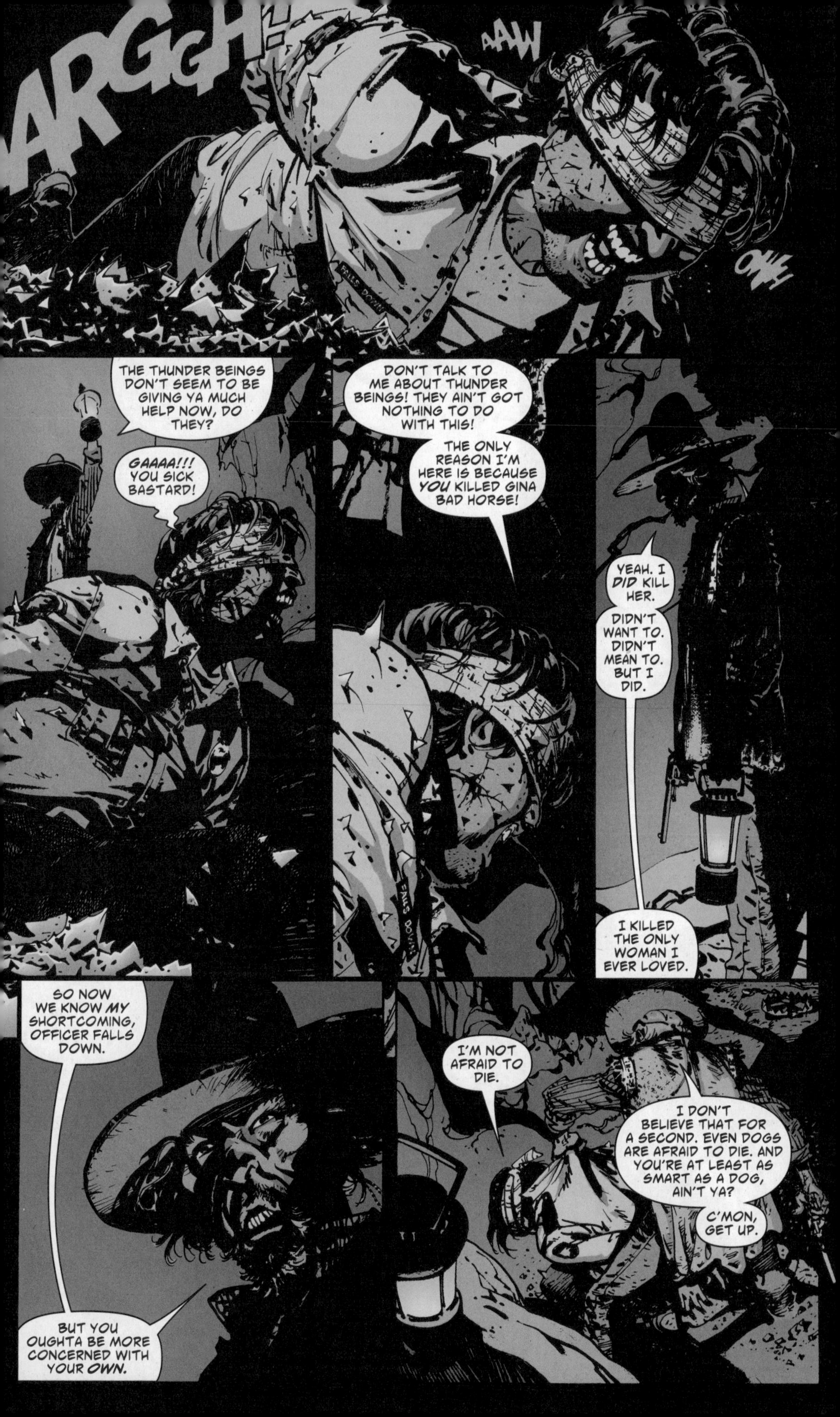
ARGGH!
AAW
OHH
FALLS DOWN
THE THUNDER BEINGS DON'T SEEM TO BE GIVING YA MUCH HELP NOW, DO THEY?
GAAAA!!! YOU SICK BASTARD!
DON'T TALK TO ME ABOUT THUNDER BEINGS! THEY AIN'T GOT NOTHING TO DO WITH THIS!
THE ONLY REASON I'M HERE IS BECAUSE YOU KILLED GINA BAD HORSE!
YEAH. I DID KILL HER.
DIDN'T WANT TO. DIDN'T MEAN TO. BUT I DID.
I KILLED THE ONLY WOMAN I EVER LOVED.
SO NOW WE KNOW MY SHORTCOMING, OFFICER FALLS DOWN.
BUT YOU OUGHTA BE MORE CONCERNED WITH YOUR OWN.
I'M NOT AFRAID TO DIE.
I DON'T BELIEVE THAT FOR A SECOND. EVEN DOGS ARE AFRAID TO DIE. AND YOU'RE AT LEAST AS SMART AS A DOG, AIN'T YA?
C'MON, GET UP.

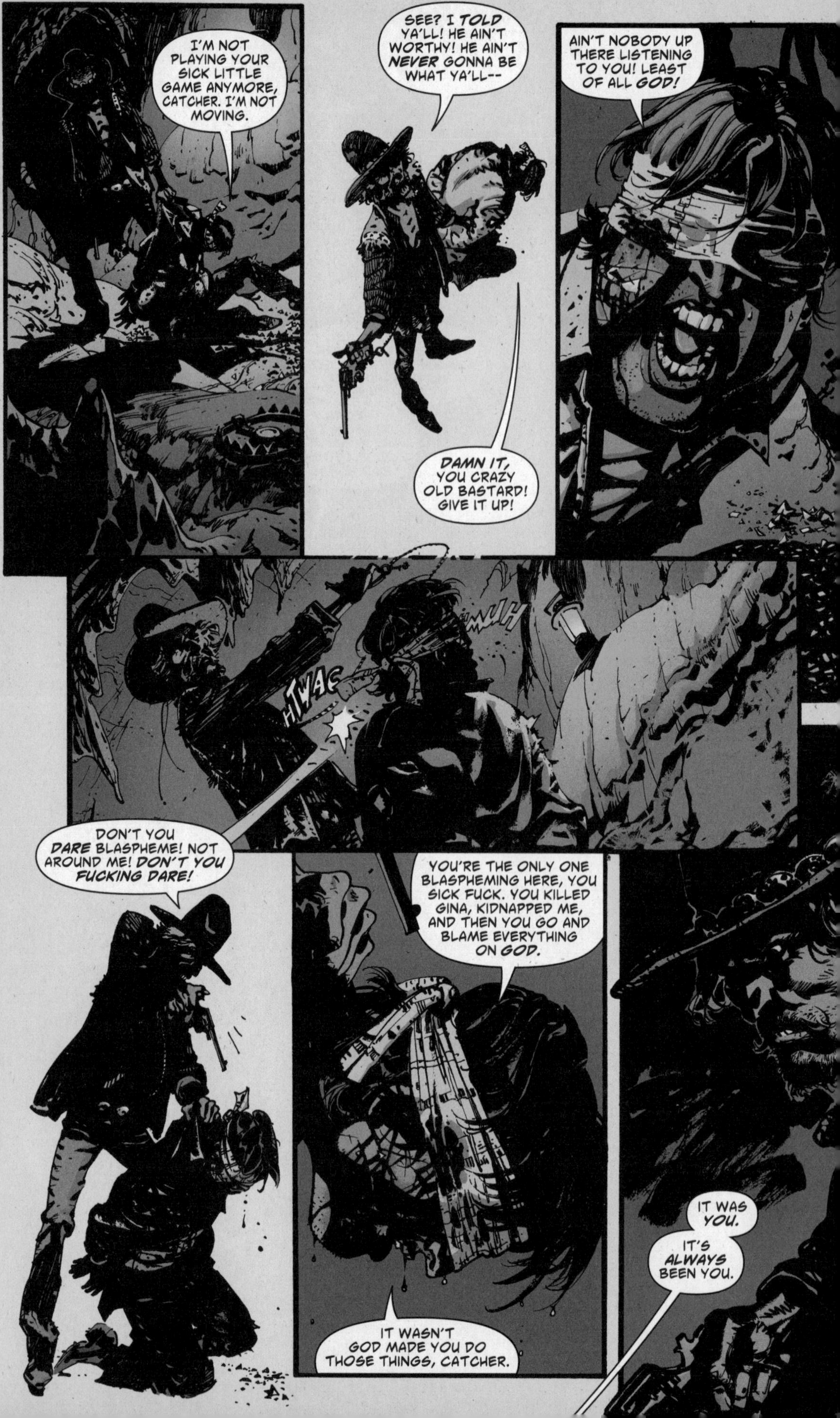
I'M NOT PLAYING YOUR SICK LITTLE GAME ANYMORE, CATCHER. I'M NOT MOVING.
SEE? I *TOLD* YA'LL! HE AIN'T WORTHY! HE AIN'T *NEVER* GONNA BE WHAT YA'LL--
DAMN IT, YOU CRAZY OLD BASTARD! GIVE IT UP!
AIN'T NOBODY UP THERE LISTENING TO YOU! LEAST OF ALL *GOD!*
DON'T YOU *DARE* BLASPHEME! NOT AROUND ME! *DON'T YOU FUCKING DARE!*
YOU'RE THE ONLY ONE BLASPHEMING HERE, YOU SICK FUCK. YOU KILLED GINA, KIDNAPPED ME, AND THEN YOU GO AND BLAME EVERYTHING ON *GOD.*
IT WASN'T GOD MADE YOU DO THOSE THINGS, CATCHER.
IT WAS *YOU.*
IT'S *ALWAYS* BEEN YOU.

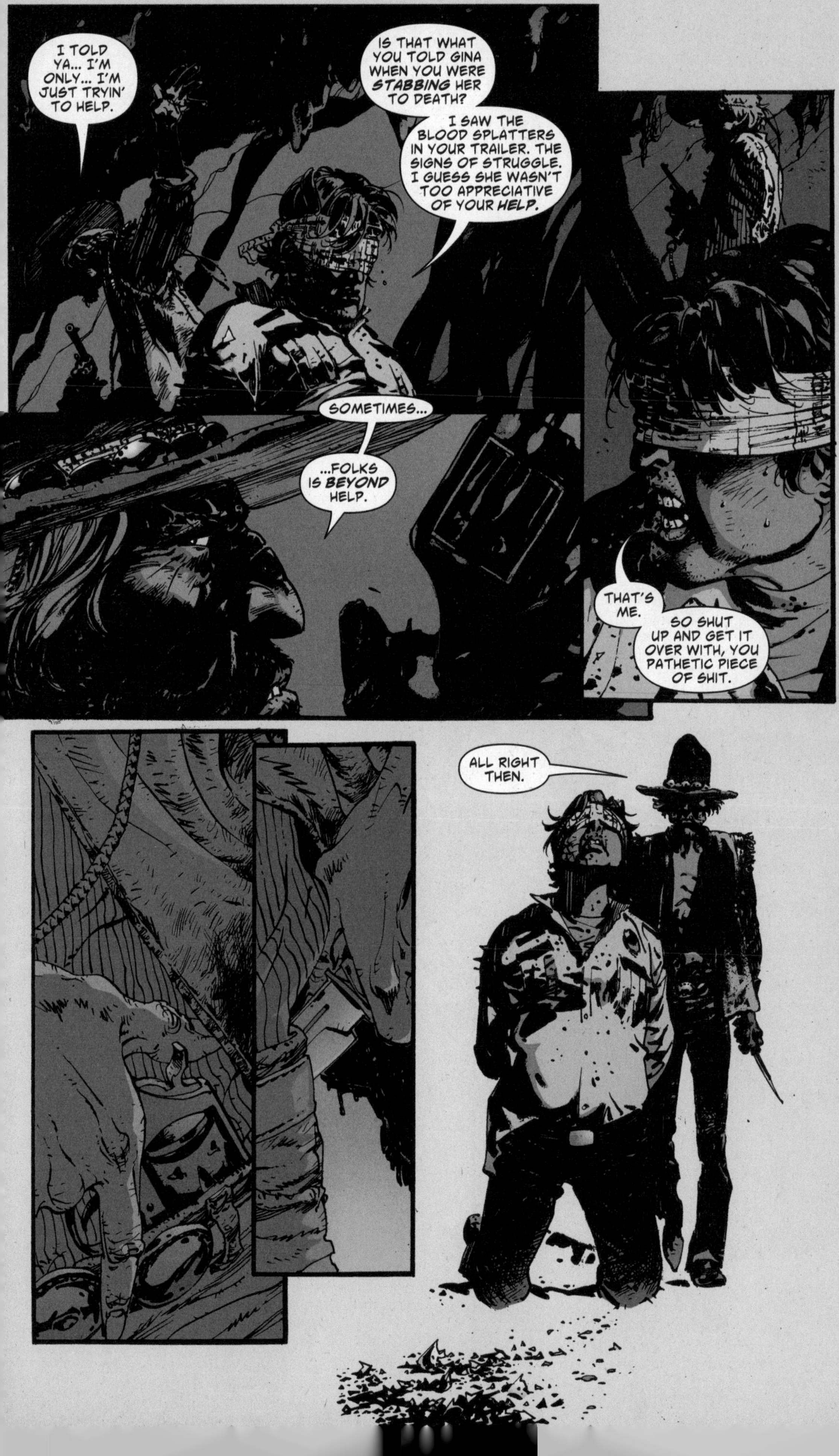
I TOLD YA... I'M ONLY... I'M JUST TRYIN' TO HELP.
IS THAT WHAT YOU TOLD GINA WHEN YOU WERE STABBING HER TO DEATH?
I SAW THE BLOOD SPLATTERS IN YOUR TRAILER. THE SIGNS OF STRUGGLE. I GUESS SHE WASN'T TOO APPRECIATIVE OF YOUR HELP.
SOMETIMES...
...FOLKS IS BEYOND HELP.
THAT'S ME.
SO SHUT UP AND GET IT OVER WITH, YOU PATHETIC PIECE OF SHIT.
ALL RIGHT THEN.

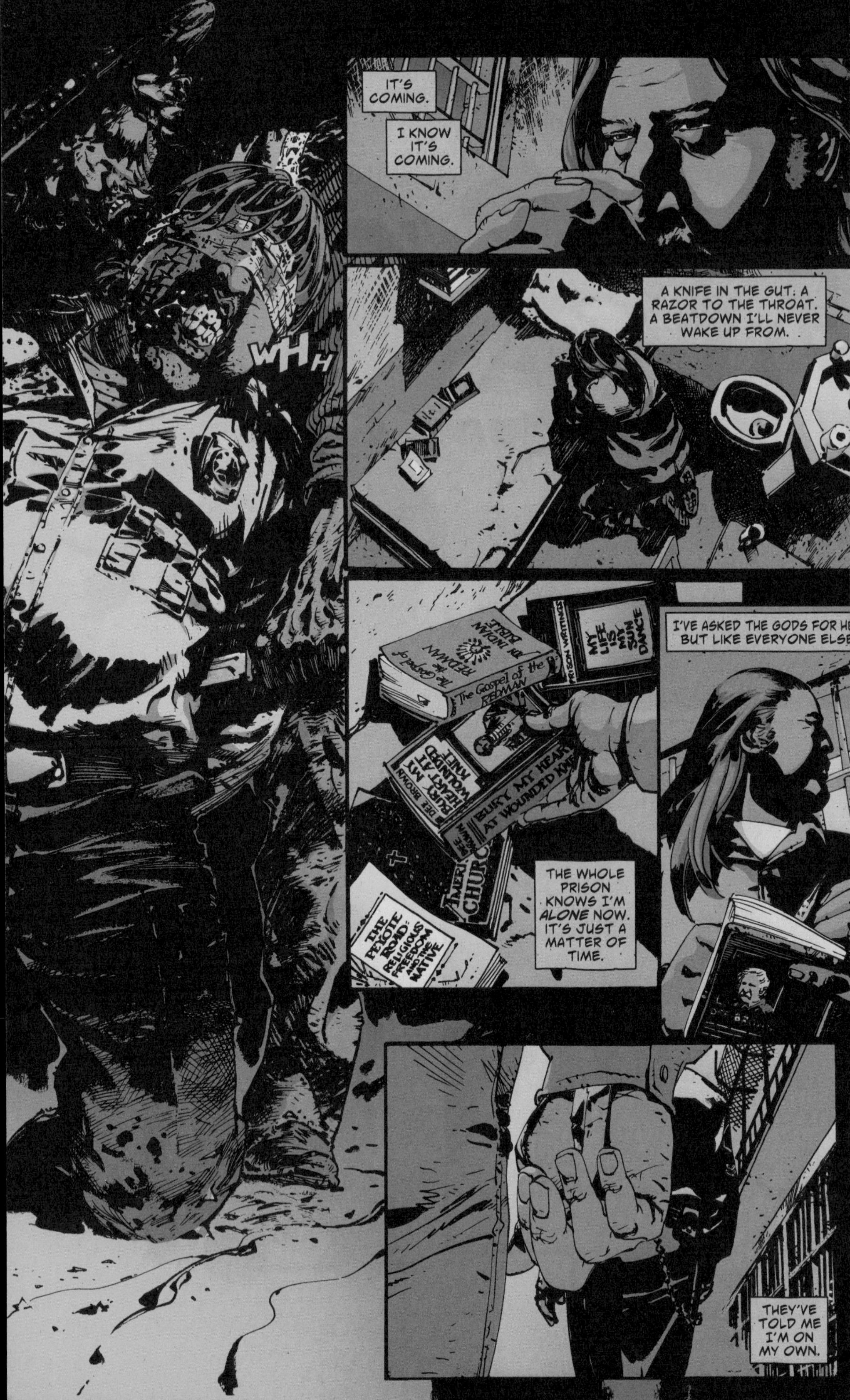
WHH
IT'S COMING.
I KNOW IT'S COMING.
A KNIFE IN THE GUT. A RAZOR TO THE THROAT. A BEATDOWN I'LL NEVER WAKE UP FROM.
I'VE ASKED THE GODS FOR HE
BUT LIKE EVERYONE ELSE
THE WHOLE PRISON KNOWS I'M ALONE NOW. IT'S JUST A MATTER OF TIME.
THEY'VE TOLD ME I'M ON MY OWN.

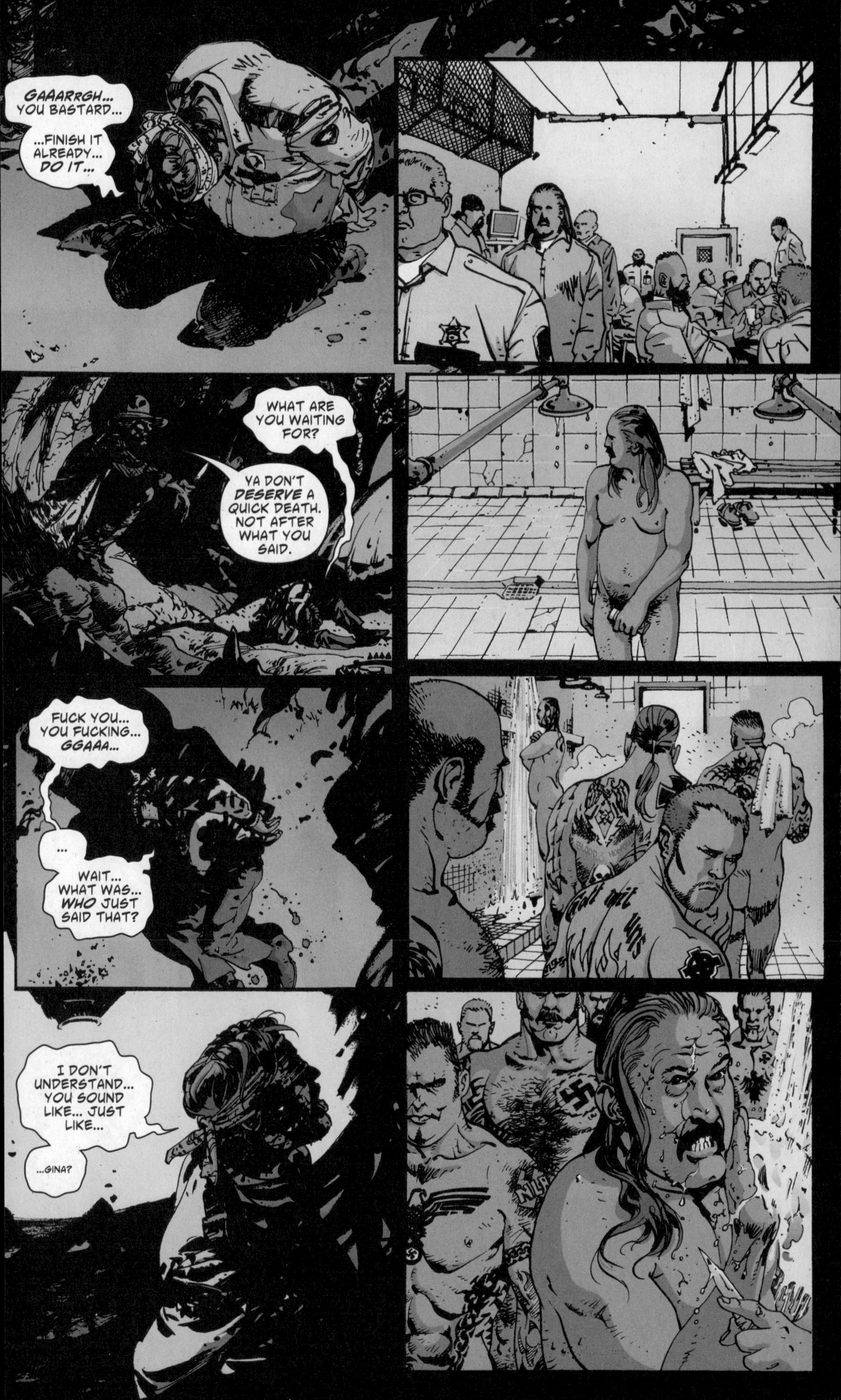
GAAARRGH... YOU BASTARD...
...FINISH IT ALREADY... DO IT...
WHAT ARE YOU WAITING FOR?
YA DON'T DESERVE A QUICK DEATH. NOT AFTER WHAT YOU SAID.
FUCK YOU... YOU FUCKING... GGAAA...
...
WAIT... WHAT WAS... WHO JUST SAID THAT?
I DON'T UNDERSTAND... YOU SOUND LIKE... JUST LIKE...
...GINA?

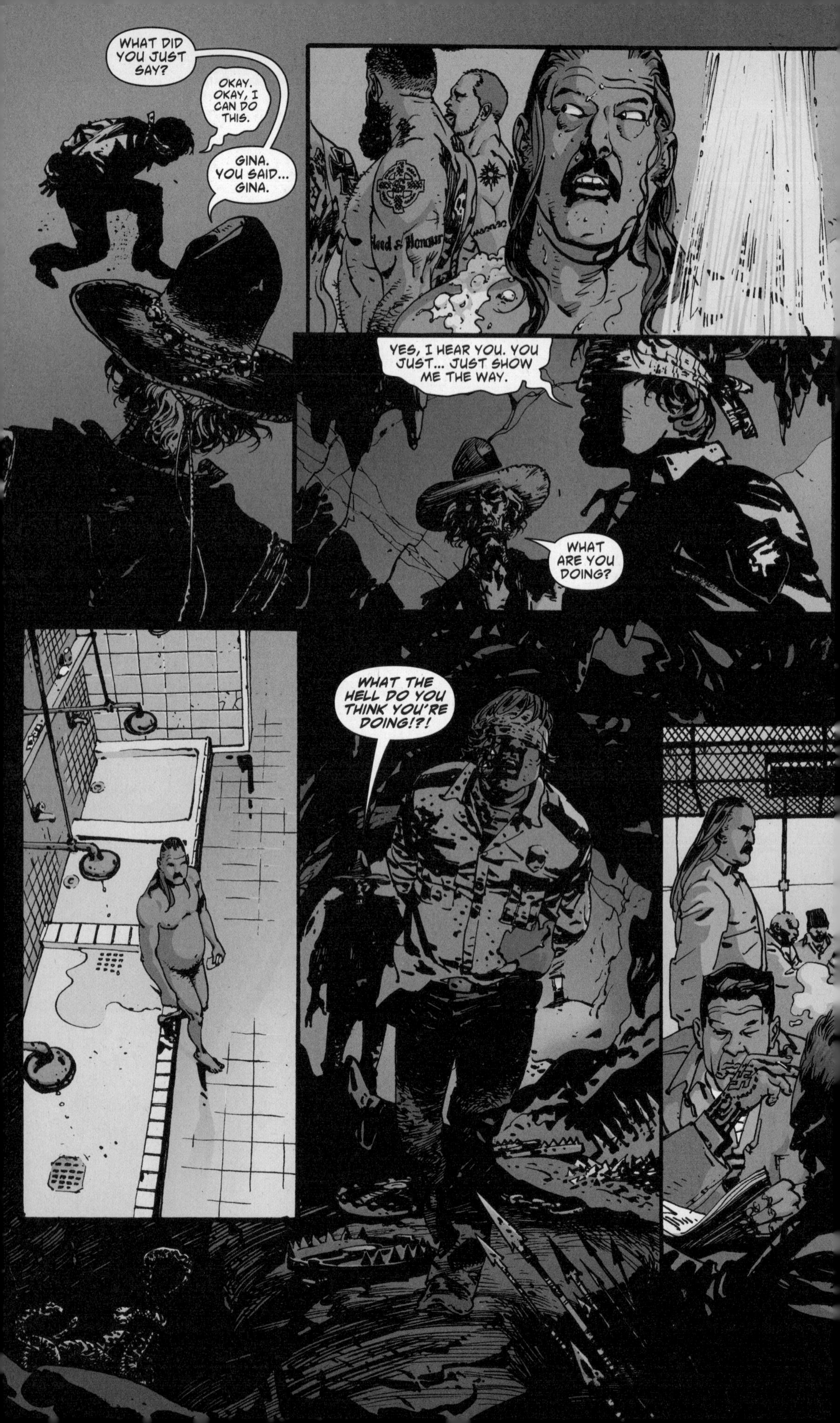
WHAT DID YOU JUST SAY?
OKAY. OKAY, I CAN DO THIS.
GINA. YOU SAID... GINA.
YES, I HEAR YOU. YOU JUST... JUST SHOW ME THE WAY.
WHAT ARE YOU DOING?
WHAT THE HELL DO YOU THINK YOU'RE DOING!?!

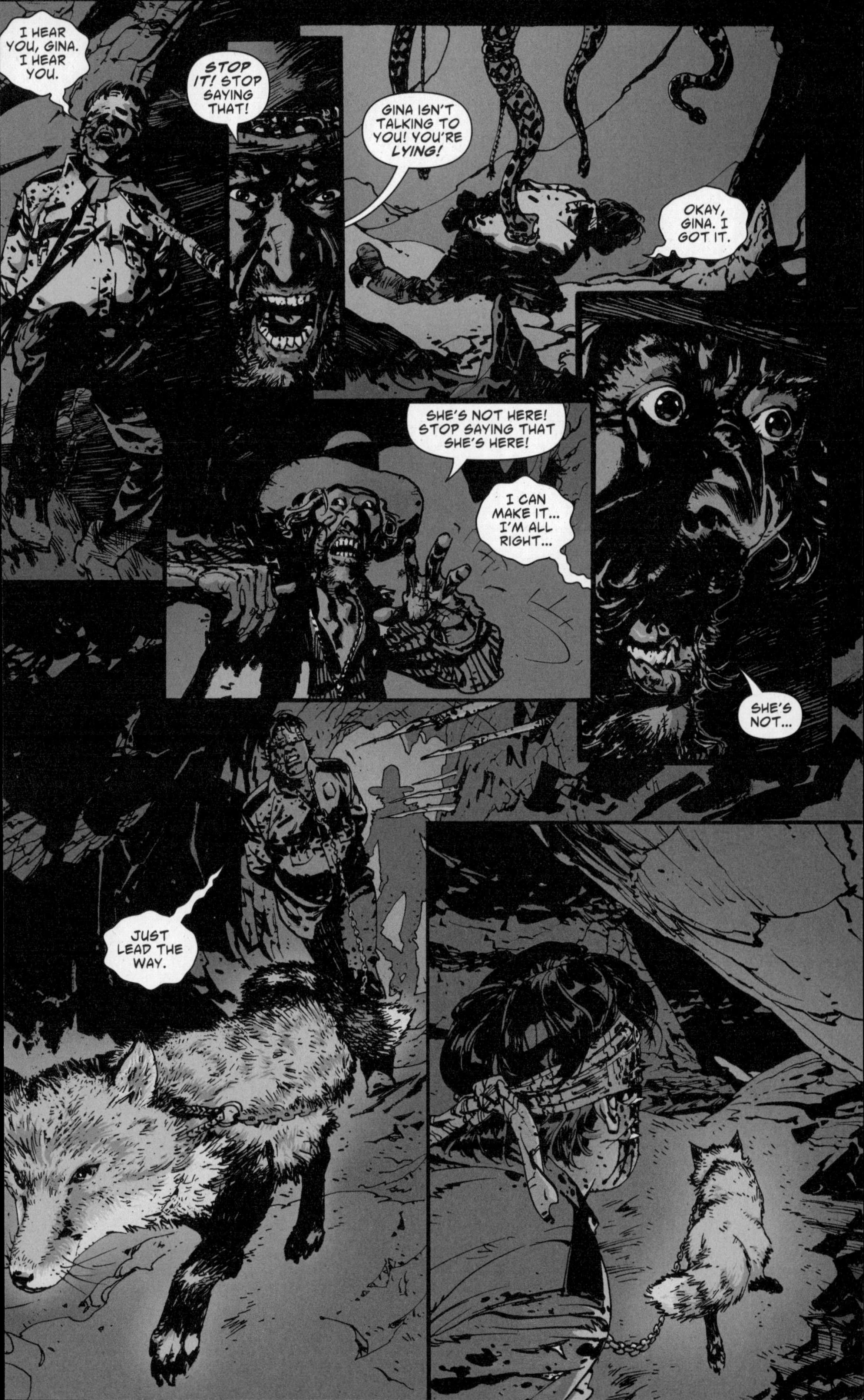
I HEAR YOU, GINA. I HEAR YOU.
STOP IT! STOP SAYING THAT!
GINA ISN'T TALKING TO YOU! YOU'RE LYING!
OKAY, GINA. I GOT IT.
SHE'S NOT HERE! STOP SAYING THAT SHE'S HERE!
I CAN MAKE IT... I'M ALL RIGHT...
SHE'S NOT...
JUST LEAD THE WAY.

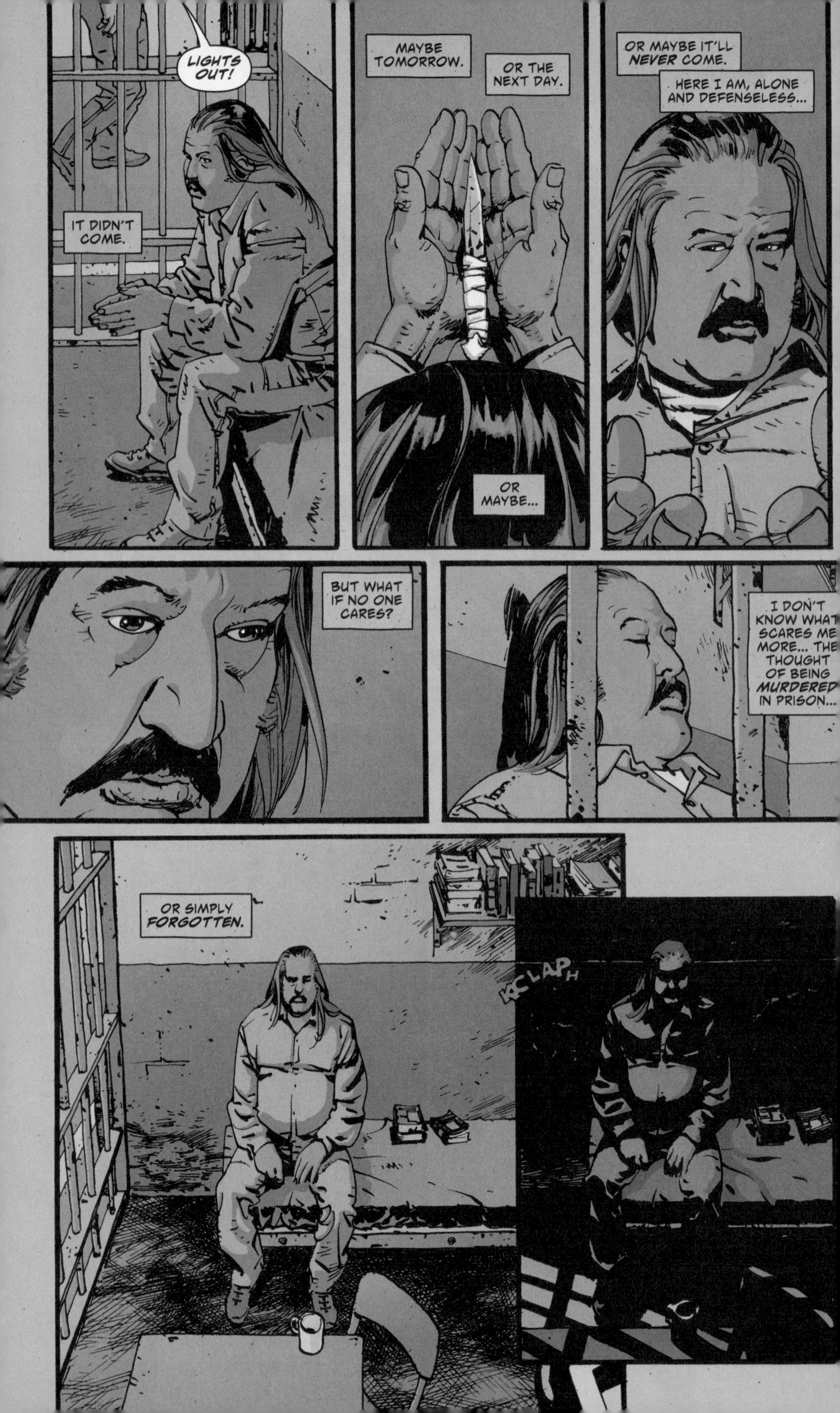
LIGHTS OUT!
IT DIDN'T COME.
MAYBE TOMORROW.
OR THE NEXT DAY.
OR MAYBE...
OR MAYBE IT'LL NEVER COME.
HERE I AM, ALONE AND DEFENSELESS...
BUT WHAT IF NO ONE CARES?
I DON'T KNOW WHAT SCARES ME MORE... THE THOUGHT OF BEING MURDERED IN PRISON...
OR SIMPLY FORGOTTEN.
KCLAPH

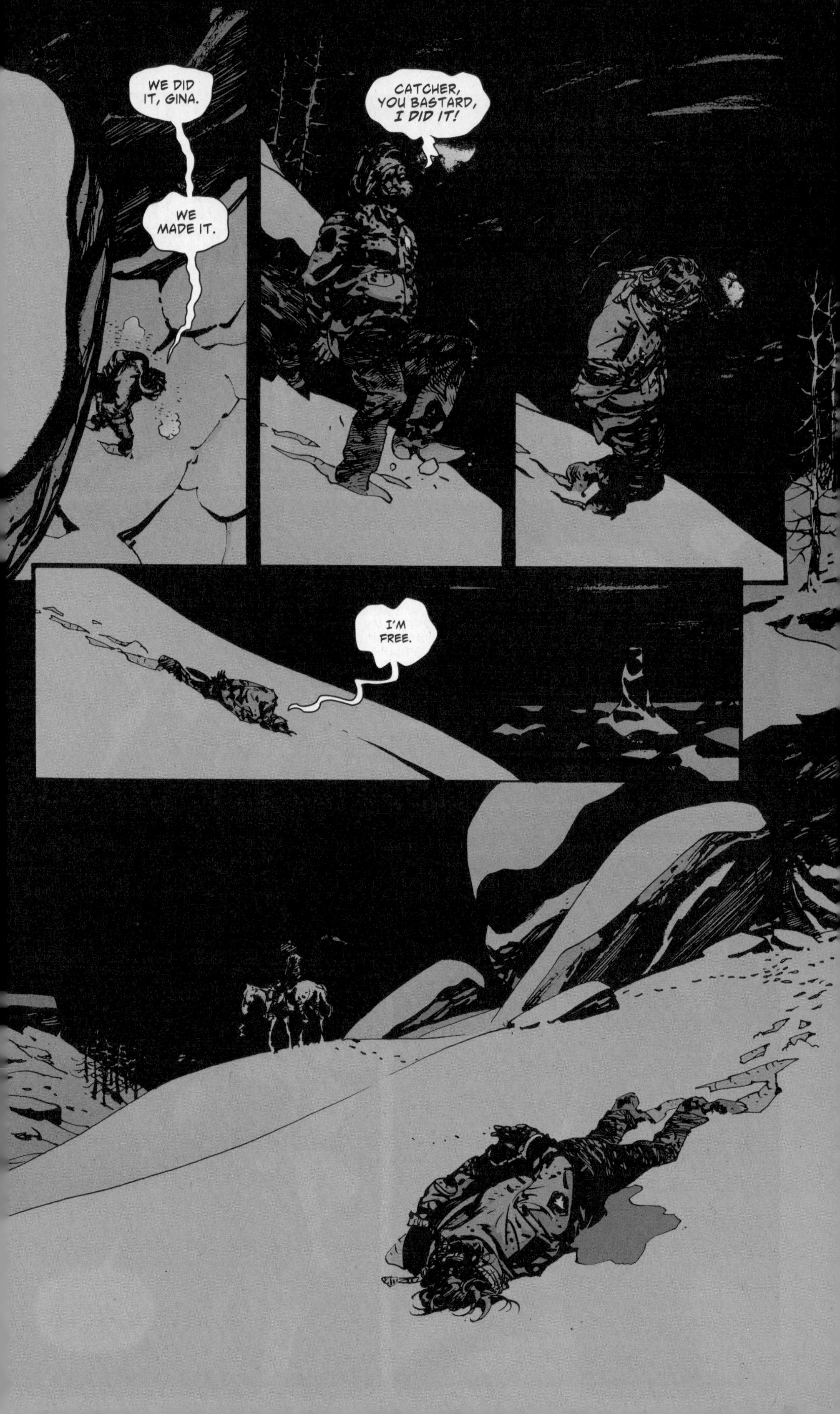
WE DID IT, GINA.
WE MADE IT.
CATCHER, YOU BASTARD, I DID IT!
I'M FREE.

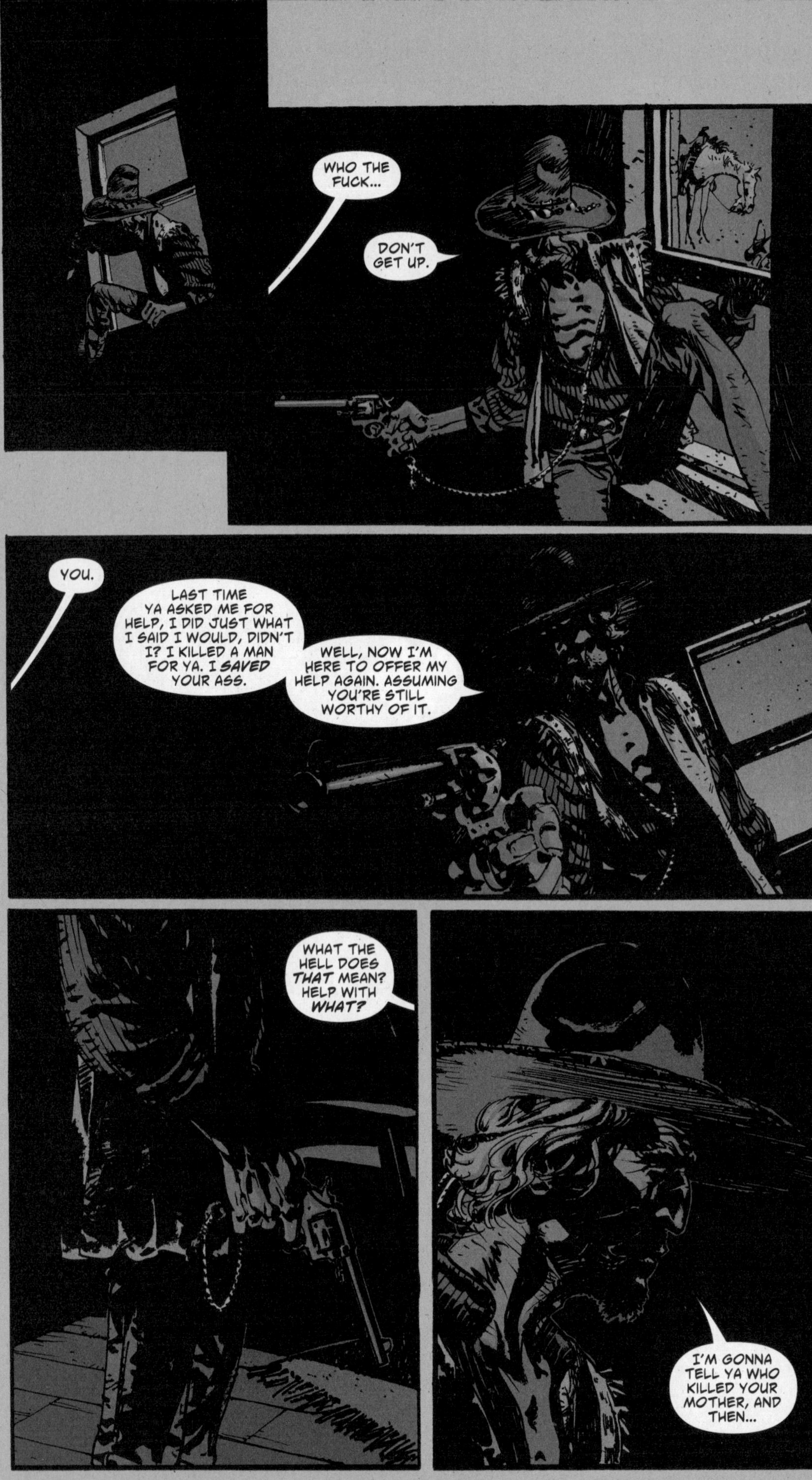
WHO THE FUCK...
DON'T GET UP.
YOU.
LAST TIME YA ASKED ME FOR HELP, I DID JUST WHAT I SAID I WOULD, DIDN'T I? I KILLED A MAN FOR YA. I *SAVED* YOUR ASS.
WELL, NOW I'M HERE TO OFFER MY HELP AGAIN. ASSUMING YOU'RE STILL WORTHY OF IT.
WHAT THE HELL DOES *THAT* MEAN? HELP WITH *WHAT?*
I'M GONNA TELL YA WHO KILLED YOUR MOTHER, AND THEN...

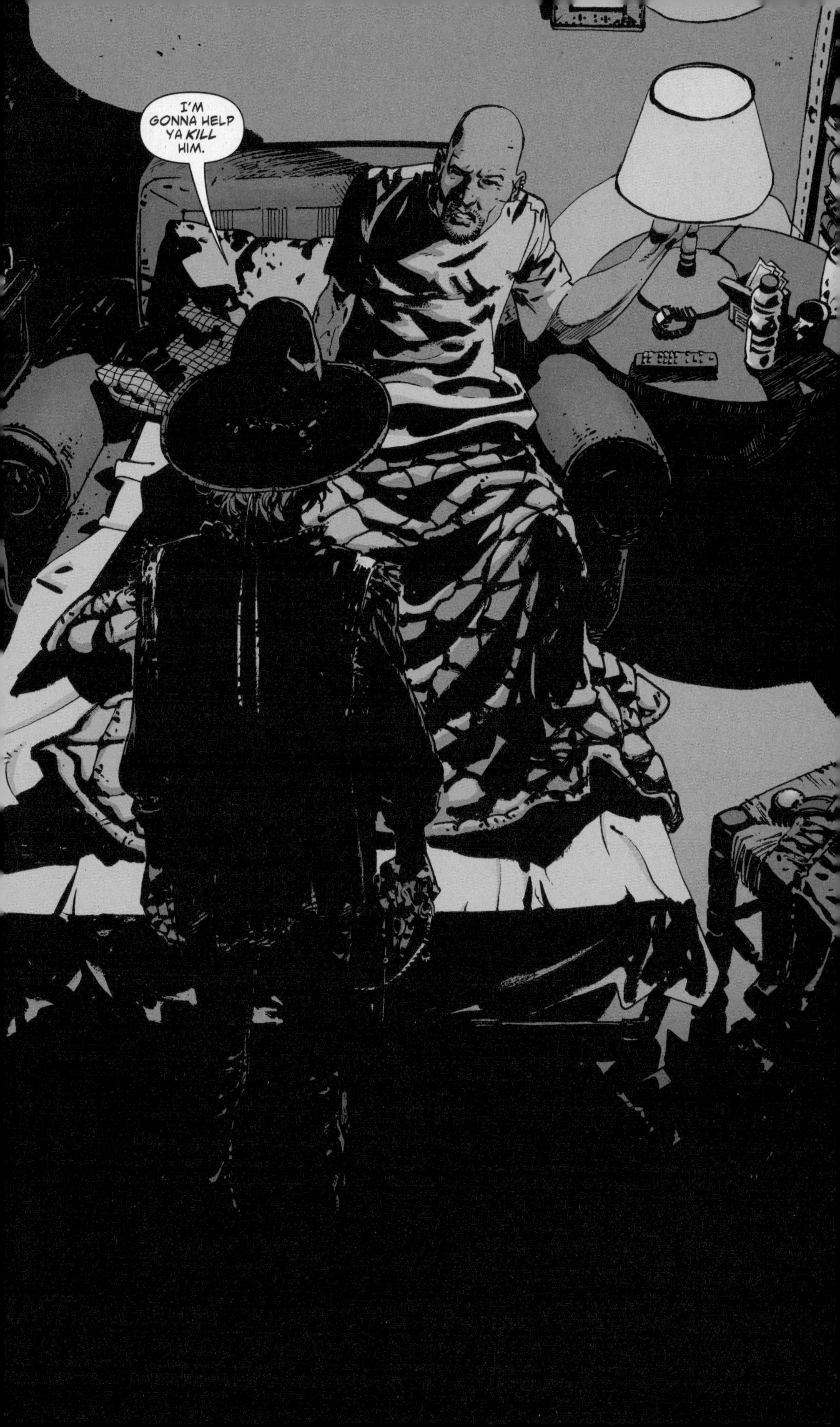
I'M GONNA HELP YA KILL HIM.

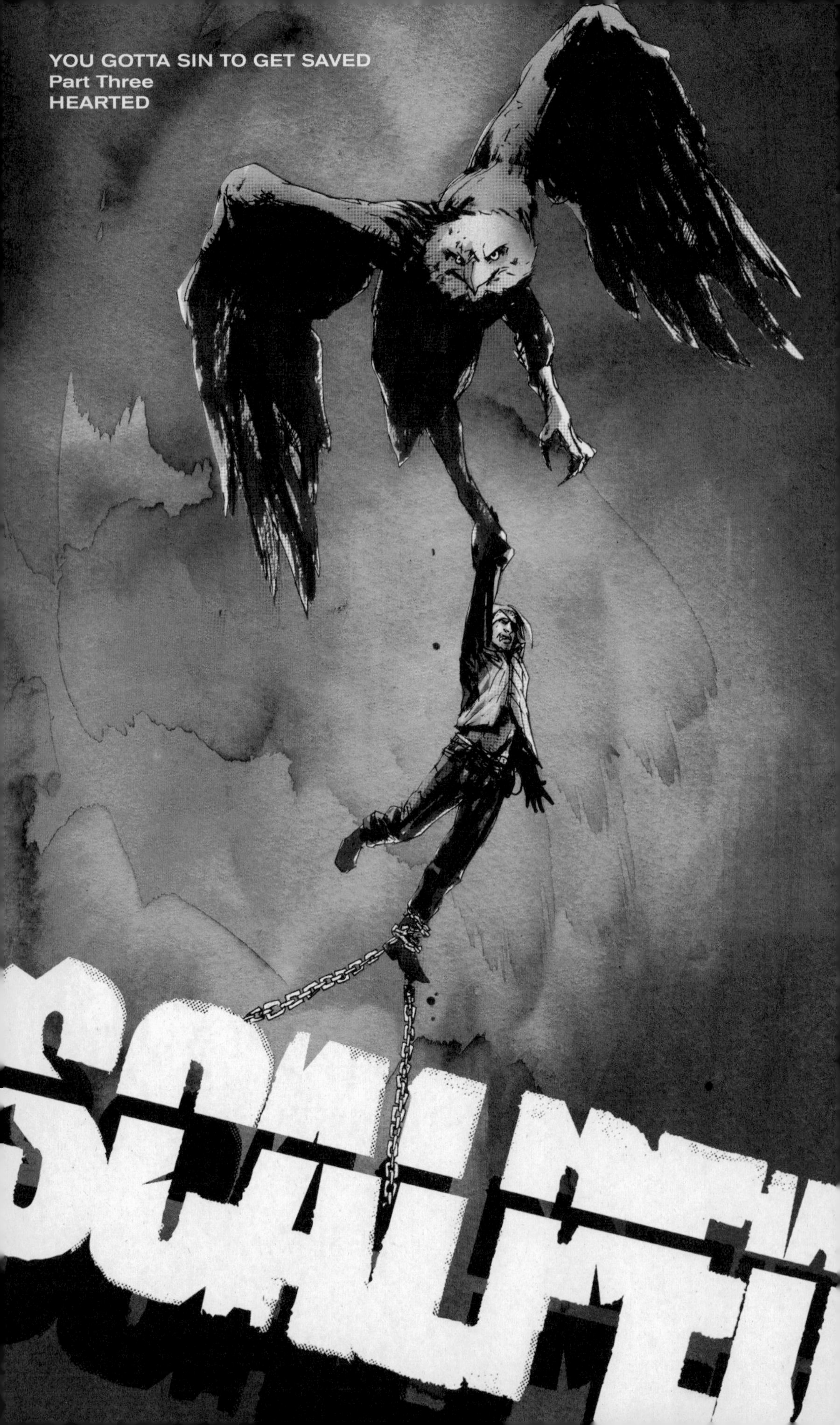
YOU GOTTA SIN TO GET SAVED
Part Three
HEARTED

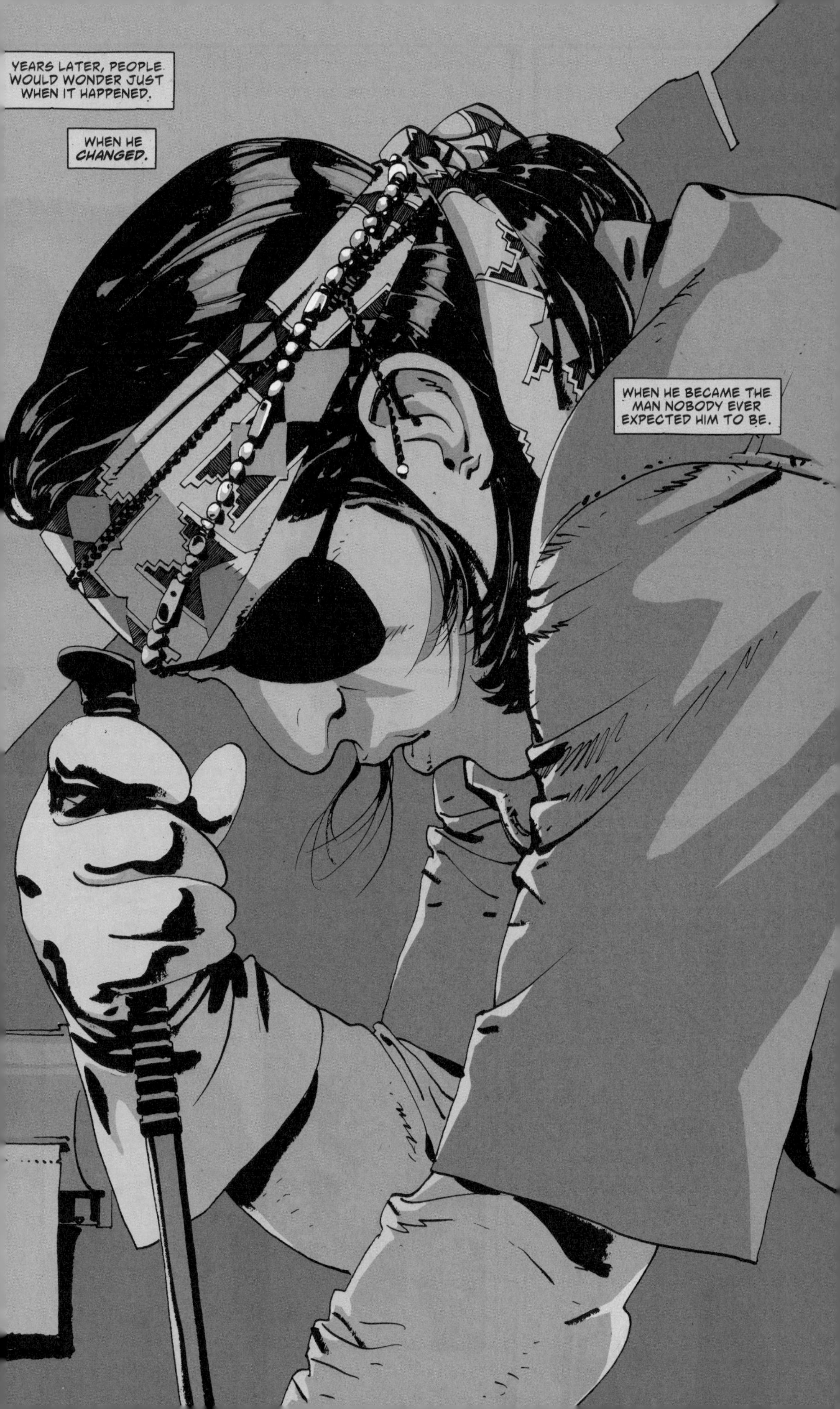

YEARS LATER, PEOPLE WOULD WONDER JUST WHEN IT HAPPENED.
WHEN HE *CHANGED.*
WHEN HE BECAME THE MAN NOBODY EVER EXPECTED HIM TO BE.

SOME WOULD SAY IT WAS WHEN HE LOST HIS *EYE*. OTHERS WOULD GUESS THE CHANGE CAME MUCH LATER, AFTER THINGS ON THE REZ GOT *REALLY* BAD.

BUT THEY'D ALL BE WRONG.

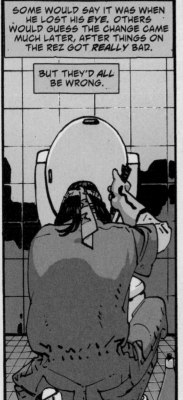

EVEN THOUGH HE DIDN'T KNOW HER, EXCEPT IN PASSING. AND EVEN THOUGH HE HAD NOTHING AT ALL TO DO WITH HER DEATH...

IT ALL HAPPENED BECAUSE OF *BRANDY TWO TREES*.

THE BODY OF 14-YEAR-OLD BRANDY TWO TREES WAS DISCOVERED THIS MORNING ALONG ROUTE 48.

WO TREES

REZ NEWS at

MS. TWO TREES, A RESIDENT OF THE *PRAIRIE ROSE INDIAN RESERVATION*, WAS APPARENTLY THE VICTIM OF A HIT AND RUN SOMETIME TUESDAY NIGHT.

ANYONE WHO MIGHT HAVE INFORMATION RELATING TO HER DEATH IS ENCOURAGED TO CONTACT TRIBAL POLICE.

"WHOA, WHERE'S THE FIRE, COWBOY?"

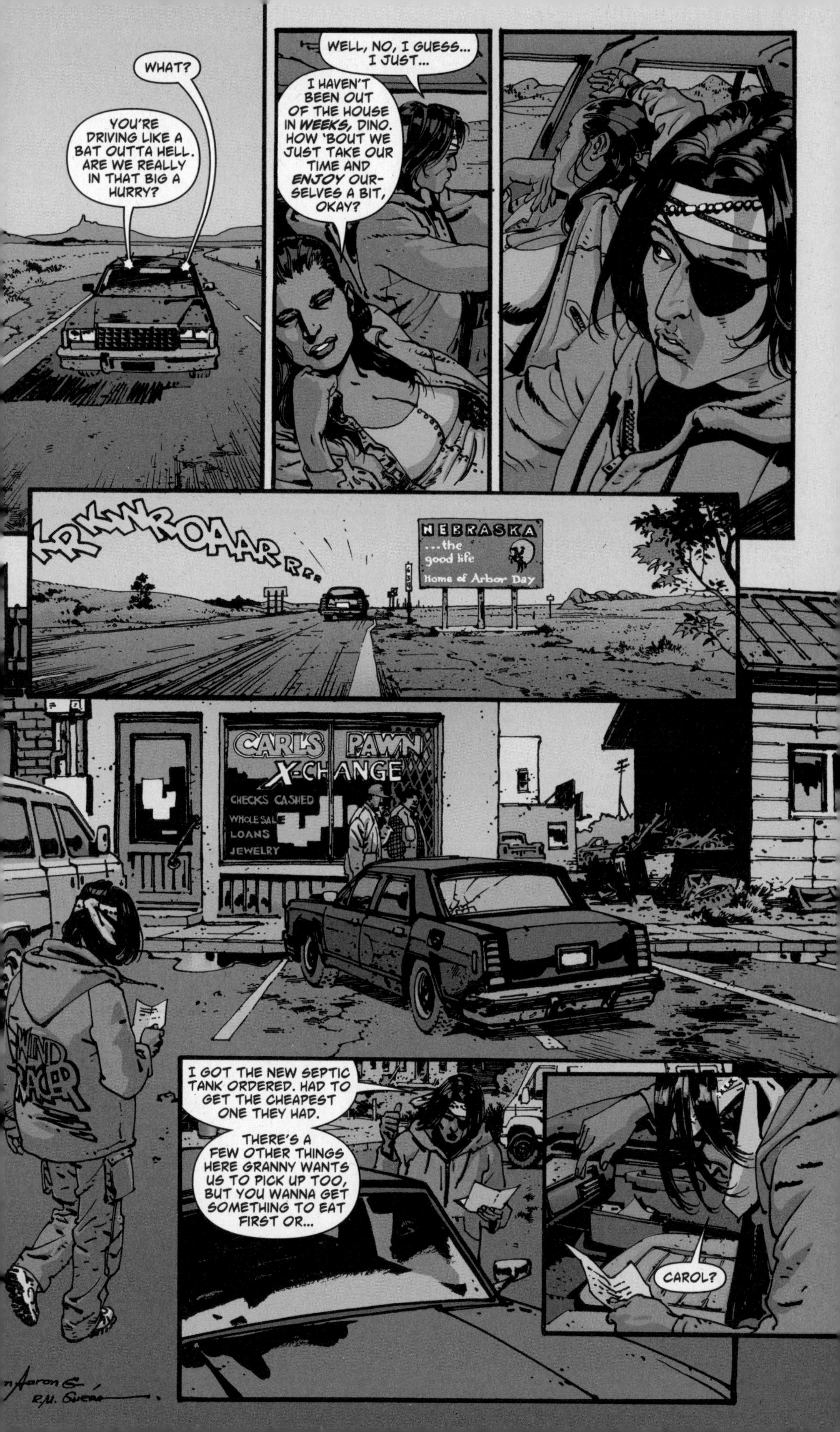
WHAT?
YOU'RE DRIVING LIKE A BAT OUTTA HELL. ARE WE REALLY IN THAT BIG A HURRY?
WELL, NO, I GUESS... I JUST...
I HAVEN'T BEEN OUT OF THE HOUSE IN WEEKS, DINO. HOW 'BOUT WE JUST TAKE OUR TIME AND ENJOY OUR-SELVES A BIT, OKAY?
KRKWROAARRRR
NEBRASKA ...the good life Home of Arbor Day
CARL'S PAWN X-CHANGE
CHECKS CASHED
WHOLESALE
LOANS
JEWELRY
WIND RACER
I GOT THE NEW SEPTIC TANK ORDERED. HAD TO GET THE CHEAPEST ONE THEY HAD.
THERE'S A FEW OTHER THINGS HERE GRANNY WANTS US TO PICK UP TOO, BUT YOU WANNA GET SOMETHING TO EAT FIRST OR...
CAROL?

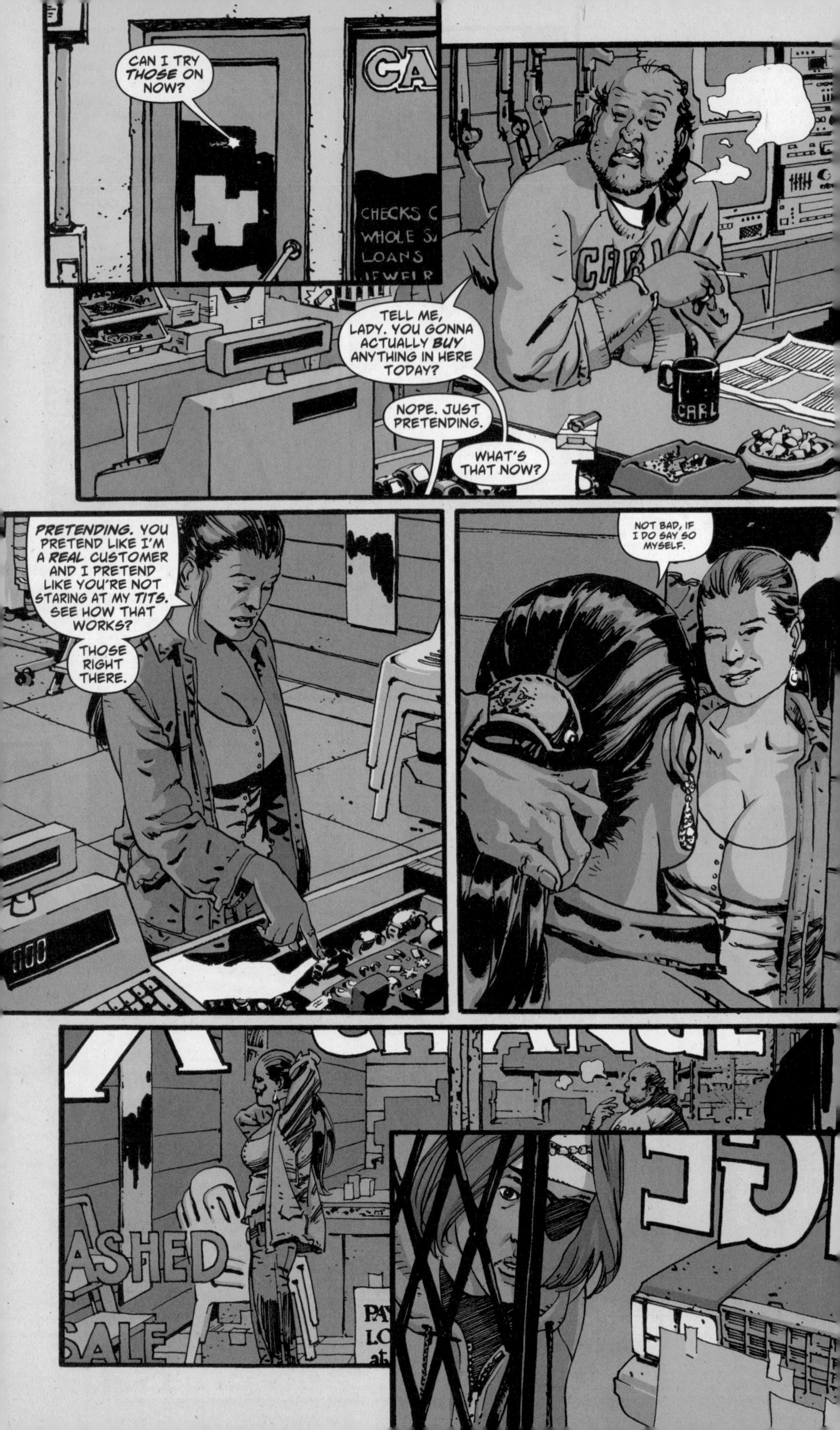
CAN I TRY THOSE ON NOW?
CA
CHECKS C
WHOLE SA
LOANS
CARL
TELL ME, LADY. YOU GONNA ACTUALLY BUY ANYTHING IN HERE TODAY?
NOPE. JUST PRETENDING.
WHAT'S THAT NOW?
CARL
PRETENDING. YOU PRETEND LIKE I'M A REAL CUSTOMER AND I PRETEND LIKE YOU'RE NOT STARING AT MY TITS. SEE HOW THAT WORKS?
THOSE RIGHT THERE.
NOT BAD, IF I DO SAY SO MYSELF.
ASHED
SALE

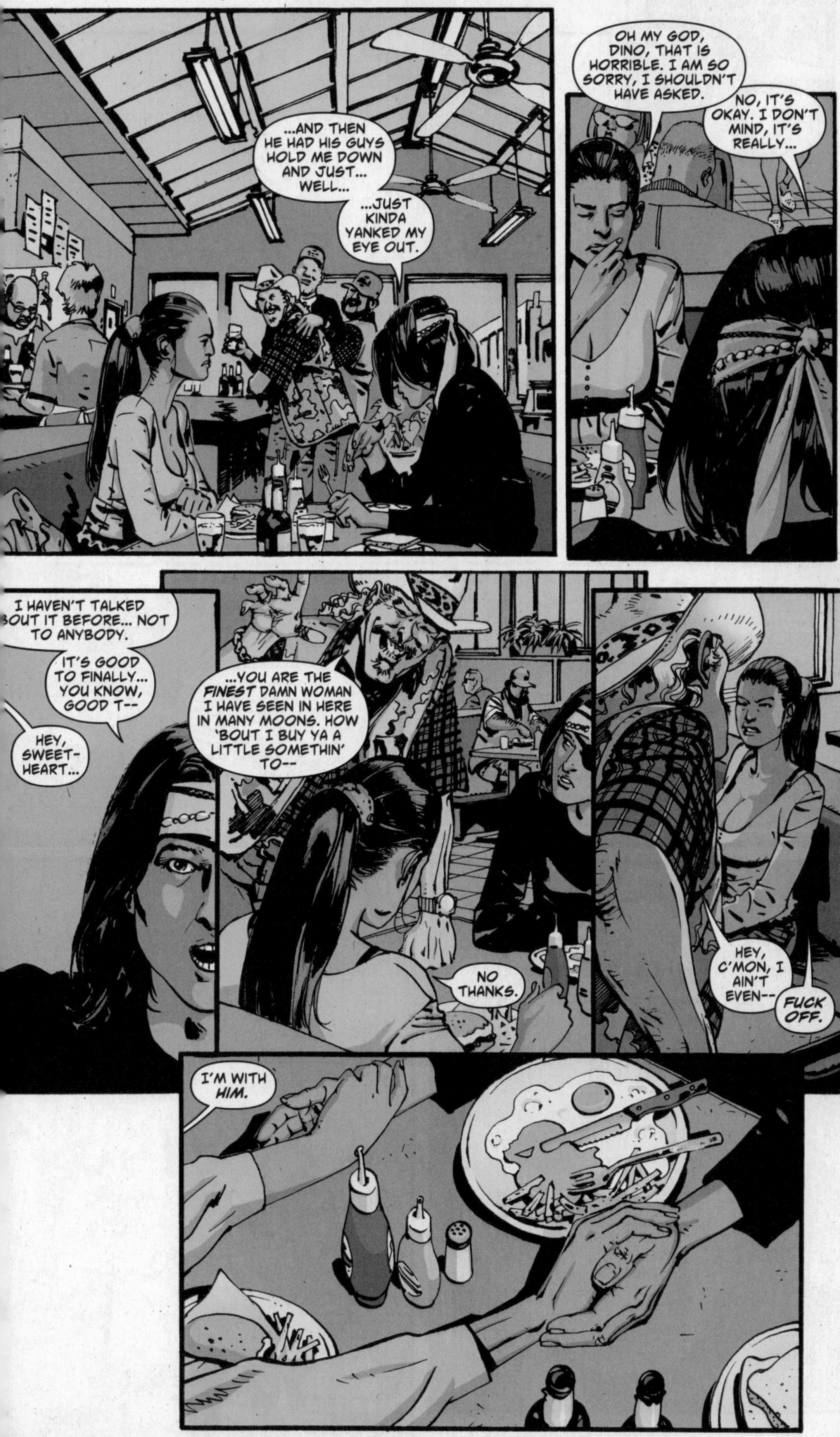
...AND THEN HE HAD HIS GUYS HOLD ME DOWN AND JUST... WELL...
...JUST KINDA YANKED MY EYE OUT.
OH MY GOD, DINO, THAT IS HORRIBLE. I AM SO SORRY, I SHOULDN'T HAVE ASKED.
NO, IT'S OKAY. I DON'T MIND, IT'S REALLY...
I HAVEN'T TALKED 'BOUT IT BEFORE... NOT TO ANYBODY.
IT'S GOOD TO FINALLY... YOU KNOW, GOOD T--
HEY, SWEET-HEART...
...YOU ARE THE *FINEST* DAMN WOMAN I HAVE SEEN IN HERE IN MANY MOONS. HOW 'BOUT I BUY YA A LITTLE SOMETHIN' TO--
NO THANKS.
HEY, C'MON, I AIN'T EVEN--
FUCK OFF.
I'M WITH *HIM.*

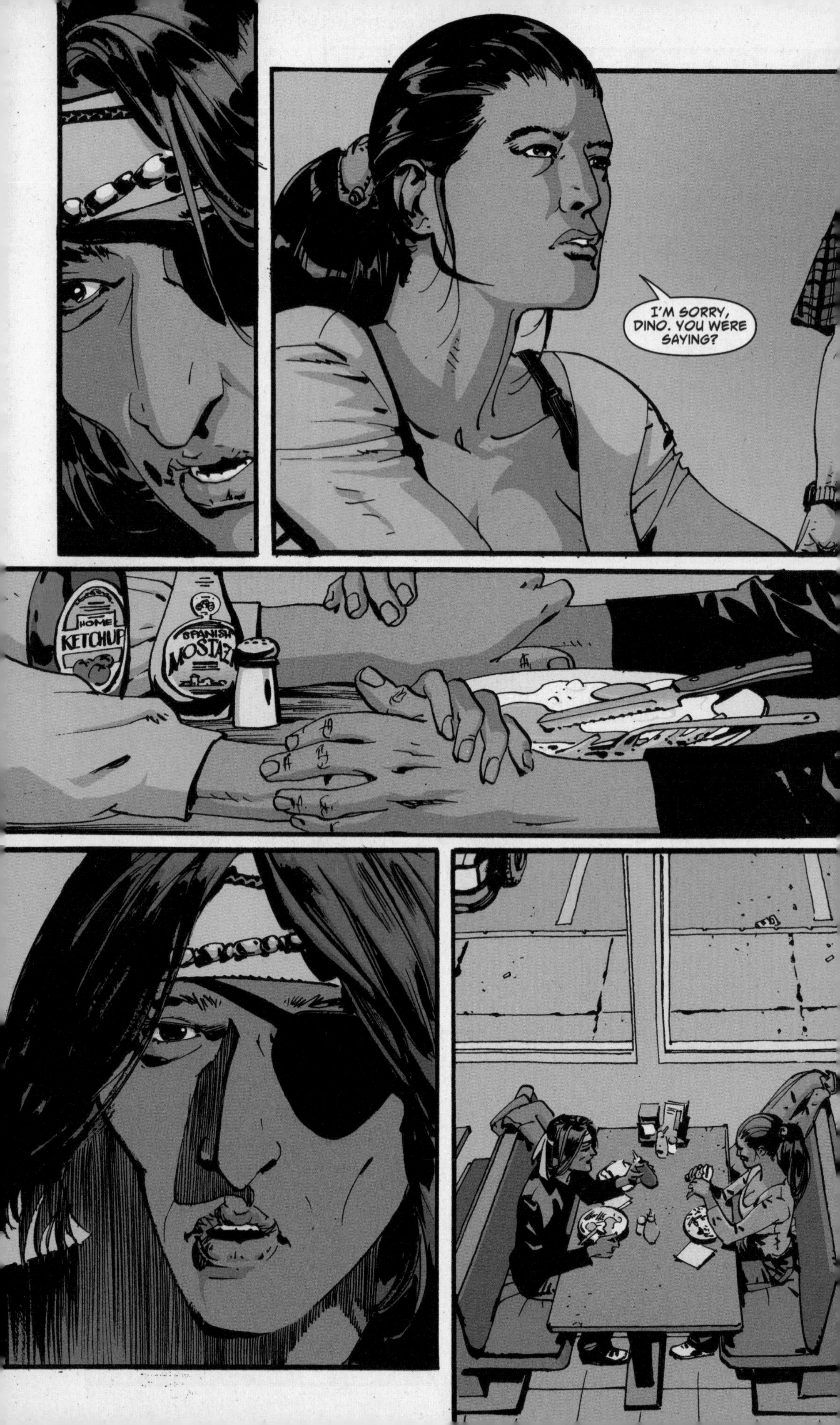

I'M SORRY, DINO. YOU WERE SAYING?
HOME KETCHUP
SPANISH MOSTAZA

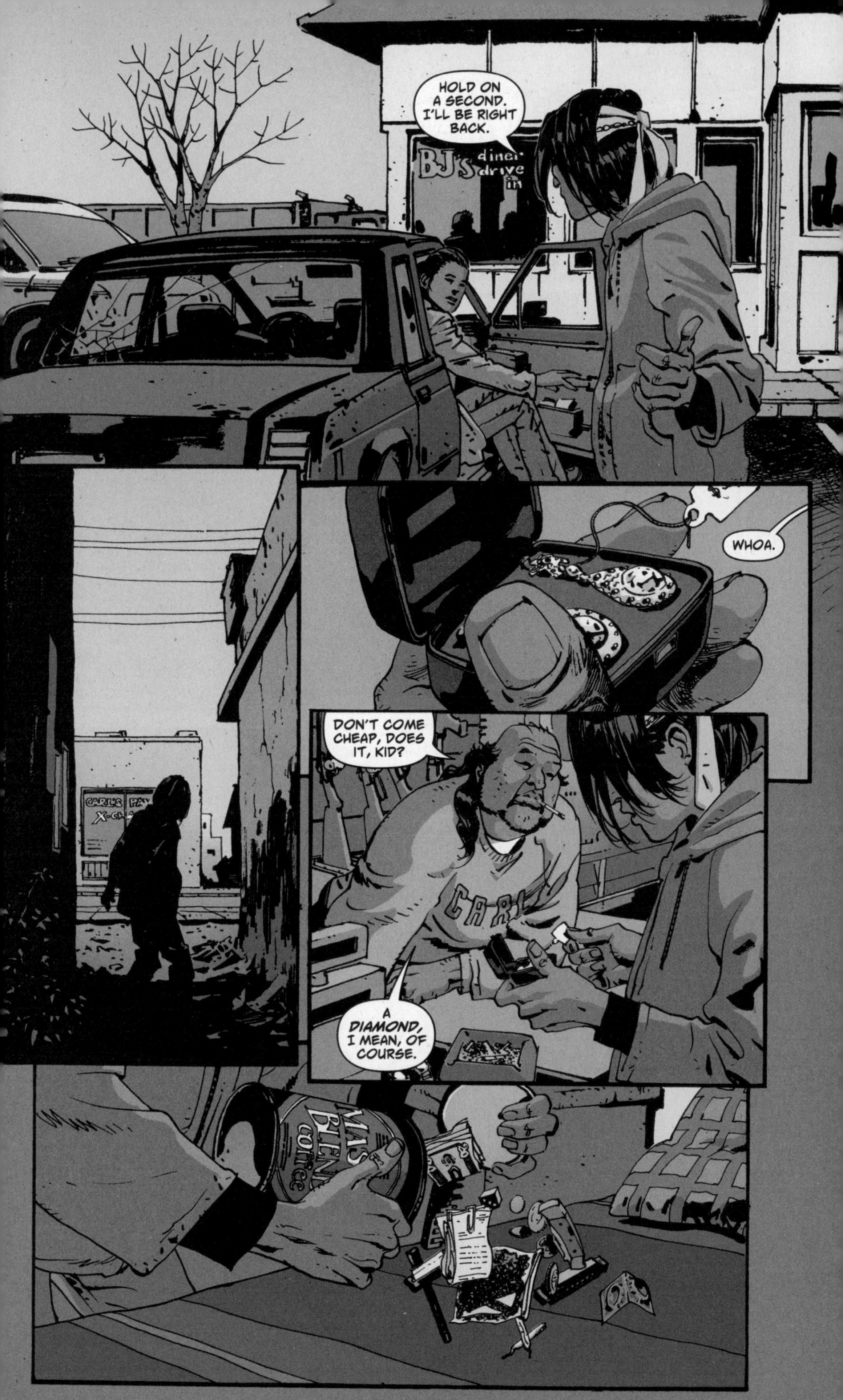
HOLD ON A SECOND. I'LL BE RIGHT BACK.
BJ's diner drive in
WHOA.
DON'T COME CHEAP, DOES IT, KID?
A *DIAMOND*, I MEAN, OF COURSE.

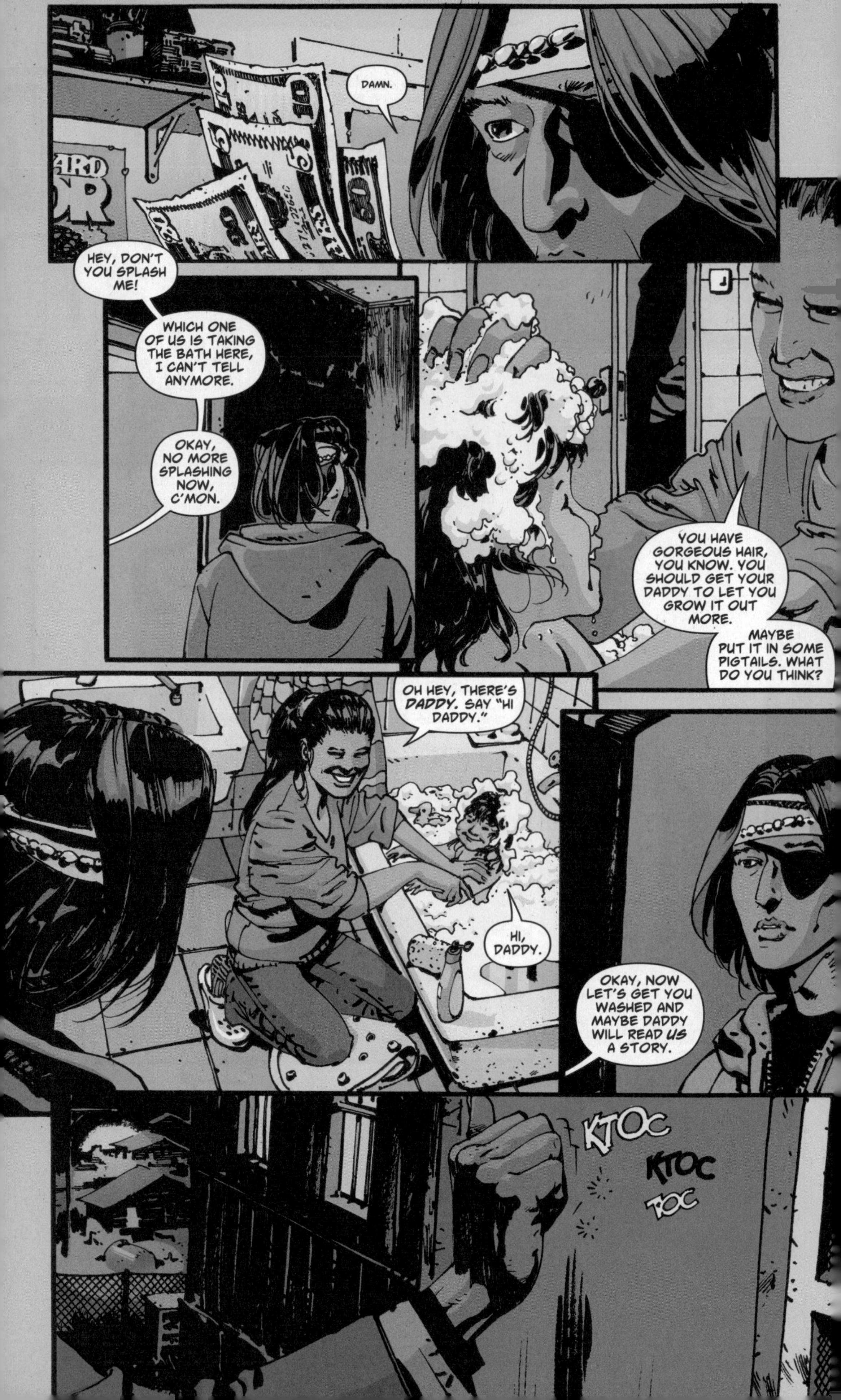
DAMN.
HEY, DON'T YOU SPLASH ME!
WHICH ONE OF US IS TAKING THE BATH HERE, I CAN'T TELL ANYMORE.
OKAY, NO MORE SPLASHING NOW, C'MON.
YOU HAVE GORGEOUS HAIR, YOU KNOW. YOU SHOULD GET YOUR DADDY TO LET YOU GROW IT OUT MORE.
MAYBE PUT IT IN SOME PIGTAILS. WHAT DO YOU THINK?
OH HEY, THERE'S *DADDY*. SAY "HI DADDY."
HI, DADDY.
OKAY, NOW LET'S GET YOU WASHED AND MAYBE DADDY WILL READ *US* A STORY.
KTOC
KTOC
TOC

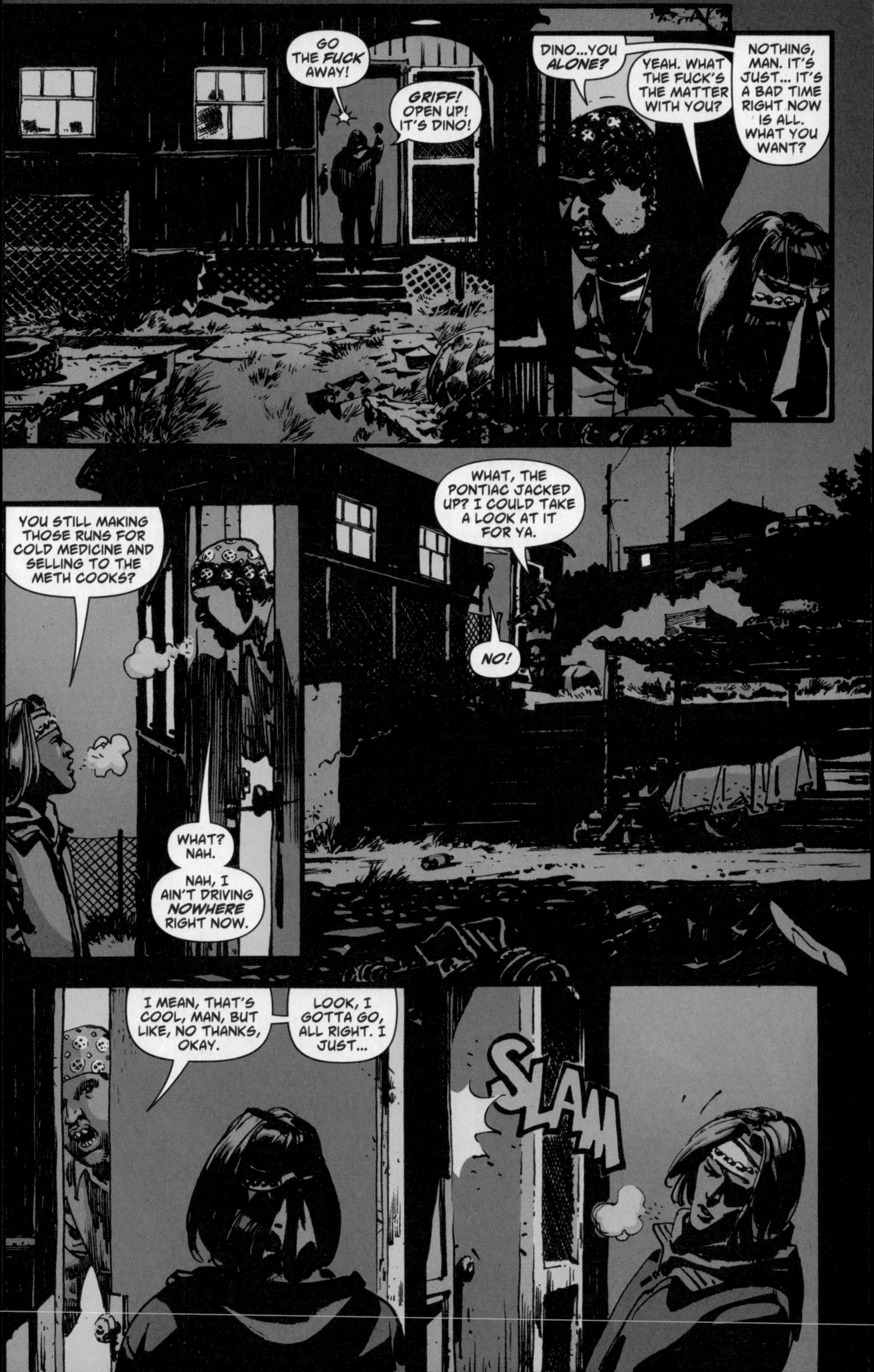
GO THE FUCK AWAY!
GRIFF! OPEN UP! IT'S DINO!
DINO...YOU ALONE?
YEAH. WHAT THE FUCK'S THE MATTER WITH YOU?
NOTHING, MAN. IT'S JUST... IT'S A BAD TIME RIGHT NOW IS ALL. WHAT YOU WANT?
YOU STILL MAKING THOSE RUNS FOR COLD MEDICINE AND SELLING TO THE METH COOKS?
WHAT? NAH.
NAH, I AIN'T DRIVING NOWHERE RIGHT NOW.
WHAT, THE PONTIAC JACKED UP? I COULD TAKE A LOOK AT IT FOR YA.
NO!
I MEAN, THAT'S COOL, MAN, BUT LIKE, NO THANKS, OKAY.
LOOK, I GOTTA GO, ALL RIGHT. I JUST...
SLAM

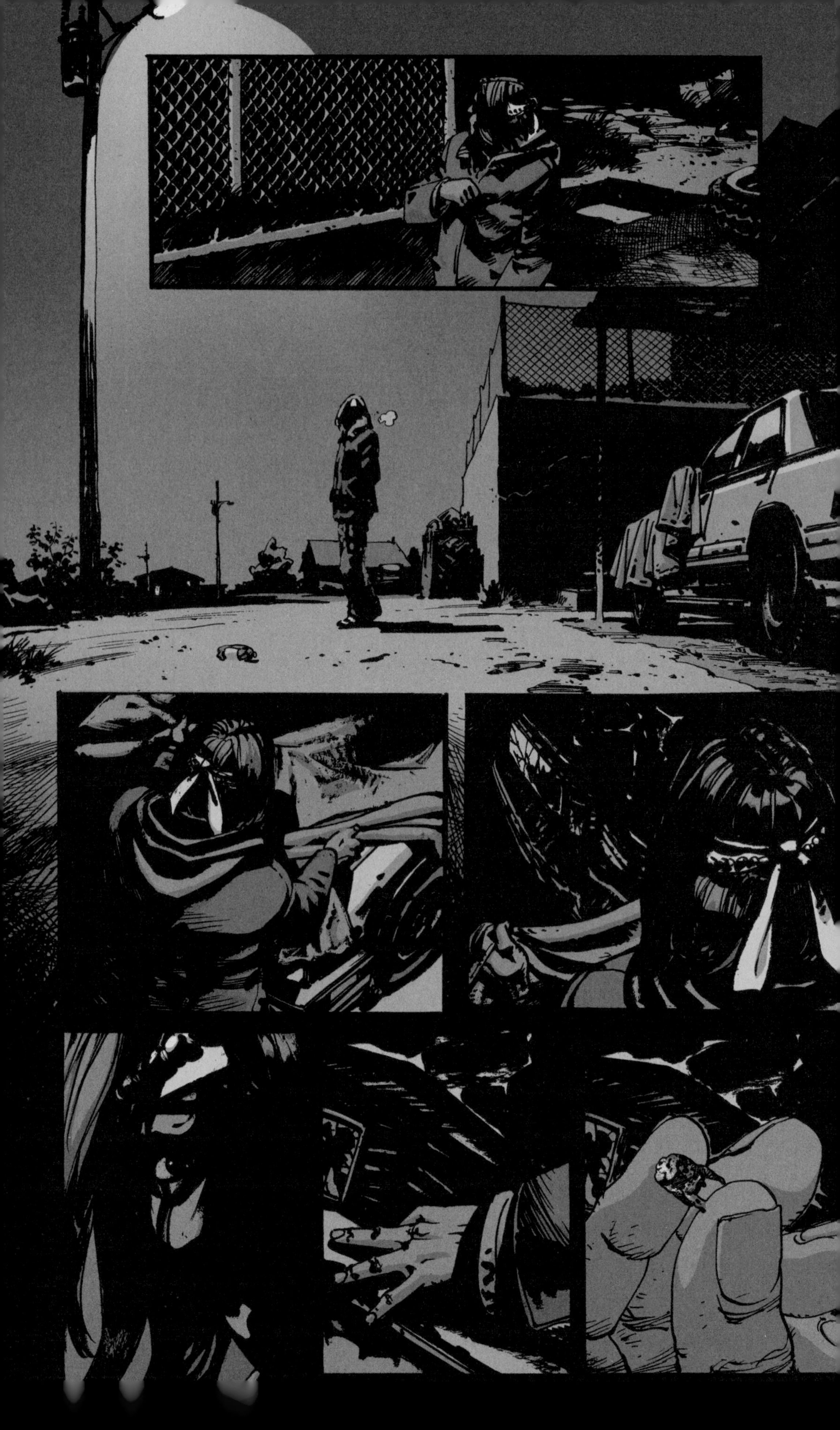

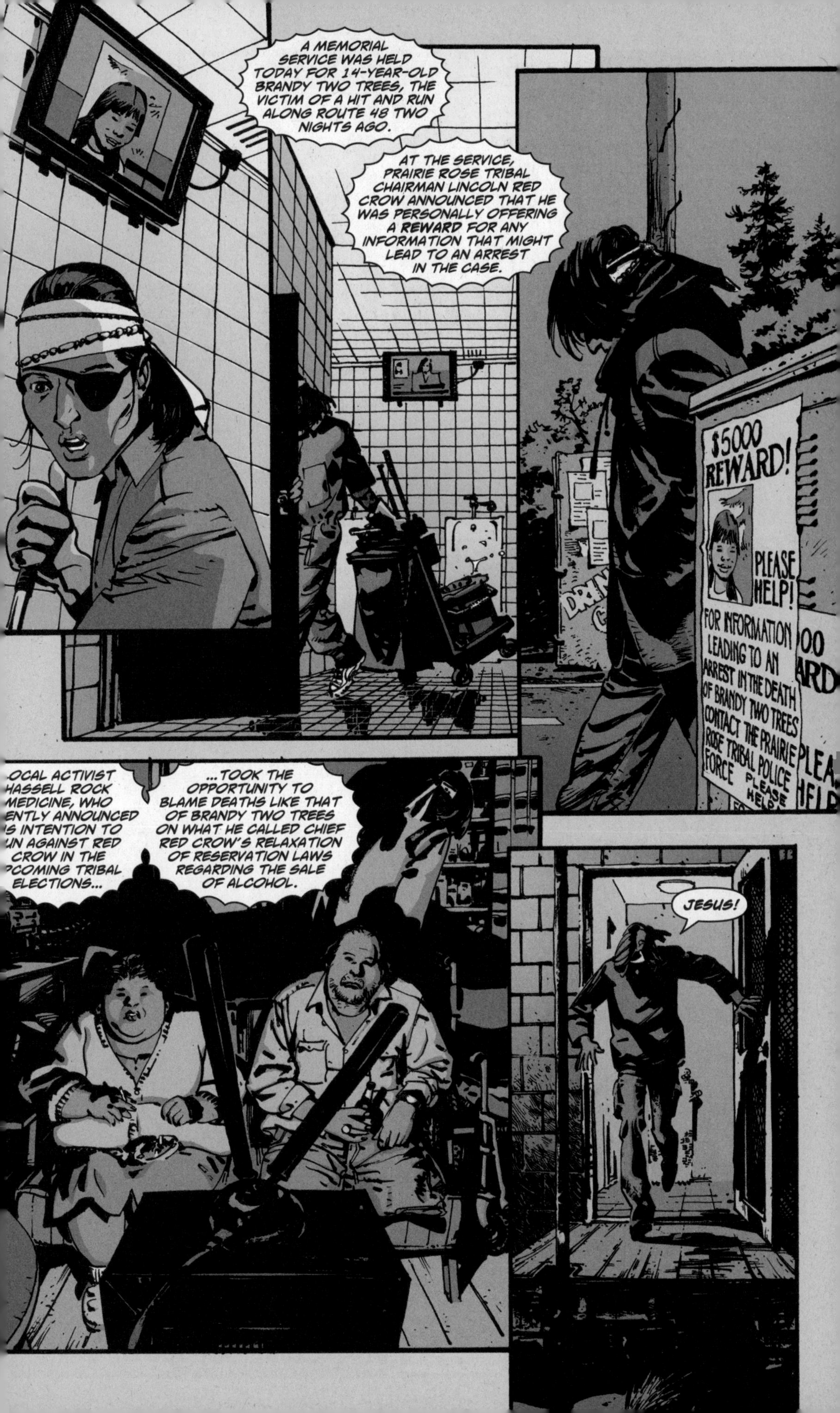
A MEMORIAL SERVICE WAS HELD TODAY FOR 14-YEAR-OLD BRANDY TWO TREES, THE VICTIM OF A HIT AND RUN ALONG ROUTE 48 TWO NIGHTS AGO.
AT THE SERVICE, PRAIRIE ROSE TRIBAL CHAIRMAN LINCOLN RED CROW ANNOUNCED THAT HE WAS PERSONALLY OFFERING A **REWARD** FOR ANY INFORMATION THAT MIGHT LEAD TO AN ARREST IN THE CASE.
$5000 REWARD!
PLEASE HELP!
FOR INFORMATION LEADING TO AN ARREST IN THE DEATH OF BRANDY TWO TREES CONTACT THE PRAIRIE ROSE TRIBAL POLICE FORCE
PLEASE HELP
OCAL ACTIVIST HASSELL ROCK MEDICINE, WHO ENTLY ANNOUNCED S INTENTION TO UN AGAINST RED CROW IN THE PCOMING TRIBAL ELECTIONS...
...TOOK THE OPPORTUNITY TO BLAME DEATHS LIKE THAT OF BRANDY TWO TREES ON WHAT HE CALLED CHIEF RED CROW'S RELAXATION OF RESERVATION LAWS REGARDING THE SALE OF ALCOHOL.
JESUS!

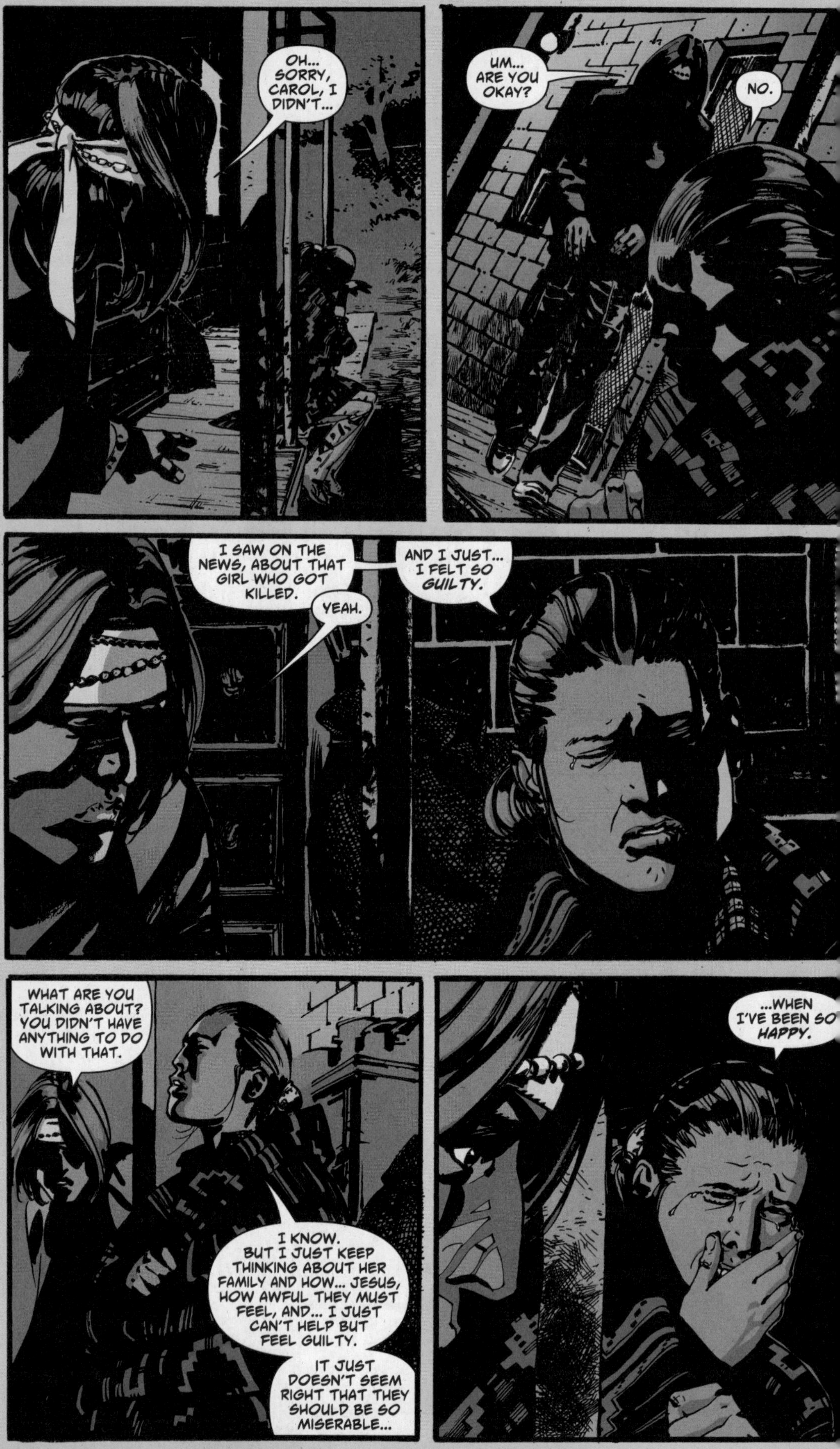
OH... SORRY, CAROL, I DIDN'T...
UM... ARE YOU OKAY?
NO.
I SAW ON THE NEWS, ABOUT THAT GIRL WHO GOT KILLED.
YEAH.
AND I JUST... I FELT SO GUILTY.
WHAT ARE YOU TALKING ABOUT? YOU DIDN'T HAVE ANYTHING TO DO WITH THAT.
I KNOW. BUT I JUST KEEP THINKING ABOUT HER FAMILY AND HOW... JESUS, HOW AWFUL THEY MUST FEEL, AND... I JUST CAN'T HELP BUT FEEL GUILTY.
IT JUST DOESN'T SEEM RIGHT THAT THEY SHOULD BE SO MISERABLE...
...WHEN I'VE BEEN SO HAPPY.

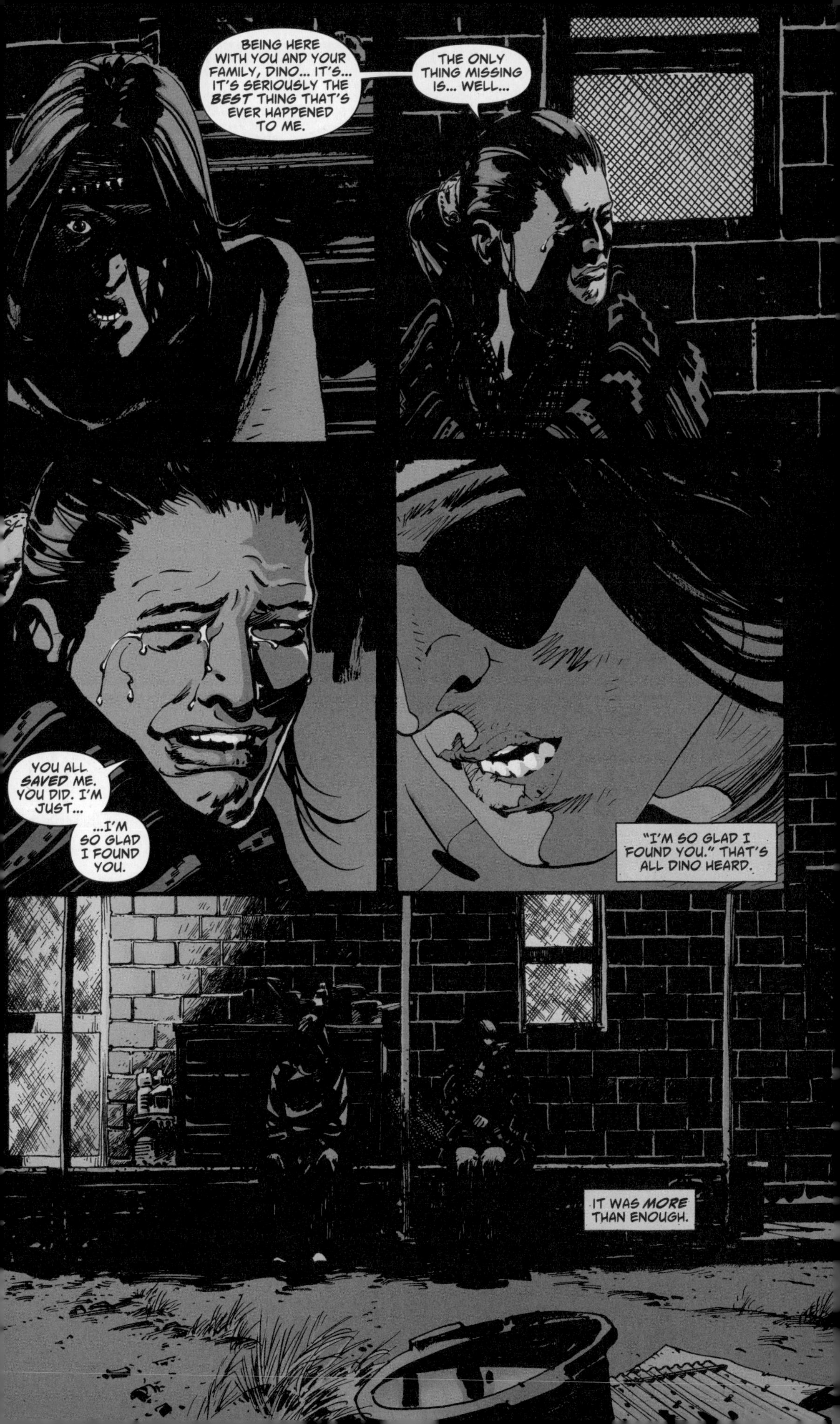
BEING HERE WITH YOU AND YOUR FAMILY, DINO... IT'S... IT'S SERIOUSLY THE BEST THING THAT'S EVER HAPPENED TO ME.
THE ONLY THING MISSING IS... WELL...
YOU ALL SAVED ME. YOU DID. I'M JUST...
...I'M SO GLAD I FOUND YOU.
"I'M SO GLAD I FOUND YOU." THAT'S ALL DINO HEARD.
IT WAS MORE THAN ENOUGH.

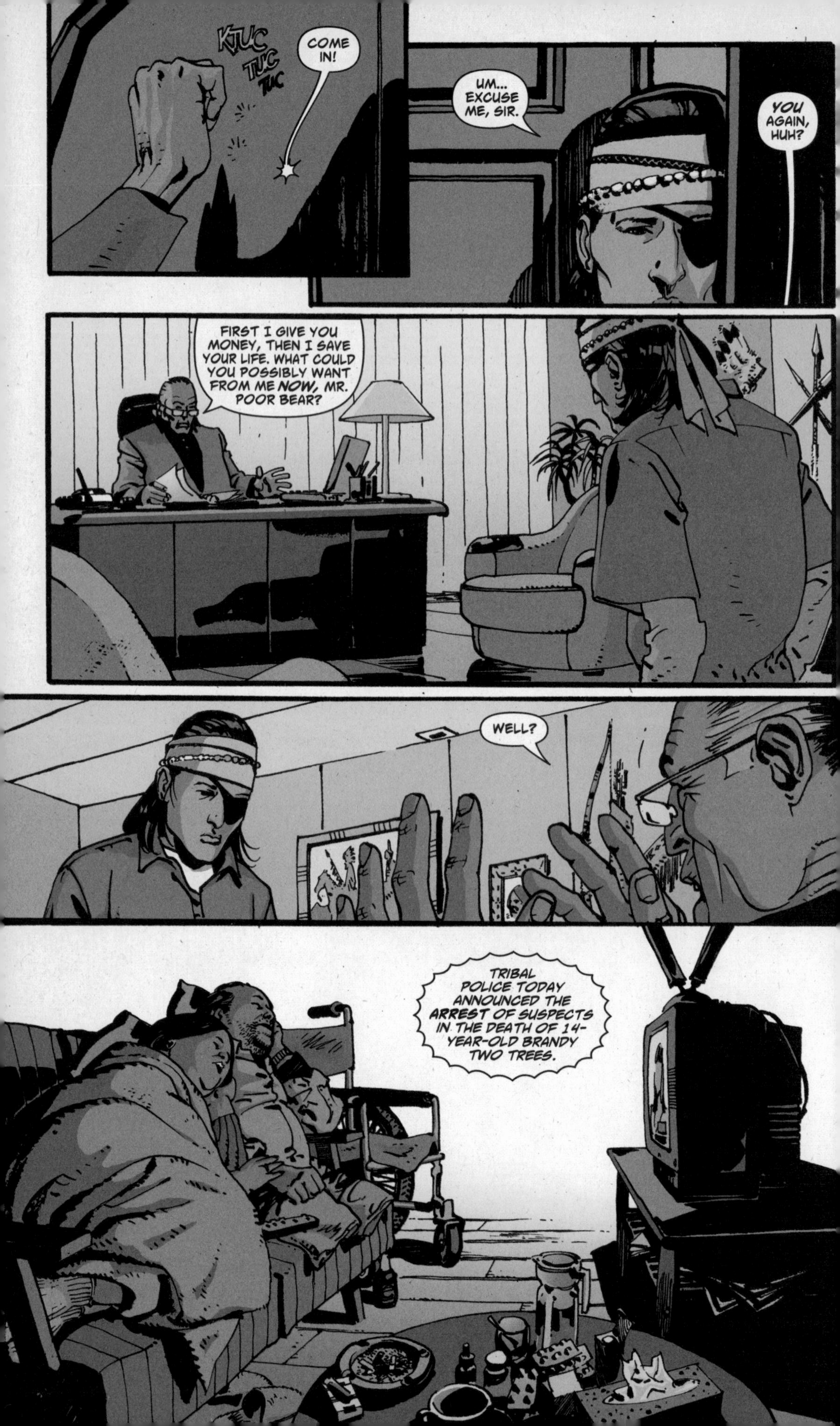
KTUC TUC TUC
COME IN!
UM... EXCUSE ME, SIR.
YOU AGAIN, HUH?
FIRST I GIVE YOU MONEY, THEN I SAVE YOUR LIFE. WHAT COULD YOU POSSIBLY WANT FROM ME NOW, MR. POOR BEAR?
WELL?
TRIBAL POLICE TODAY ANNOUNCED THE ARREST OF SUSPECTS IN THE DEATH OF 14-YEAR-OLD BRANDY TWO TREES.

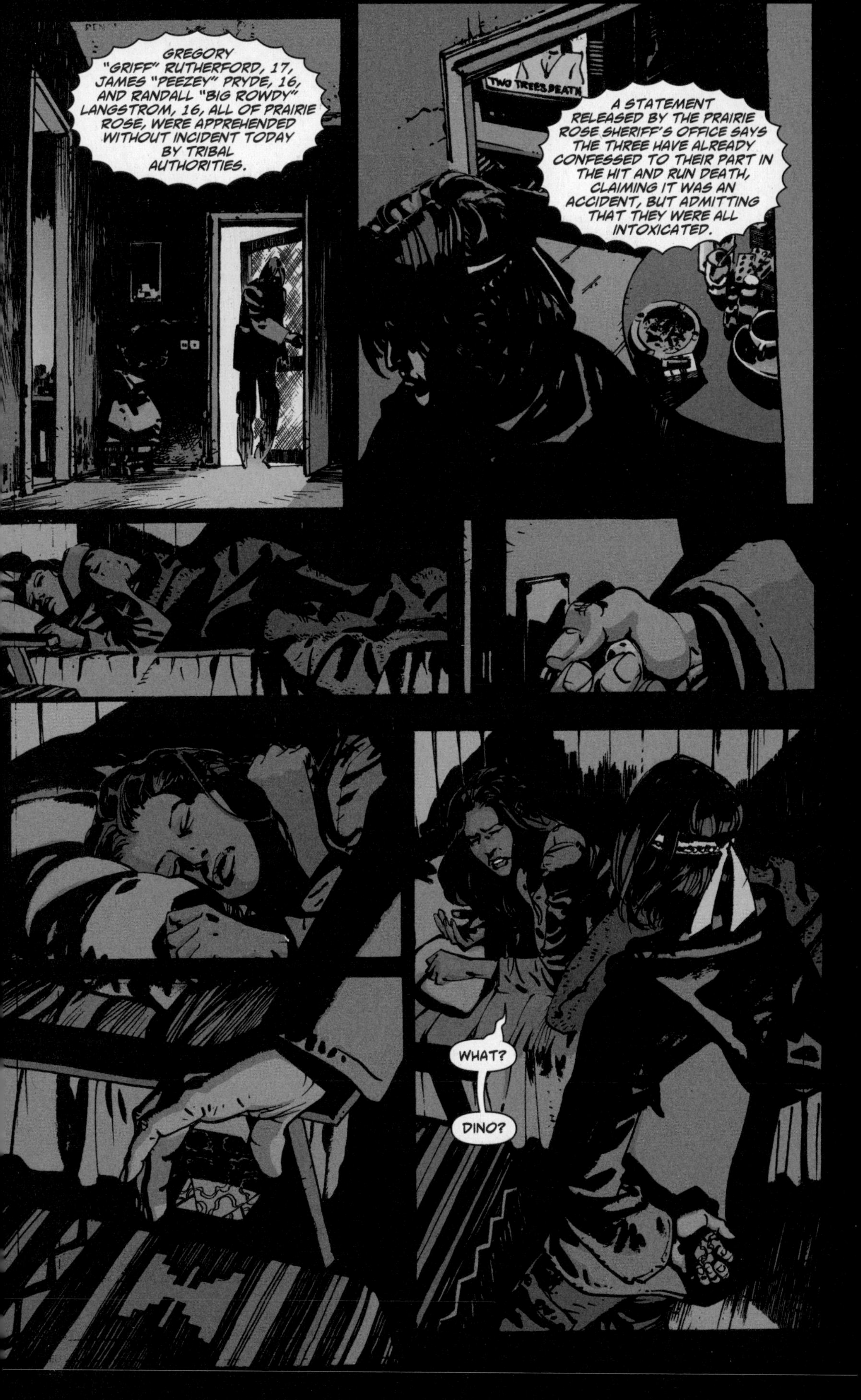
GREGORY "GRIFF" RUTHERFORD, 17, JAMES "PEEZEY" PRYDE, 16, AND RANDALL "BIG ROWDY" LANGSTROM, 16, ALL OF PRAIRIE ROSE, WERE APPREHENDED WITHOUT INCIDENT TODAY BY TRIBAL AUTHORITIES.
TWO TREES DEATH
A STATEMENT RELEASED BY THE PRAIRIE ROSE SHERIFF'S OFFICE SAYS THE THREE HAVE ALREADY CONFESSED TO THEIR PART IN THE HIT AND RUN DEATH, CLAIMING IT WAS AN ACCIDENT, BUT ADMITTING THAT THEY WERE ALL INTOXICATED.
WHAT?
DINO?

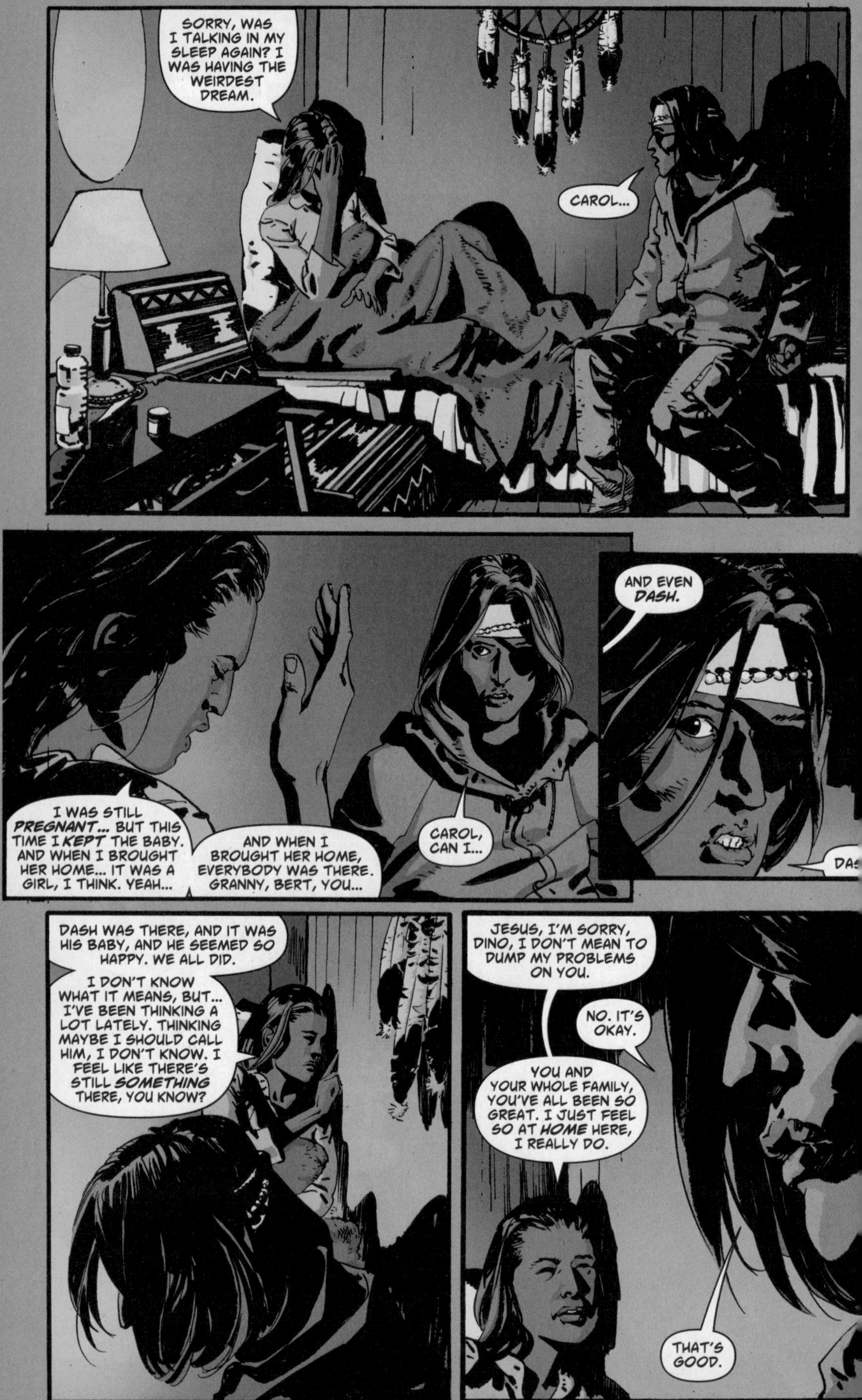
SORRY, WAS I TALKING IN MY SLEEP AGAIN? I WAS HAVING THE WEIRDEST DREAM.
CAROL...
I WAS STILL *PREGNANT*... BUT THIS TIME I *KEPT* THE BABY. AND WHEN I BROUGHT HER HOME... IT WAS A GIRL, I THINK. YEAH...
AND WHEN I BROUGHT HER HOME, EVERYBODY WAS THERE. GRANNY, BERT, YOU...
CAROL, CAN I...
AND EVEN *DASH*.
DASH WAS THERE, AND IT WAS HIS BABY, AND HE SEEMED SO HAPPY. WE ALL DID.
I DON'T KNOW WHAT IT MEANS, BUT... I'VE BEEN THINKING A LOT LATELY. THINKING MAYBE I SHOULD CALL HIM, I DON'T KNOW. I FEEL LIKE THERE'S STILL *SOMETHING* THERE, YOU KNOW?
JESUS, I'M SORRY, DINO, I DON'T MEAN TO DUMP MY PROBLEMS ON YOU.
NO. IT'S OKAY.
YOU AND YOUR WHOLE FAMILY, YOU'VE ALL BEEN SO GREAT. I JUST FEEL SO AT *HOME* HERE, I REALLY DO.
THAT'S GOOD.

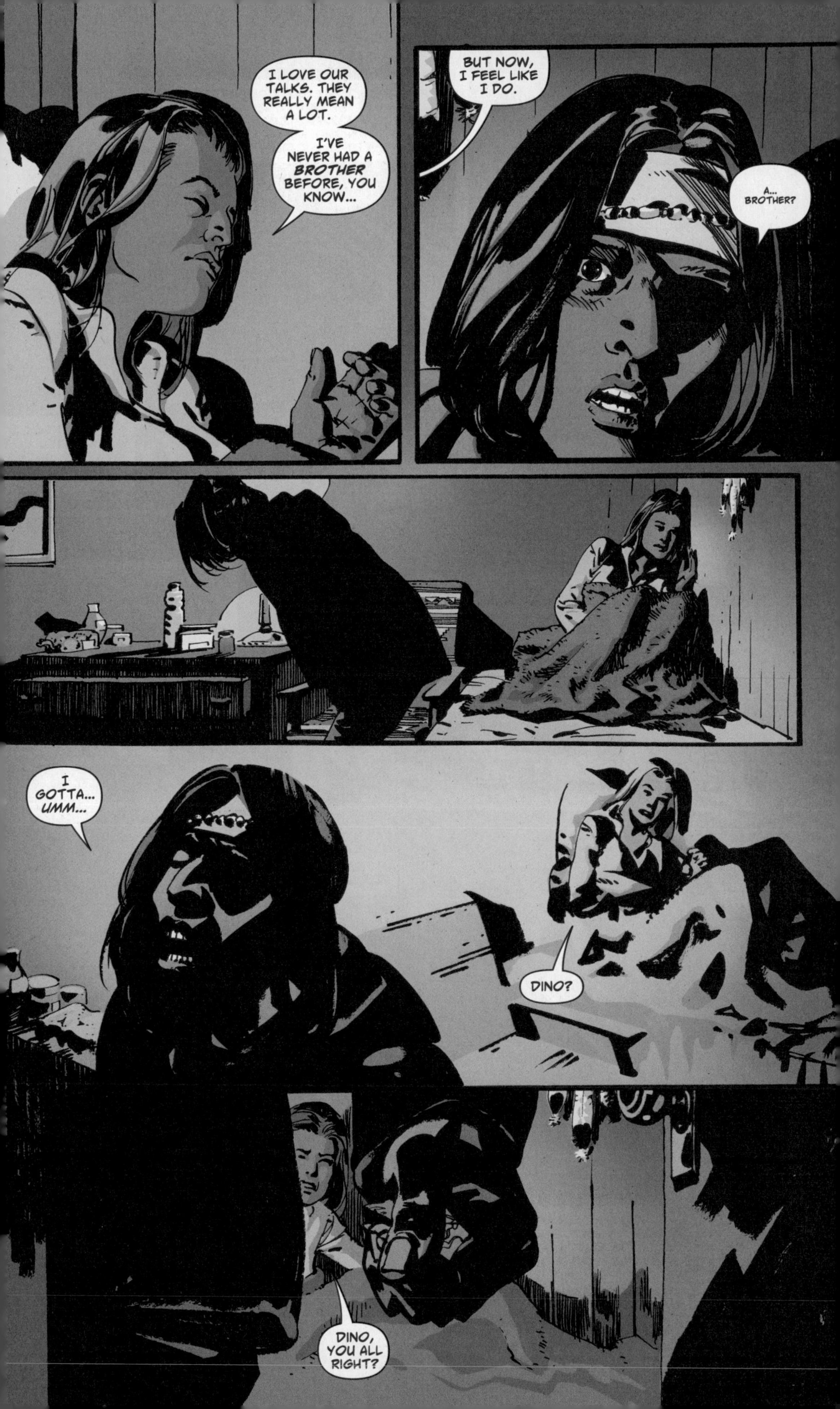
I LOVE OUR TALKS. THEY REALLY MEAN A LOT.
I'VE NEVER HAD A BROTHER BEFORE, YOU KNOW...
BUT NOW, I FEEL LIKE I DO.
A... BROTHER?
I GOTTA... UMM...
DINO?
DINO, YOU ALL RIGHT?

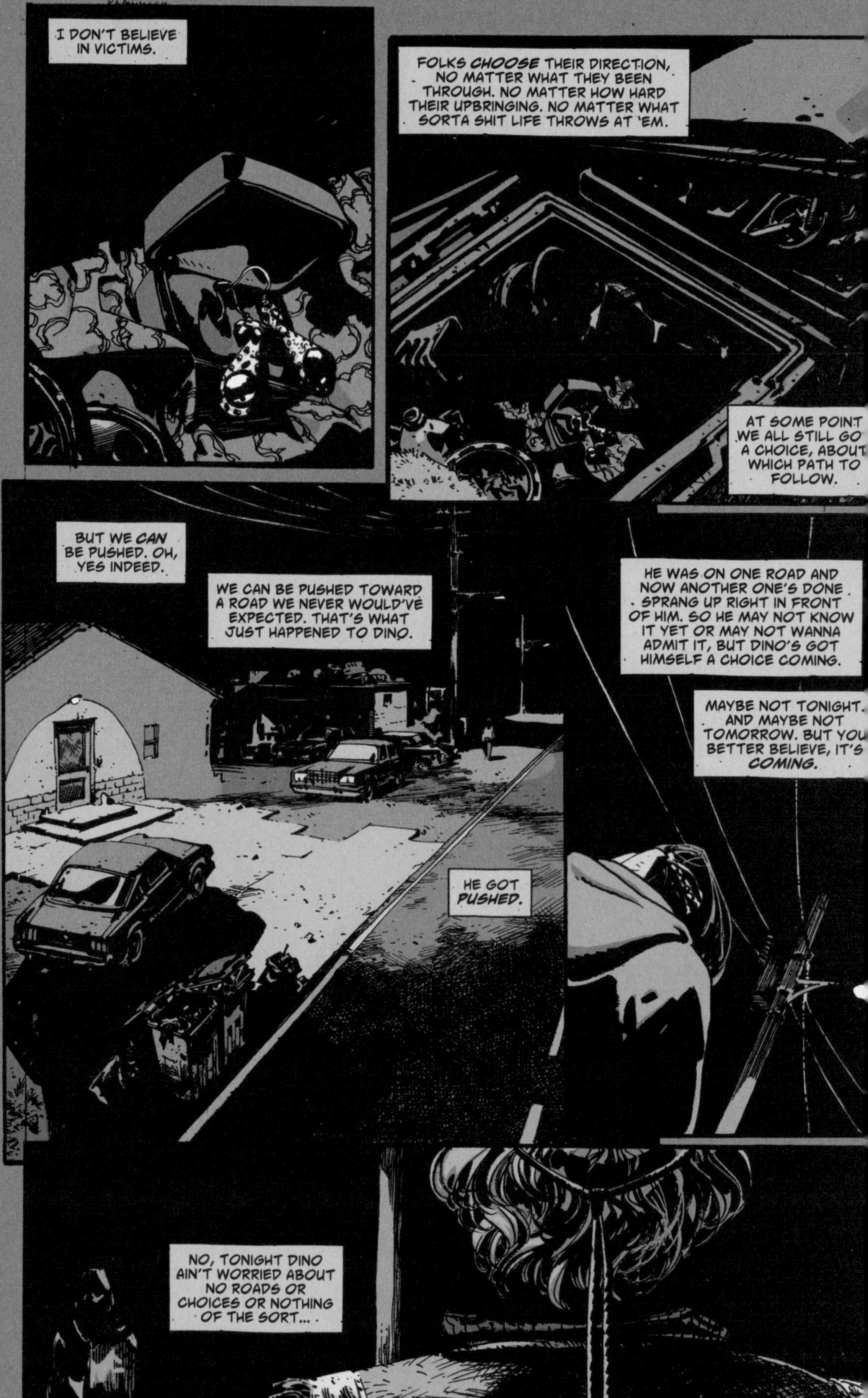
I DON'T BELIEVE IN VICTIMS.
FOLKS *CHOOSE* THEIR DIRECTION, NO MATTER WHAT THEY BEEN THROUGH. NO MATTER HOW HARD THEIR UPBRINGING. NO MATTER WHAT SORTA SHIT LIFE THROWS AT 'EM.
AT SOME POINT WE ALL STILL GOT A CHOICE, ABOUT WHICH PATH TO FOLLOW.
BUT WE *CAN* BE PUSHED. OH, YES INDEED.
WE CAN BE PUSHED TOWARD A ROAD WE NEVER WOULD'VE EXPECTED. THAT'S WHAT JUST HAPPENED TO DINO.
HE GOT *PUSHED.*
HE WAS ON ONE ROAD AND NOW ANOTHER ONE'S DONE SPRANG UP RIGHT IN FRONT OF HIM. SO HE MAY NOT KNOW IT YET OR MAY NOT WANNA ADMIT IT, BUT DINO'S GOT HIMSELF A CHOICE COMING.
MAYBE NOT TONIGHT. AND MAYBE NOT TOMORROW. BUT YOU BETTER BELIEVE, IT'S *COMING.*
NO, TONIGHT DINO AIN'T WORRIED ABOUT NO ROADS OR CHOICES OR NOTHING OF THE SORT...

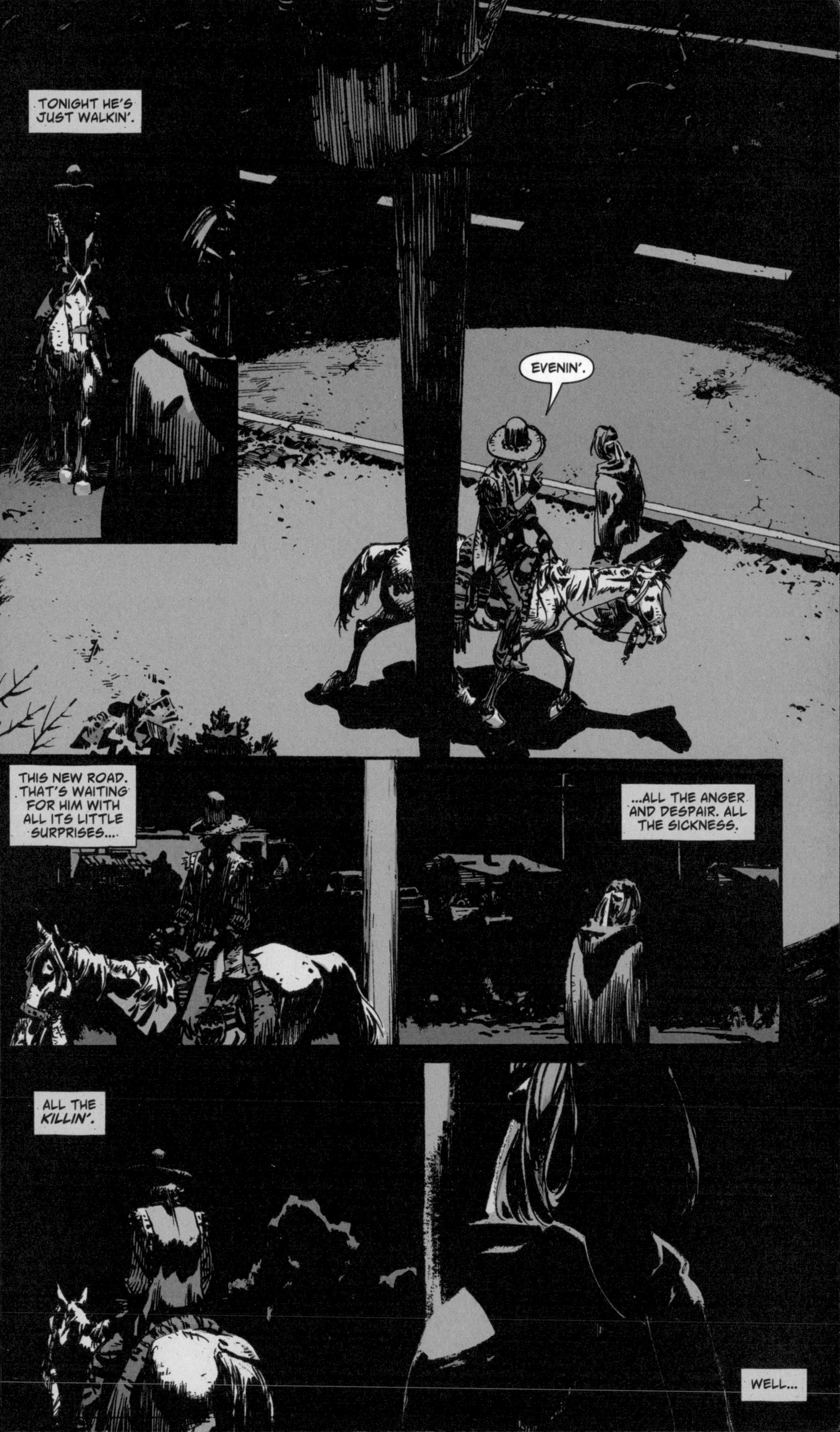
TONIGHT HE'S JUST WALKIN'.
EVENIN'.
THIS NEW ROAD. THAT'S WAITING FOR HIM WITH ALL ITS LITTLE SURPRISES....
...ALL THE ANGER AND DESPAIR. ALL THE SICKNESS.
ALL THE *KILLIN'*.
WELL...

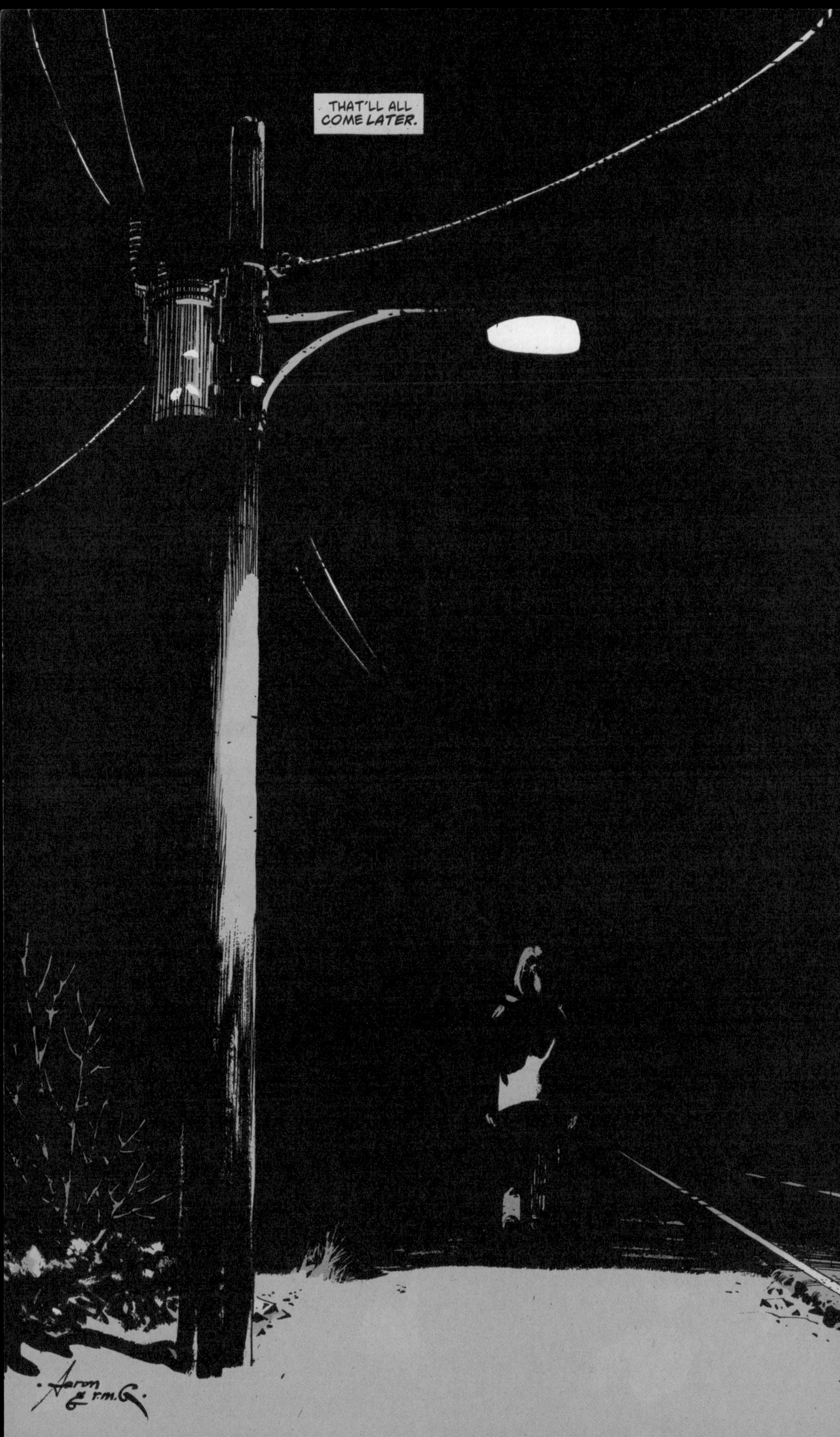
THAT'LL ALL COME LATER.
Aaron & r.m.G.

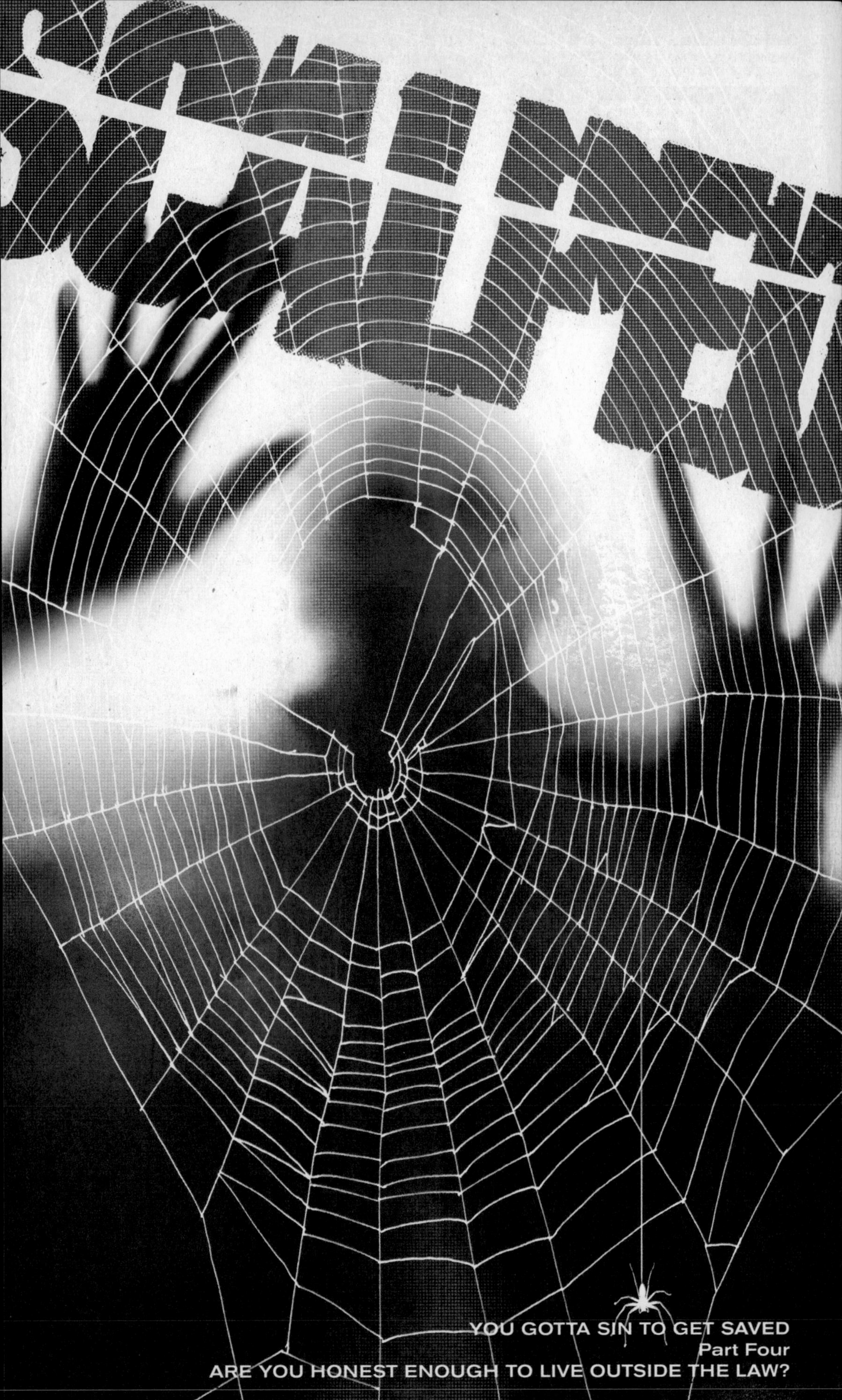
YOU GOTTA SIN TO GET SAVED
Part Four
ARE YOU HONEST ENOUGH TO LIVE OUTSIDE THE LAW?

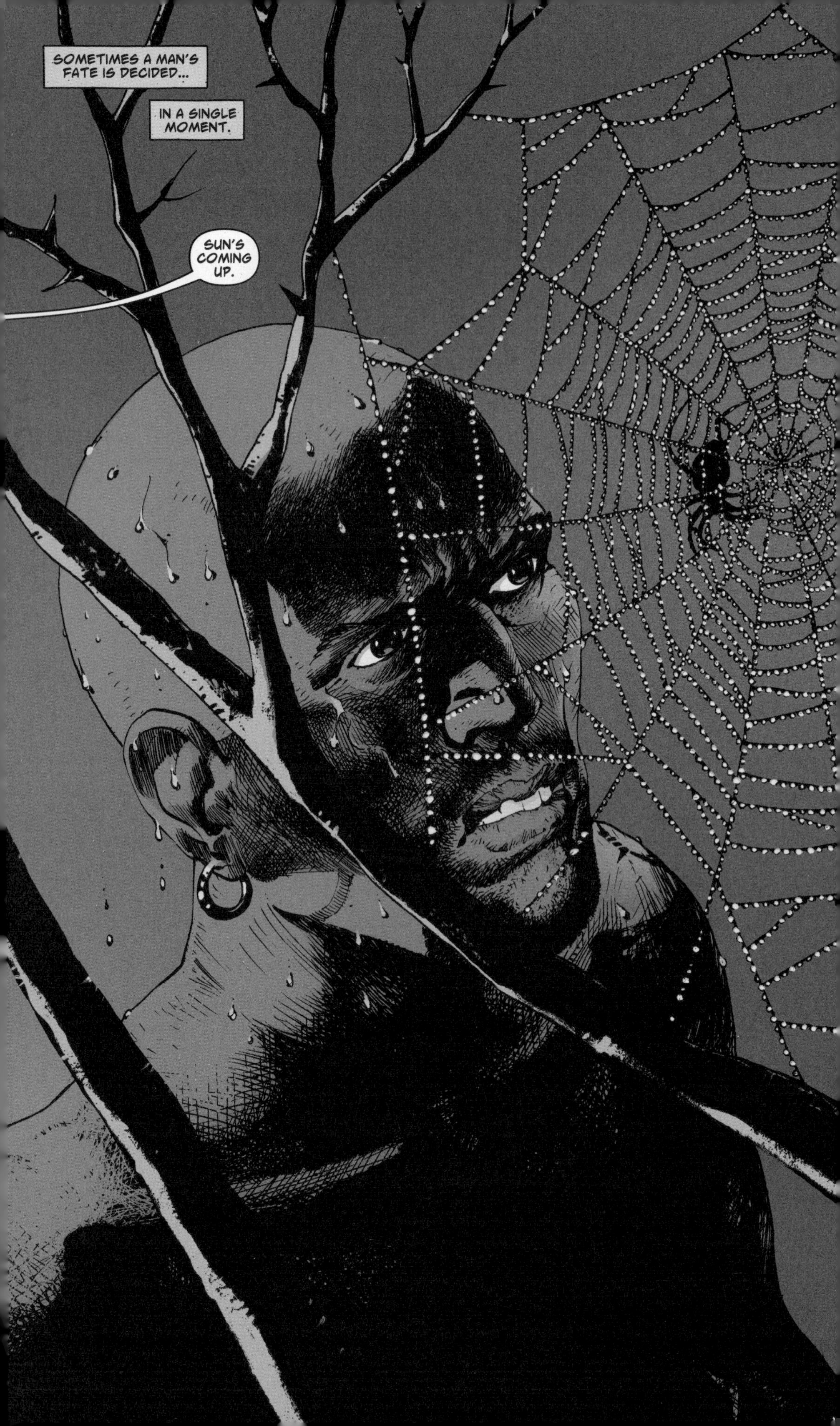
SOMETIMES A MAN'S FATE IS DECIDED...
IN A SINGLE MOMENT.
SUN'S COMING UP.

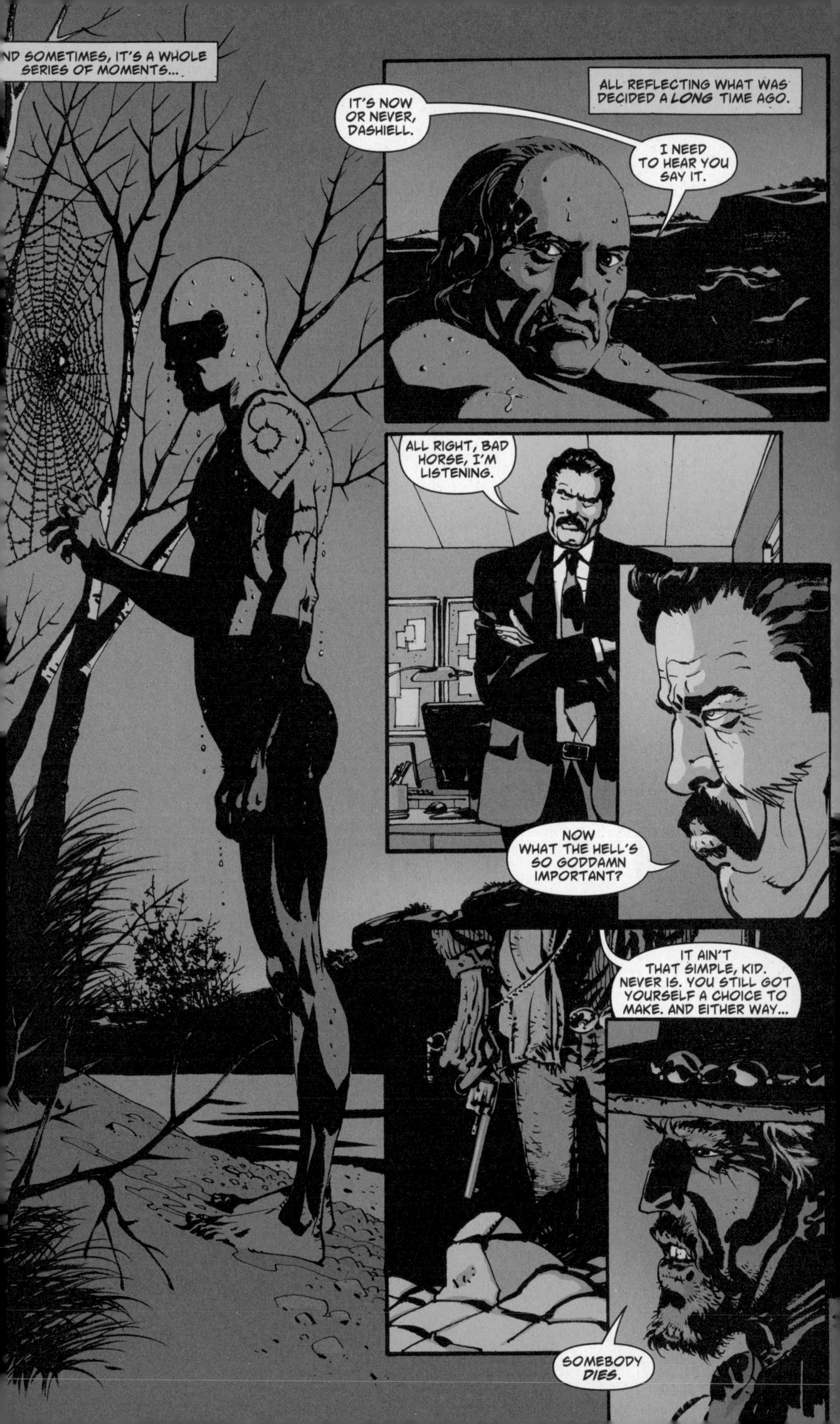
ND SOMETIMES, IT'S A WHOLE SERIES OF MOMENTS...
ALL REFLECTING WHAT WAS DECIDED A LONG TIME AGO.
IT'S NOW OR NEVER, DASHIELL.
I NEED TO HEAR YOU SAY IT.
ALL RIGHT, BAD HORSE, I'M LISTENING.
NOW WHAT THE HELL'S SO GODDAMN IMPORTANT?
IT AIN'T THAT SIMPLE, KID. NEVER IS. YOU STILL GOT YOURSELF A CHOICE TO MAKE. AND EITHER WAY...
SOMEBODY DIES.

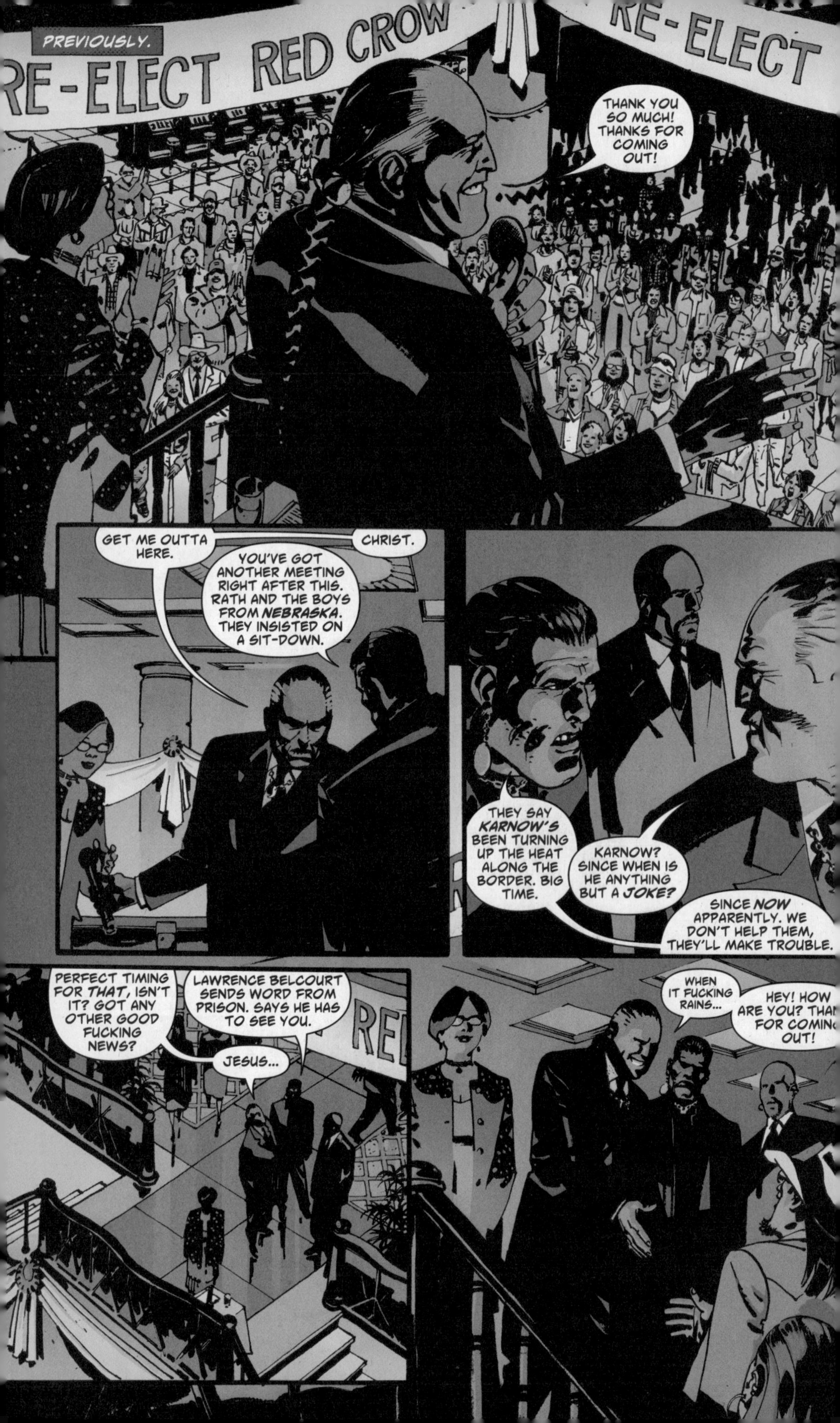
PREVIOUSLY.
RE-ELECT RED CROW
RE-ELECT
THANK YOU SO MUCH! THANKS FOR COMING OUT!
GET ME OUTTA HERE.
CHRIST.
YOU'VE GOT ANOTHER MEETING RIGHT AFTER THIS. RATH AND THE BOYS FROM NEBRASKA. THEY INSISTED ON A SIT-DOWN.
THEY SAY KARNOW'S BEEN TURNING UP THE HEAT ALONG THE BORDER. BIG TIME.
KARNOW? SINCE WHEN IS HE ANYTHING BUT A JOKE?
SINCE NOW APPARENTLY. WE DON'T HELP THEM, THEY'LL MAKE TROUBLE.
PERFECT TIMING FOR THAT, ISN'T IT? GOT ANY OTHER GOOD FUCKING NEWS?
LAWRENCE BELCOURT SENDS WORD FROM PRISON. SAYS HE HAS TO SEE YOU.
JESUS...
WHEN IT FUCKING RAINS...
HEY! HOW ARE YOU? THAN FOR COMIN OUT!

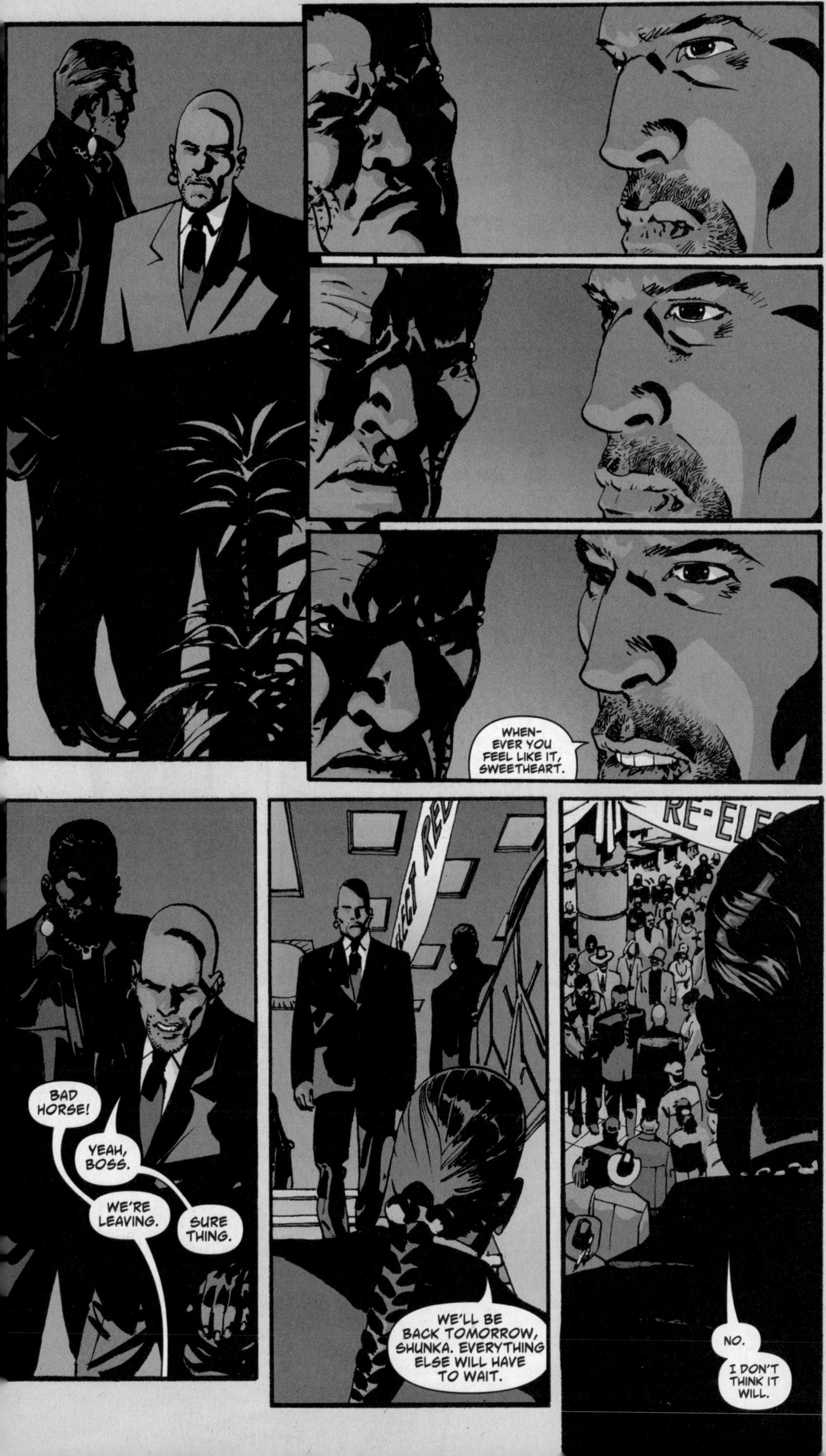
WHEN-EVER YOU FEEL LIKE IT, SWEETHEART.
BAD HORSE!
YEAH, BOSS.
WE'RE LEAVING.
SURE THING.
WE'LL BE BACK TOMORROW, SHUNKA. EVERYTHING ELSE WILL HAVE TO WAIT.
NO.
I DON'T THINK IT WILL.

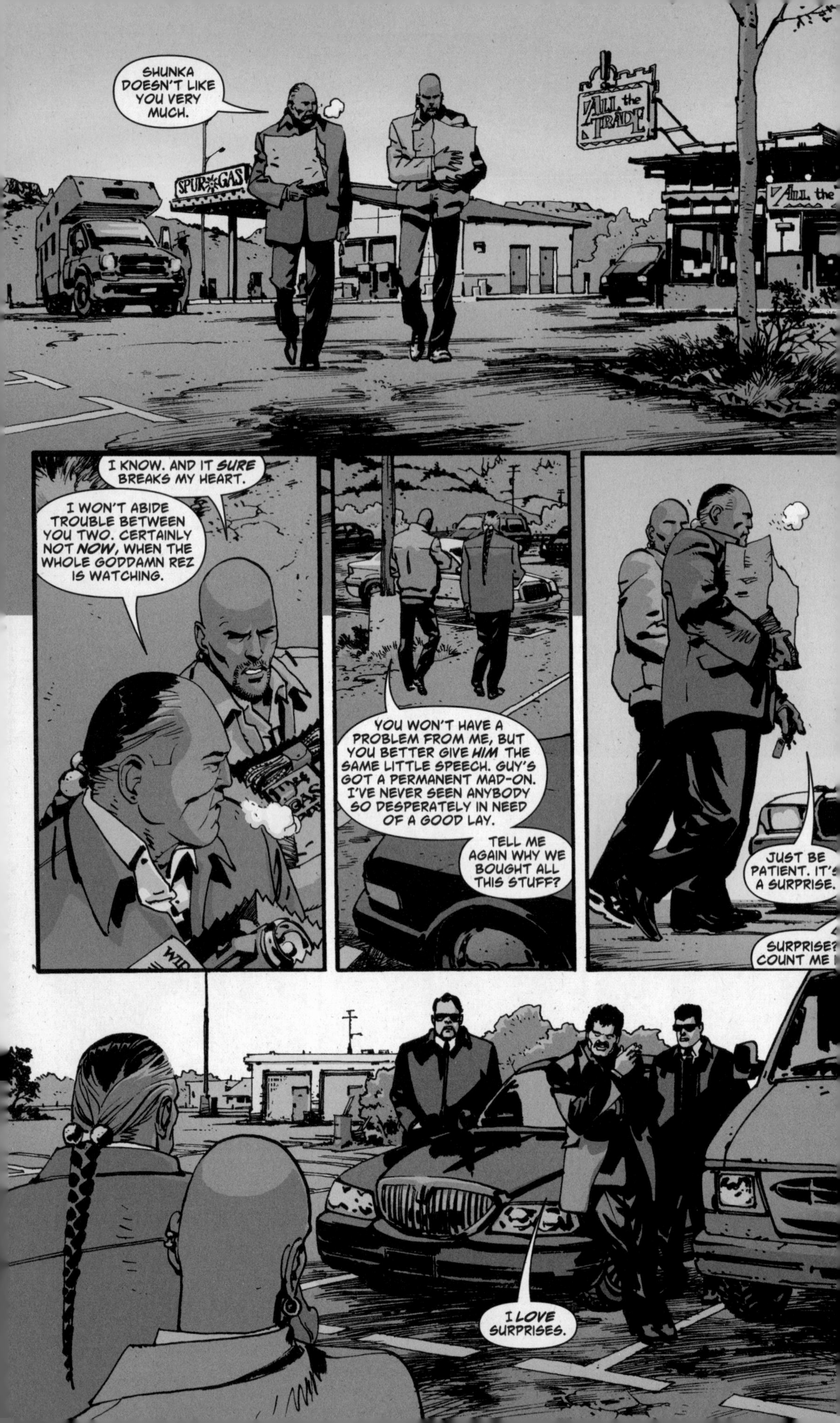
SHUNKA DOESN'T LIKE YOU VERY MUCH.
SPUR GAS
ALL the TRADE
I KNOW. AND IT SURE BREAKS MY HEART.
I WON'T ABIDE TROUBLE BETWEEN YOU TWO. CERTAINLY NOT NOW, WHEN THE WHOLE GODDAMN REZ IS WATCHING.
YOU WON'T HAVE A PROBLEM FROM ME, BUT YOU BETTER GIVE HIM THE SAME LITTLE SPEECH. GUY'S GOT A PERMANENT MAD-ON. I'VE NEVER SEEN ANYBODY SO DESPERATELY IN NEED OF A GOOD LAY.
TELL ME AGAIN WHY WE BOUGHT ALL THIS STUFF?
JUST BE PATIENT. IT'S A SURPRISE.
SURPRISE? COUNT ME
I LOVE SURPRISES.

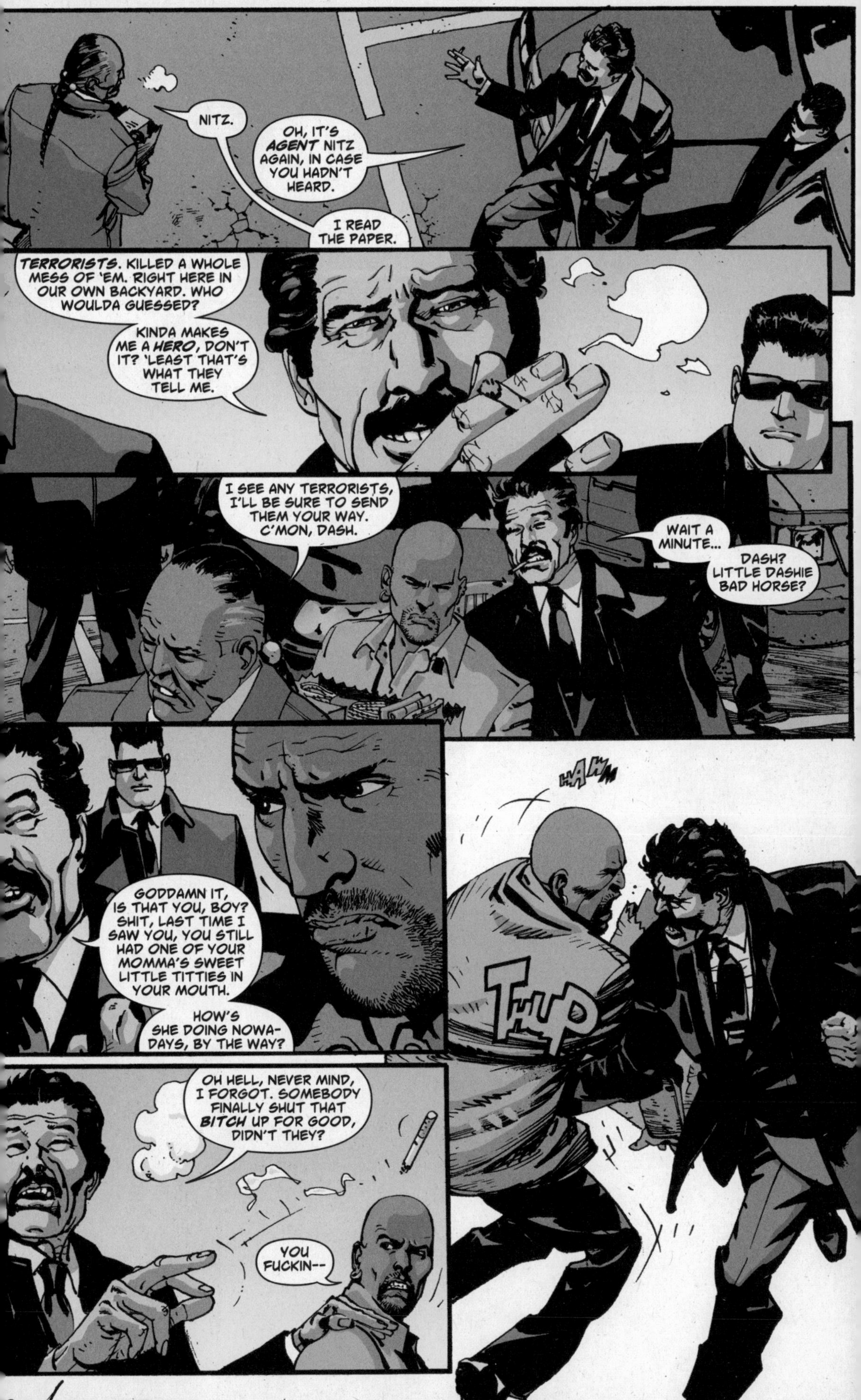
NITZ.
OH, IT'S AGENT NITZ AGAIN, IN CASE YOU HADN'T HEARD.
I READ THE PAPER.
TERRORISTS. KILLED A WHOLE MESS OF 'EM. RIGHT HERE IN OUR OWN BACKYARD. WHO WOULDA GUESSED?
KINDA MAKES ME A HERO, DON'T IT? 'LEAST THAT'S WHAT THEY TELL ME.
I SEE ANY TERRORISTS, I'LL BE SURE TO SEND THEM YOUR WAY. C'MON, DASH.
WAIT A MINUTE...
DASH? LITTLE DASHIE BAD HORSE?
GODDAMN IT, IS THAT YOU, BOY? SHIT, LAST TIME I SAW YOU, YOU STILL HAD ONE OF YOUR MOMMA'S SWEET LITTLE TITTIES IN YOUR MOUTH.
HOW'S SHE DOING NOWA-DAYS, BY THE WAY?
OH HELL, NEVER MIND, I FORGOT. SOMEBODY FINALLY SHUT THAT BITCH UP FOR GOOD, DIDN'T THEY?
YOU FUCKIN--
HAHH
THUP

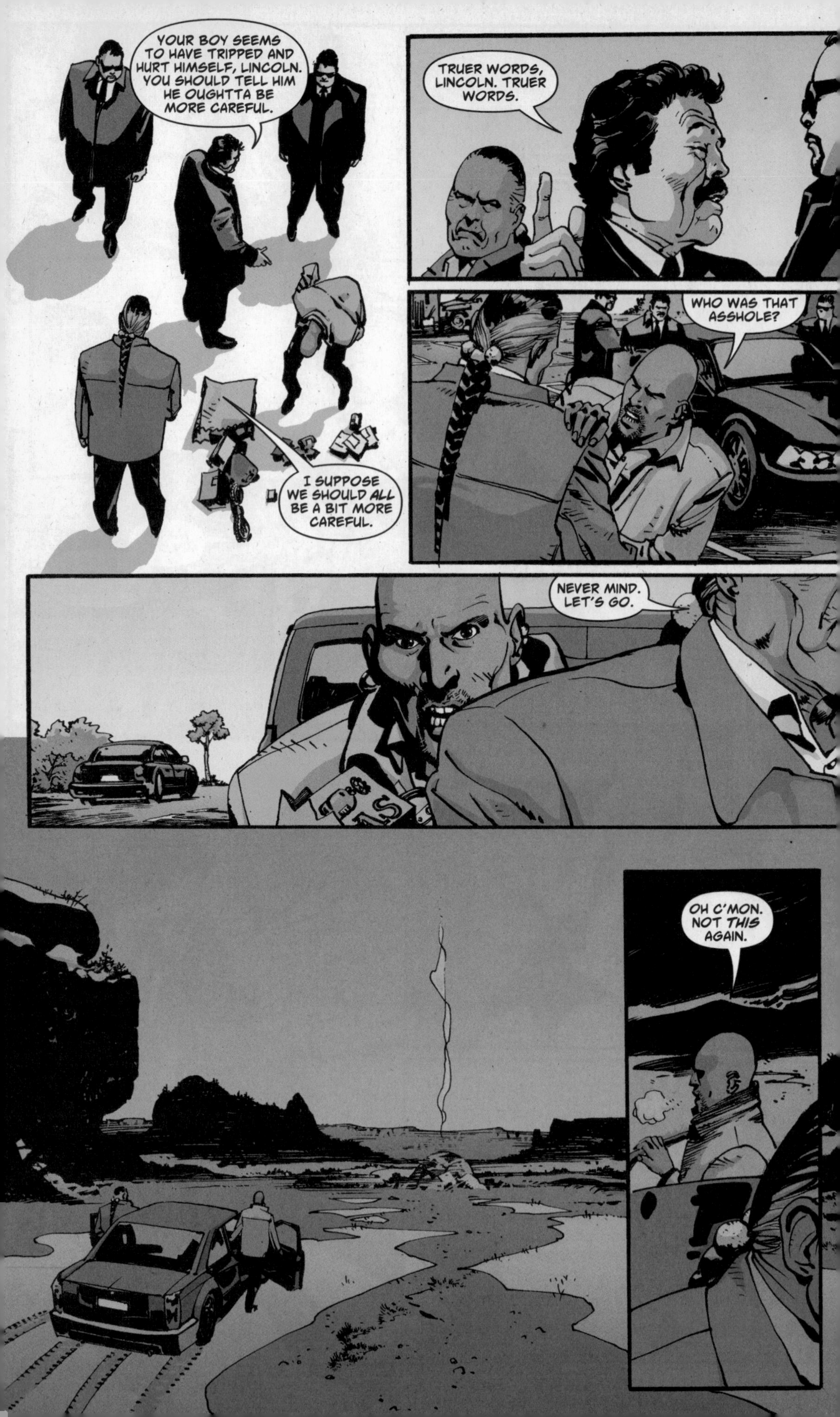
YOUR BOY SEEMS TO HAVE TRIPPED AND HURT HIMSELF, LINCOLN. YOU SHOULD TELL HIM HE OUGHTTA BE MORE CAREFUL.
I SUPPOSE WE SHOULD ALL BE A BIT MORE CAREFUL.
TRUER WORDS, LINCOLN. TRUER WORDS.
WHO WAS THAT ASSHOLE?
NEVER MIND. LET'S GO.
OH C'MON. NOT THIS AGAIN.

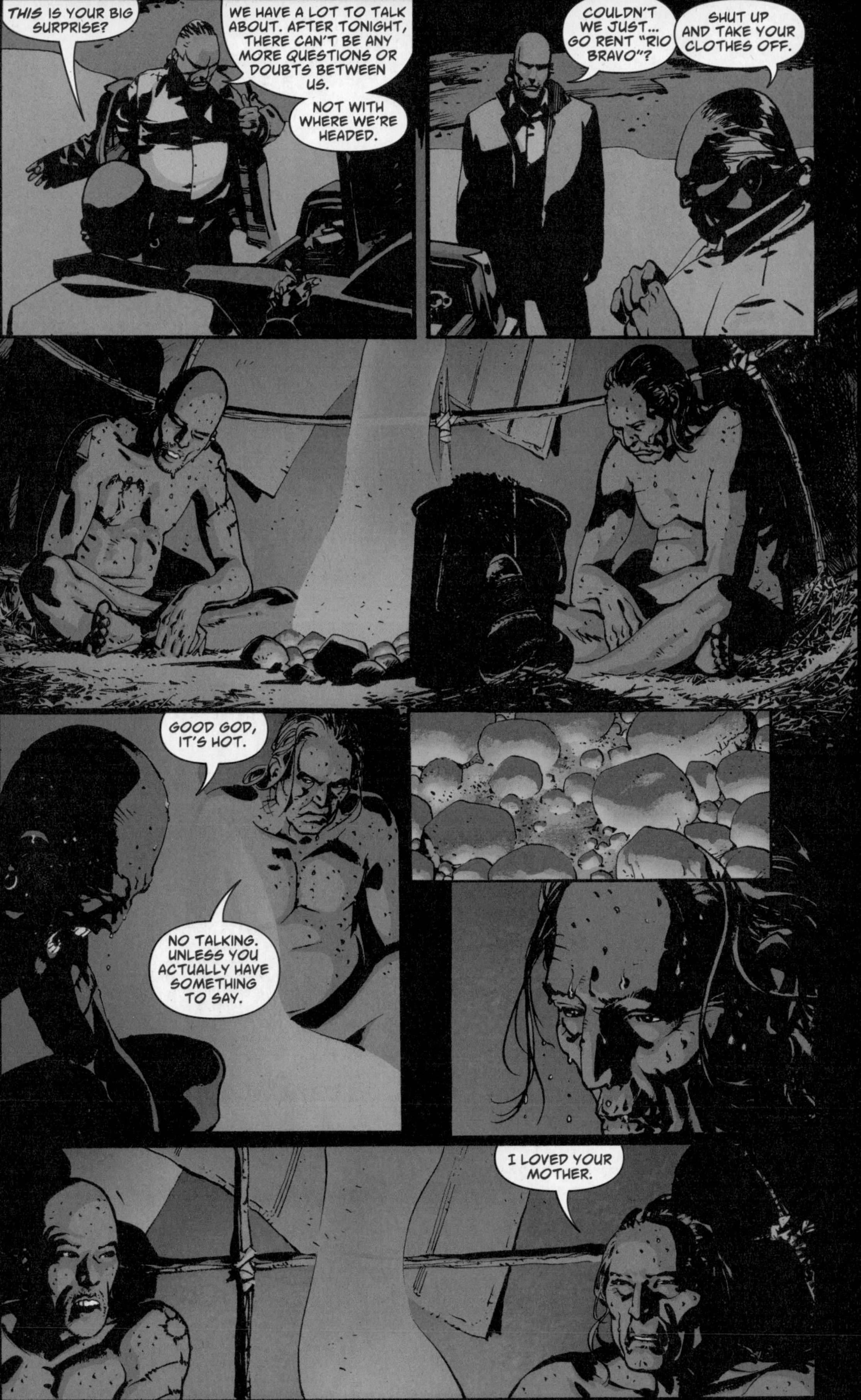
THIS IS YOUR BIG SURPRISE?
WE HAVE A LOT TO TALK ABOUT. AFTER TONIGHT, THERE CAN'T BE ANY MORE QUESTIONS OR DOUBTS BETWEEN US.
NOT WITH WHERE WE'RE HEADED.
COULDN'T WE JUST... GO RENT "RIO BRAVO"?
SHUT UP AND TAKE YOUR CLOTHES OFF.
GOOD GOD, IT'S HOT.
NO TALKING. UNLESS YOU ACTUALLY HAVE SOMETHING TO SAY.
I LOVED YOUR MOTHER.

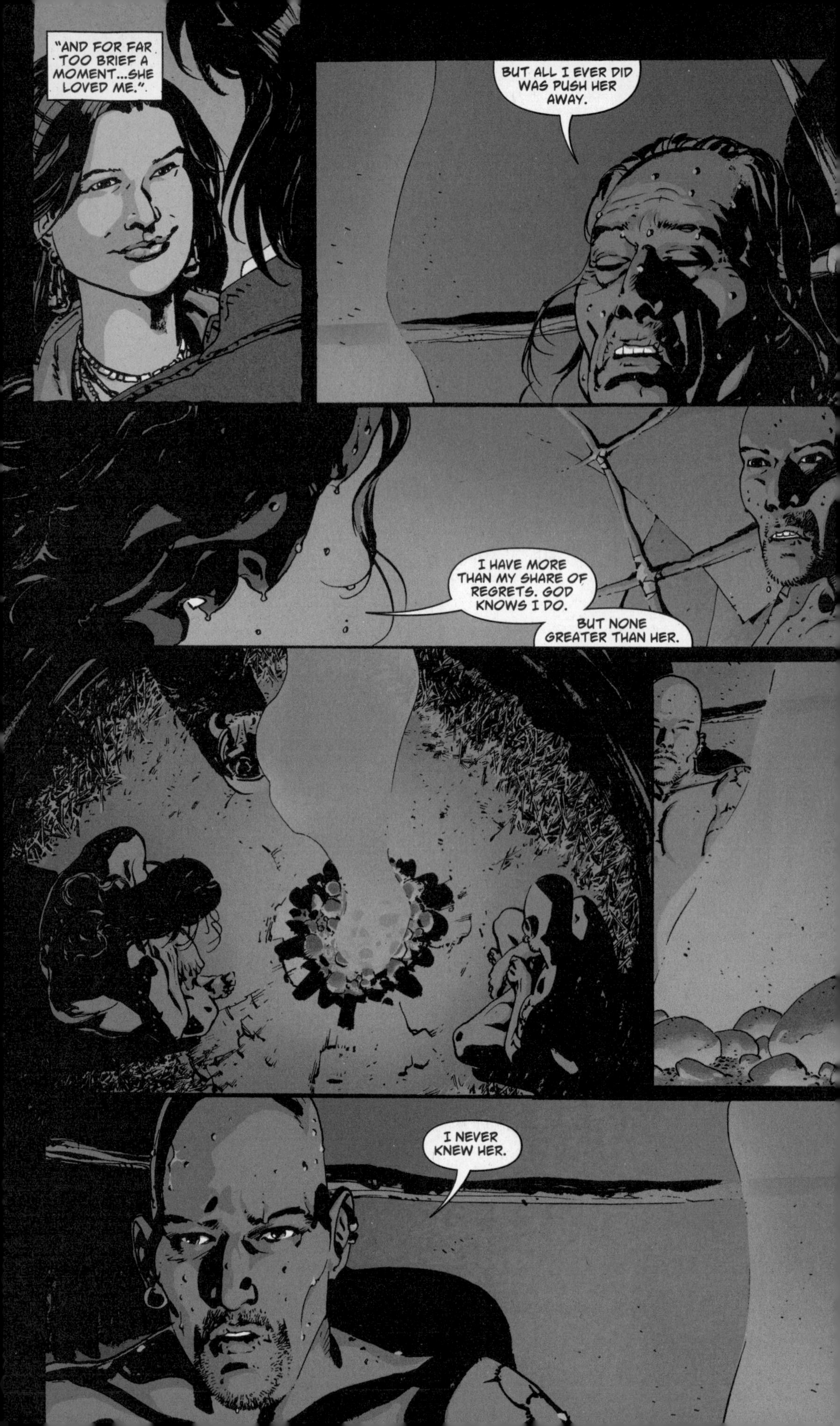
"AND FOR FAR TOO BRIEF A MOMENT...SHE LOVED ME."
BUT ALL I EVER DID WAS PUSH HER AWAY.
I HAVE MORE THAN MY SHARE OF REGRETS. GOD KNOWS I DO.
BUT NONE GREATER THAN HER.
I NEVER KNEW HER.

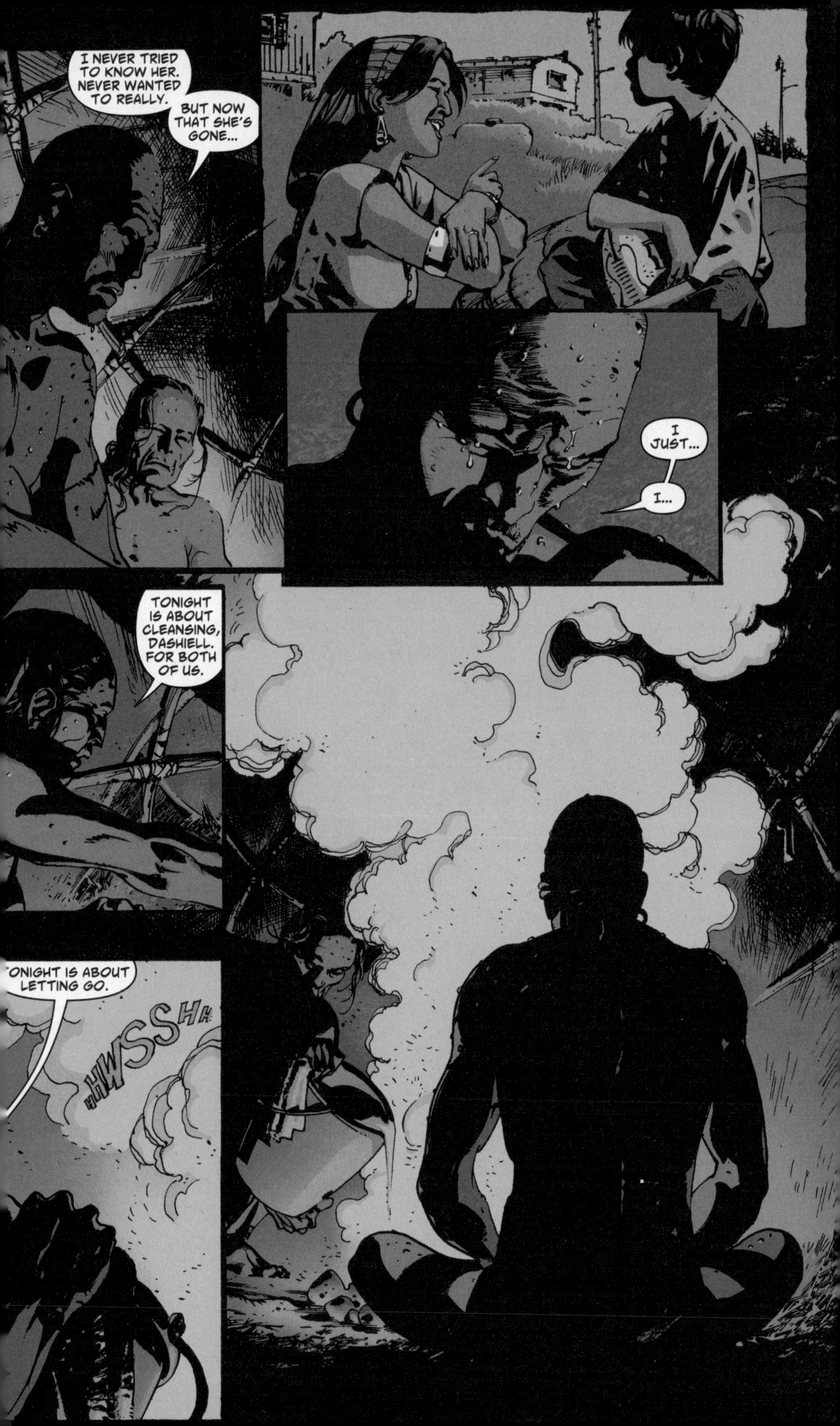
I NEVER TRIED TO KNOW HER. NEVER WANTED TO REALLY.
BUT NOW THAT SHE'S GONE...
I JUST...
I...
TONIGHT IS ABOUT CLEANSING, DASHIELL. FOR BOTH OF US.
TONIGHT IS ABOUT LETTING GO.
HWSSHH

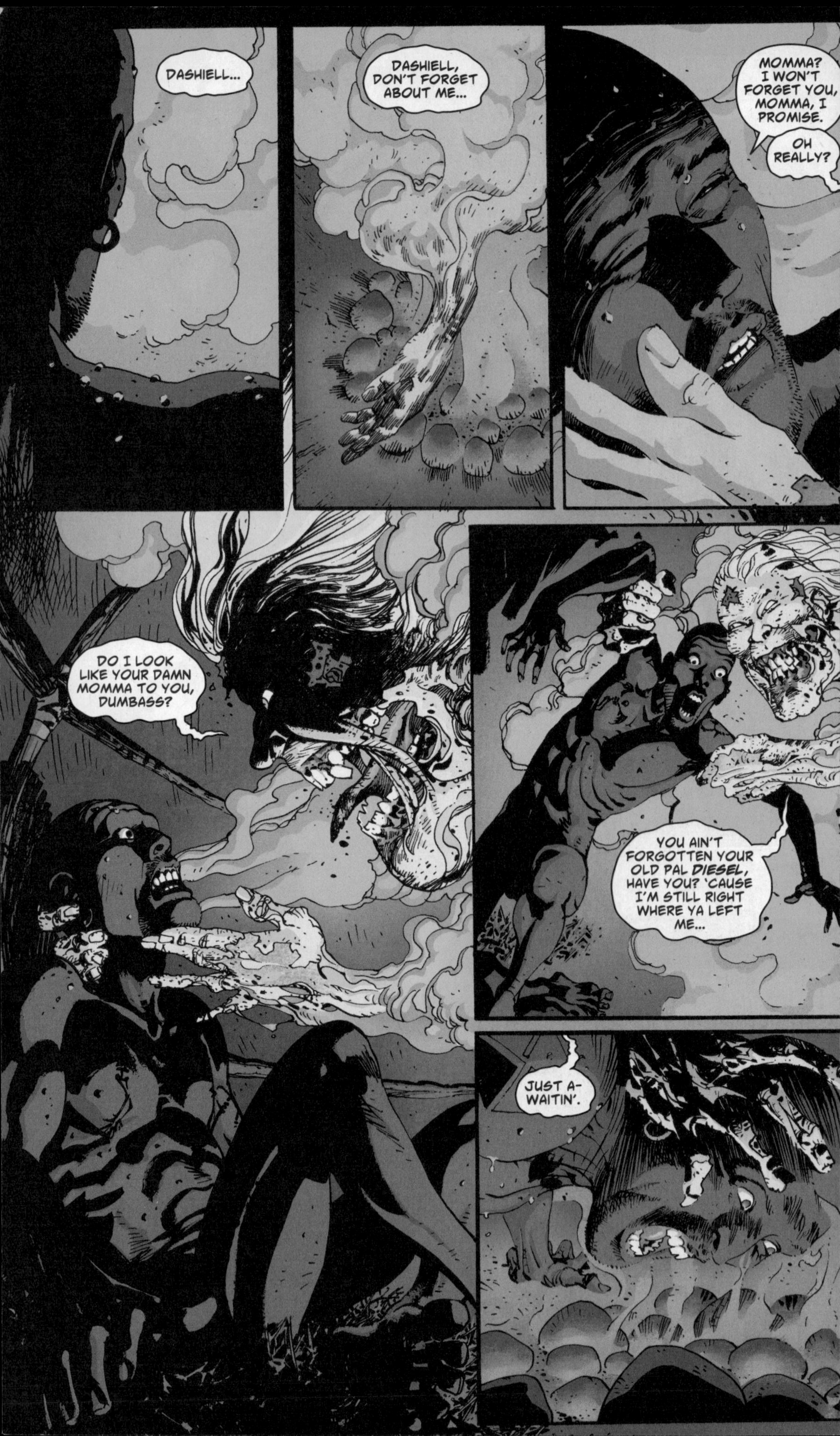
DASHIELL...
DASHIELL, DON'T FORGET ABOUT ME...
MOMMA? I WON'T FORGET YOU, MOMMA, I PROMISE.
OH REALLY?
DO I LOOK LIKE YOUR DAMN MOMMA TO YOU, DUMBASS?
YOU AIN'T FORGOTTEN YOUR OLD PAL DIESEL, HAVE YOU? 'CAUSE I'M STILL RIGHT WHERE YA LEFT ME...
JUST A-WAITIN'.

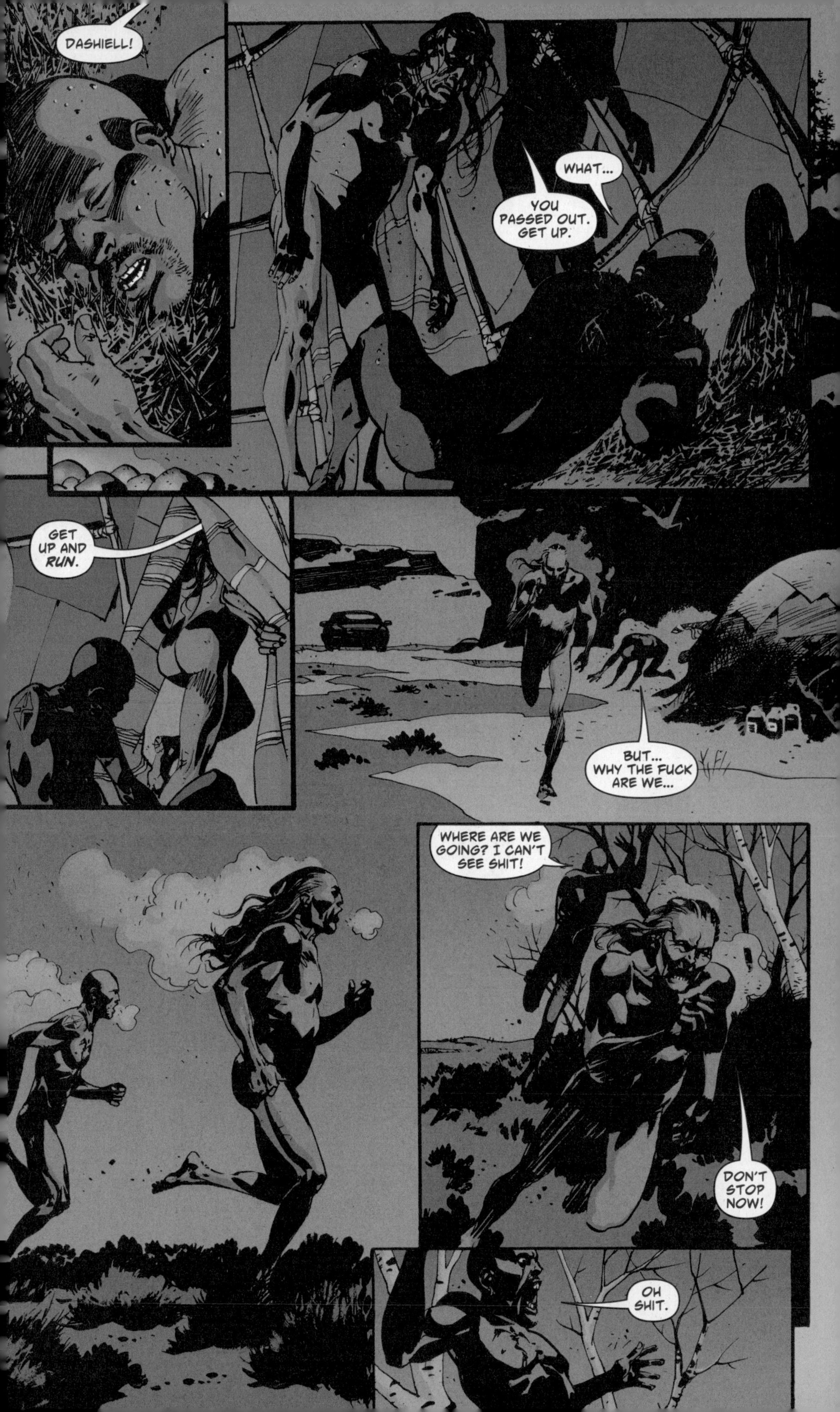
DASHIELL!
WHAT...
YOU PASSED OUT. GET UP.
GET UP AND RUN.
BUT... WHY THE FUCK ARE WE...
WHERE ARE WE GOING? I CAN'T SEE SHIT!
DON'T STOP NOW!
OH SHIT.

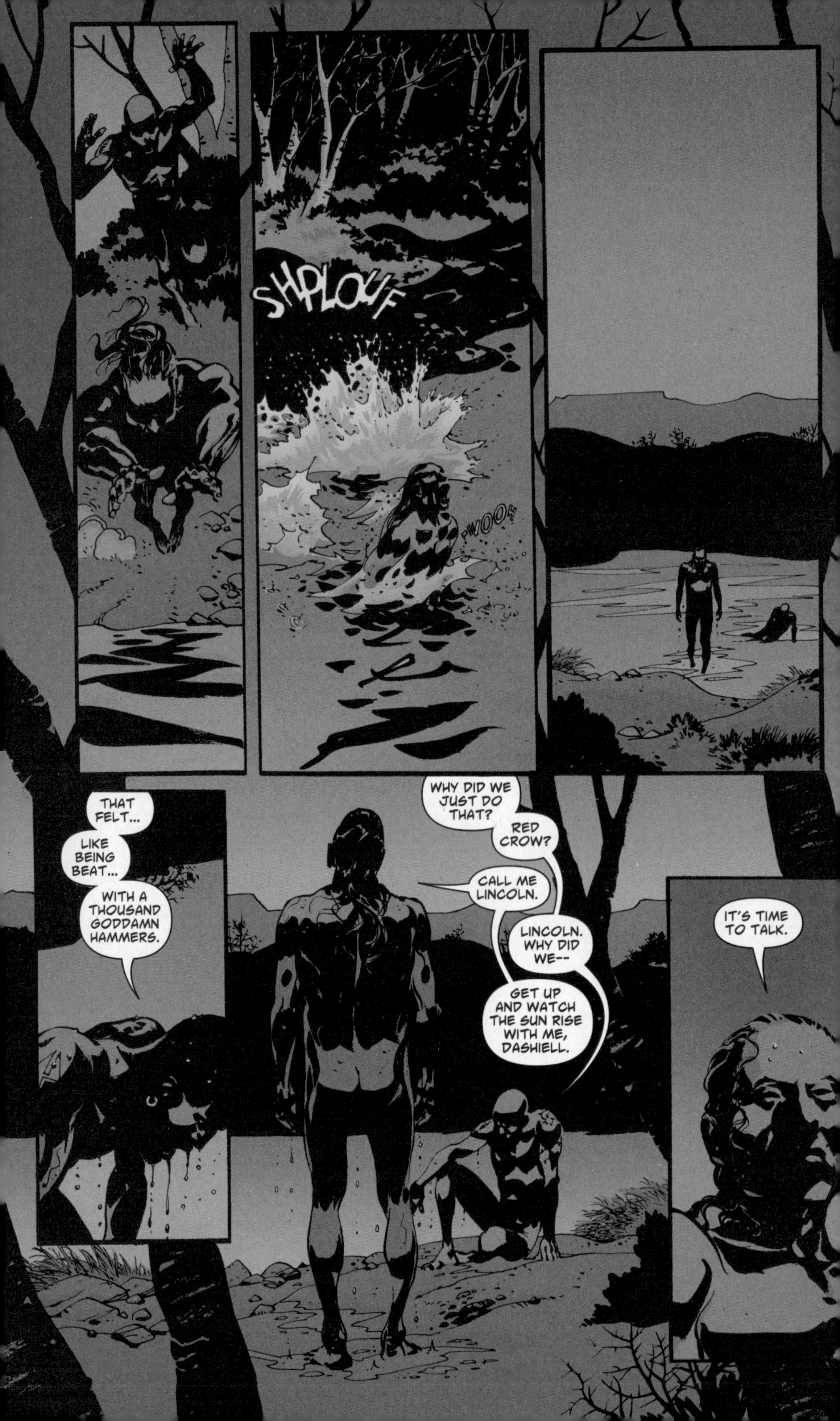
SHPLOUF
PWOOH
THAT FELT...
LIKE BEING BEAT...
WITH A THOUSAND GODDAMN HAMMERS.
WHY DID WE JUST DO THAT?
RED CROW?
CALL ME LINCOLN.
LINCOLN. WHY DID WE--
GET UP AND WATCH THE SUN RISE WITH ME, DASHIELL.
IT'S TIME TO TALK.

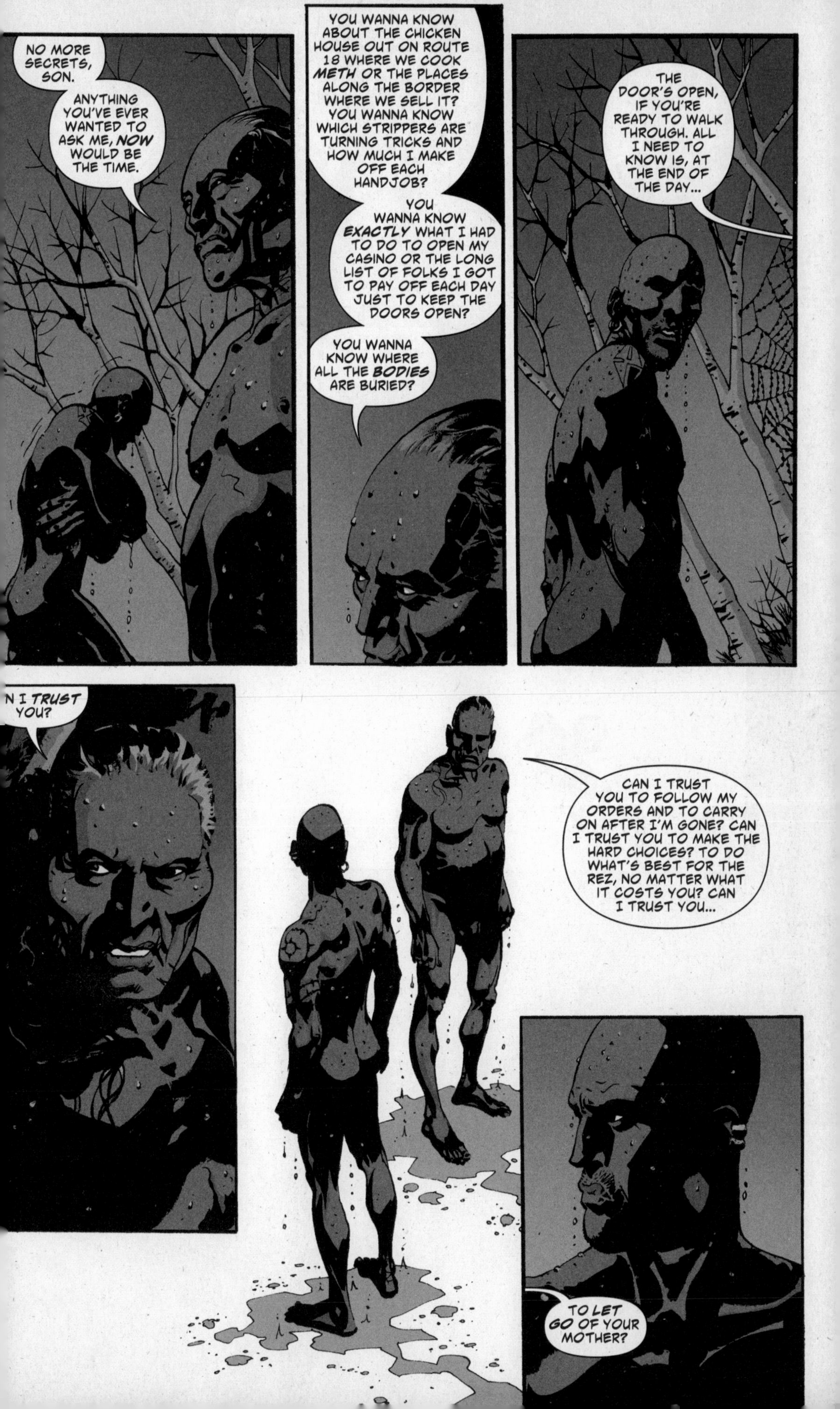
NO MORE SECRETS, SON.
ANYTHING YOU'VE EVER WANTED TO ASK ME, NOW WOULD BE THE TIME.
YOU WANNA KNOW ABOUT THE CHICKEN HOUSE OUT ON ROUTE 18 WHERE WE COOK METH OR THE PLACES ALONG THE BORDER WHERE WE SELL IT? YOU WANNA KNOW WHICH STRIPPERS ARE TURNING TRICKS AND HOW MUCH I MAKE OFF EACH HANDJOB?
YOU WANNA KNOW EXACTLY WHAT I HAD TO DO TO OPEN MY CASINO OR THE LONG LIST OF FOLKS I GOT TO PAY OFF EACH DAY JUST TO KEEP THE DOORS OPEN?
YOU WANNA KNOW WHERE ALL THE BODIES ARE BURIED?
THE DOOR'S OPEN, IF YOU'RE READY TO WALK THROUGH. ALL I NEED TO KNOW IS, AT THE END OF THE DAY...
N I TRUST YOU?
CAN I TRUST YOU TO FOLLOW MY ORDERS AND TO CARRY ON AFTER I'M GONE? CAN I TRUST YOU TO MAKE THE HARD CHOICES? TO DO WHAT'S BEST FOR THE REZ, NO MATTER WHAT IT COSTS YOU? CAN I TRUST YOU...
TO LET GO OF YOUR MOTHER?

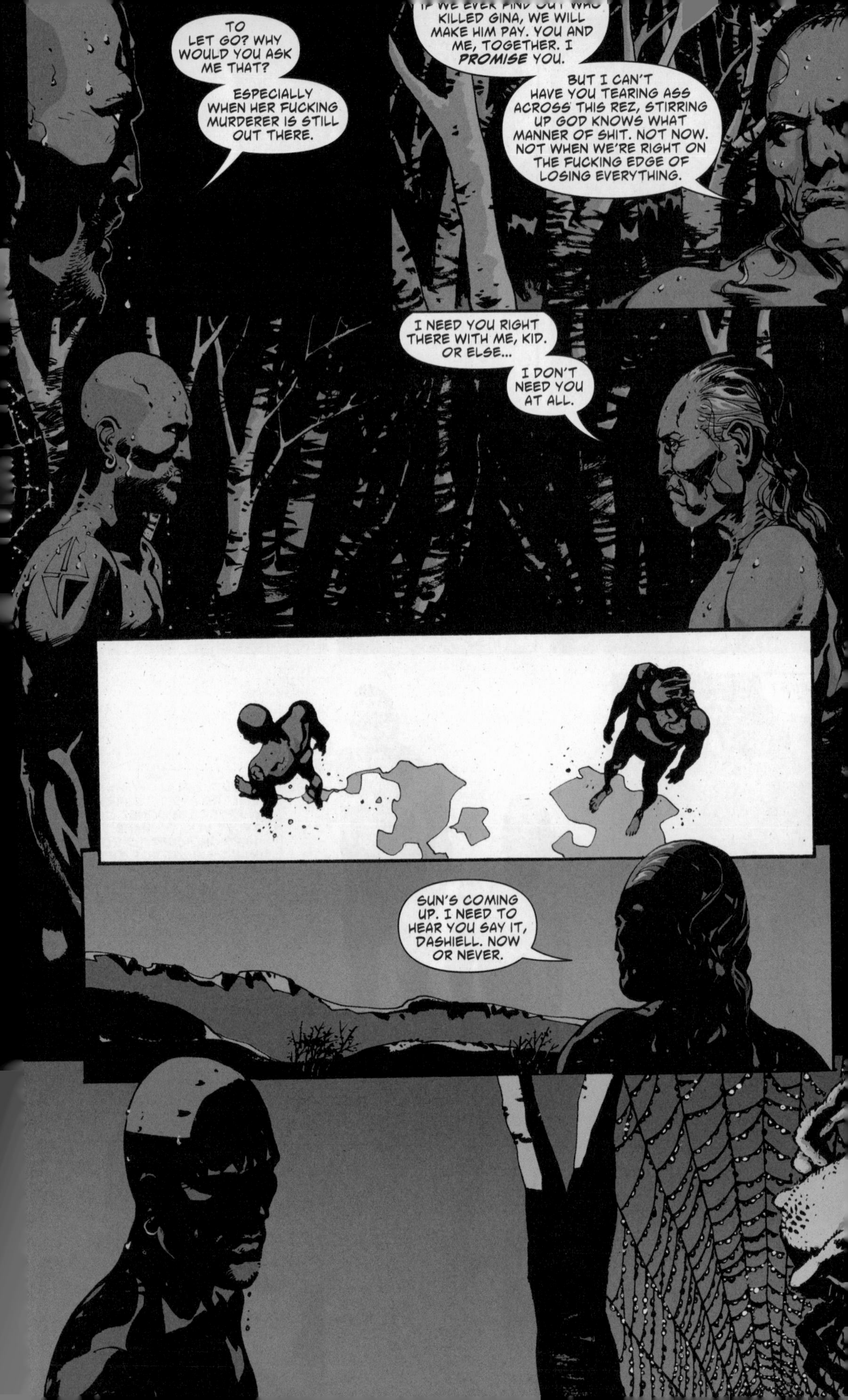
TO LET GO? WHY WOULD YOU ASK ME THAT?
ESPECIALLY WHEN HER FUCKING MURDERER IS STILL OUT THERE.
KILLED GINA, WE WILL MAKE HIM PAY. YOU AND ME, TOGETHER. I PROMISE YOU.
BUT I CAN'T HAVE YOU TEARING ASS ACROSS THIS REZ, STIRRING UP GOD KNOWS WHAT MANNER OF SHIT. NOT NOW. NOT WHEN WE'RE RIGHT ON THE FUCKING EDGE OF LOSING EVERYTHING.
I NEED YOU RIGHT THERE WITH ME, KID. OR ELSE...
I DON'T NEED YOU AT ALL.
SUN'S COMING UP. I NEED TO HEAR YOU SAY IT, DASHIELL. NOW OR NEVER.

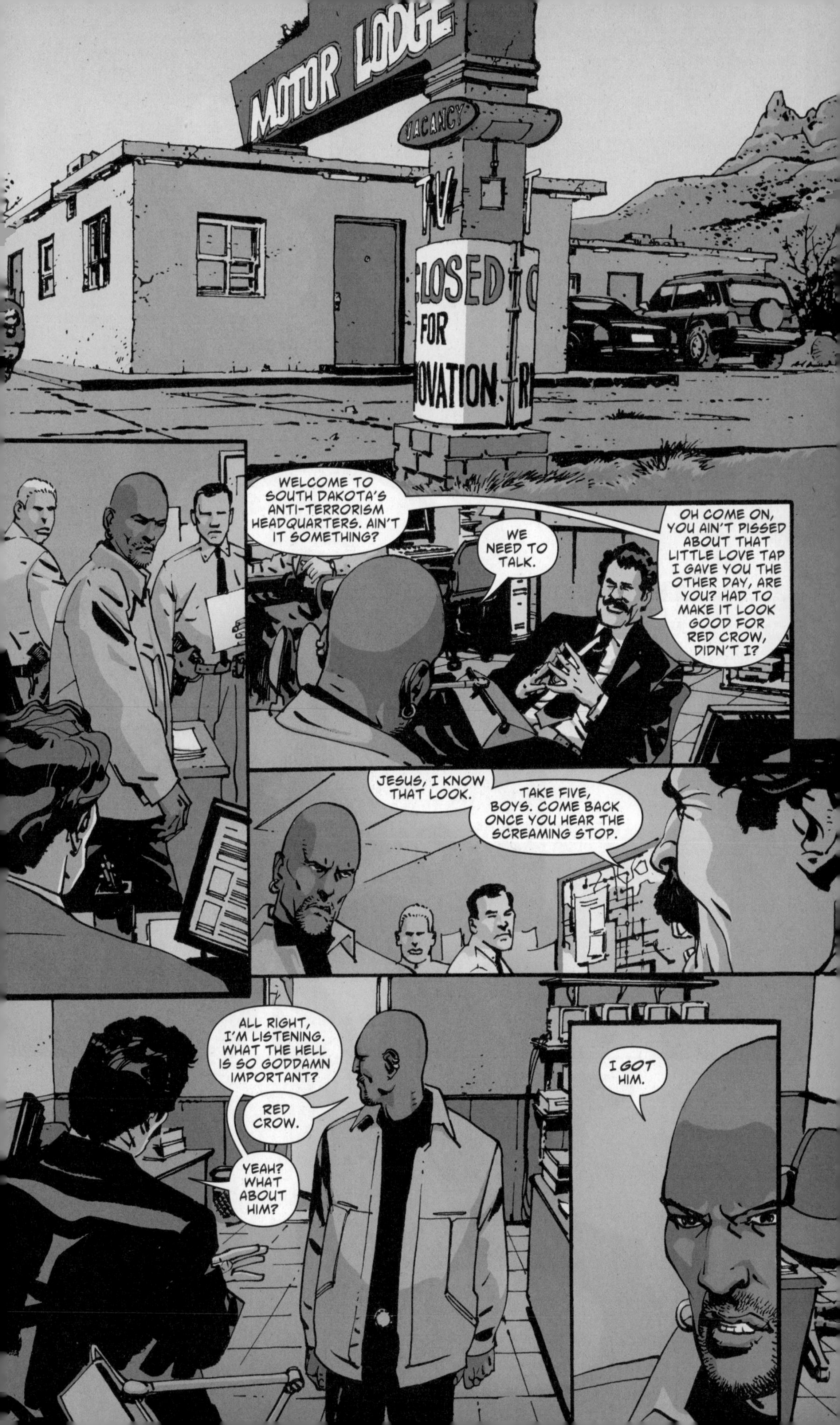
MOTOR LODGE
VACANCY
CLOSED
FOR
OVATION
WELCOME TO SOUTH DAKOTA'S ANTI-TERRORISM HEADQUARTERS. AIN'T IT SOMETHING?
WE NEED TO TALK.
OH COME ON, YOU AIN'T PISSED ABOUT THAT LITTLE LOVE TAP I GAVE YOU THE OTHER DAY, ARE YOU? HAD TO MAKE IT LOOK GOOD FOR RED CROW, DIDN'T I?
JESUS, I KNOW THAT LOOK.
TAKE FIVE, BOYS. COME BACK ONCE YOU HEAR THE SCREAMING STOP.
ALL RIGHT, I'M LISTENING. WHAT THE HELL IS SO GODDAMN IMPORTANT?
RED CROW.
YEAH? WHAT ABOUT HIM?
I GOT HIM.

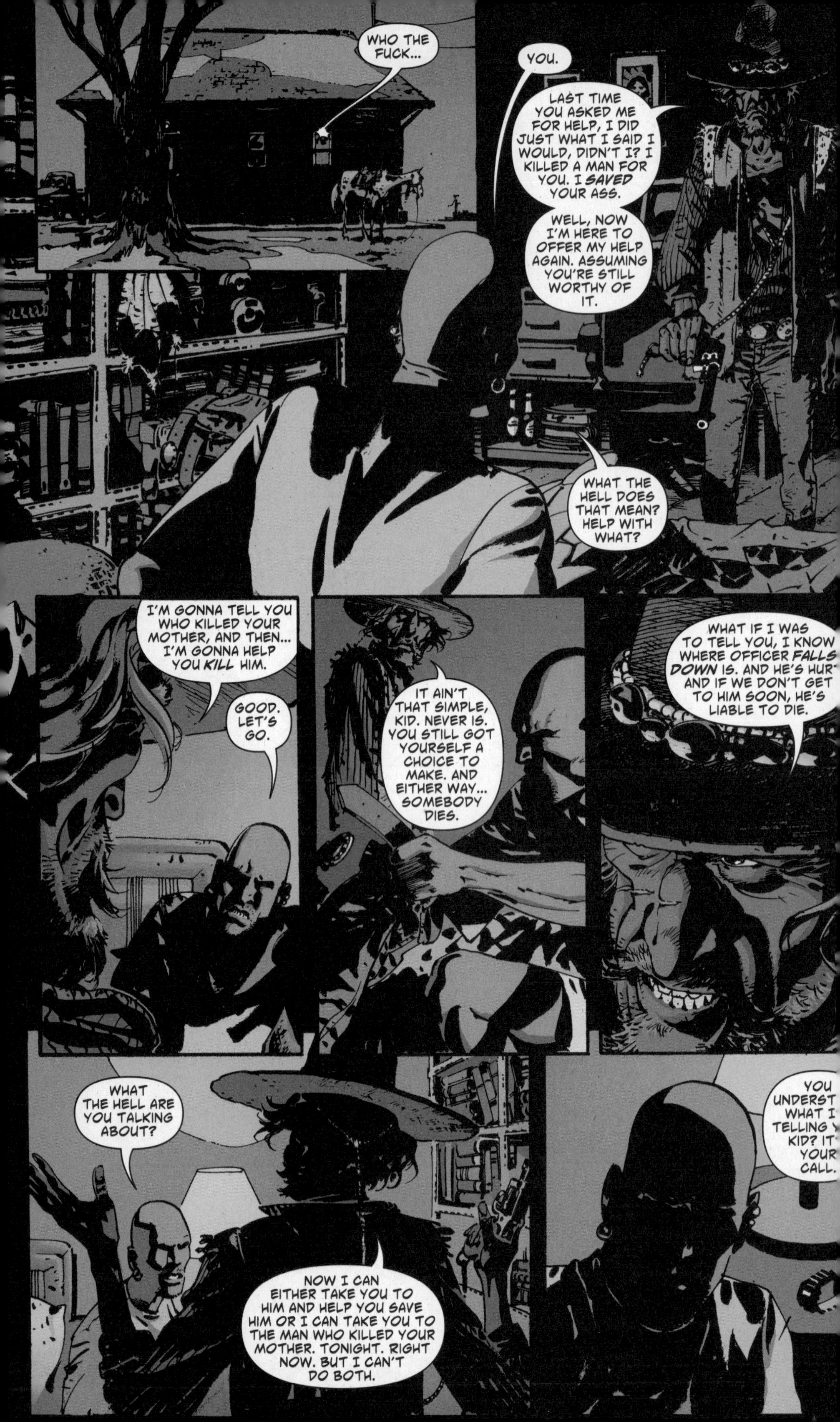
WHO THE FUCK...
YOU.
LAST TIME YOU ASKED ME FOR HELP, I DID JUST WHAT I SAID I WOULD, DIDN'T I? I KILLED A MAN FOR YOU. I SAVED YOUR ASS.
WELL, NOW I'M HERE TO OFFER MY HELP AGAIN. ASSUMING YOU'RE STILL WORTHY OF IT.
WHAT THE HELL DOES THAT MEAN? HELP WITH WHAT?
I'M GONNA TELL YOU WHO KILLED YOUR MOTHER, AND THEN... I'M GONNA HELP YOU KILL HIM.
GOOD. LET'S GO.
IT AIN'T THAT SIMPLE, KID. NEVER IS. YOU STILL GOT YOURSELF A CHOICE TO MAKE. AND EITHER WAY... SOMEBODY DIES.
WHAT IF I WAS TO TELL YOU, I KNOW WHERE OFFICER FALLS DOWN IS. AND HE'S HUR- AND IF WE DON'T GET TO HIM SOON, HE'S LIABLE TO DIE.
WHAT THE HELL ARE YOU TALKING ABOUT?
NOW I CAN EITHER TAKE YOU TO HIM AND HELP YOU SAVE HIM OR I CAN TAKE YOU TO THE MAN WHO KILLED YOUR MOTHER. TONIGHT. RIGHT NOW. BUT I CAN'T DO BOTH.
YOU UNDERST WHAT I TELLING KID? IT YOUR CALL.

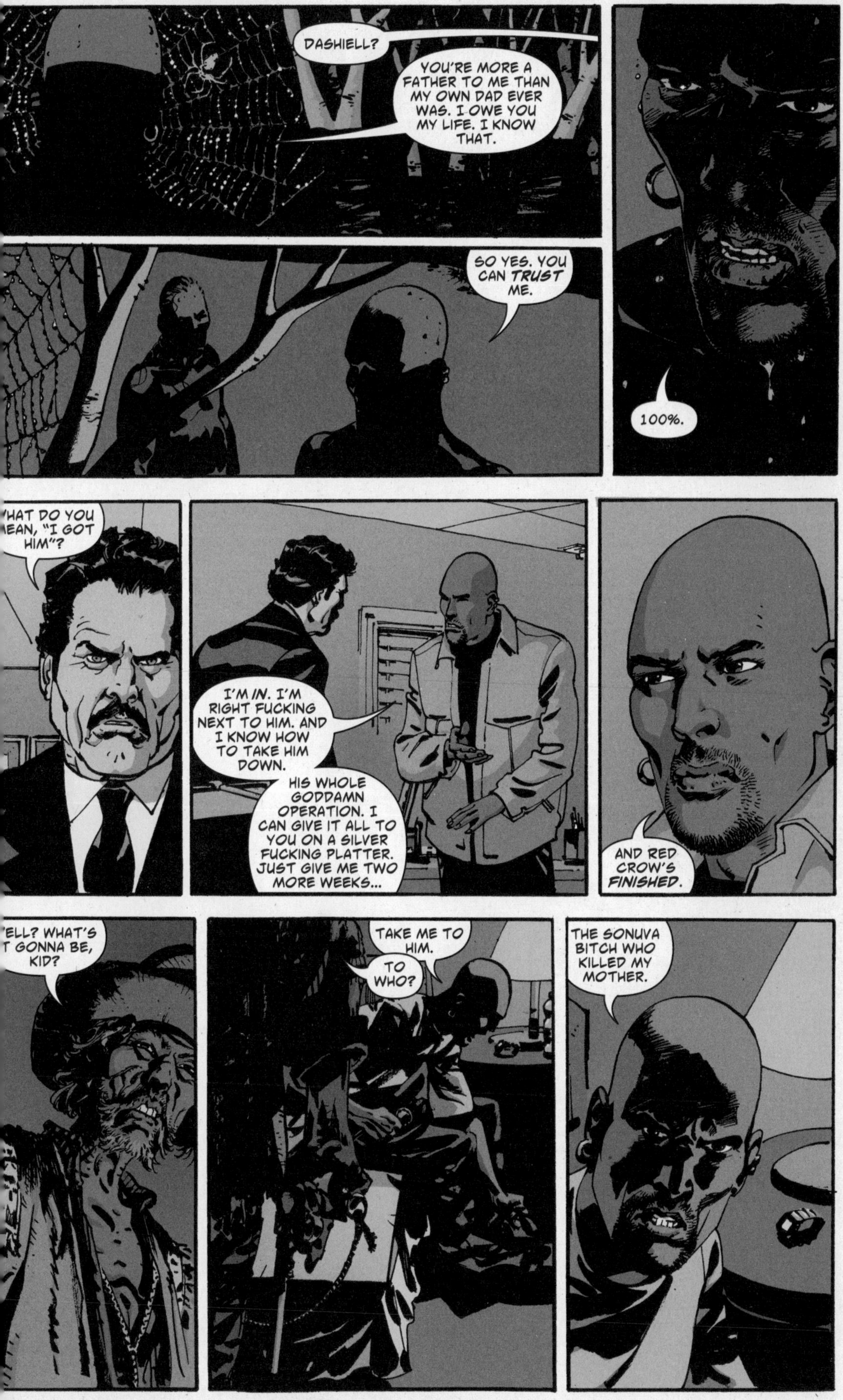
DASHIELL?
YOU'RE MORE A FATHER TO ME THAN MY OWN DAD EVER WAS. I OWE YOU MY LIFE. I KNOW THAT.
SO YES. YOU CAN *TRUST* ME.
100%.
HAT DO YOU EAN, "I GOT HIM"?
I'M *IN*. I'M RIGHT FUCKING NEXT TO HIM. AND I KNOW HOW TO TAKE HIM DOWN.
HIS WHOLE GODDAMN OPERATION. I CAN GIVE IT ALL TO YOU ON A SILVER FUCKING PLATTER. JUST GIVE ME TWO MORE WEEKS...
AND RED CROW'S *FINISHED*.
ELL? WHAT'S T GONNA BE, KID?
TAKE ME TO HIM.
TO WHO?
THE SONUVA BITCH WHO KILLED MY MOTHER.

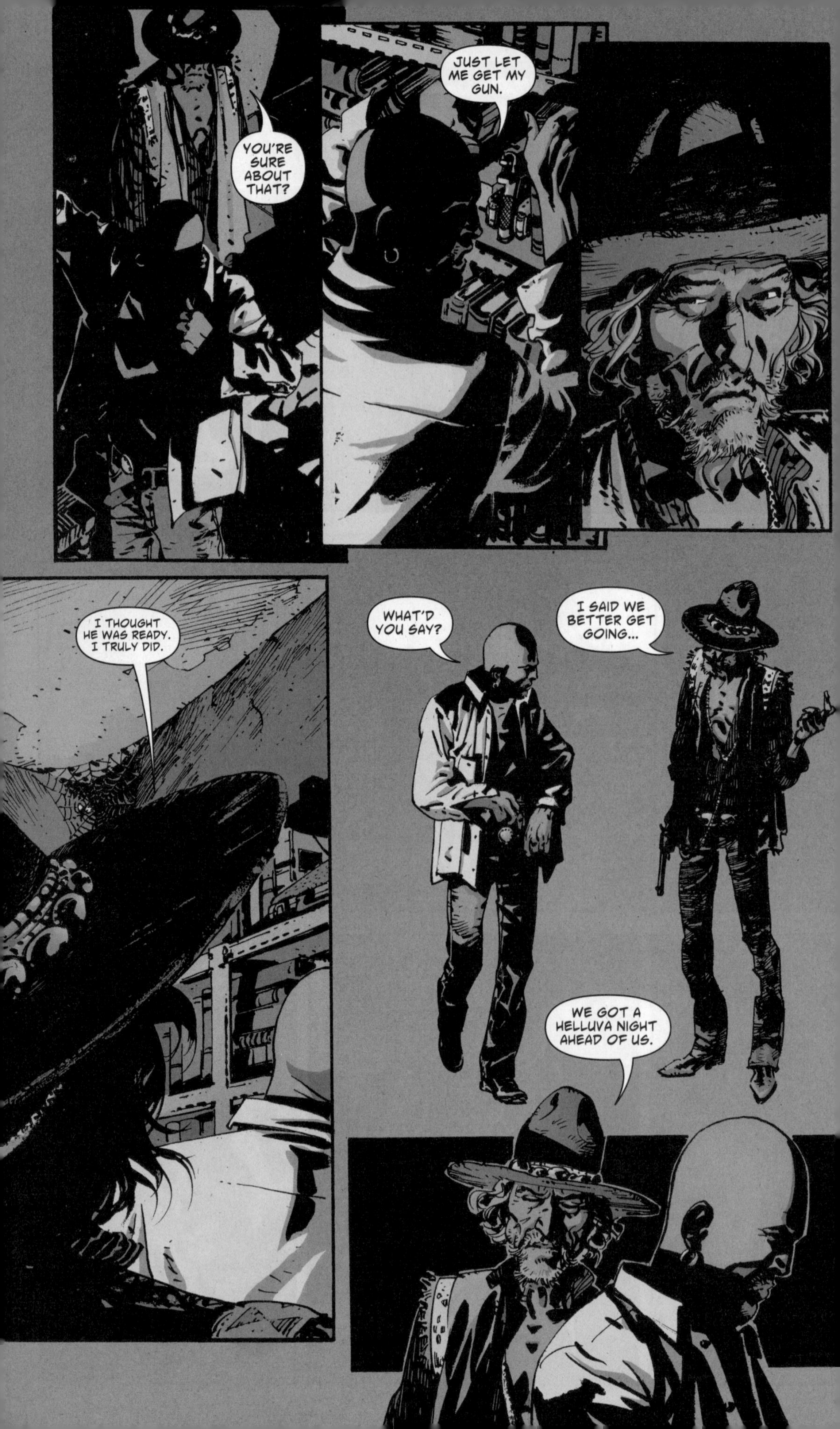

YOU'RE SURE ABOUT THAT?
JUST LET ME GET MY GUN.
I THOUGHT HE WAS READY. I TRULY DID.
WHAT'D YOU SAY?
I SAID WE BETTER GET GOING...
WE GOT A HELLUVA NIGHT AHEAD OF US.

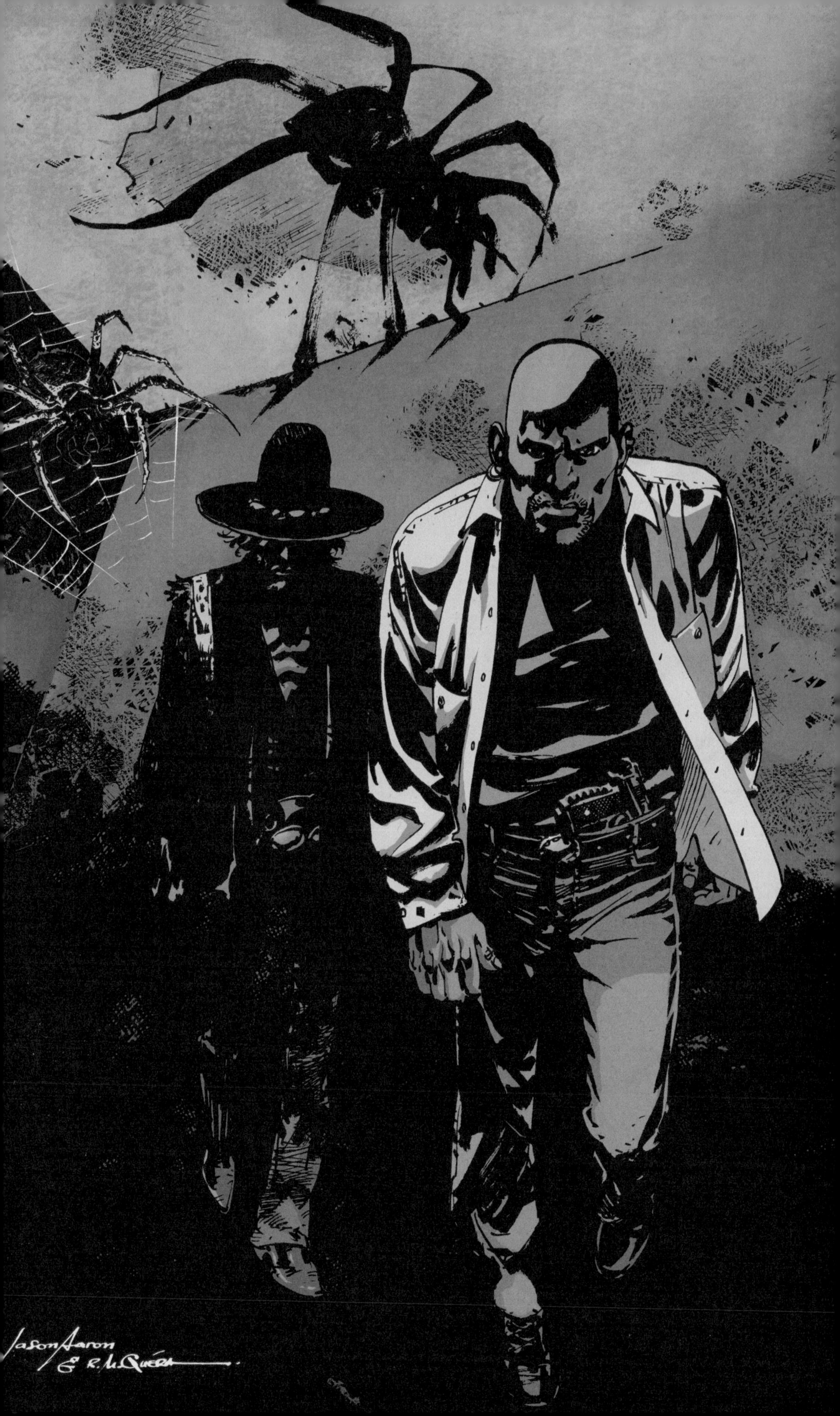
Jason Aaron
R. M. Guéra

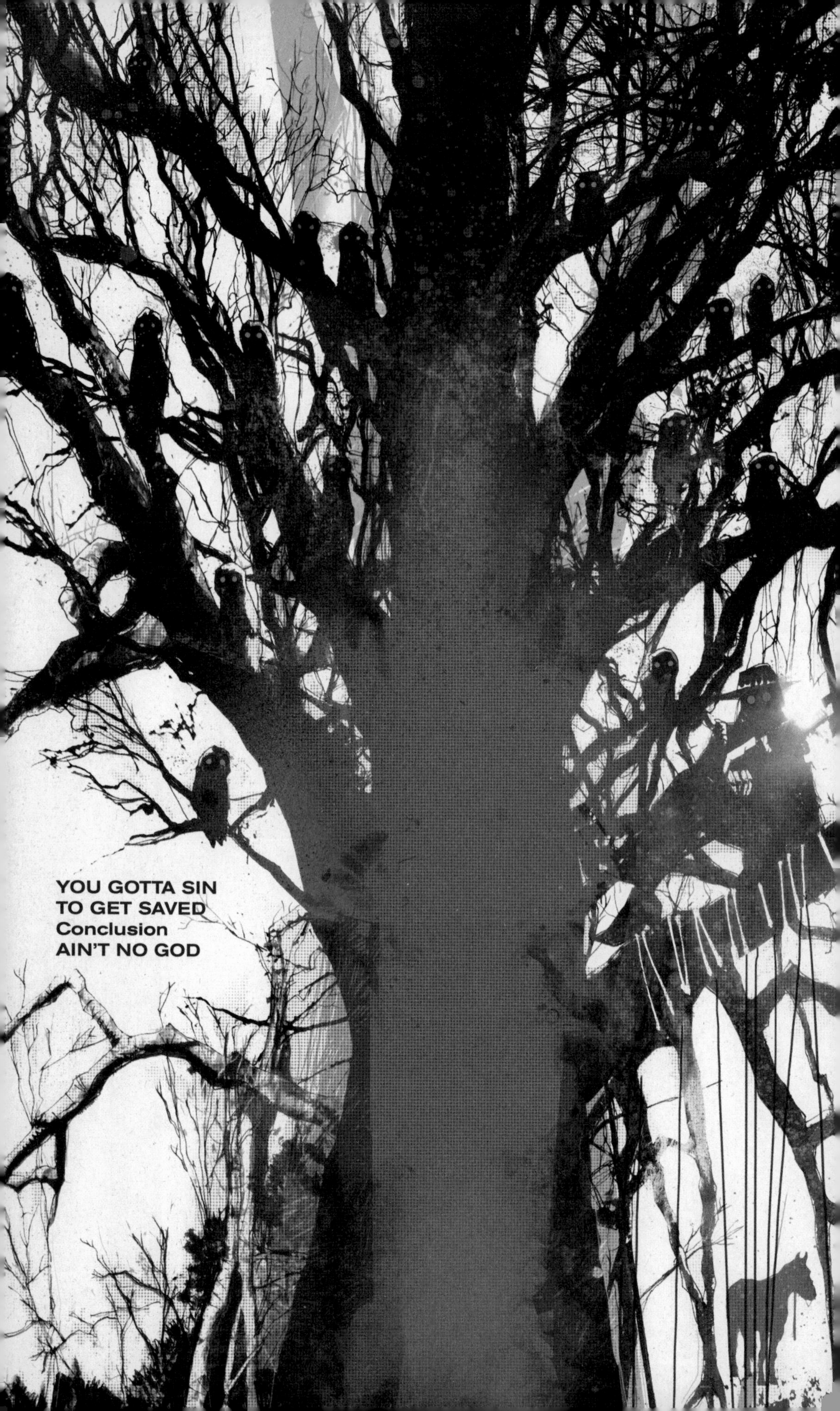
YOU GOTTA SIN
TO GET SAVED
Conclusion
AIN'T NO GOD

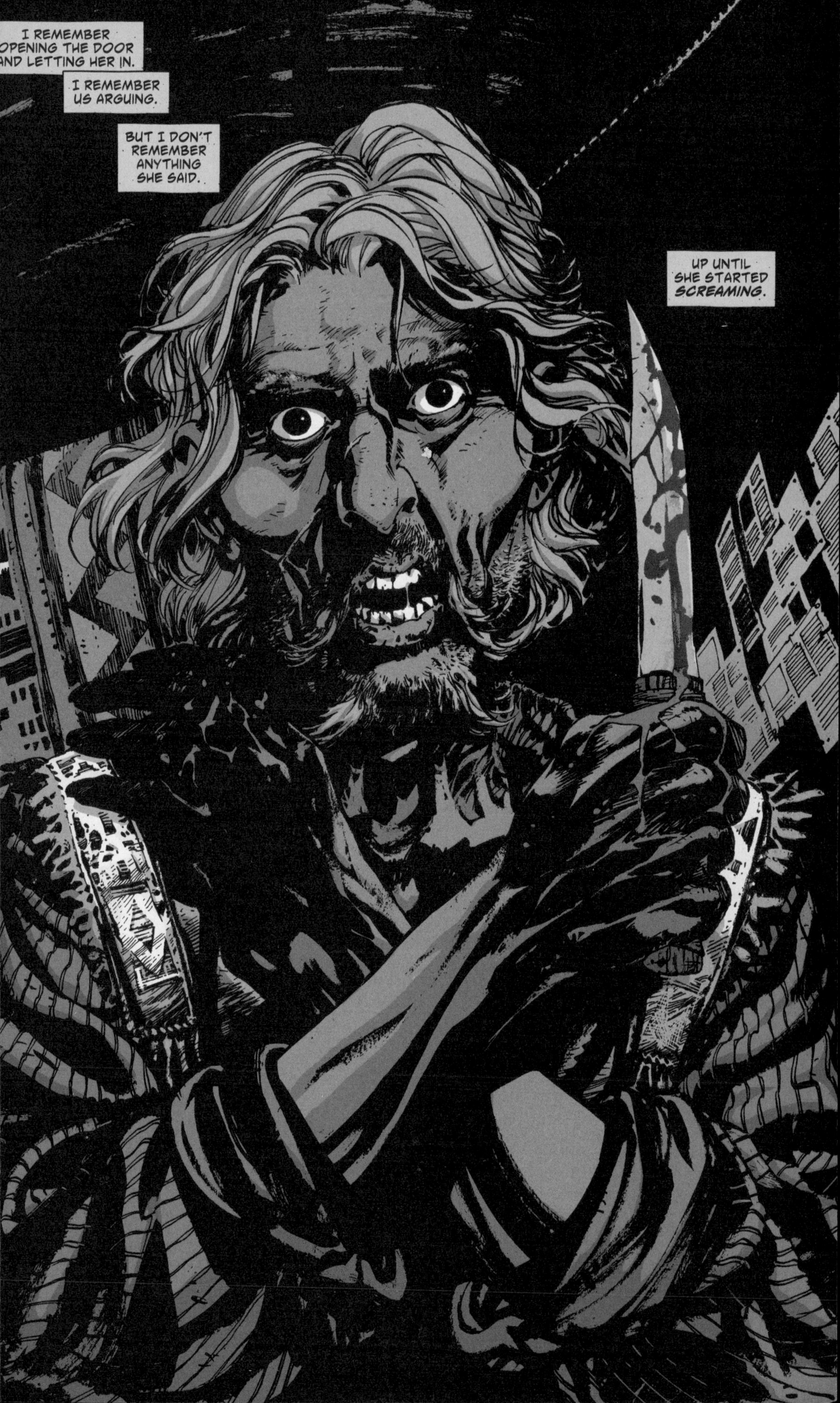
I REMEMBER OPENING THE DOOR AND LETTING HER IN.
I REMEMBER US ARGUING.
BUT I DON'T REMEMBER ANYTHING SHE SAID.
UP UNTIL SHE STARTED *SCREAMING*.

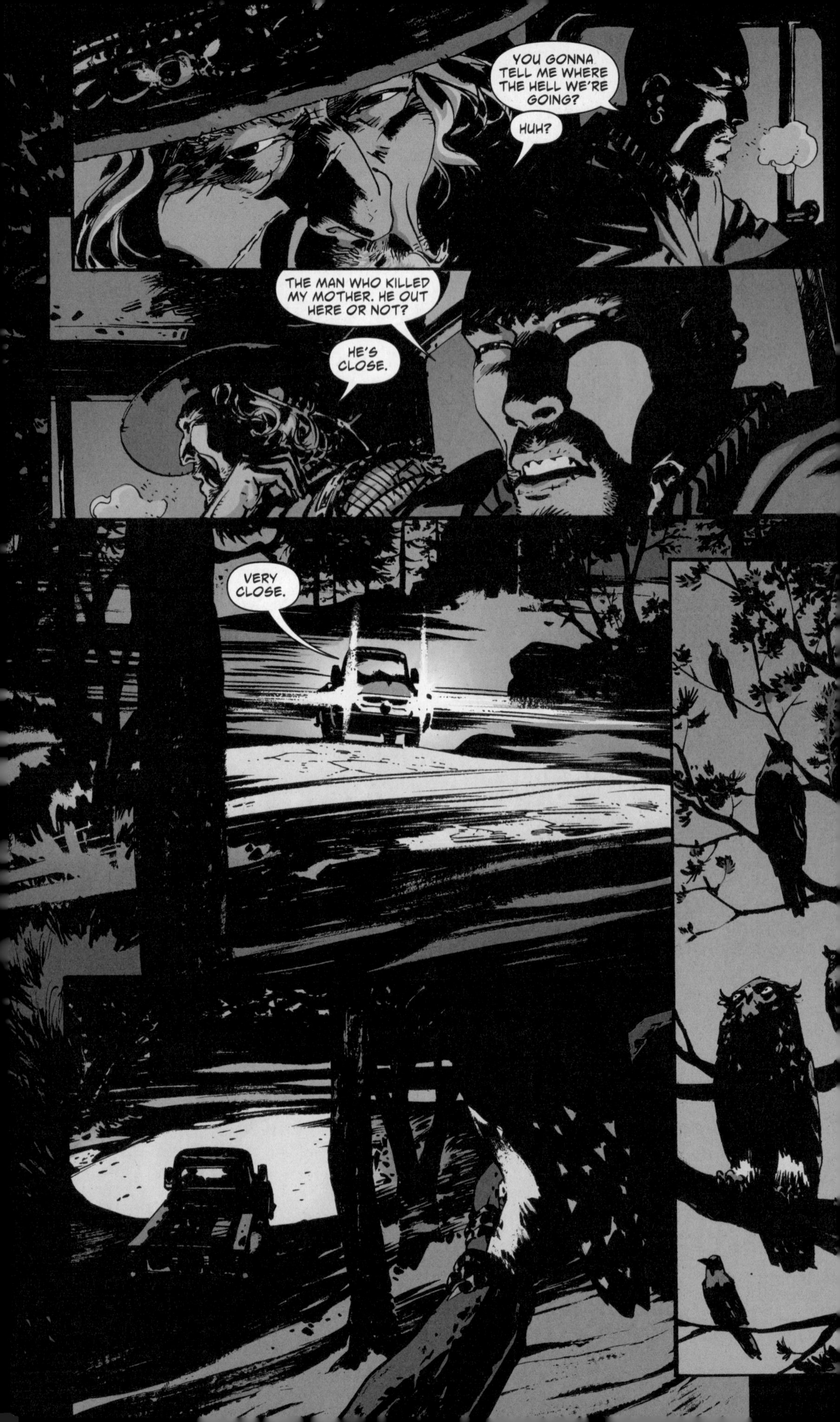
YOU GONNA TELL ME WHERE THE HELL WE'RE GOING?
HUH?
THE MAN WHO KILLED MY MOTHER. HE OUT HERE OR NOT?
HE'S CLOSE.
VERY CLOSE.

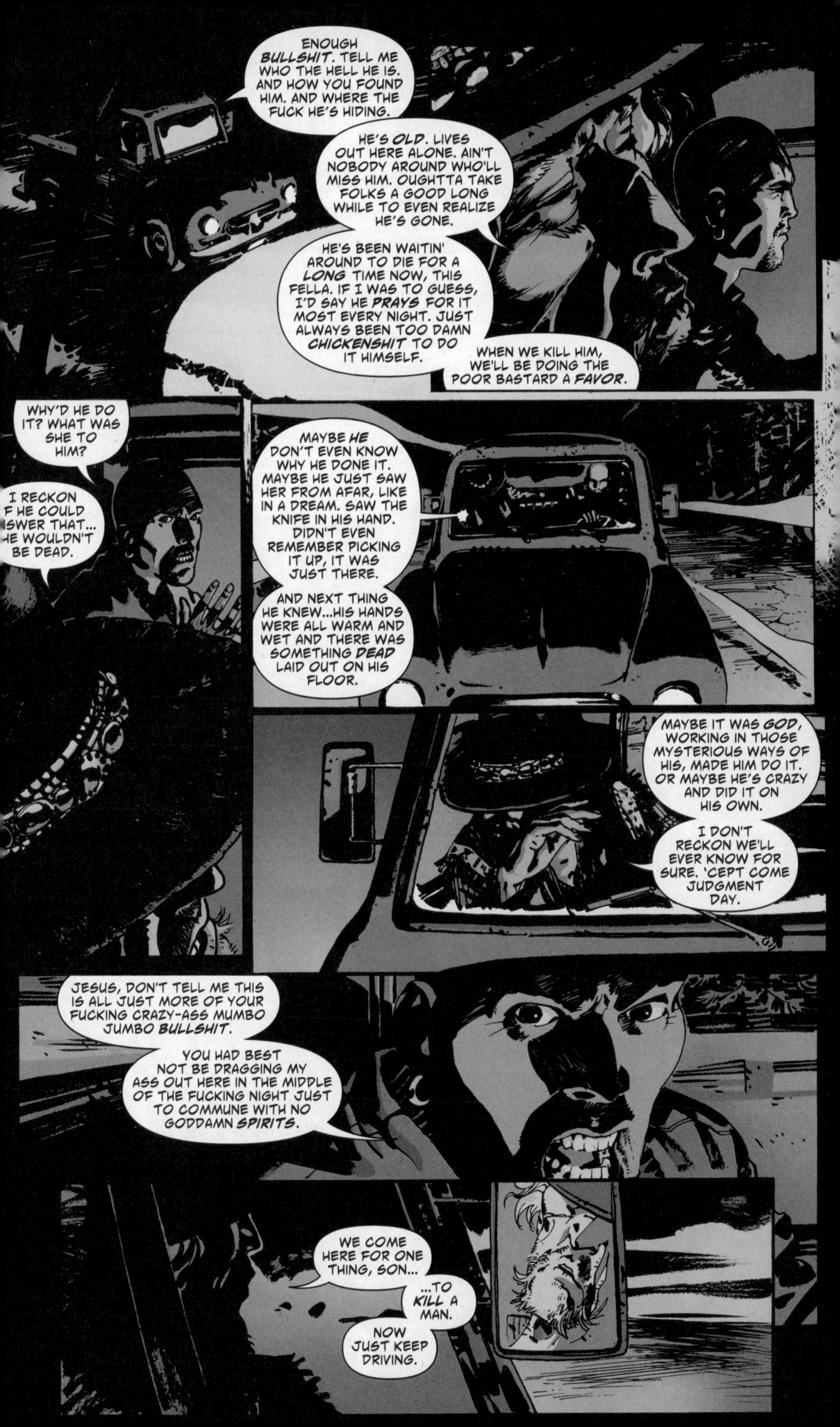
ENOUGH BULLSHIT. TELL ME WHO THE HELL HE IS. AND HOW YOU FOUND HIM. AND WHERE THE FUCK HE'S HIDING.
HE'S OLD. LIVES OUT HERE ALONE. AIN'T NOBODY AROUND WHO'LL MISS HIM. OUGHTTA TAKE FOLKS A GOOD LONG WHILE TO EVEN REALIZE HE'S GONE.
HE'S BEEN WAITIN' AROUND TO DIE FOR A LONG TIME NOW, THIS FELLA. IF I WAS TO GUESS, I'D SAY HE PRAYS FOR IT MOST EVERY NIGHT. JUST ALWAYS BEEN TOO DAMN CHICKENSHIT TO DO IT HIMSELF.
WHEN WE KILL HIM, WE'LL BE DOING THE POOR BASTARD A FAVOR.
WHY'D HE DO IT? WHAT WAS SHE TO HIM?
I RECKON F HE COULD SWER THAT... HE WOULDN'T BE DEAD.
MAYBE HE DON'T EVEN KNOW WHY HE DONE IT. MAYBE HE JUST SAW HER FROM AFAR, LIKE IN A DREAM. SAW THE KNIFE IN HIS HAND. DIDN'T EVEN REMEMBER PICKING IT UP, IT WAS JUST THERE.
AND NEXT THING HE KNEW...HIS HANDS WERE ALL WARM AND WET AND THERE WAS SOMETHING DEAD LAID OUT ON HIS FLOOR.
MAYBE IT WAS GOD, WORKING IN THOSE MYSTERIOUS WAYS OF HIS, MADE HIM DO IT. OR MAYBE HE'S CRAZY AND DID IT ON HIS OWN.
I DON'T RECKON WE'LL EVER KNOW FOR SURE. 'CEPT COME JUDGMENT DAY.
JESUS, DON'T TELL ME THIS IS ALL JUST MORE OF YOUR FUCKING CRAZY-ASS MUMBO JUMBO BULLSHIT.
YOU HAD BEST NOT BE DRAGGING MY ASS OUT HERE IN THE MIDDLE OF THE FUCKING NIGHT JUST TO COMMUNE WITH NO GODDAMN SPIRITS.
WE COME HERE FOR ONE THING, SON...
...TO KILL A MAN.
NOW JUST KEEP DRIVING.

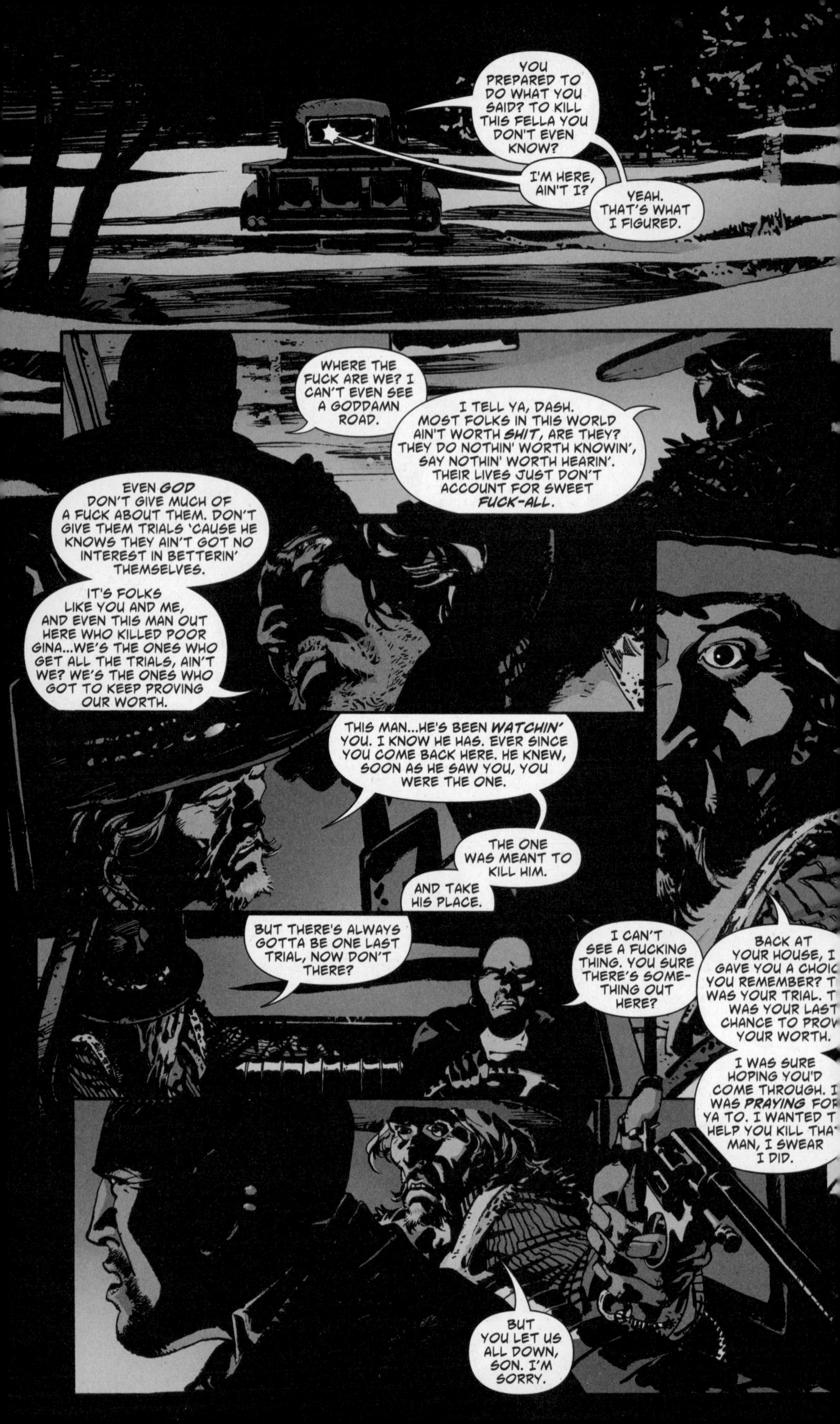

YOU PREPARED TO DO WHAT YOU SAID? TO KILL THIS FELLA YOU DON'T EVEN KNOW?
I'M HERE, AIN'T I?
YEAH. THAT'S WHAT I FIGURED.
WHERE THE FUCK ARE WE? I CAN'T EVEN SEE A GODDAMN ROAD.
I TELL YA, DASH. MOST FOLKS IN THIS WORLD AIN'T WORTH *SHIT*, ARE THEY? THEY DO NOTHIN' WORTH KNOWIN', SAY NOTHIN' WORTH HEARIN'. THEIR LIVES JUST DON'T ACCOUNT FOR SWEET *FUCK-ALL*.
EVEN *GOD* DON'T GIVE MUCH OF A FUCK ABOUT THEM. DON'T GIVE THEM TRIALS 'CAUSE HE KNOWS THEY AIN'T GOT NO INTEREST IN BETTERIN' THEMSELVES.
IT'S FOLKS LIKE YOU AND ME, AND EVEN THIS MAN OUT HERE WHO KILLED POOR GINA...WE'S THE ONES WHO GET ALL THE TRIALS, AIN'T WE? WE'S THE ONES WHO GOT TO KEEP PROVING OUR WORTH.
THIS MAN...HE'S BEEN *WATCHIN'* YOU. I KNOW HE HAS. EVER SINCE YOU COME BACK HERE. HE KNEW, SOON AS HE SAW YOU, YOU WERE THE ONE.
THE ONE WAS MEANT TO KILL HIM.
AND TAKE HIS PLACE.
BUT THERE'S ALWAYS GOTTA BE ONE LAST TRIAL, NOW DON'T THERE?
I CAN'T SEE A FUCKING THING. YOU SURE THERE'S SOME-THING OUT HERE?
BUT YOU LET US ALL DOWN, SON. I'M SORRY.

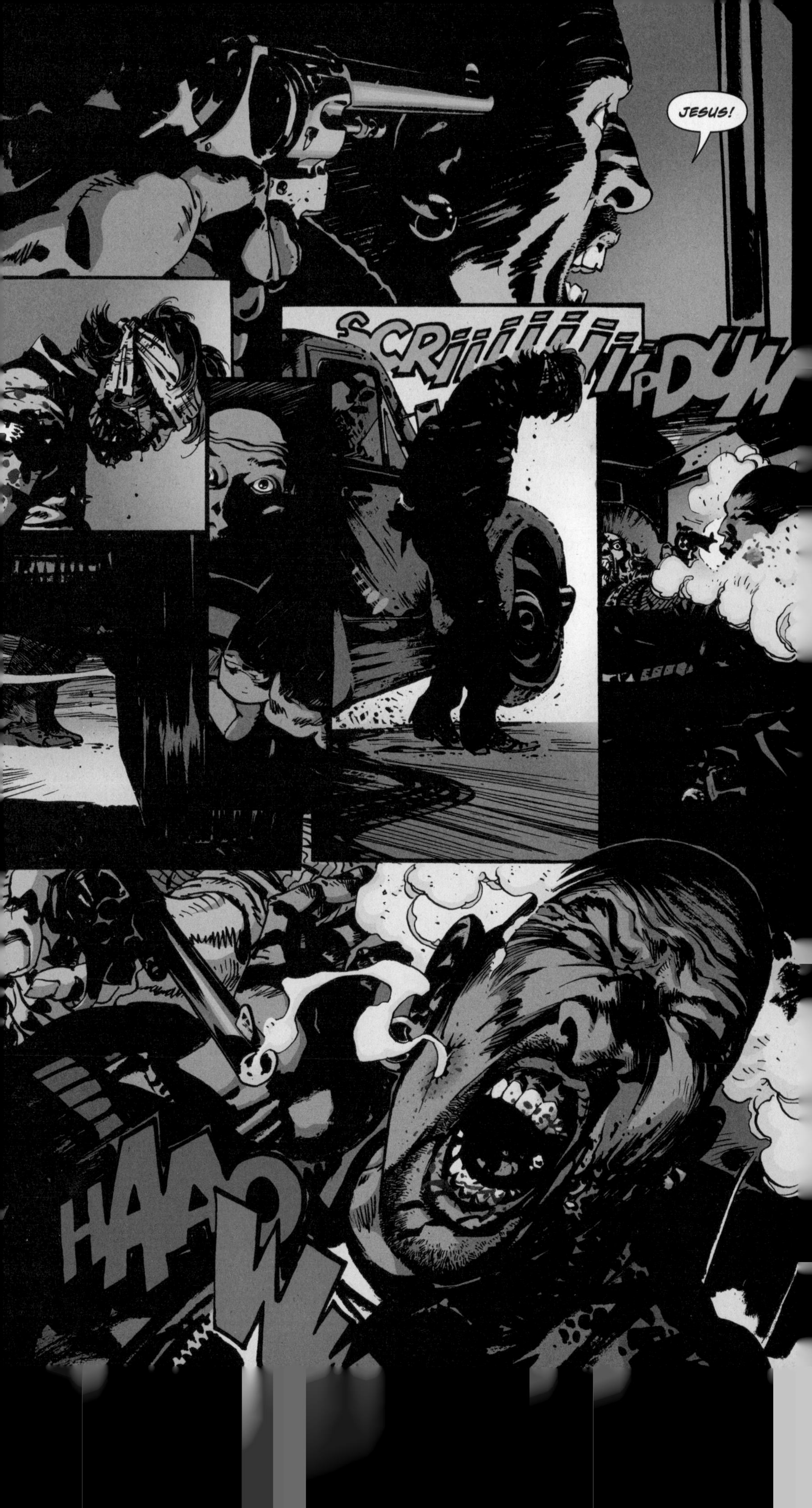
JESUS!

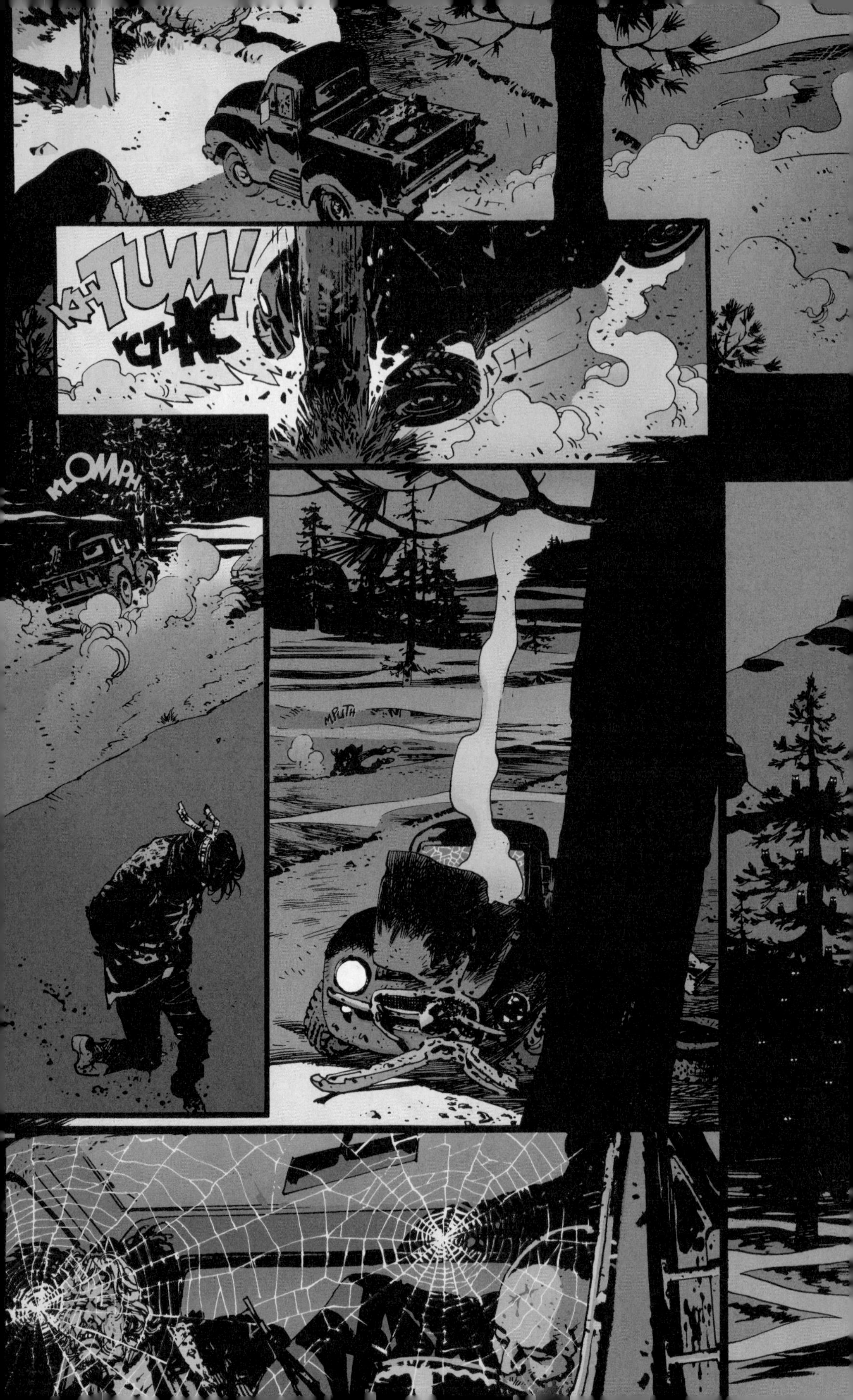
KA-TUNK!
K'CHAK
KLOMPH
MPUTH

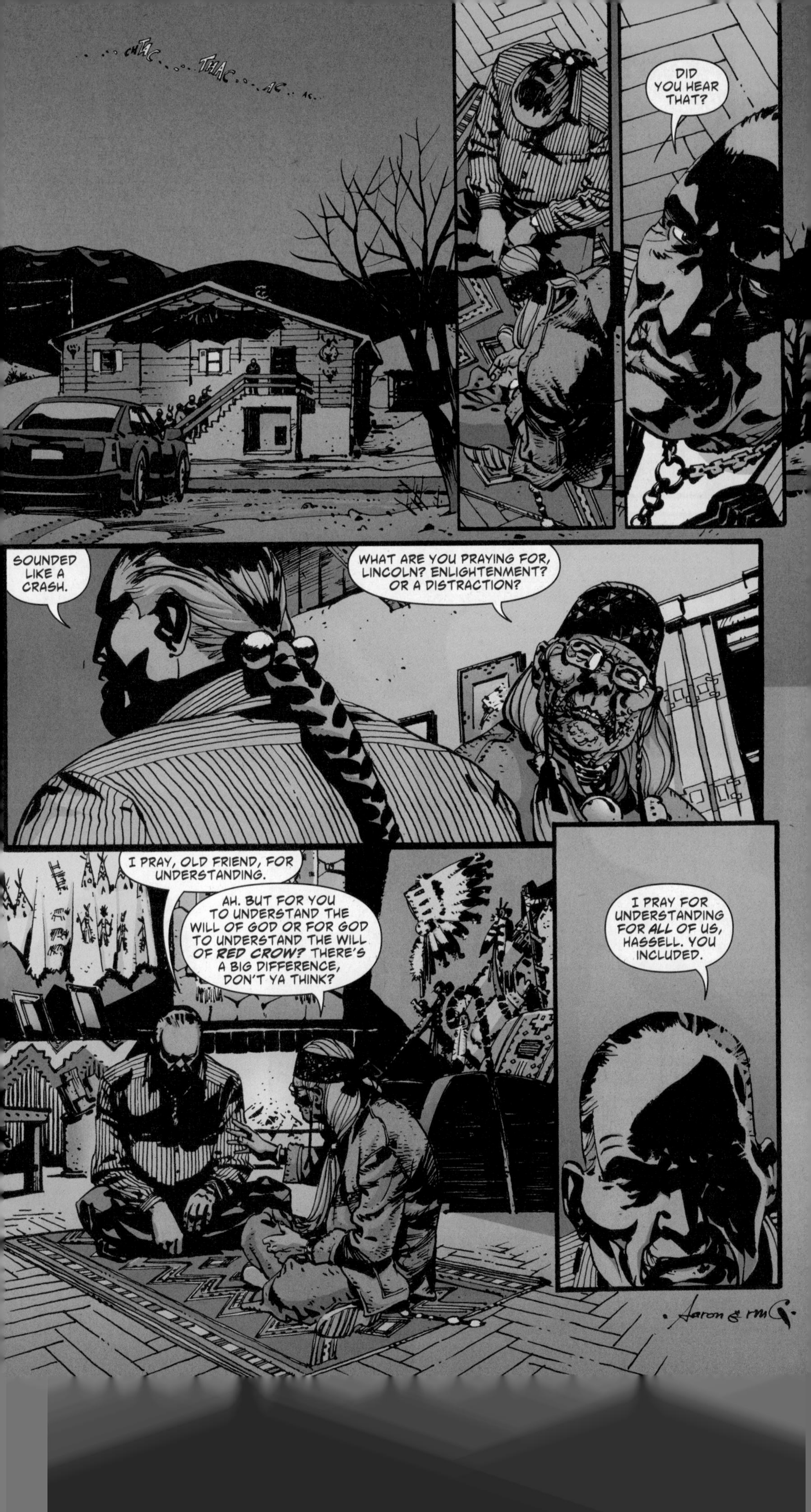
...CHTAC...THAC...AC..AC..
DID YOU HEAR THAT?
SOUNDED LIKE A CRASH.
WHAT ARE YOU PRAYING FOR, LINCOLN? ENLIGHTENMENT? OR A DISTRACTION?
I PRAY, OLD FRIEND, FOR UNDERSTANDING.
AH. BUT FOR YOU TO UNDERSTAND THE WILL OF GOD OR FOR GOD TO UNDERSTAND THE WILL OF RED CROW? THERE'S A BIG DIFFERENCE, DON'T YA THINK?
I PRAY FOR UNDERSTANDING FOR ALL OF US, HASSELL. YOU INCLUDED.
Aaron & rmG

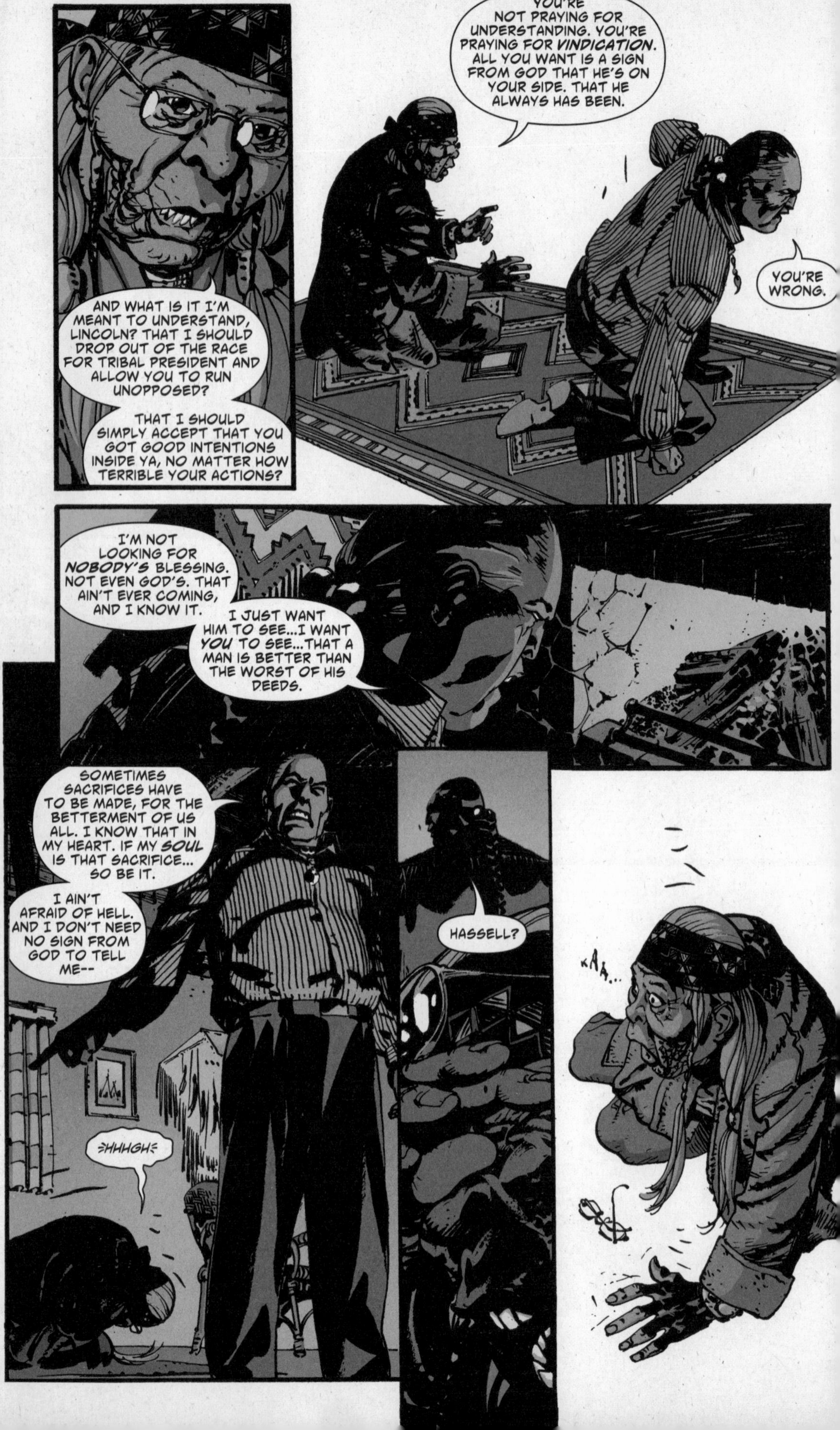
AND WHAT IS IT I'M MEANT TO UNDERSTAND, LINCOLN? THAT I SHOULD DROP OUT OF THE RACE FOR TRIBAL PRESIDENT AND ALLOW YOU TO RUN UNOPPOSED?
THAT I SHOULD SIMPLY ACCEPT THAT YOU GOT GOOD INTENTIONS INSIDE YA, NO MATTER HOW TERRIBLE YOUR ACTIONS?
YOU'RE NOT PRAYING FOR UNDERSTANDING. YOU'RE PRAYING FOR VINDICATION. ALL YOU WANT IS A SIGN FROM GOD THAT HE'S ON YOUR SIDE. THAT HE ALWAYS HAS BEEN.
YOU'RE WRONG.
I'M NOT LOOKING FOR NOBODY'S BLESSING. NOT EVEN GOD'S. THAT AIN'T EVER COMING, AND I KNOW IT.
I JUST WANT HIM TO SEE...I WANT YOU TO SEE...THAT A MAN IS BETTER THAN THE WORST OF HIS DEEDS.
SOMETIMES SACRIFICES HAVE TO BE MADE, FOR THE BETTERMENT OF US ALL. I KNOW THAT IN MY HEART. IF MY SOUL IS THAT SACRIFICE... SO BE IT.
I AIN'T AFRAID OF HELL. AND I DON'T NEED NO SIGN FROM GOD TO TELL ME--
HHHGH
HASSELL?
KAA...

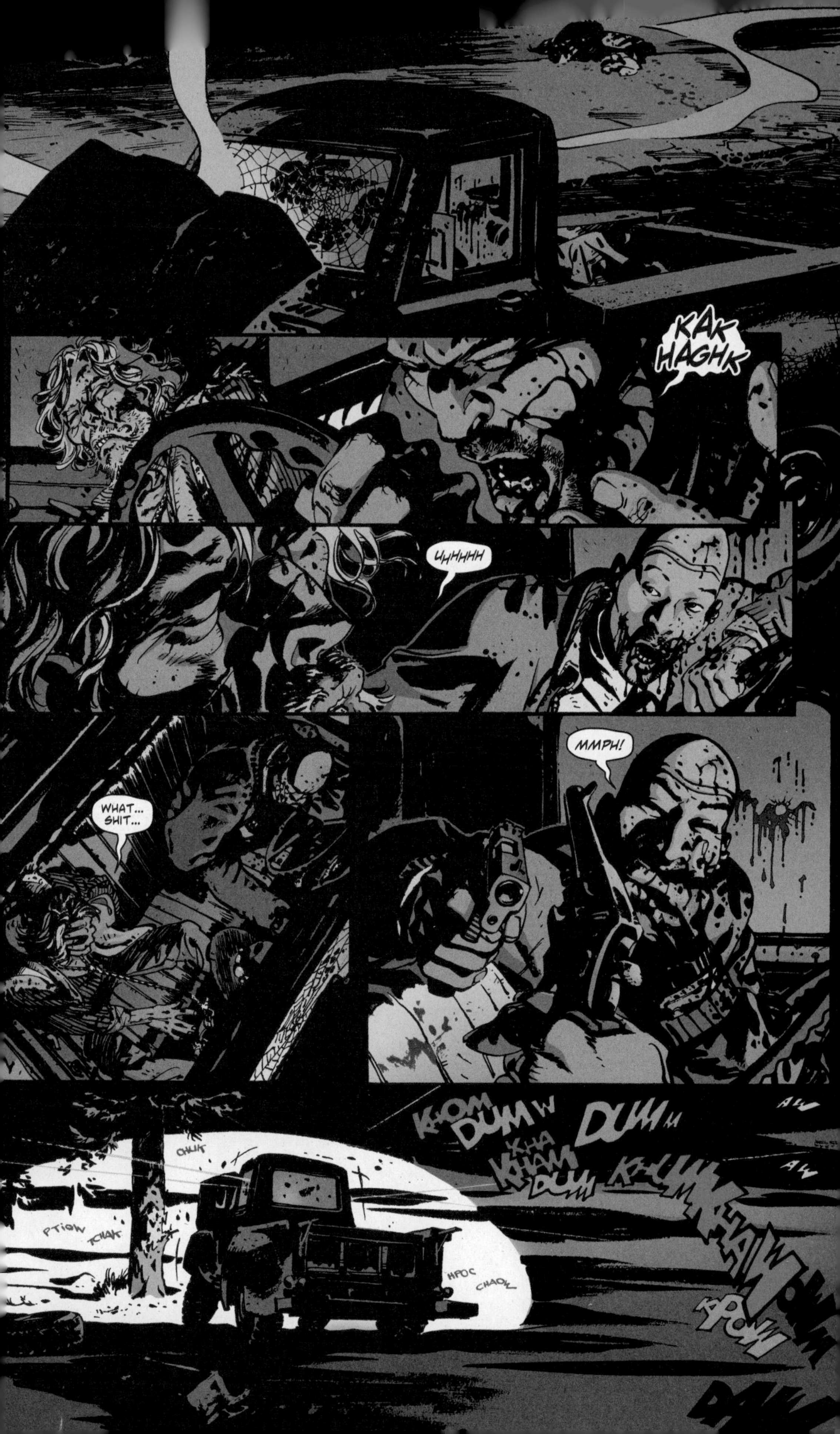
KAK HAGHK
UHHHHH
WHAT... SHIT...
MMPH!
CHUK
PTIOW
TCHAK
HPOC
CHAOW
DUMM
KHA
KHAM
AW
AW
KPOW

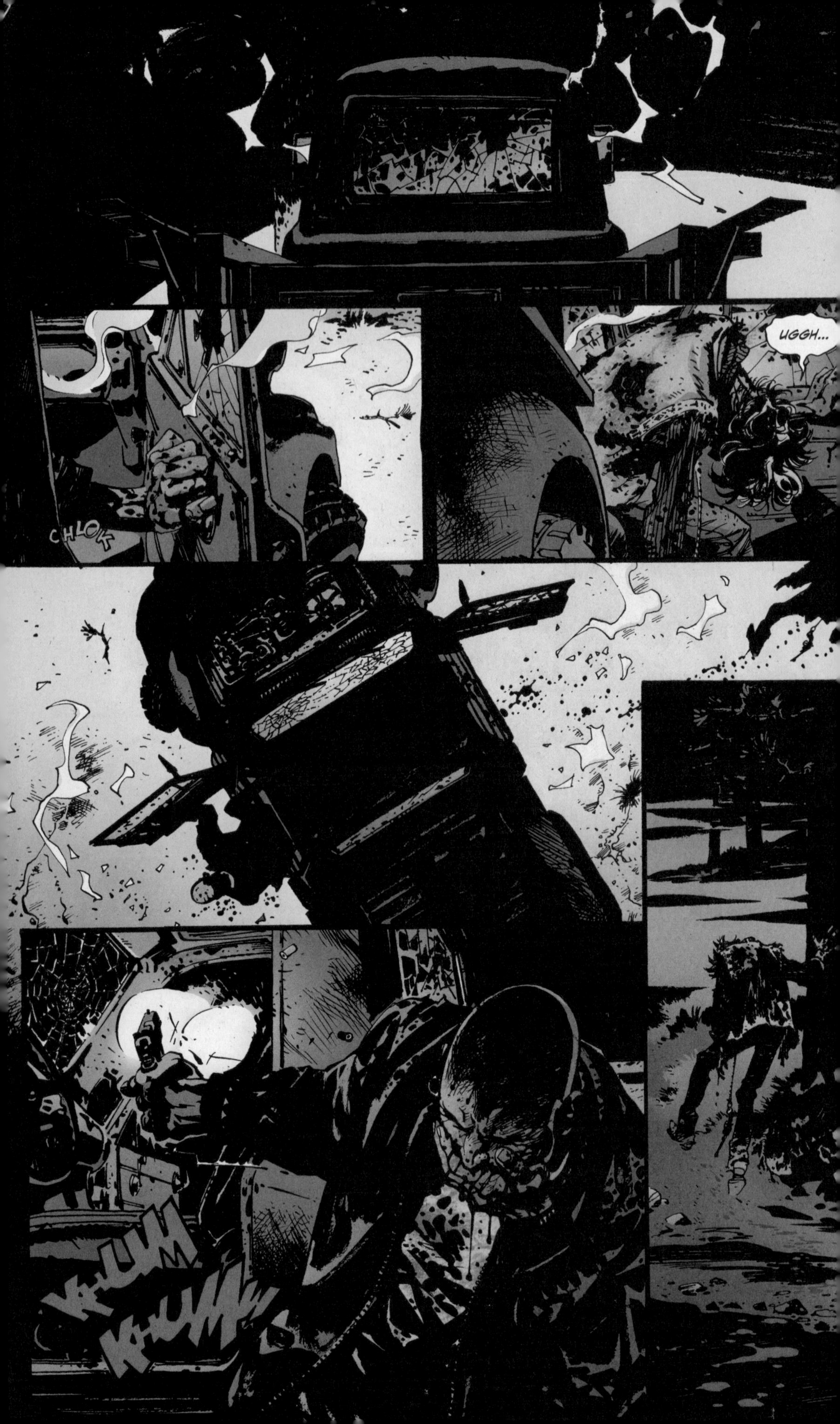
CHLOK
UGGH...

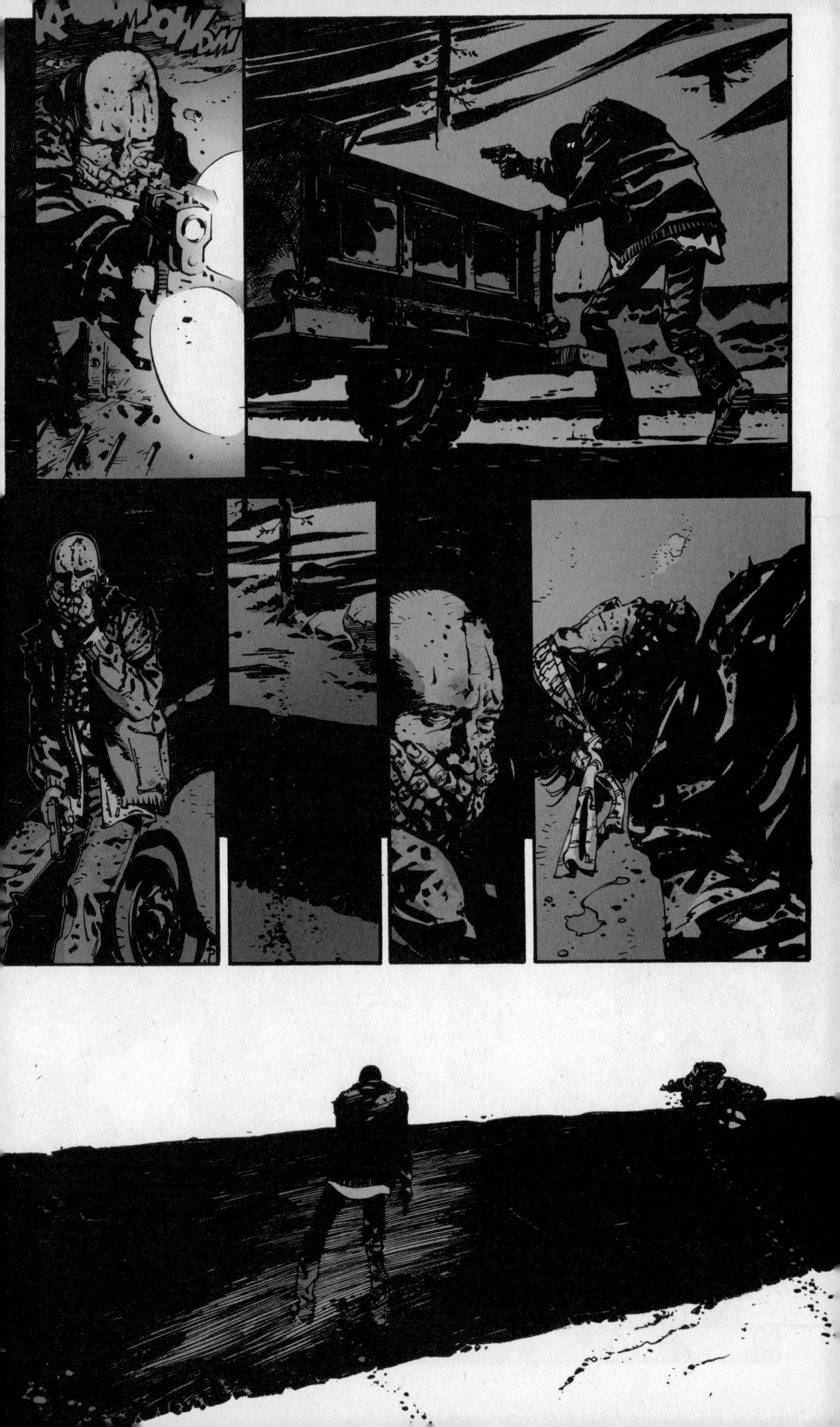

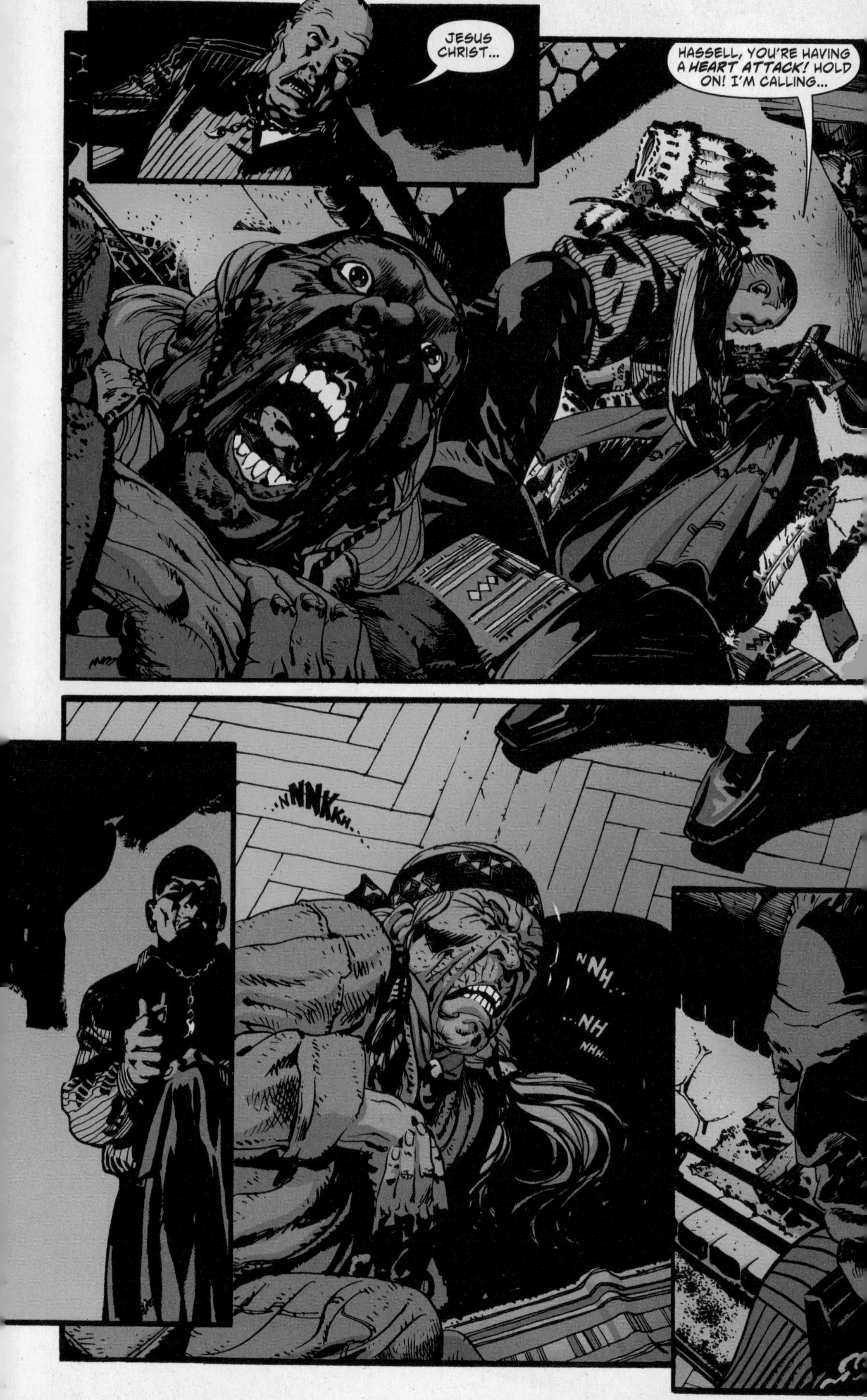
JESUS CHRIST...
HASSELL, YOU'RE HAVING A HEART ATTACK! HOLD ON! I'M CALLING...
NNNKKH...
NNH...
...NH
NHH...

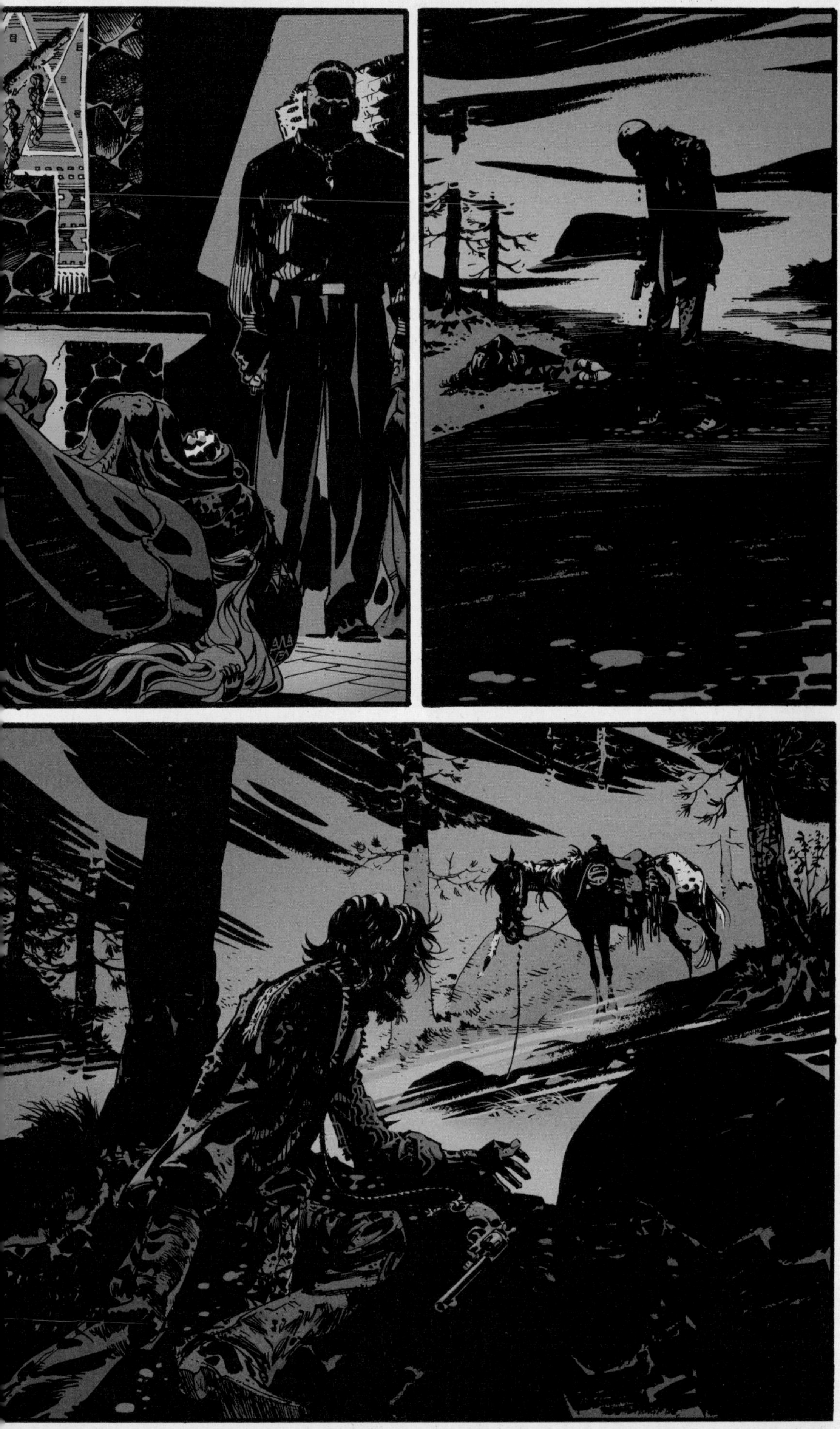

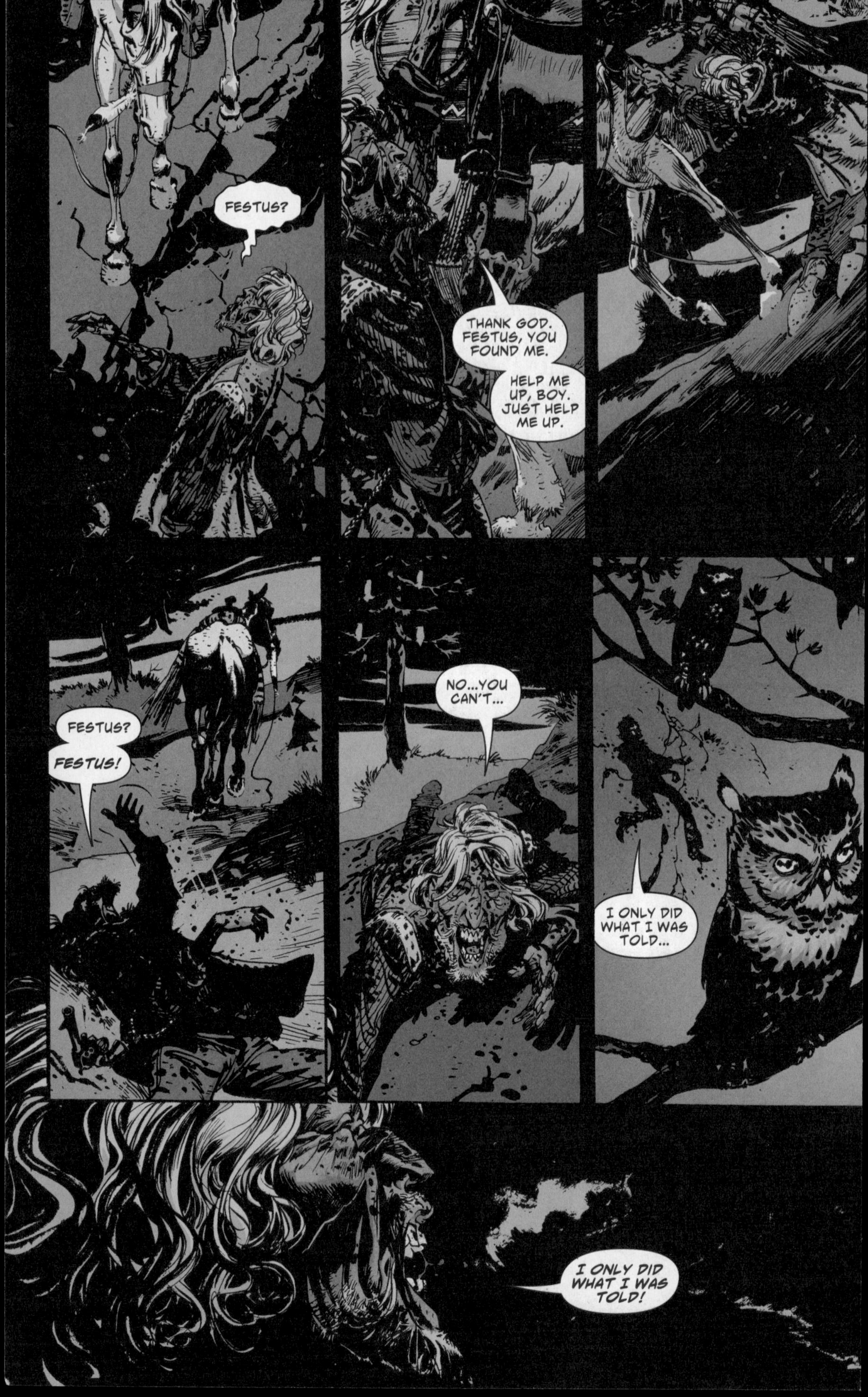
FESTUS?
THANK GOD. FESTUS, YOU FOUND ME.
HELP ME UP, BOY. JUST HELP ME UP.
FESTUS?
FESTUS!
NO...YOU CAN'T...
I ONLY DID WHAT I WAS TOLD...
I ONLY DID WHAT I WAS TOLD!

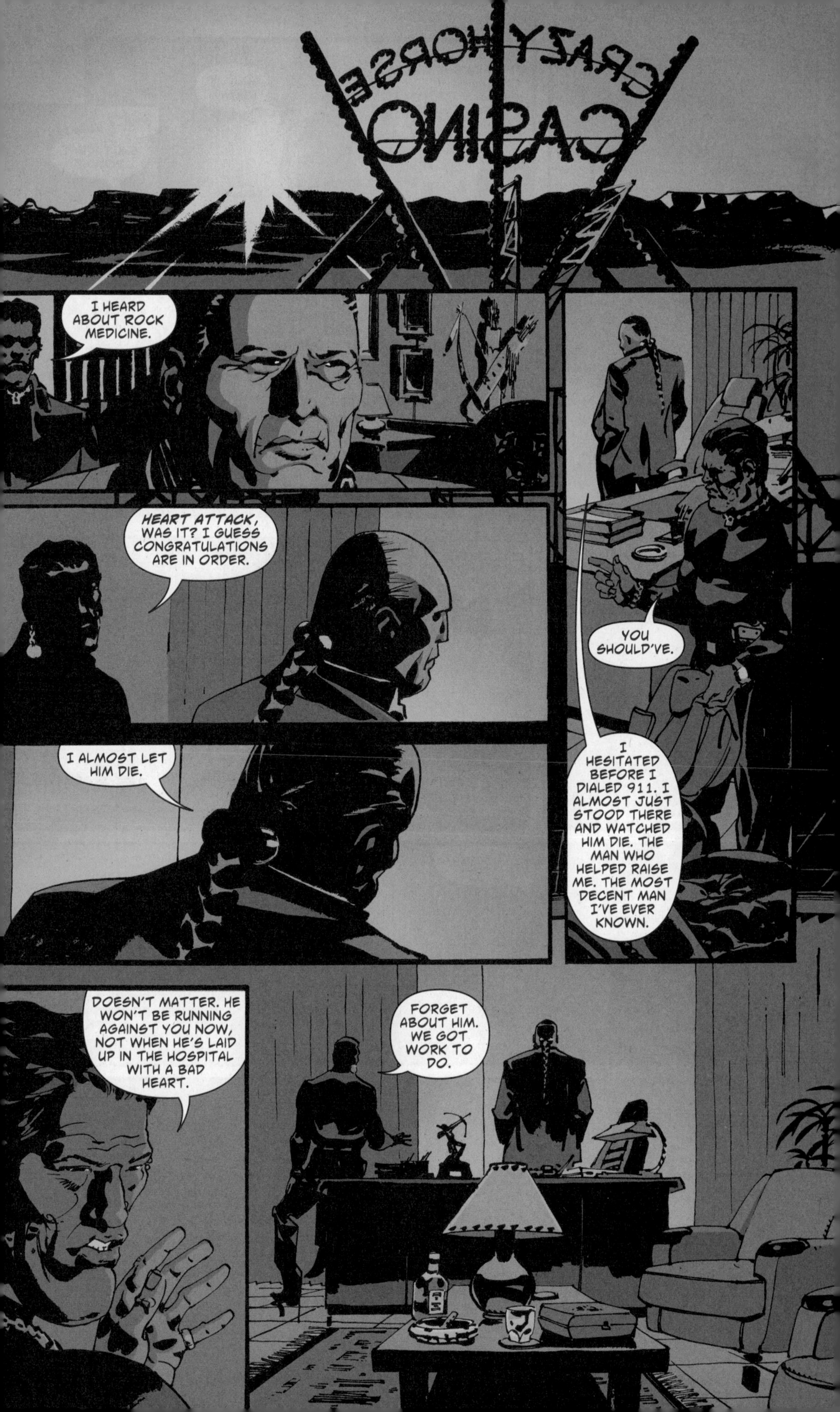

CRAZY HORSE CASINO
I HEARD ABOUT ROCK MEDICINE.
HEART ATTACK, WAS IT? I GUESS CONGRATULATIONS ARE IN ORDER.
I ALMOST LET HIM DIE.
YOU SHOULD'VE.
I HESITATED BEFORE I DIALED 911. I ALMOST JUST STOOD THERE AND WATCHED HIM DIE. THE MAN WHO HELPED RAISE ME. THE MOST DECENT MAN I'VE EVER KNOWN.
DOESN'T MATTER. HE WON'T BE RUNNING AGAINST YOU NOW, NOT WHEN HE'S LAID UP IN THE HOSPITAL WITH A BAD HEART.
FORGET ABOUT HIM. WE GOT WORK TO DO.

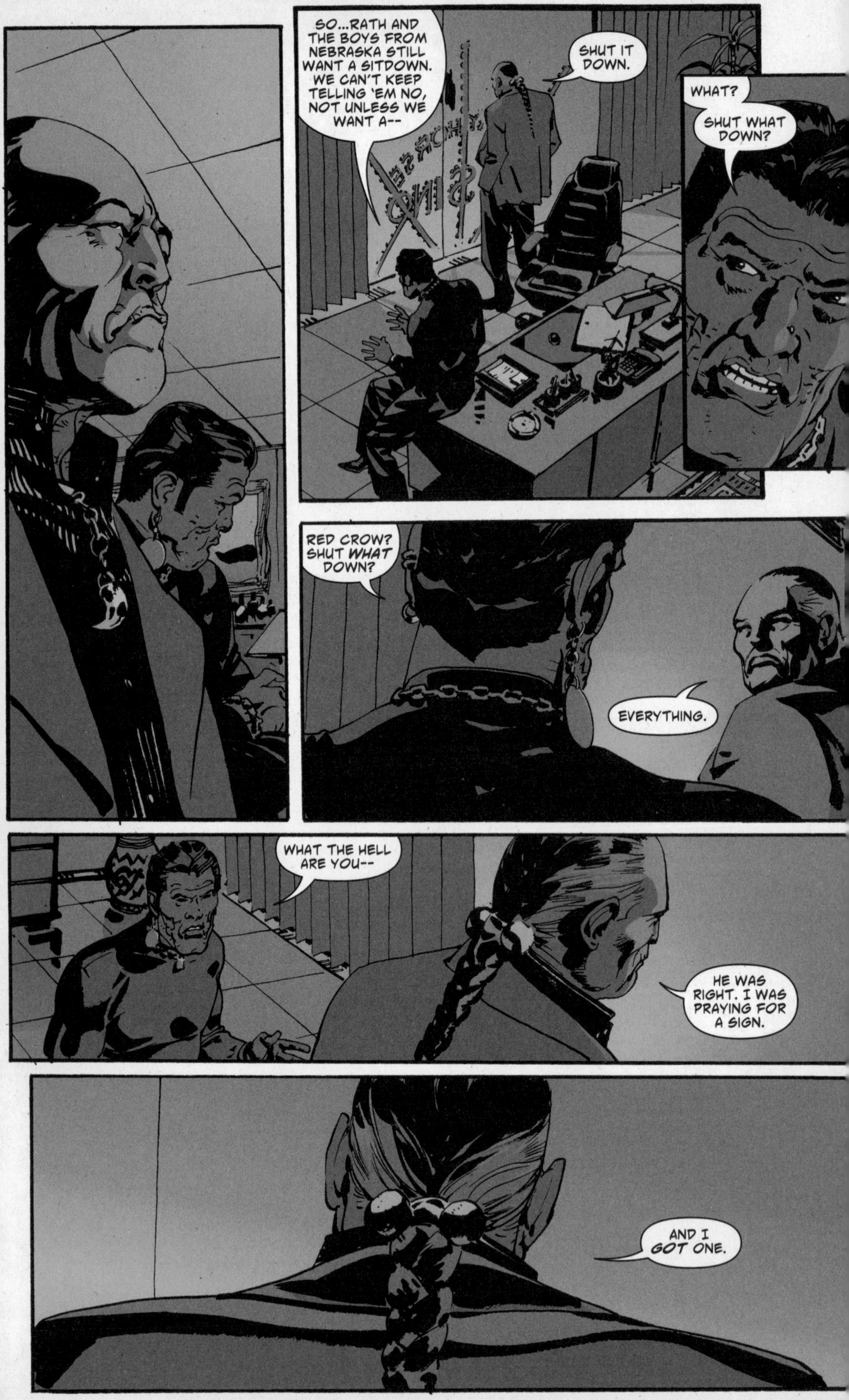
SO...RATH AND THE BOYS FROM NEBRASKA STILL WANT A SITDOWN. WE CAN'T KEEP TELLING 'EM NO, NOT UNLESS WE WANT A--
SHUT IT DOWN.
WHAT?
SHUT WHAT DOWN?
RED CROW? SHUT *WHAT* DOWN?
EVERYTHING.
WHAT THE HELL ARE YOU--
HE WAS RIGHT. I WAS PRAYING FOR A SIGN.
AND I *GOT* ONE.

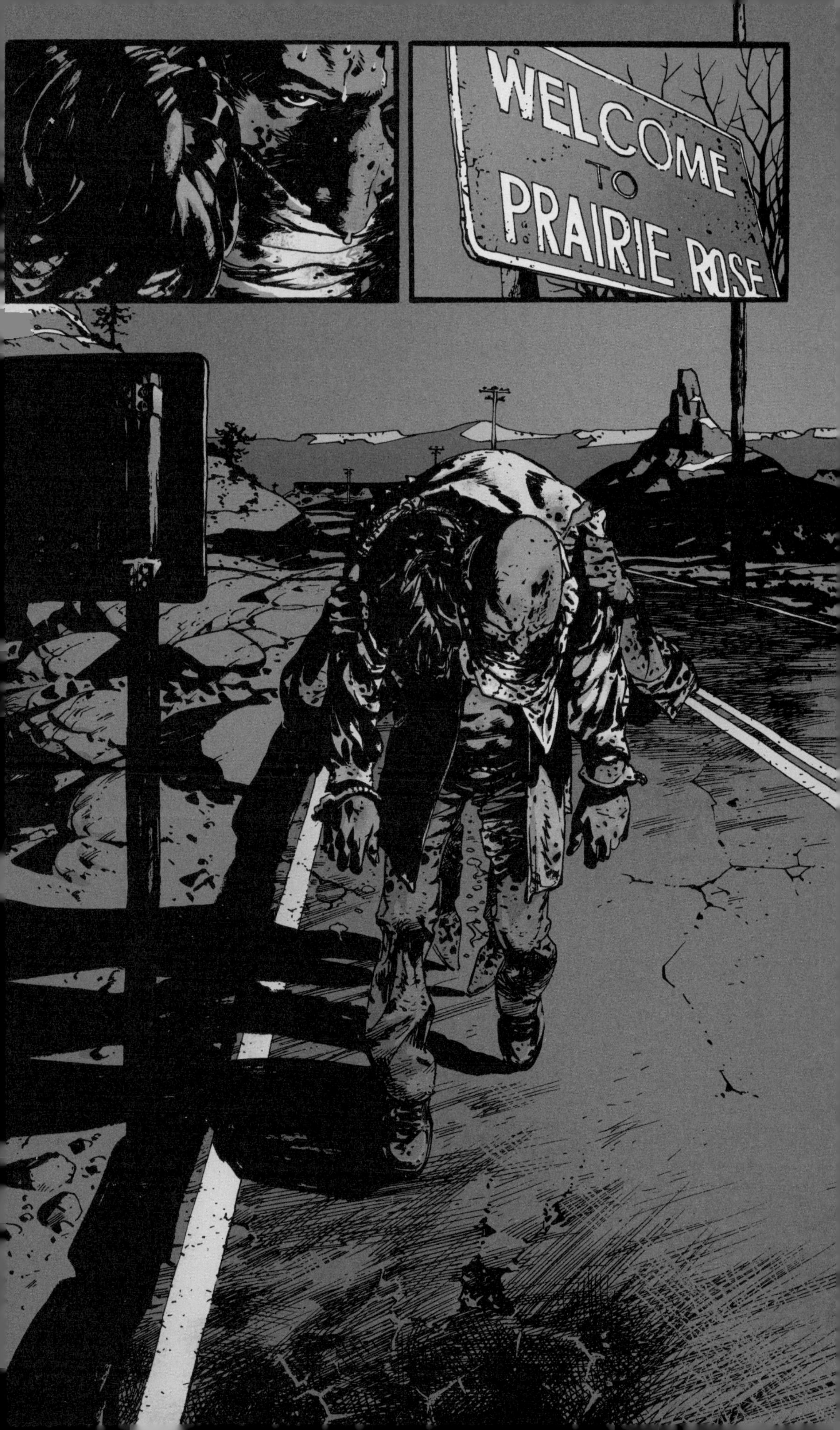
WELCOME
TO
PRAIRIE ROSE

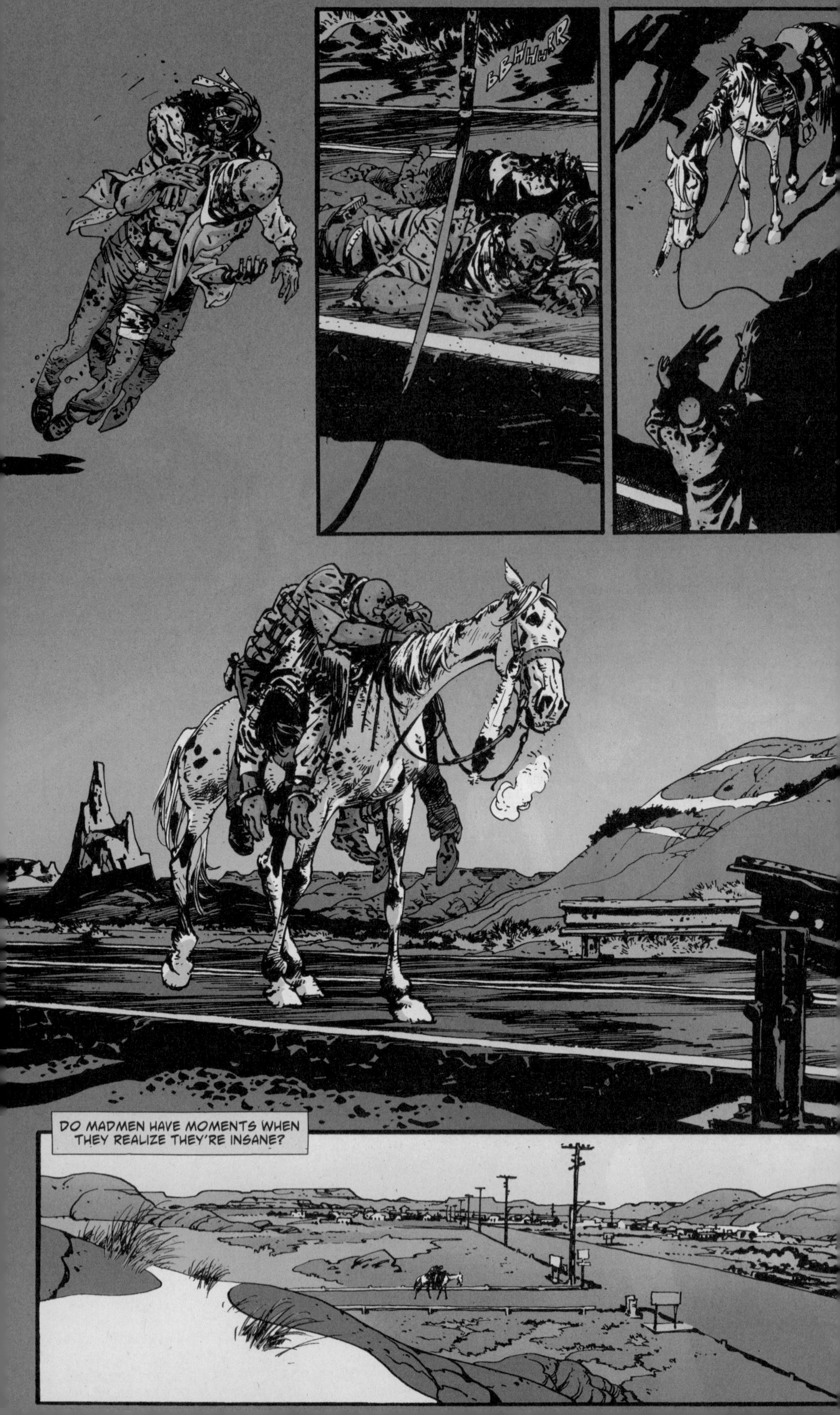
BBHHHRR
DO MADMEN HAVE MOMENTS WHEN THEY REALIZE THEY'RE INSANE?

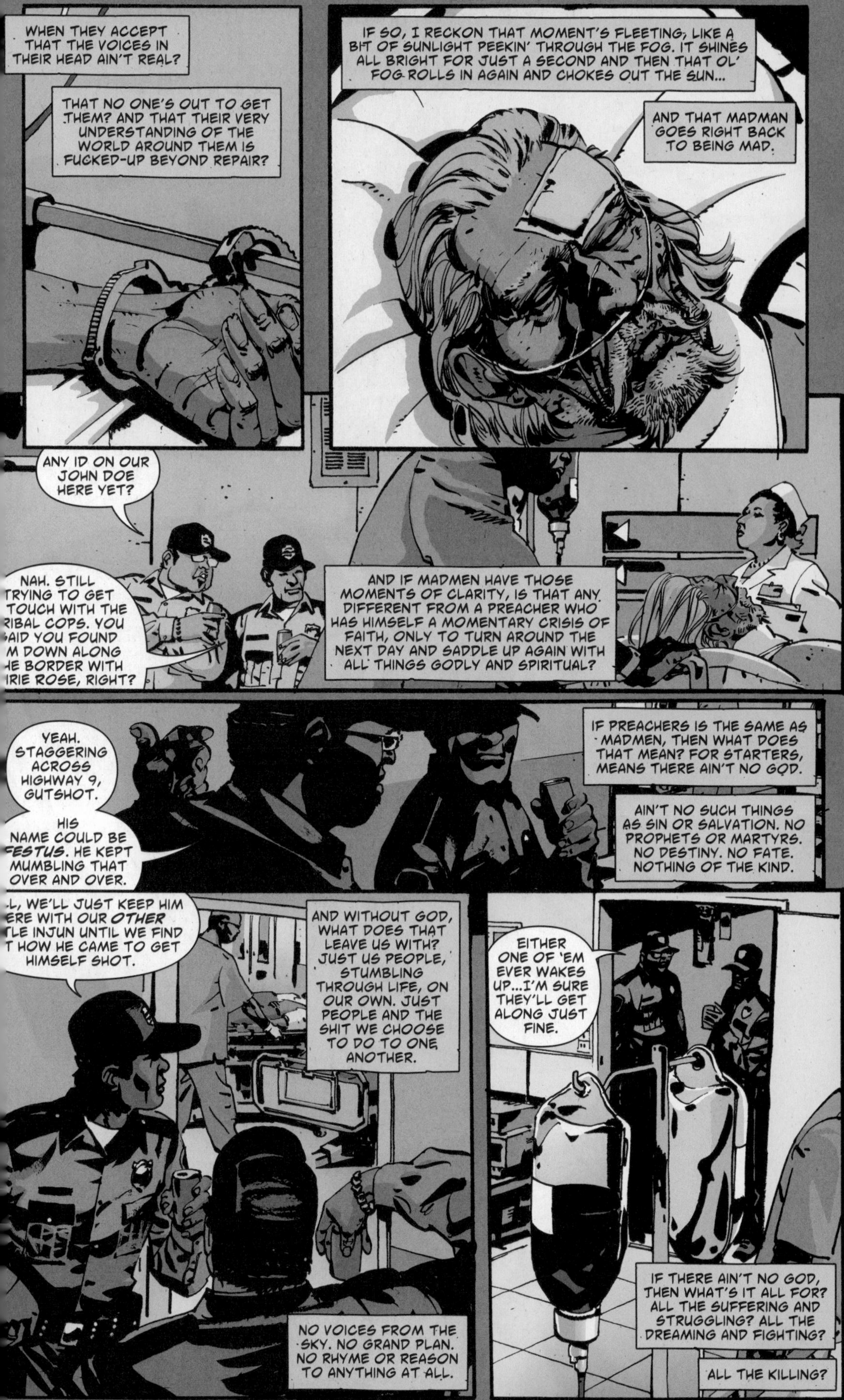
WHEN THEY ACCEPT THAT THE VOICES IN THEIR HEAD AIN'T REAL?
THAT NO ONE'S OUT TO GET THEM? AND THAT THEIR VERY UNDERSTANDING OF THE WORLD AROUND THEM IS FUCKED-UP BEYOND REPAIR?
IF SO, I RECKON THAT MOMENT'S FLEETING, LIKE A BIT OF SUNLIGHT PEEKIN' THROUGH THE FOG. IT SHINES ALL BRIGHT FOR JUST A SECOND AND THEN THAT OL' FOG ROLLS IN AGAIN AND CHOKES OUT THE SUN...
AND THAT MADMAN GOES RIGHT BACK TO BEING MAD.
ANY ID ON OUR JOHN DOE HERE YET?
NAH. STILL TRYING TO GET TOUCH WITH THE RIBAL COPS. YOU SAID YOU FOUND M DOWN ALONG HE BORDER WITH RIE ROSE, RIGHT?
AND IF MADMEN HAVE THOSE MOMENTS OF CLARITY, IS THAT ANY DIFFERENT FROM A PREACHER WHO HAS HIMSELF A MOMENTARY CRISIS OF FAITH, ONLY TO TURN AROUND THE NEXT DAY AND SADDLE UP AGAIN WITH ALL THINGS GODLY AND SPIRITUAL?
YEAH. STAGGERING ACROSS HIGHWAY 9, GUTSHOT.
HIS NAME COULD BE FESTUS. HE KEPT MUMBLING THAT OVER AND OVER.
IF PREACHERS IS THE SAME AS MADMEN, THEN WHAT DOES THAT MEAN? FOR STARTERS, MEANS THERE AIN'T NO GOD.
AIN'T NO SUCH THINGS AS SIN OR SALVATION. NO PROPHETS OR MARTYRS. NO DESTINY. NO FATE. NOTHING OF THE KIND.
L, WE'LL JUST KEEP HIM ERE WITH OUR OTHER TLE INJUN UNTIL WE FIND T HOW HE CAME TO GET HIMSELF SHOT.
AND WITHOUT GOD, WHAT DOES THAT LEAVE US WITH? JUST US PEOPLE, STUMBLING THROUGH LIFE, ON OUR OWN. JUST PEOPLE AND THE SHIT WE CHOOSE TO DO TO ONE ANOTHER.
NO VOICES FROM THE SKY. NO GRAND PLAN. NO RHYME OR REASON TO ANYTHING AT ALL.
EITHER ONE OF 'EM EVER WAKES UP...I'M SURE THEY'LL GET ALONG JUST FINE.
IF THERE AIN'T NO GOD, THEN WHAT'S IT ALL FOR? ALL THE SUFFERING AND STRUGGLING? ALL THE DREAMING AND FIGHTING?
ALL THE KILLING?

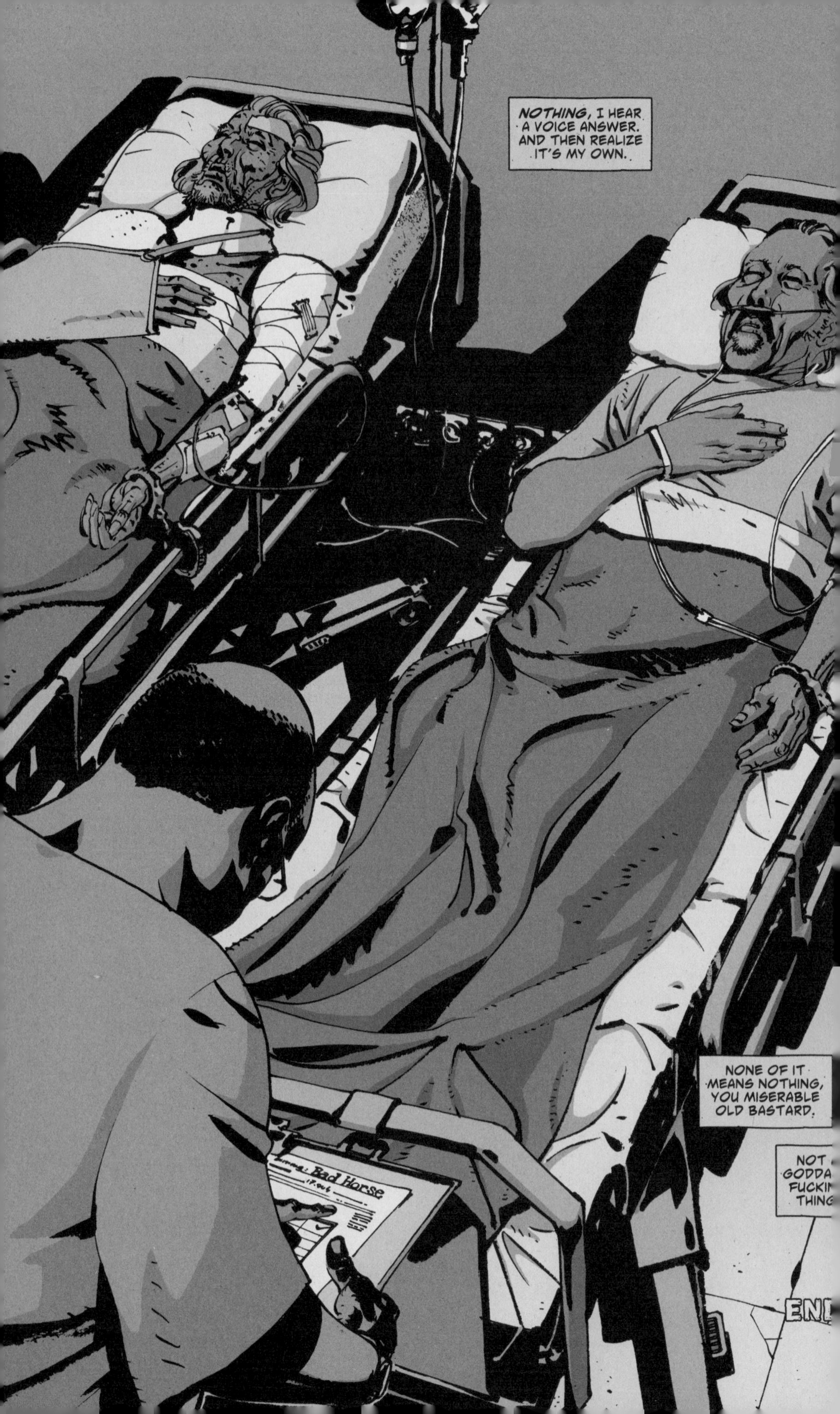
NOTHING, I HEAR A VOICE ANSWER. AND THEN REALIZE IT'S MY OWN.
Bad Horse
NONE OF IT MEANS NOTHING, YOU MISERABLE OLD BASTARD.
NOT GODDA FUCKI THING

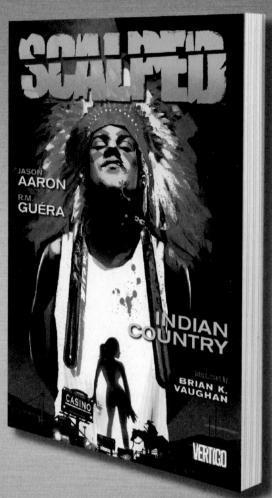

FROM INDIE COMICS SENSATION

BRIAN WOOD

DMZ
BRIAN WOOD RICCARDO BURCHIELLI
INTRODUCTION BY BRIAN AZZARELLO
"Gut-wrenchingly portrays the chaotic reality of life in a war zone." — WASHINGTON POST
ON THE GROUND
PRESS
VERTIGO

"Measures up to any summer blockbuster."
–TIME OUT NEW YORK

"The dramatic images recall the nightly news, and stories of warzone life ring true. GRADE: A-"
– ENTERTAINMENT WEEKLY

"One of the strongest ongoing series to come out of DC's Vertigo line in some time. GRADE: A-"
–THE ONION

VOL. 1: ON THE GROUND
VOL. 2: BODY OF A JOURNALIST
VOL. 3: PUBLIC WORKS
VOL. 4: FRIENDLY FIRE
VOL. 5: THE HIDDEN WAR
VOL. 6: BLOOD IN THE GAME
VOL. 7: WAR POWERS
VOL. 8: HEARTS AND MINDS

DMZ VOL. 2:
BODY OF A JOURNALIST

DMZ
BRIAN WOOD RICCARDO BURCHIELLI KRISTIAN DONALDSON
BODY OF A JOURNALIST
VERTIGO

DMZ VOL. 3:
PUBLIC WORKS

DMZ
BRIAN WOOD RICCARDO BURCHIELLI
PUBLIC WORKS
VERTIGO

DMZ VOL. 4:
FRIENDLY FIRE

DMZ
BRIAN WOOD / RICCARDO BURCHIELLI / NATHAN FOX
FRIENDLY FIRE
"a disturbing and challenging success"
"increasingly relevant"
VERTIGO

GO TO
VERTIGOBOOKS.COM
FOR FREE SAMPLES OF THE FIRST ISSUES OF OUR GRAPHIC NOVELS

Suggested for Mature Readers

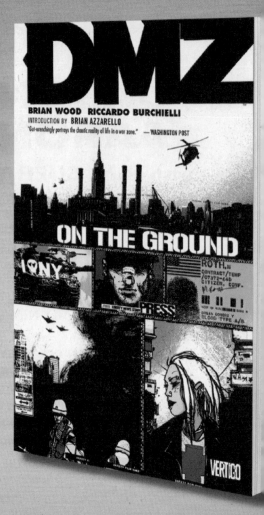

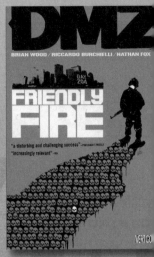

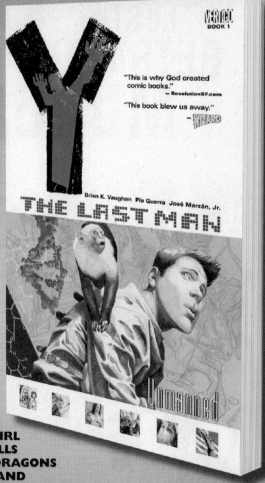

DECEPTION
LUST
BETRAYAL
MURDER

DONT MISS THESE OTHER TITLES FROM VERTIGO CRIME

THE CHILL
By JASON STARR Author of
PANIC ATTACK and THE FOLLO
Art by MICK BERTILORENZI
JANUARY 20

THE BRONX KILL
By PETER MILLIGAN
Author of GREEK STREET
Art by JAMES ROMBERGER
MARCH 2010

AREA 10
By CHRISTOS N. GAG
Art by CHRIS SAMNEE
APRIL 2010

SUGGESTED FOR MATURE READERS

VERTIGO
CRIME